BEANS

BEANS

More Than 200 Delicious, Wholesome Recipes from Around the World

BY ALIZA GREEN

Foreword by
William Woys Weaver

Photography by Steve Legato

RUNNING PRESS
PHILADELPHIA · LONDON

9 8 7 6 5 4 3 2
Digit on the right indicates the number of this printing

Library of Congress Control Number: 2004102735

ISBN 0-7624-1931-8

Photography by Steve Legato
Food styling by Aliza Green
Cover and interior design by Alicia Freile
Edited by Janet Bukovinsky Teacher
Typography: Sabon and Helvetica Neue

This book may be ordered by mail from the publisher.
Please include $2.50 for postage and handling.
But try your bookstore first!

Running Press Book Publishers
125 South Twenty-second Street
Philadelphia, Pennsylvania 19103-4399

Visit us on the web!
www.runningpress.com

To my husband, Don Reiff, who gave me the benefit of his highly evolved design sense and critical palate throughout this project. He never objected to endless nights of bean meals and was an unfailingly willing (and appreciative) subject for my culinary experiments.

And thanks go to my mom, Vivian Green, who taught me to never give up and kept encouraging me to write. I've learned so much from her as a writer—she is an accomplished playwright—and as a person.

Acknowledgments

My deepest appreciation and thanks go to Mary McGuire Ruggiero, my editor. Her constant encouragement and good humor made the occasionally rocky going a little smoother. After spending a week in her stimulating and entertaining company at the 1997 International Association of Culinary Professionals conference in Chicago, it became clear to me that I was ready to write a cookbook about legumes. I've also counted on Mary to make me look good and not to let the mistakes I've made slip through the cracks.

Janet Bukovinsky Teacher has made working on the new edition a true pleasure. Not many writers have the chance to revisit a book and make it even better; Janet gave me just the right amount of suggestions, corrections, and encouragement so that I know this book is "as good as it gets."

I would like to thank wholeheartedly my good friend, fellow foodie, and stalwart recipe tester, Linda Gellman, who was always cheerfully willing to try another recipe. I couldn't have written this book without her help and insightful recipe comments. I only hope she'll agree to work with me again.

I want to thank my chef and cookbook-writer friends who have generously shared their recipes for my book, including French-Asian Chef Philippe Chin; restaurateur and master of the dining room Toto Schiavone; Chef Guillermo Pernot; Certified Master Chef and 2000 U.S. Culinary Olympic Team Captain Alfonso Contrisciani; restaurateurs Amin and Jude Bitar; cookbook authors Fred and Linda Griffiths; and Lyonnais Chef Pierre Orsi.

I thank my two children, Zachary and Ginevra, who have been totally supportive of me and my crazy food work, even when it has meant that they had to FFY—fend for yourself—for dinner (unless they wanted yet another dish of beans).

Contents

My first encounter with Aliza Green left a remarkable impression. It occurred almost 20 years ago when we met at The Garden restaurant with owner Kathleen Mulhern to discuss the establishment of a Delaware Valley chapter of the American Institute of Wine and Food. Even then Aliza's personal commitment to good food came through with all the enthusiasm she has since devoted to so many other worthwhile projects. We became instant friends, I guess because we believe in the same things, even though our professional lives move along slightly different paths. I have written about food from the perspective of history, from the perspective of the dining room. Aliza now writes from the heart of the kitchen. This is her bailiwick, and her huge store of creative energy seems to thrive on it. During her stint as chef at the White Dog Cafe, Aliza experimented with a long list of exciting farm-fresh products; indeed I shall never forget the memorable meal that she once cooked for me and for several of my guests from Colonial Williamsburg. For those Virginians, it was their first exposure to the culinary renaissance then under way in Philadelphia, but it was also a firsthand taste of the kind of high-quality produce that our restaurants were seeking out in the Pennsylvania countryside. The marriage of farm garden and restaurant kitchen has been one of the lasting themes in Aliza's quest for good food that not only benefits the palate and healthful eating, but also gives something back to the land. That is Aliza's special touch.

I should have realized then that lurking among all her dishes of chickpeas and lentils, all her bowls of velvety bean soup, all her smoking casseroles of flavorful favas, were the makings of this book. She calls it a bible, but I would also call it *The Essential Aliza,* for in every respect it is a guidebook to her philosophy of cuisine, plus some. For a person like myself, who is a gardener who cooks, and a cook who also writes, this is definitely the sort of exacting cookbook that needed writing long ago. I can well appreciate the love and care and no small amount of labor that went into it, for this is a huge subject and there are not many books that have tackled the bean and a host of other legumes in such a head-on, hands-on manner. Bravo Aliza!

I should know. I grow many of these vegetables in my own kitchen garden—at last count, over 200 sorts of beans, over 50 sorts of peas, perhaps 40 sorts of favas and cowpeas, and quite a few of the more unusual legumes that are now only coming back into vogue among aficionados—such as chickling vetch, lupine seeds, and those delightful popping beans from Peru. By bean collectors' standards, my collection is small, but I have tried to make it extremely high quality in terms of culinary merits. So oftentimes, when I have come in from the garden with a bowl full of picture-perfect flageolet chevrier verts, or African bambaras, or our own native Blue Shackamaxon beans, I have asked myself where it is I might turn to get some ideas on how to cook them. Aliza's book offers just such a refreshing perspective. Many readers will thoroughly enjoy the tidbits on bean history, and the other legumes as well. I think the legume primer, which forms the bulk of chapter two, is especially helpful because it introduces us to some of the truly good varieties that are now available, with far more detailed and useful information than what is normally provided on a typical supermarket label. That took homework, but cooks need to know their materials in order to use them to best advantage, so I think this is one part of the cookbook that will fill up quickly with the little notes and flags one finds in the cookbooks people use most. I could go on. I could crow about the delicious recipes, but words cannot replace the wonderful way they taste. They must be tried. I know there are several dishes I am going to make quite often. But what I like most about this book is that Aliza's recipes work two ways. You can follow them verbatim for easy-to-follow, great-tasting results, or you can tinker with them and use them as the basis for your own delightful creations. That, by the way, is how I like to cook, so I am especially grateful that she has jam-packed this book with nifty tips and useful advice about flavor combinations, cooking techniques, and a host of other details so important to readers who are feeling their way through certain types of dishes for the very first time. In this respect, this book is indeed a bible and an indispensable companion to anyone who wants to put good food on his or her table—and help the farmers who grew it as well.

—William Woys Weaver

When I told my friends about my bean cookbook project, they reacted in one of two ways. Either they'd laugh with a bit of embarrassment mixed in and repeat one of the bean-related folk rhymes of childhood, "Beans, beans, the musical fruit . . ." Or else they'd exclaim, "Oh, I just love beans; I'm so glad you're writing this book!"

It seems that beans are a subject that inspires a lot of controversy. Unfortunately, many people have a bad association with beans—memories of eating pork and beans from a can for dinner or endless nights of baked beans, simply because these were cheap and easy dishes. I'm ashamed to admit that even I have bad memories of a classic bean dish, the Sabbath *cholent* (large lima beans cooked slowly with the meat and potatoes) that my mother (and her mother) made for cold-weather Shabbat afternoon dinners. As a child I absolutely loathed this dish. If I discovered that we were having it after Saturday morning synagogue services, I would make sure to get myself invited to a friend's house for lunch that day. Later, as a young woman and a budding chef, I was introduced to the great southwest French country-style masterpiece, cassoulet. I tasted the crusty, steaming hot, garlicky cassoulet and loved it. Only later, while doing research for this book, did I realize that the two dishes actually shared the same origin. Both *cholent* and cassoulet are one-pot meals (or casseroles) slow-cooked in the residual heat of the baker's oven overnight and served hot the next day. Their difference can be traced directly to religious beliefs. The Jewish dish *cholent* contains only beef (and sometimes goose), while the strongly French Catholic cassoulet normally contains a variety of pork products. Try the recipes for both French cassoulet and Jewish *cholent* (Jewish Sabbath casserole) to find out just how delicious these dishes are.

In 1991, I conducted a legume workshop sponsored by our local chapter of the American Institute of Wine and Food. During the class I demonstrated and sampled three of the recipes included in this book. I truly enjoyed the class and the participants loved the recipes. Because of this positive experience, I was inspired to take a more comprehensive look at bean cookery. I realized beans had been a leitmotif in my culinary career, and that I had developed a broad and imaginative base of delicious legume recipes from around the world.

I wanted to share with readers my firm belief that beans are a culinary delight with the bonus of being nutritional powerhouses. We now know that everyone can benefit from adding more legumes to their diet, but especially women that are pregnant, need more iron in their diet, or want to help prevent breast cancer, or osteoporosis in later years. People with diabetes, high-blood pressure, or anyone that wants to help prevent cancer and heart attacks should also eat more legumes.

While I'm not a vegetarian, I love vegetables and this book is chock-full of wonderfully flavorful recipes and all the basic legume cookery information you'd ever need to know. I've also included vegetarian variations for many of the recipes. The recipes in this book come from many sources and represent the cuisines of more than twenty-five countries that have strong repertoires of legume dishes. Some I developed during my long career as a chef and food consultant; others I tasted in my travels and just had to re-create. My chef and foodie friends were also generous enough to share their own recipes.

Beans and legumes can be as fancy as Georges Perrier's Velouté of Giant White Coco Beans with its requisite garnish of black truffles. Lentilles du Puy, the tiny French green lentils, and flageolets, the pale green ovals beloved by legendary French chef Auguste Escoffier, are both strictly controlled as to their origin and fetch a high price. Legumes can be as down-to-earth as Ful-Medames, the Egyptian porridge of fava beans with egg, or the Spanish and Mexican Earthenware-Cooked Beans *(Frijoles de Olla)*. They can be as complex as the Brazilian national dish, Feijoada Completa, or my own Spiced Duck in Port Wine Sauce with Green Lentils. They can be as simple as a split yellow mung bean dal from India, or a dish of the chickpea and sesame dip, hummus. They can be as exotic as the fermented lentil and rice pancakes from Bombay called dosa or the Indonesian bean salad Gado Gado. But don't be scared off by all the international-sounding dishes; beans can also be as homey and familiar as Diner-Style Split Pea Soup or Boston Baked Beans with Steamed Brown Bread. And, be sure to try the recipes for bean ice cream, bean torte, and bean pie—you'll be amazed at how good they are.

I've come to adore bean cookery, though I found that a surprisingly large number of American chefs have trouble cooking beans and other legumes. If I saw an interesting-looking bean dish on a menu, I'd always order it. But many times the beans would turn out to be mushy and bland (obviously from a can). Other times they would be hard and indigestible, probably because the chef got creative and cooked the beans with hardening substances, such as sugar, salt, and acid prior to the necessary precooking step. It was rare that I'd find legumes prepared as perfectly as I would like in America, though chefs and cooks in Europe and Latin America prepared them expertly.

But, I'm happy to say that the picture has changed. These days, American chefs are incorporating all sorts of American-grown heirloom and imported specialty legumes into their menus, while home cooks are buying and cooking more legumes all the time. And everyone seems to know how nutritious beans and other legumes are. Being so enthusiastic about this topic, I decided to "spill the beans" about how wonderful bean cuisine really can be. I hope you'll agree. —*"Bean" Appétit!*

CHAPTER ONE

The History, Gastronomy, and Nutritional Importance of Legumes

Legumes, which include beans, peas, lentils, and peanuts, are one of the most ancient human food-stuffs. They have been a dietary staple in many parts of the world since the days of our hunter-gatherer ancestors, about 12,000 years ago. And for good reason: they are versatile, easy to grow, easy to store, inexpensive, and are packed with essential nutrients. No part of the bean is wasted, from its sprouts, tender young pods, and green seeds to its dry seeds, which are stored for cold winter days.

Though we may think of beans as lowly, they have enjoyed high status and been credited with possessing great powers in other eras and cultures.

According to history, the followers of the Greek philosopher Pythagoras were prohibited from eating beans due to the belief that to consume beans was to consume the souls of one's ancestors thus preventing them from being reincarnated. In Rome, the natural historian Pliny wrote of the belief that the souls of the dead resided in beans. Greeks and Romans reportedly banished ghosts by spitting beans at them, and at Roman funeral banquets (probably for the same reason) beans were an important part of the offering made to dead relatives.

In ancient Rome, an annual ritual was conducted during the period of Lemuria, to placate the ever-restless ghosts of the dead. The head of the household walked through the rooms of the house at midnight throwing small dark fava beans behind him, while reciting a special chant. In Japan, a parallel rite was practiced at the beginning of each new year. At midnight, the head of the house scattered roasted beans in all the rooms to drive out the demons and bring in good luck.

Indeed, legumes have a stronghold in the traditions and, of course, the customs of most cultures. Native Americans, such as the Algonquins, depended on corn and kidney beans for making their traditional succotash (cooked in bear fat)—a dish that's been adapted across America. Chickpeas, sesame, and lemon combine to make the Lebanese *hummus bi tahina,* now an American vegetarian staple. No East Indian meal would be complete without a bowl of dal, split lentils or mung beans that can be served as a soup or side dish. Mexican cooks spoon a dollop of pinto or black bean frijoles onto every plate and serve them refried the next day. And where would Israelis be without their national street food, the chickpea (and sometimes fava) fritters called falafel, Egyptian in origin but now often served with a Yemenite sauce containing ground fenugreek seeds (also a legume).

Beans have been around so long that many techniques have evolved for improving their flavor and digestibility. In Germany and Switzerland, savory is known as *bohnenkraut* (the bean herb), and is always included when cooking a pot of beans. Mexican cooks invariably add sprigs of epazote to the *olla,* or earthenware pot, when cooking black beans, because the special resinous oil contained in this wild wormseed plant helps reduce some of the beans' gaseous effects. Cooks in rural Italy faithfully add alkaline-rich greens like wild chicory, dandelion, spinach, or chard to balance the acidity of the beans. And according to cookbook author Madhur Jaffrey, spices used in Indian cuisine, such as ginger, fennel seed, and carom or lovage seed, function as nutrition and flavor enhancers as well as carminatives (antiflatulents).

SMALL BUT MIGHTY LEGUMES ARE NUTRITIONAL POWERHOUSES

The worldwide importance of legumes has much to do with their nutritional richness. They are second only to cereal grasses in their importance in the human diet. Beans and other legumes are high in protein, fiber, and complex carbohydrates, low in calories and sodium, and cholesterol-free. Beans derive only 2 to 5 percent of their calories from fat. (Soybeans, though, are about 34 percent fat, and peanuts—also legumes—are 40 to 50 percent fat.) Dried or canned beans have the same nutritional benefits, but green beans and peas contain less protein or fiber than dried legumes, which have been allowed to mature on the plant.

Beans Are the Best Source of Vegetable Protein

Dry beans are the richest source of vegetable protein (21 to 27 percent when cooked). Except for soybeans, however, the protein they contain is incomplete. Soybeans have the highest protein of any plant (35 percent), and are the only legume to contain all nine essential amino acids needed to form a complete protein, though peanuts are not far behind (20 to 30 percent protein). Other legumes contain eight amino acids, missing only methionine, which is plentiful in grains; grains lack tryptophan and lysine, which are found in beans. So all you have to do to get complete protein is eat beans with complementary foods like grains or nuts, and it doesn't even have to be in the same meal. Ultimately, most of us eat more than enough complete protein to overcome any deficiency in beans.

Beans Are a High-Energy Food with a Low to Moderate Glycemic Index

Beans have long been valued as an energy source because they are full of complex carbohydrates, but have a low or moderate glycemic index. In other words, the complex carbohydrates in dry beans are digested more slowly than those in simple carbohydrate foods, like bread or rice, thus satisfying hunger longer.

Eat Beans and Add More Fiber to Your Diet

Those who need more fiber (both soluble and insoluble) in their diet will find few sources better than legumes. Insoluble fiber, or roughage, helps promote a healthy digestive tract and can reduce the risk of certain types of cancer. Soluble fiber is known for its cholesterol-fighting ability and helps the body handle fats and carbohydrates. The fiber in beans is especially beneficial for diabetics, because it helps to maintain healthy blood glucose levels.

BEANS ARE RICH IN VITAMINS AND MINERALS

All legumes contain high amounts of B vitamins and are the best source of folate, especially important for women before and during pregnancy because it plays an important role in cell development. Folate may also help reduce the risk of certain birth defects and several types of cancer, and may protect against heart disease. (Lentils are particularly high in folate.) Legumes contain an abundance of potassium, which regulates body fluid and may help reduce the risk of high blood pressure and stroke. They provide significant amounts of other minerals, such as potassium, zinc, iron, calcium, and magnesium.

THE FOUR ROMAN FAMILIES

In his tome of kitchen science and lore, *On Food and Cooking*, Harold McGee says, "A remarkable and as yet unexplained sign of their status in the ancient world is the fact that each of the four major legumes known to Rome lent its name to a prominent Roman family: Fabius comes from the faba bean, Lentulus from the lentil, Piso from the pea, and Cicero from the chickpea."

Beans Have Calcium and Iron for Strong Bones and Red Blood

Beans are high in the iron needed to build red blood cells, which is especially important for women. While dried legumes are a good source of iron, they should be combined with foods rich in vitamin C, such as dark leafy greens, tomatoes, and peppers in order to increase the body's ability to absorb this iron. Chile peppers contain lots of vitamin C. Beans provide almost as much calcium as milk, which is necessary to maintain strong bones and teeth and help prevent osteoporosis in later years.

Eat Beans with Tomatoes, Peppers, and Chiles

Throughout the Mediterranean, India, Latin America, and the American Southwest, beans are combined with vegetables high in vitamin C like tomatoes, peppers, and especially chiles. Look for recipes like Crostini with Cannellini Bean Spread and Oven-Roasted Tomatoes, Texas Stuffed Tomatoes with Black-Eyed Pea Salad, Southwest Black Bean Salad with Baked Spiced Goat Cheese, Fresh Tomato and White Bean Soup, Portuguese Salt Cod and Kidney Bean Salad, and Tunisian Fava Bean Stew with Merguez Lamb Sausage to increase iron and calcium in your diet.

Eat Beans with Greens

There is a long tradition of combining beans and dark leafy greens, particularly in soups and pastas, throughout the Mediterranean. These greens are also alkaline, neutralizing the beans' acidity and making them more easily digestible. Try these recipes to provide more iron and calcium to your diet: Country-Style Ziti; Chicory and Cannellini Bean Soup; Spring Greens Ravioli with

Creamy White Bean Sauce, Ragout of Flageolets, Chicken-Basil Sausage, and Spinach; and Mustard-Crusted Rack of Lamb with Spinach and Cranberry Bean Ragout.

Eat Beans and Lower Your Risk of Heart Disease and Cancer

A study conducted at Tulane University in New Orleans found that people who ate beans at least four times a week were 19 percent less prone to heart disease than those who ate beans once a week. Bean eaters lowered their overall risk of cardiovascular disease by 9 percent. Other studies have shown that Hispanic women have a significantly lower risk of breast cancer than Caucasian women do; the difference is believed to be due to their high consumption of beans. Another study, conducted at the University of Kentucky, showed that increasing bean intake for only three weeks lowered men's cholesterol by an average of 19 percent, reducing their risk of heart attack by almost 40 percent.

Go for Colorful Beans and More Antioxidants

Beans contain flavonoids, plant substances that give many fruits and vegetables their color and act as antioxidants to protect against certain cancers and heart

COMPLEMENTARY FOODS

Pairing legumes with complementary foods to make them nutritionally complete has a long tradition around the world, and many examples can be found in the recipe section of this book. Pasta and *fagioli* (often cannellini or borlotti) are combined throughout Italy; *frijoles* (black or pinto beans) are served with corn or wheat tortillas in Mexico; rice and beans (red, black, and pink beans, cowpeas, pigeon peas, and black-eyed peas) are cooked together all over the Caribbean. In Lebanon and other parts of the Middle East, hummus (mashed chickpeas) is mixed with sesame seeds, and falafel (chickpea fritters) are served in pita bread. All manner of highly nutritious dals (soupy split lentils, mung beans, chickpeas, or pigeon peas) are served over rice in India. Native Americans combined kidney beans and corn to make succotash while the colonists served their Sabbath-day baked beans with steamed brown bread.

disease. In general, darker-colored seed coats are associated with higher levels of flavonoids and higher antioxidant activity. Black beans contain the highest flavonoid levels, followed by red, brown, yellow, and white beans. When you cook beans, the flavonoids leach into the liquids but aren't destroyed, so the liquid left over from cooking beans is worth saving for your next pot of soup.

LEGUMES AND GAS: WHY IT OCCURS AND HOW TO PREVENT IT

Let wind and water go free, then healthy thou wilt be.
—An old Wiltshire saying

The profound effects of beans on the digestive system have generated great concern and controversy throughout the ages, and much has been written about it. According to Saint Augustine, flatulence was an unmistakable sign of man's fall from grace. Saint Jerome forbade beans to the nuns in his charge on the grounds that "they tickle the genitals." These notions of the erotic persisted for some time. Many centuries later an English writer, Henry Buttes, wrote of beans' "flatulencie, whereby they provoke to lecher." It seems that beans were considered an aphrodisiac precisely because of the powerful aftereffects of eating them.

Pleasure of another sort is probably at the root of the perennial children's rhyme that begins "Beans, beans, the musical fruit . . ." and ends with the perverse wish ". . . so let's have beans for every meal!" The Victorian Italian culinary authority Pellegrino Artusi wrote in his influential cookbook *La Scienza en Cucina (Science in the Kitchen),* "It seems to me that the taste of lentils is more delicate than that of beans in general and that, as for the threat of bombardment, they are less dangerous than ordinary beans and equal to the black-eyed pea." But the French writer Clement-Marius Morard claimed that a frequent diet of lentils "produced a revolution in the organs, disturbed the head, deranged the mind, and ruined the sight."

Most of us know from experience that eating beans causes gas, but few know why. It turns out that oligosaccharides, a chemical constituent in legumes, are responsible for the embarrassing consequence of their consumption. Oligosaccharides are complex sugar molecules linked together in such a way that human enzymes cannot digest them easily. As a result, the oligosaccharides leave the upper intestines unchanged and enter the lower intestines in a form that the body cannot absorb. Here the large resident bacterial population does the job the upper intestines are unable to do, and in the process gives off various gases as waste products.

It is this sudden increase in bacterial action, caused by the arrival of a food supply available only to the bacteria, that results in flatulence after eating legumes. Oligosaccharides are especially common in seeds because they are a form in which sugars can be stored for future use. They accumulate in the final stages of bean development, so it seems that green, or immature, beans are much less troublesome than dry beans. Fresh shelled beans from the current year's crop are also low in oligosaccharides.

There must be other factors that cause flatulence because white or navy beans have a lower oligosaccharide content than soybeans, but a higher gas activity. Apparently some seeds contain an antiflatulence factor that inhibits bacterial growth. The precise amount and composition of gas produced by a particular person on a particular occasion (such as the middle of a fancy dinner party) depends on many different factors, such as how the food is swallowed, the bacteria present in the intestine, the general activity of the gastrointestinal tract, and the food being eaten. Current knowledge can be boiled down to two statements: Soy, navy, black turtle, and lima beans are generally the most troublesome legumes. Peanuts generate little activity.

There are numerous opinions on the subject of flatulence and how to solve it. Author Patience Gray has several suggestions to offset what she calls "the explosive effects of the bean." First, she recommends using the most recent crop of beans. Second, she believes cooking beans in earthenware helps (as is done in many places such as southern Italy, Spain, Greece, Mexico, North Africa, and Cuba) because the clay absorbs distressing elements. Third, she recommends cooking the beans with alkaline ingredients like wild chicory, dandelion, spinach, or chard that has been blanched, squeezed dry, then finely chopped and added during the last 15 minutes of cooking to neutralize the acidity of the beans.

Julie Sahni, author of *Classic Indian Cooking*, believes that our troubles with beans arise because beans contain vegetable proteins that are harder to digest than animal proteins. Those present in certain types of unhulled beans and peas, such as black gram beans, kidney beans, and chickpeas, require more time

CAN BEANS MAKE YOU BETTER IN BED?

In the southern Italian province of Puglia, women believe that cooking dried fava beans "in their coats" (with their skins on) gives the beans special powers to increase one's physical potency. According to their folklore, fava beans cooked in their coats make the men stronger both in the fields and in the marriage bed.

and effort to digest. Beans are ideal for people who work outdoors and do heavy physical labor, especially if they are vegetarian, as are many Indians. For those of us who lead a modern, sedentary urban life but still want to eat beans, Sahni recommends serving them in moderate portions and including digestive spices, such as asafetida (a powerfully aromatic combination of tree resins), fresh ginger, fennel seed, and ajwain (the seeds of a lovage plant, also called carom seeds). The smaller split beans, peas, and lentils collectively called dal in India present less of a digestion problem. In fact, according to Sahni, these skinless lentils "are among the easiest to digest legumes."

Make it Easy on Yourself: Add Beans Gradually

If you're not accustomed to eating beans and other legumes, add them gradually to the diet, starting with small amounts combined with other foods. To help reduce flatulence, drink lots of liquids at the same time. And be sure to check out the Anti-Flatulence Cooking Tips (on page 51) for natural methods for reducing the flatulence factor of eating beans—they really work! Start with lentils and split peas and work your way up to kidney and soybeans, which are considered the most difficult to digest. Your body will eventually be able to digest legumes more easily.

WHAT IS A LEGUME, ANYWAY? DEFINING TERMS

Despite their long history and culinary significance, many of us are still confused about exactly what are and are not beans. The Greeks called them *pháselos*, from their resemblance to a type of small, swift sailing boat, which became the Latin *Phaseolus* and the botanical name for the New World bean family. The Romans called them *faba* (now *fava* in Italian, *fève* in French, and *fabas* in Spanish) and the Anglo-Saxons called them simply "beans."

According to *Webster's New World Dictionary of Culinary Arts,* a bean is "any of various legumes (mostly from the genus Phaseolus) with a double-seamed pod containing a single row of seeds (sometimes also called beans); some are used for their edible pods, others for shelling fresh, and some for their dried seeds." This includes Old World legumes, such as lentils, chickpeas, peas, soybeans, and the black-eyed pea family, and New World varieties, such as limas, kidney beans, black turtle beans, cranberry beans, cannellini or white kidney beans, and peanuts.

The secondary meaning of bean is "the ovoid or kidney-shaped dried seed." "Pulse" is a general term for edible seeds obtained from leguminous plants, such as peas, beans, and lentils. So, it seems as though bean plants are "legumes" and the seeds are "pulses." However, the word "pulse" is often used to refer to lentils and peas, rather than beans.

To add to the confusion, the French and Italians also use the terms "legumes" and "legumini" to refer to all

BEAN STOCK

Be sure to save the nutritious and fiber-rich bean cooking liquid. Use it as a quick stock. Chickpea broth is delicious, versatile, and rich in soluble fiber—so much fiber, in fact, that the broth gels when chilled.

manner of vegetable dishes. In a kitchen run according to the strict French brigade system, the chef in charge of all vegetables and starches is the *legumier*. In American English, it's a bit more complicated. We differentiate among peas, beans, and lentils and consider them very different, though they are all close relatives and meet the criterion of a plant that forms a single row of seeds in a double-seamed pod.

Without getting lost in semantics, in this book "legume" refers to all the members of the larger family, which includes peas, common beans, lentils, and chickpeas. I use "beans" when referring mainly to New World members of the common bean family, such as limas and kidney beans, and to favas, which are the most important Old World bean.

CHAPTER TWO

A Legume Primer

This chapter identifies more than 120 of the most popular and important legumes and their characteristics and culinary uses, along with some fascinating heirloom and imported varieties. Purchasing, preparation, and storage information are also included. Recipes using particular beans are listed in their sections.

Legumes included:

Adzuki Bean (Azuki, Aduki)
Anasazi Bean
Anhar Pigeon Pea
Appaloosa Bean
Baby White Lima Bean (Small Lima Bean, Butter Bean, Sieva Bean, Civet Bean, Dixie Speckled Butter Bean, Calico Bean, Florida Speckled Pole Bean)
Beluga Lentil
Black Appaloosa Bean (Cave Bean)
Black Calypso (Yin Yang, Orca)
Black Chickpea (Black Garbanzo Bean)
Black Gram Bean
Black Runner Bean
Black Turtle Bean
Black-Eyed Pea
Blue Pod Capucijner
Blue Shackamaxon Bean
Bolita Bean
Borlotti Bean (Tuscan Bean)
Brown Lazy Wife Bean (Lentil Bean)
Brown Lentil
Calypso Bean (Steuben Yellow Eye, Molasses Face, Maine Yellow Eye, Butterscotch Calypso)
Cannellini Bean
Castelluccio Lentil
Ceci Siciliani
Christmas Lima Bean (Chestnut Lima)
Cicerchie
Coco (French Navy Bean)
Corona Grande
Cowpeas
Cranberry Bean (Roman Bean)
Cream Pea
Crowder Pea
Dark Green Chickpea
Dark Red Kidney Bean
Desi Chickpea
Edamame
European Soldier Bean
Eye of Goat Bean (Ojo de Cabra)
Fabada Bean

Fagioli Pavoni
Fagioli Scritti
Fagioli Sorana
Flageolet de Chevrier
French Green Lentil (Lentille du Puys)
French Horticultural Bean (October Bean)
Fresh Cranberry Bean
Fresh Green Lima
Giant White Coco Bean
Gigante Bean (Gigandes, Hija)
Golden Split Fava
Goober Pea
Good Mother Stallard
Great Northern Bean
Green Bean
Green Fava Bean
Green Mung Bean
Green Romano Bean
Green Split Pea
Haricot Blanc de Soisson
Haricot Lingot
Haricots Verts
Hopi Orange Lima Bean
Jackson Wonder Bean
Judiós Bean (Judias)
Kabuli Chickpea
Kidney Bean
Lady Pea
Large Brown Fava
Large White Lima (Madagascar Bean, Burma Bean, Rangoon Bean, Habas Grandes, Fagioli della Nonna, Fagioli di Spagna, Grandma's Bean)
Lupini Bean
Madeira (Madera) Bean
Marrowfat Pea
Monstoller Wild Goose Bean
Mortgage Lifter Bean (Aztec, Pueblo Bean)
Munsi Wolf Bean
Navy Bean
Nuna Bean (Poroto, Numia, Popping Bean, Toasting Bean)
Painted Pony Bean

Pea Shoots
Pea Sprouts
Pebble Bean
Petite Crimson Lentil
Pigeon Pea (Gandule)
Pink Bean
Pinto Bean
Purple Hyacinth Bean
Rattlesnake Bean
Red Lima Bean
Red Valentine Bean
Rice Bean
Scarlet Runner Bean
Small Brown Fava
Small Red Bean
Snow Pea
Southern Checker Pea
Spanish Peanut
Split Red Lentil
Split White Lentil (Urud Dal)
Split Yellow Lentil
Sugar Snap Pea
Swedish Brown Bean
Sweet Green Pea
Tall Telephone Pea
Tarbais Bean
Tepary Beans
Tocomares (Chocolate Runner)
Tolosana Bean (Prince Bean)
Tongues of Fire Bean
Toor Pigeon Pea
Trout Bean (Jacob's Cattle Bean, Coach Bean, Dalmatian Bean, Forellen-German)
Virginia Peanut
Wax Bean (Crystal White Wax Bean)
White Emergo Bean (Sweet White, White Runner)
Winged Bean
Yam Bean
Yard-Long Bean
Yellow Indian Woman Bean
Yellow Split Chickpea (Channa Dal)
Yellow Split Pea
Zebra Bean (Amethyst Bean)
Zolfino Pratomagno

One could devote an entire book to the botanical relationships of all legumes, of which there are literally thousands. This chart represents the major branches of the legume family and the most commonly used beans, peas, and lentils. Methods of classification vary greatly, ranging from seed type to culinary characteristics, and they change according to new research findings. In this book legumes have been categorized by their botanical relationships in the primer section and by their culinary uses in the cooking charts.

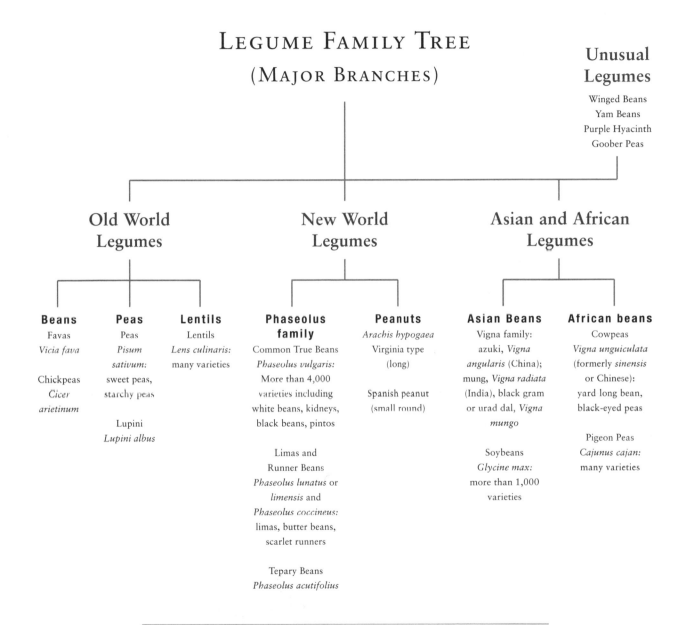

LEGUME FAMILY TREE
(MAJOR BRANCHES)

Unusual Legumes
Winged Beans
Yam Beans
Purple Hyacinth
Goober Peas

Old World Legumes

Beans
Favas
Vicia fava

Chickpeas
Cicer arietinum

Peas
Peas
Pisum sativum:
sweet peas,
starchy peas

Lupini
Lupini albus

Lentils
Lentils
Lens culinaris:
many varieties

New World Legumes

Phaseolus family
Common True Beans
Phaseolus vulgaris:
More than 4,000
varieties including
white beans, kidneys,
black beans, pintos

Limas and
Runner Beans
Phaseolus lunatus or
limensis and
Phaseolus coccineus:
limas, butter beans,
scarlet runners

Tepary Beans
Phaseolus acutifolius

Peanuts
Arachis hypogaea
Virginia type
(long)

Spanish peanut
(small round)

Asian and African Legumes

Asian Beans
Vigna family:
azuki, *Vigna angularis* (China);
mung, *Vigna radiata* (India), black gram
or urad dal, *Vigna mungo*

Soybeans
Glycine max:
more than 1,000
varieties

African beans
Cowpeas
Vigna unguiculata
(formerly *sinensis*
or Chinese):
yard long bean,
black-eyed peas

Pigeon Peas
Cajunus cajan:
many varieties

NEW SCIENTIFIC NAMES FOR BEANS
According to Alan Davidson in his magnum opus, *The Oxford Companion to Food*, many of the beans familiar in the West that were formerly classified in the genus *Phaseolus* have now been assigned to the genus *Vigna*.

Specific Legume Descriptions and Characteristics

OLD WORLD LEGUMES

BEANS

Favas
Vicia faba

Green Fava Bean: The venerable broad bean (fava or faba) was the only bean known to Europe until the discovery of the New World, though other legumes like chickpeas, lentils, and peas were well known. Favas have been cultivated since ancient times everywhere from Britain to Sicily and Egypt. Favas are quite hardy and come in green, purple, deep tan, and pale beige varieties. In England, large dried brown favas are known as horse beans, because they were fed to horses. Other names for the fava are *faba* in Spanish, *fève* in French, *fava* in Italian, broad and Windsor bean in British English.

Fava beans grow inside large green pods about eight inches long and one inch wide with a string running down the inner side. Pull off the string, open up the pod and you'll find a row of beans nestled inside a protective white, spongy material. Each fava bean is enclosed in a second skin, which is normally removed before eating. Fresh favas range in color and size from the young beans that are a springtime delicacy to large, starchy, yellow-white mature beans. When picked young enough, these thumbnail-sized, brilliant green beans may be enjoyed raw dipped in salt as a snack.

To eat fresh favas, bend back the tips of the pods, and then pull down along the side to remove the string. The pods will then open easily. Remove the beans and discard the pods. Remove the second inner skin before the final cooking stage. Bring a pot of salted water to a boil. Add the shelled favas and cook them just until the water comes back to a boil. Drain and then refresh them in a bowl of ice water or under cold running water to set the color. Peel off and discard the outer skins, revealing the bright green inner beans. If your fresh favas are overly mature and yellow inside rather than bright green, you'll need to cook them again in boiling water until tender. Otherwise set aside the green favas and eat as is or continue with your recipe. Because fresh favas take a fair amount of time to prepare, enjoy a few favas as a garnish for all sorts of dishes.

Green Fava Bean Recipes

Provençal Artichokes with Fava Beans
Minted Fresh Fava Beans
Broad Bean and Nasturtium Soup
Trio of Savory Beans
Raw Baby Favas with Salt
Roasted Pigeons with Baby Fava Beans

Suggested Uses

• Sprinkle green favas at the last minute into any sauté of fish, seafood, or poultry to add a colorful and tasty accent.
• When cooking starches such as rice, couscous, or wheat berries, stir in favas just before serving.
• Add favas to fresh tomato sauce, brown butter and Parmesan sauce, or even cream-based sauces for pasta.

Dried Fava Bean: Dried favas come in many sizes, shapes, and colors. The two basic kinds are those in their skins and split favas with their inner skins removed.

Large Brown Fava Bean: These whole dried favas are the most common kind. They have a noticeably granular texture and a strong flavor with a slightly bitter quality. Favas in their skins take longer to cook than the split, skinned varieties, which are also easier to digest.

Small Brown Fava Bean: These small reddish brown favas in their skins are almost round in shape. They take less time to cook then their larger cousins.

Golden Split Fava Bean: My favorite kind of dried fava is the large, split golden type that I buy at a Lebanese grocery. They are available from Middle Eastern groceries and from the Sadaf Company (see Sources, page 341). They cook quickly and evenly and the golden color is a real plus when making bean dips.

Dried Fava Bean Recipes

Egyptian Fava Bean Soup
Bitar's Pan-Grilled Falafel
Tunisian Fava Bean Stew with Merguez Lamb Sausage
Crunchy Fried Favas with Pimentón

Chickpeas
Cicer arietinum

It is said that an ancestor of the family of the Roman orator Cicero had a wart on his face that resembled a chickpea, hence the root of his name. *Ariteinum* is Latian for "ramlike" (as in the zodiac sign Aries) and refers to the chickpea's resemblance to a ram's head, complete with curling horns. There are many names for chickpeas including the Spanish *garbanzo,* the Old English *calavance,* the Italian *ceci,* the Portuguese *grao-de-bico,* and the Indian *gram,* a term used for whole, rather than split legumes.

Dry chickpeas are notoriously hard and the most challenging of beans to cook. Check that your chickpeas come from a source that sells its stock quickly. Shriveled, dried-out chickpeas will never get soft, no matter how long you cook them. I buy mine from a Mexican, Latino, Indian, or Middle Eastern grocery. Cooked chickpeas packed in glass jars imported from Spain are of excellent quality; dried chickpeas from Spain are especially plump and thin-skinned.

Soak chickpeas for at least 10 hours and as long as 24 hours before cooking. Many cooks recommend skinning cooked chickpeas before proceeding further with recipes. While skinning will improve the digestibility of chickpeas, for aesthetic reasons I prefer to use unskinned cooked chickpeas. To skin, place the cooked chickpeas in a large bowl of cold water. Rub vigorously between your fingers to loosen the skins, which will rise to the surface of the water. Using a wire skimmer (or your cupped hands) remove and discard the skins.

Black Chickpea (Black Garbanzo, Black Gram): This small chickpea is the size of a large pea and has black skin that bleeds slightly when cooked, although the center remains toffee colored. It has an earthy, smoky flavor with a subtle sweet note and a firm texture. When skinned and split, they are known in Indian cooking as *channa dal,* or split yellow chickpeas.

Ceci Siciliani: This special variety is imported from Sicily. Chickpeas were a staple food of the Roman Empire, especially in Sicily. There, a moderately intense feeling is ironically referred to as *Amuri e brodu di ciciri:* "love and chickpea broth." This saying dates back to the thirteenth century, when rebellious Sicilians could identify French overlords by having them pronounce the word "ciciri" (chickpeas), whose sound they could never reproduce correctly.

Cicerchie: This variety of chickpea dates back to ancient Rome and is cultivated primarily in Puglia and Umbria. Tiny and irregular in shape and ranging in color from gray to brown, they look like miniature fava beans. They have a delicate flavor and tender skin and make a great accompaniment to game and can also be prepared in a puree to serve with bitter greens. Cicerchie are high in iron.

Dark Green Chickpea: Small dark green, skinned whole chickpeas are available in Indian groceries. In India, chickpeas have been part of the diet since the second millennium BCE. These and other types of chickpeas have a nutlike chewy texture that makes them satisfying in one-dish meals or hearty soups.

Desi Chickpea: These chickpeas are smaller and darker and have a thicker skin, so they take a longer time to cook.

Kabuli Chickpea (Garbanzo): This common variety is tan to light brown when raw and golden brown when cooked. Called garbanzos in Spanish-speaking countries, they are plump and creamy with a relatively thin skin.

Yellow Split Chickpea: These bright golden-yellow split chickpeas are the most popular legume in India, where they are called *channa dal.* Black-skinned in their unhulled form, these same chickpeas are found whole in Indian markets, under the name black gram beans.

Split Baby Garbanzo: This chickpea variety cooks in less than fifteen minutes and looks like a yellow corn kernel when cooked. It has a nutty texture, delicate flavor, and lots of protein. It is also easily digested because

Chickpea Recipes

Crunchy Falafel with Yemenite Fenugreek Sauce
Spicy Hummus Dip
Pan-Grilled Falafel with Salad in Garlic Dressing
Provençal Chickpea Salad with Tuna Caviar
Spanish One-Pot Soup
Spanish Chickpea Soup with Garlic-Mint Pesto
Niçoise Pasta Shell Salad with Green Beans, Chickpeas, and Tuna
Indian-Spiced Chickpeas
Seven Vegetable and Chicken Couscous
Chickpea and Eggplant Moussaka with Goat Cheese Topping
Chile-Spiced Fried Chickpeas
Israeli Couscous with Eggplant Rolls and Chickpeas

Chickpea Flour Recipes

Chickpea Fries Riviera Style
Indian Vegetable Tempura in Chickpea Batter
Socca Niçoise with Roasted Peppers and Goat Cheese
Chickpea Spaetzle
Tunisian Chickpea Cookies

it is skinless. The firm, almost crunchy texture is excellent in salads. In their whole form, these chickpeas are called black chickpeas or Bengal gram in India.

Chickpea Flour: Chickpeas come in many forms, including flour, which is used in India for making fritters and pancakes, fried crunchy sticks called *panisses* in Nice and around the Riviera, and for the snack "bread" called *socca*.

Chickpea flour, much of which comes from Canada, may be found under the name Bengal gram or besan flour in Indian groceries, and is sometimes available roasted. Milder tasting, extra-fine ground chickpea flour is imported from France. Store chickpea flour in the refrigerator or freezer as it is prone to insect infestation.

THE PEA FAMILY
PISUM SATIVUM,
PISUM CULINARIS

Starchy Peas

Blue Pod Capucijner: This large, grayish brown pea becomes quite leathery when mature, but is decorative with beautiful rose-pink and wine-red flowers. The deep maroon pods change to inky blue as the peas mature. A Dutch or French variety that dates back to the 17th century, these peas were developed by Capuchin monks, who gave them their name. They are known as *pois à cross violette* (purple cross peas) in France.

Green Split Pea: Both the Greeks and Romans cultivated shelling peas for drying. Pease porridge was the English wintertime staple for centuries because it "sticks to the ribs." Yellow split pea soup still serves the same purpose for the inhabitants of Quebec. Two types of peas are now grown: the wrinkly skinned sweet peas for eating green and the smooth-skinned starchy peas for drying as whole and split peas. Green split peas, an old-fashioned

---

Split Pea Recipes

Diner-Style Split Pea Soup

Dutch Green Split Pea Soup

Quebeçois Yellow Split Pea Soup

Moroccan Golden Split Pea and Pumpkin Soup

Dosa (Yellow Split Pea Pancakes) with Cucumber-Yogurt Raita

EIGHTY YEARS OF FROZEN PEAS

In the 1920s and 1930s peas became one of the earliest successes in frozen vegetables. Their evanescent sweetness, which starts to disappear soon after being picked, is fixed and preserved by freezing.

starchy pea variety without any skins, are split in half for ease of cooking. They are sometimes found in whole form, which take longer to cook. There is also a third type of wild Mediterranean pea called the oasis or maquis pea.

Marrowfat Pea: This sought-after old English variety was thought to taste as good and rich as the cherished marrow fat from meat bones. A plump mature pea, which dries naturally in the field, this name was recorded by the *Oxford English Dictionary* as early as 1733. It is grown mainly in Britain, but many are exported to the Far East, especially Japan, where one of the oldest export varieties, called Maro, has been known for 100 years.

Tall Telephone Pea: This wrinkled type of marrow pea grows on seven- to eight-foot vines with huge pods almost five inches long and containing eight to ten peas that hang straight down. It is also known as the Dwarf Telephone Pea, Alderman Pea, and Carter's Daisy Pea and is noted for its high quality, fine flavor, and excellent production.

Yellow Split Peas: A starchy pea variety in an attractive golden color, yellow split peas are commonly used for soups and are especially popular in Sweden, Canada, and India. In Sweden, thick yellow split pea soup is the traditional Thursday night supper, which commemorates King Eric XIV, who was poisoned with arsenic in his yellow split pea soup. Canada is now the largest source of yellow split peas in the world. Called *channa dal* in India (although this name also refers to split yellow chickpeas), yellow split peas are sometimes roasted, then ground and used to bind ground meat kebabs. They can also be fried or used to thicken sauces.

Sweet Peas

Pea Shoot and Pea Sprout: Pea shoots, the very top tiny leaves and curly tendrils of snow pea vines, are a great delicacy in Chinese cooking and often the most expensive vegetables in the market. Add them to soup just before serving or at the last minute to a stir-fry of vegetables. They have a fresh, sweet flavor and make an outstanding garnish for any light dish. Companies that specialize in sprouts are now selling pea sprouts: the stem and first green leaves sprouted from peas. They are less expensive than pea shoots, and though not as sweet and spring-green in color—only the leaf portion is green—they make a good substitute.

Snow Pea and Sugar Snap Pea: Snow peas were probably first cultivated in Holland and were originally known as Dutch peas. Sugar or snap peas are to garden peas as green string beans are to shelling beans. Sugar snaps and snow peas are both types of sugar peas, with tender, edible pods. The difference is that snow peas are completely flat with underdeveloped inner seeds, while sugar snaps are full rounded, and closely resemble a garden pea in its pod. Other names for snow peas include *mangetout* (eat-them-alls) in France, Chinese pea, Chinese snow pea, Chinese pea pod, and sugar pea. These flat-podded peas are hand picked and are available fresh or frozen. They are especially popular in Asian stir fries because they cook within minutes in the high heat that maintains their bright color and fleeting crispness.

Look for barely discernible miniature peas inside snow peas. Snow peas should be light green in color and smooth and firm. Be sure to inspect the pods carefully for small circles of rot on their surface, a dead giveaway that they've been sitting too long on the shelf. Since people buy snow peas in small quantities, these peas tend to sell slowly at many supermarkets. Instead, try to buy them from Asian markets, which tend to sell them quickly and maintain a fresh inventory.

Sugar snaps and snow peas couldn't be easier to prepare. Hold the pod just below the stem between thumb and forefinger and break back the stem end. To remove the stem and attached strings on either side of the pod, grasp the tip of the stem and pull it down parallel to the pod. Steam or pan-fry snow peas, but always cook them quickly at high heat (for brightest color) and serve them right away.

A relatively new type of edible pod pea is the fantastically popular sugar snap pea developed in the United States by Dr. C. Lamborn of Gallatin Valley Seed Co. (now Rogers NK Seed Co.) and introduced to gardeners in 1979. Sugar snaps are round-podded and similar to standard pea pods in appearance. However, they are fleshier and free from pod-wall fiber when mature, and some are stringless.

Most sugar snaps are purchased fresh, though they are also available frozen and can be used as an alternative to either sweet garden peas or snow peas. Snap peas should be brilliant green in color with the same smooth, firm skin as snow peas. Stay away from sugar snaps with shriveled tops or spotted sides. To maintain their brilliant color and crisp, juicy texture, cook at high heat for a very short time. They don't take well to blanching (precooking and then reheating), which is not even a timesaver because they cook so quickly. Once sugar snaps are cooked, serve them as quickly as possible because they will start to shrivel and darken within minutes.

Sweet Green Pea: Italian Renaissance gardeners originally cultivated the sweet green pea, leading to a craze for this new delicacy in the French royal court. In fact, in Louis XIV's court, the ladies would eat peas just before going to bed, in spite of the danger of indigestion. In the north and west of France, the towns of Saint-Germain and Clamart were so famous for the quality of their tiny peas that their names came to be used as culinary terms for any dishes made with *petit pois*. The people of France and Italy still celebrate spring by eating sweet young peas. Eating *risi e bisi,* a dish of creamy rice mixed with tiny peas *(piselli),* is the traditional rite of spring in Venice. The French cook the same petits pois for a matter of minutes with spring onions and butter lettuce for a dish of exquisite delicacy. Common names include garden pea, sweet pea, and English pea. Special decorative varieties of green peas are grown for their lovely and colorful blossoms.

Sweet peas are the familiar "peas-in-a-pod." Their parchment-like pods are normally too stringy to eat, though they can be used to make a soup broth. Choose pearl-shaped peas that perfectly fill their pods, the way you'd like your trousers to fit: close to the body, but not showing any bulges. Stay away from overgrown, starchy peas that are flattened against each other and resemble a set of teeth. For the ultimate in sweet succulence, eat peas just after they're picked. But don't despair if this isn't possible. Peas will maintain almost all of their sweetness for 3 to 4 days if placed in a closed plastic bag and refrigerated.

Lupini
Lupini albus

Lupini Beans: These flat, coin-shaped, yellow-brown beans have a small round hole at one end and are most commonly purchased already cooked and pickled. They are enjoyed as a snack with beverages in Lebanon, southern Italy, Spain, and Portugal, where they are called *tremoços*. To serve the lupini, drain the liquid from the jar and place the beans in a bowl. Invite guests to suck the inner beans from their skins, discarding the skins in bowls.

Members of the pea family, lupini or lupins are grown mainly for their flowers. The seeds or beans of certain species, though toxic and bitter when fresh, are treated to make them edible, and then roasted or boiled. In spite of the lengthy preparation needed to make them edible, lupini have been part of the Old World diet for more than 2,000 years. Some varieties now grown can be used without preliminary preparation. The variety called tarwi is high in protein.

The Lentil Family
Lens esculenta,
Lens culinaris

An important, indeed essential, plant in the ancient world, lentils have been cultivated for close to 10,000 years in the Middle East. Whole lentils are made up of two lens-shaped sides, hence the origin of its name. India accounts for about half the world's consumption of lentils and therefore has developed its own lexicon and classification for their most popular legumes, based on culinary use rather than botanical category. *Gram* is an Indian term used for legumes that are whole, rather than split, such as black gram or mung bean, green chickpea, and green mung bean. Split legumes, such as red lentils, split golden chickpeas, and split white inner seeds of black mung beans called *urud*, are all called dal.

While common lentils are small, round, and earth-brown in color, lentils come in a variety of colors and sizes. There are two main types of lentils: those that are relatively large and light or yellow-colored, and those that are small and brown, pink, or gray. In the north of India and Pakistan, the Muslim population mainly eats whole pink lentils; in the south split lentils are more popular. Next to soybeans, lentils have the highest protein content of all vegetables, about 25 percent. This may account for their being a favorite food during Lent in Roman Catholic countries, along with their decidedly meaty character.

All lentils are thin-skinned so they cook quickly without soaking. Vegetable proteins, particularly those present in certain types of unhulled beans and peas, can be very difficult to digest, but the smaller shelled peas and beans present less of a problem. Lentils are among the easiest of all legumes to digest.

Beluga Lentil: These fancy black lentils are petite and fetch a high price. Their name is a play on their resemblance to beluga caviar, the smallest, blackest, and most expensive sturgeon caviar.

Brown Lentil: These are the most common and inexpensive lentils with a mild flavor and soft texture. They are best used for soups where they will turn soft, almost melting in character, and help to thicken the soup. They can easily become mushy if overcooked

Castelluccio Lentil: These small brown lentils are famed in Italy for their delicate taste and tiny size. Lentils produced in Castelluccio di Norcia in Umbria have been awarded the I.G.T., or Protected Geographical Indication. Cultivation has always been organic, using centuries-old traditions of crop rotation.

French Green Lentil: Called "Lentilles du Puy," these special lentils are raised in Puy, a region of southwest France. They are small, speckled deep green, and firm when cooked, which only takes a short time. Because of their attractive appearance, nutty flavor, and ease of cooking, they are the darlings of French and American chefs, especially in the classic nouvelle cuisine dish of salmon on a bed of lentils.

Petite Crimson Lentil: These tiny red lentils, about one-third the size of regular lentils, are originally from Turkey, Egypt, and India. They are now domestically grown and cook in 5 minutes. They can be mixed with rice or made into soups.

Spanish Pardina Lentil: Known as Spanish brown lentils or continental lentils, they are small and richly colored (ranging from earthy brown to moss green with streaks of black), and hold their shape very well when cooked.

Split Red Lentil: These salmon-colored small split lentils are also called red chief lentils, pink lentils, Egyptian lentils, and *masoor dal* in India. They turn golden and very soft when cooked and are ideal for soups and purées.

Split Yellow Lentil: (See Pigeon Peas, page 45.)

Split White Lentil: (See Black Chick Pea, page 25.)

Lentil Recipes

Crispy Lentil Wafers with Coconut-Cilantro Chutney

Tabbouli Salad with Lentils, Lemon, and Mint

Spanish Lentil Salad with Salt Cod Fritters and Preserved Lemon Aïoli

Curried Red Lentil Soup

Faki (Greek Lentil Soup)

Black Sea Bass with French Green Lentils and Tarragon

French Lentil and Foie Gras Stuffed Won Ton Ravioli with Tomato and Truffle Oil

French Green Lentils with Black Truffles and Caramelized Shallots

Spiced Duck in Port Wine Sauce with Green Lentils and Savoy Cabbage

Grilled Cured Tuna on a Bed of Beluga Lentils

French Green Lentil Salad with Bacon and Tomato

NEW WORLD LEGUMES

THE *PHASEOLUS* FAMILY: COMMON TRUE BEANS AND LIMAS

Common True Beans Popular in America

Green Beans: We might take green beans for granted, but they are a consistently satisfying, good-looking green vegetable choice. The best are bright grass-green in color (rather than faded or yellowish) and have a soft, velvety skin. Check the end where the bean has been broken off the stem; if the scar is hard and dark, it was picked too long ago. Fresh-picked beans should be crisp enough to make a "snap" sound when broken in half. Ideally, choose slender pods with small, uniform-size seeds inside so they will cook evenly.

Green beans are still known as string beans because old-fashioned varieties had strings to remove. Because fresh-picked green beans make a crisp snapping sound when the ends are broken off, they are also called snap beans. It's your choice whether to break off both ends (the stem and the pointy tip) or to just trim off the stem ends. I prefer to leave the pointy tips on for aesthetics, though they are slightly tougher than the rest of the bean. Because the pointy end deteriorates first, becoming shriveled and unsightly, green beans with their sprightly tips intact can display their freshness.

For a fancier look, line up the green beans and use a sharp knife to cut off both the tops and bottoms so that the beans are all the same length. You can also French-cut the beans by slicing them on a sharp diagonal into two inch lengths, exposing the inner flesh and tiny seeds.

Green beans react quickly to acidity, losing their attractive color and becoming more olive-colored than emerald. To cook green beans, there are several good choices. The first is to steam them using a basket steamer. The second method is to bring a large pot of salted water to a boil and blanch, or partially cook, the beans, bringing the water back to a boil as quickly as possible. Be sure to stir the beans so they cook and color evenly. Cook 2 to 3 minutes, or until bright green and crisp-tender; then drain.

The third method is to bring one to two inches of salted water to a boil in a large skillet and then add the beans, stirring them occasionally and bringing the water back to a boil as quickly as possible; cook for 2 to 3 minutes. If you're seasoning the beans with anything acidic like lemon, vinegar, white wine, or even tomatoes, add them at the last minute to preserve their color. In Greece, India, and Spain, green beans are cooked slowly in a sauce that is often tomato based until they are meltingly tender Though olive in color, these beans have an appetizing quality all their own.

Wax Bean (Crystal White Wax Bean): Hybridized by Dutch plant breeders, wax beans were first grown in England as a forcing bean for hothouses. Also called ice bean, this is a light green to white variety of green or snap bean that tends to be a little tougher, more like an old-fashioned green bean variety. Heirloom varieties have a string running the length of their pods, which must be removed before cooking.

Follow the cooking directions for green beans (see page 29) if the wax beans are young with a lemon-yellow to greenish color rather than a creamy white. Colorful purple wax beans are available in markets between May and October. If your wax beans are more mature with prominent inner seeds, follow the cooking directions for romano beans (see page 34).

Black Turtle Bean: Also called black beans or frijoles negros, turtle beans, and Mexican or Spanish black beans, these popular legumes are medium to small in size and maintain a dramatic shiny black color when cooked, though they are actually a very deep purple. The best

black beans are considered to be the heirloom black Valentines, actually a deep purple-black. All black beans, which are closely related to kidney beans, turn purplish when cooked. They have a meaty texture and a rich, earthy flavor.

Black beans are beloved in Cuba, Trinidad, Brazil, Mexico, and in the American Southwest, and some describe the flavor as slightly mushroom-like, with a velvety texture. Note that the black bean used in Chinese cooking (often fermented for a funky taste) is completely different. The Chinese bean is a soybean, possibly though not necessarily black until fermented, whereas the black turtle bean is a variety of common bean.

Dried black turtle beans are very likely to contain foreign matter, because dirt clumps or little stones are easily disguised. Always be sure to pick them over carefully. There are innumerable versions of black bean soup, including two in this book. Black beans make an exceptionally smooth purée.

Some find black beans to be particularly treacherous when it comes to creating noxious gas. To cook black beans, soak them overnight in cold water; then drain and rinse under cold water. Place in a large pot and cover generously with cold water. Bring the water to a boil; then drain, discarding the water. Add the flavoring ingredient of your choice (see Basic Cooking Chart, page 58). Cover with fresh cold water (or stock, diluted with water if concentrated). Bring to a boil again, skimming off any white foam impurities. Reduce the heat and simmer for about 2 hours; then stir in the salt. Continue to cook for 1 hour longer or until tender to the bite.

PUTTING THE TURTLE IN BLACK TURTLE BEAN

In the United States, black beans were first raised in the Gulf Coast areas near Mexico, where they were an important food in the diet of local slaves. Because many people associated these beans with slave food and didn't like the fact that they stained every food cooked with them an inky color, black beans were not well received at first. The name "black turtle bean" seems to have resulted from a marketing effort by a 19th-century seed company that tried to popularize them by selling them as "turtle soup beans," suitable to add to or use as a substitute for turtle in the soup then considered the utmost in luxury foods. As a result, soups like Black Turtle Bean Purée with Madeira, Lemon, and Egg Mimosa are made with all the traditional flavorings for turtle soup.

Black Bean Recipes

Black Bean Nachos with Salsa and Guacamole
Black Bean Quesadillas with Pepita-Tomatillo Sauce
Tex-Mex Seven-Layer Salad with Homemade Tortilla Chips
Black Bean Paté with Tequila
Southwest Black Bean Salad with Baked Spiced Goat Cheese
Cuban Black Bean Soup with Sofrito and Smoked Turkey
Black Turtle Bean Purée with Madeira, Lemon, and Egg
 Mimosa
Black Bean Burgers on Garlic Toasted Buns
Black Bean and Hazelnut Cakes with Steamed Clams
Bean-Pebbled Paella
Black Turtle Beans with Epazote and Cotija Cheese
Cuban Black Turtle Beans and Rice
Oaxacan Corn Tortillas in Black Bean Sauce

Kidney Bean Recipes

Red Bean Dip with Crunchy Pita Chips and Vegetables
Kidney Bean Salad in Mustard Vinaigrette
Pennsylvania Dutch Chow-Chow
Portuguese Salt Cod and Kidney Bean Salad
Three-Bean Salad Ring with Avocado Mousse
Bean-Pebbled Paella
Red Bean and White Hominy Chili
Five-Way Cincinnati-Style Chili
Sabbath Beef, Bean, and Barley Casserole

Great Northern Bean: One of the most popular and versatile varieties in the United States and Canada, these all-purpose, medium-sized oblong beans with white skins have a slightly nutty flavor and a powdery texture. Although they are slightly larger than the pea-sized navy bean, Great Northern beans can be substituted for them in soups and baked bean dishes.

Kidney Bean: These large, kidney-shaped beans have a robust, full-bodied flavor and a soft, though meaty, texture. They take a long time to cook, hold up well in slow-cooked casseroles, and cook to a light pinkish red. A thick skin means these beans require long cooking, and they can be harder to digest, but they also hold their shape well in long-simmered dishes like chili con carne.

Dark Red Kidney Bean: These large, kidney-shaped beans with a robust, full-bodied flavor and soft texture are dark, almost purple-red, and cook up to a beautiful crimson. In India, where they are called *badi rajma*, dark red kidney beans are very popular because their heartiness makes them a satisfying meat substitute. The smaller red chile bean *(pequeño)* and the pink bean, popular in Puerto Rico and sold by Goya and other companies, are close substitutes.

I enjoy using the gorgeous, dark red kidney beans sold in the can by the S & W Company; a similarly deep-colored bean imported from Spain is sold in glass jars at Whole Foods. I find that in bean salads and other dishes where color is important, it's hard to match the brilliant color of dark red kidney beans. By using the dried dark red kidney beans sold by Whole Foods and Vann's Spices, I can now achieve this same desirable color

Navy Bean: This white bean was served so often to sailors that it became forever associated with the navy. Being small, it took less time to cook in the ships' galleys than larger beans. For a similar reason, navy beans are often used by commercial baked bean manufacturers. They have many names, including haricot, Boston bean, white coco, pea bean, white pea bean, and *alubias chicas* in Spanish. Navy beans are perfect for baked beans, salads, soups, stews, and purées.

Pink Bean: This oval pink-skinned bean with a very creamy texture is beloved in Puerto Rican cookery, where it is called *habichuela roja,* or red bean. Pink beans can be used in all pinto and cranberry bean recipes. Pinquitos are small, rounded pink beans that retain their firm texture even after long, slow cooking. They are traditional for Santa Maria–style tri-tip beef barbecue popular in California.

Pinto Bean: This medium-sized, oval, mottled beige and brown bean common throughout the American Southwest has an earthy flavor and powdery texture. It is related to the kidney bean and turns reddish brown when cooked. The best pintos are raised at high altitude; they are quicker cooking and easier to digest. These beans are used in chili and all types of southwestern dishes, including refried beans. *Pinto* means "painted" in Spanish. Other colorful names include crabeye bean and gunga pea.

Small Red Bean: These rounded, burgundy-red beans, called Mexican red beans and *rojos pequeños* in Spanish, are good lookers and good cookers. Because they are small, they cook quickly and evenly. Popular among Hispanic people in the United States, they are sold in large quantities by Goya. Use them in any Creole dishes or in recipes that call for kidney beans, such as chili and baked beans.

Heirloom Common True Bean Varieties
Phaseolus vulgaris

Bean seeds are probably the easiest seeds of all to save from the vegetable garden, and will remain viable for years if stored in a dry, cool place. Many of the heirloom varieties listed here have striking markings or special characteristics that farmers wanted to save and share. Saving heirloom bean seeds promotes genetic diversity in our crops, thus helping our food supply stay robust. Because beans are self-pollinating, insect cross-pollination is not common. Therefore, gardeners can save seeds of common beans and peas and expect them to remain true to type.

The greater the diversity of seeds we have, the greater is the possibility of overcoming problems with any one plant. Generations of gardeners and small regional growers have saved seeds to preserve some of these heirloom varieties of common beans. These plants performed best for them, developed resistances to local insect and disease problems, and became adapted to specific soils and climates.

Anasazi Bean: These burgundy and white mottled beans have a sweet flavor and meaty texture and are a close relative of appaloosa beans. "Anasazi" is a Navajo word meaning "the ancient ones," and refers to the Anasazi cliff dwelling Indians who lived in the Four Corners area (now Colorado, Utah, Arizona, and New Mexico) around A.D. 130. This bean variety was originally found in the ruins of cliff dwellings by settlers in the early 1900s and is now registered to and grown exclusively for Adobe Milling of Dove Creek, Colorado. Grown at high altitude (about 7,000 feet), Anasazi are said to contain 75 percent less of the gas-causing carbohydrates than pinto beans. They make good baked beans.

Appaloosa Bean: Though sometimes referred to as Anasazi beans, growers insist the two beans are different. Also called red appaloosa, these beans have markings that are reminiscent of those on the appaloosa pony. Slender and oval with mottled burgundy to purple markings, this bean is recommended for dishes like Southwest Baked Beans because it holds its shape well and has a rich flavor. Appaloosas make a good substitute for black-eyed peas in Smoked Turkey Chili, and may also be substituted for pintos, a close relation.

Black Appaloosa Bean (Cave Bean): These striking black-and-white beans with a distinctive flat, angular shape were supposedly found in the desert soil near ancient cave dwellings in the Southwest. Because of their visual appeal, they are best suited for salads and baked bean dishes, where the bean will remain whole.

Black Calypso Bean (Yin Yang, Orca): This boutique bean with its dramatic black-and-white color patterns was developed by growers in Europe, where it's become quite popular. It is smooth in texture with a mild vegetable-like flavor similar to yet milder than the black turtle bean. Cooking these beautiful beans in lots of water helps keep their distinctive coloring. They can add visual flair to many recipes and will expand two times when cooked.

Blue Shackamaxon Bean: This old variety of pole beans, preserved among Quaker farmers of southeastern Pennsylvania and southern New Jersey, is said to be of Lenape Indian origin. Named after a place called Shackamaxon along the Delaware River, now in the city of Philadelphia, the bean was never grown commercially. The seeds were preserved by a seedsman in Bucks County, Pennsylvania. When freshly shelled, the beans are bright navy blue; as they dry, they turn purplish blue.

Bolita Bean: This Western heirloom bean was grown by Native Americans throughout the Southwest. The Spanish who settled in northern New Mexico developed them. This warm brown bean is rich-tasting, with more depth of flavor than its close relative the pinto bean, and can be used in Southwest-style dishes.

Brown Lazy Wife Bean: Known as "lentil beans" among the Pennsylvania Dutch, these small brown beans are named for how quickly they cook, and are commonly grown in the hills of western Pennsylvania, Maryland, West Virginia, and Ohio, where they may have originated. They are also popular as a soup bean in Germany, Switzerland, and northern Italy. Believed to have been taken from Pennsylvania to Switzerland almost 300 years ago, they are often combined with lentils in cooking.

Calypso Bean (Steuben Yellow Eye): This thin-skinned, medium white bean with mustard colored splotches or "eyes" is a 400-year-old variety with many names, including Steuben yellow eye, molasses face, Maine yellow eye, and butterscotch calypso. It has a velvety texture and mellow flavor, plumps up well, and becomes ivory to brown after cooking, making it excellent for salads and baked dishes. This may be the original bean used in colonial Boston for baked beans. This bean is preferred for Hoppin' John in parts of the South.

Eye of Goat Bean (Ojo de Cabra): This cranberry-type bean is rounded in shape and with long brown stripes that inspired its name. Sweet with a smooth texture, this bean stays firm and richly colored after cooking. Ojo de Cabra plants will also produce a few blue and purple beans. They are a favorite in Baja, California, and are used as a side dish or in salads.

European Soldier Bean: For perhaps obvious reasons, these oval, medium-size white beans with red markings in the "eye" reminiscent of a European toy soldier were well known in early New England where the term "red coats" referred to the uniforms of the British soldiers. The distinctive markings are also said to resemble a soldier in Napoleon's army. They have a slightly mealy texture and should be cooked whole to maintain their markings in slow-cooked dishes and soups.

French Horticultural Bean: An heirloom variety in the cranberry family, this tasty bean is also known as the October bean. It is delicious in soups, stews, and salads. Its firm texture and sweet, nutty flavor make this a favorite among bean aficionados.

Good Mother Stallard Bean: This beautiful maroon and white colored bean is relatively large and round in shape. While some color is lost in cooking, the subtle mottled lines remain. It is a meaty, sweet, somewhat granular bean with a nutty, slightly herbal taste, and it makes great comfort food.

Jackson Wonder Bean: This bean comes in mottled shades of beige and purplish brown. It was popularized in Atlanta, Georgia, in the 1880s, where it became known as a good soup bean because of its creamy texture.

Madeira (Madera) Bean: This mottled brown, flat, oval-shaped bean is the largest member in the large cranberry family. These beans, originally from South America, were brought to Portugal, where they became important in that nation's cuisine. They were then brought back to the United States by Portuguese and Italian immigrants. Madeiras have a floury texture and chestnutlike flavor. Though smaller, cranberry or scarlet runner beans are acceptable substitutes.

Monstoller Wild Goose Bean: The story of Civil War veteran John Monstoller, who was said to have shot down a wild goose with these beans in its craw, is very well known among heirloom seed savers. The beans were planted in 1866 and preserved ever since then by the same family. Excellent baked and in soups, this bean is very large, white on the bottom, heavily speckled with brown and maroon, and has an orange patch around the "eye."

Mortgage Lifter Bean (Aztec, Pueblo Bean): This extremely large white heirloom bean tastes similar to butter beans, or large limas. The name comes from a farmer who was about to lose his land to the bank. Instead, his good crop of beans lifted his mortgage. Perhaps another reason the farmer could pay off his mortgage was that these beans dramatically increase volume when cooked, allowing the use of fewer beans.

Munsi Wolf Bean: This heirloom variety was grown by the Lenape Indians in Delaware Water Gap not far from Philadelphia. It is also called Speckled Minisink Bean.

Nuna Bean (Poroto, Numia, Popping, Toasting Bean): A thick-skinned variety of common bean, grown in the high Andes, the nuna bean was found at pre-Inca archaeological sites. It is a staple in many areas of Ecuador and Peru. At the high altitudes where nuna beans are cultivated, water boils at a lower temperature—closer to 195°F than 212°F—which would make cooking beans a slow process. Instead, nuna beans are heated in a thin layer of oil until the beans pop. The popped beans resemble popcorn, with a flavor reminiscent of peanuts. At least thirty-three varieties of nuna bean have been developed. Especially popular are grey and white speckled (*nuna azul*) and light red (*nuna mani*) varieties. The white nuna called *huevo de paloma* (pigeon's egg) is highly regarded. "Q'osco Poroto," the first variety of popping bean released by the Peruvian Ministry of Agriculture, became available in 2000. To my knowledge, these beans are not yet available commercially in the United States.

Painted Pony Bean: Similar to the appaloosa bean in that they also resemble the markings of a pony, these beans are closely related to the pinto as well. Of Mexican origin, they are slender and oval in shape, and in shades from cream and beige all the way to brown and black. Rich and nutty in flavor, they are excellent in chili or other slow-cooked bean dishes.

Pebble Bean: This remarkable heirloom bean is being propagated by the people at The Bean Bag (see Sources, page 341). Colorful beans in every pod range in color from brown, to tan, red, white, and even black, all on the same plant. Pebble beans cook evenly with a great spectrum of color variation. They are subtly flavored with creamy texture and delicate skins. They are outstanding for soup, salad, or chili.

Rattlesnake Bean: These slender, oval beans are speckled brown over a tan background. The pods twist around like rattlesnakes as they grow, hence their name. A relatively new variety, rattlesnake beans are closely related to pintos but with a richer, more intense flavor that makes them excellent in casseroles and chili.

Red Valentine Bean: These six-inch-long narrow pods are ideal substitutes for green beans. They are heavily speckled in deep wine red over a pink background. In Germany, they are called Turkish date beans. In its dried form, the bean is called one-thousand-for-one, purple-speckled valentine, and refugee bean.

Swedish Brown Bean: Swedish immigrants who settled in Montana introduced these toasty, pale brown beans, a staple of Swedish cooking, to the northern United States about 100 years ago. They continue to be popular there because they mature early in the season, before the frost. When cooked, they turn honey brown and have a rich, slightly sweet, nutty flavor. They are most often used in soups, especially Swedish brown bean soup, and for "Bruna Bonor" (baked beans with bacon). They blend well with Indian spices.

Tongues of Fire: This cranberry-type, mottled beige and brown marked bean is grown from a seed variety originally collected from Tierra del Fuego, on the southern tip of South America. This variety later found its way to Italy. The pods are ivory and develop red "flames" as they mature, with ivory white blossoms. This bean tenderizes easily while absorbing aromatic herbs and spices well. It is used for New England succotash, Italian pasta dishes, and Portuguese sausage and beans.

Trout Bean (Jacob's Cattle Bean, Coach Bean, Dalmatian Bean, Forellen-German): The white and maroon-spotted heirloom Tepary beans do indeed resemble spotted Dalmatian dogs or cattle. Originally brought to the United States from Germany, where it is called Forellen, the trout bean has been grown in New England since colonial times. These beans are suitable for growing in desert climates, and they have a relatively short growing season. When cooked, the texture is velvety, perfect for salads, relishes, and soups.

Yellow Indian Woman Bean: Native Americans in Montana grew this gold-colored bean and passed down through generations of families. It is a very delicate type of runner bean. A distant cousin to the pinto family with a very flavorful taste, it is appropriate for most Western-style recipes.

Zebra Bean: This heirloom variety, also known as the amethyst bean, is white with dark streaks that resemble a zebra's markings. It is highly prized for its superior creamy texture and full-bodied flavor, especially in Spain.

Common True Bean Varieties Popular in Europe

Green Romano Bean: This fresh Italian green bean, once only found frozen in the United States, is now a seasonal treat, especially in neighborhoods with a large Italian population. It is a flat and wide green bean with a pronounced beany flavor. When young, these beans are quite tender, but they are often larger (as long as six inches) with visible inner bean seeds. Larger beans should be treated more like dried beans and cooked for a longer period of time until tender. Romano beans hold up well and don't disintegrate when cooked. They take well to strong flavorings, such as tomato sauce with lots of garlic or lemon, capers, and chopped anchovies. Dragon tongue beans are another type of romano with pale yellow pods and decorative markings in deep purple.

Choose the smallest romano beans you can find. Ideally they should be flattened in shape and only slightly wider than common green beans. The brighter the green color and the less apparent the inner bean seed, the more tender the bean. Pale or yellow beans are likely to be overgrown and tough. Using a sharp knife, trim off the stem end on a slight angle. It's your choice whether to cut off the pointy end. It will be slightly tough but adds visual interest and demonstrates the fresh-picked quality of the beans. I like to cut romano beans on the diagonal into even lengths before cooking.

If the beans vary in size, separate them into two piles: one of larger beans and one with smaller beans. Cook each size separately and then mix them back together. Follow the basic cooking instructions for green beans (page 29), allowing more time for larger-seeded beans.

Green Romano Bean Recipes

Romano Bean and Navel Orange Salad
Summer Minestrone with Pesto alla Genovese
Frittata with Romano Beans, Prosciutto, and Fontina
Golden Garlic Aïoli with Romano Beans and Sugar Snaps

Suggested Uses

• Add to minestrone soup or risotto.
• Partially cook (blanch) and toss in a pan with bacon or pancetta bits.
• Serve cooked and chilled with a bowl of mayonnaise-based dipping sauce.
• Add to pasta salad.

Haricots Verts: *Haricots verts,* which simply means "green beans" in French, are fashionably thin and hand-picked at just the right size. These pencil-thin green beans are a great delicacy in France. Most *haricots verts* sold in America come from Central America because of lower labor costs, but the sweetest and plumpest I've found came from a local organic farm. Other descriptive names include *haricots filets* (string beans) and *haricots aiguilles* (needle beans).

Prepare the *haricots verts* by trimming off the stem end only. If the beans are not at their peak and their pointy tips are shriveled, trim them off also. To cook, set up a vegetable steamer basket with boiling water underneath and steam them for 3 to 5 minutes or until they turn a brilliant emerald green. Turn off the heat, lift out the steamer basket, and refresh the beans under cold running water to set the color. You can also cheat and add a tiny pinch of baking soda to the water when boiling. This will make them slightly less nutritious, but will ensure their eye appeal.

Haricots Verts Recipes

Haricots Verts and Beet Salad with White Truffle Vinaigrette, Goat Cheese, and Olivada Crostini
Haricots Verts and Fried Quail Eggs in Black Truffle Vinaigrette
Provençal-Style Green Beans

Suggested Uses

• Steam and refresh under cold running water and dress with vinaigrette or flavored aioli.
• Steam, drain, and immediately toss in a small pan of butter or olive oil.
• Steam, drain, and season with a little sea salt, fresh ground black pepper, and fresh squeezed lemon juice.

Borlotti Bean: Borlotti or Tuscan beans are the most popular beans in Tuscany, the land of the "bean eaters." Normally found in their dried form in this country, borlotti are plump and rounded in shape. Their background color is pinkish tan with crimson speckles and streaks. Look for them in Italian groceries. They are similar to cranberry beans and interchangeable in use. In fact, cranberry beans grown in the United States are exported to Italy as borlotti beans. In Italy many members of this family of medium-sized, kidney-shaped speckled beans, including *lamon, stregoni, scritti,* and *saluggia,* are sought after in the specific regions where they are grown. All of them share a meaty flavor and mild earthiness. Look for these heirloom varieties at the Republic of Beans (see Sources, page 341).

Cannellini Bean: These large, white, kidney-shaped beans are used extensively in Italy, and often found canned. They have a creamy smooth, firm texture and a mild, nutty flavor that makes them extremely versatile. They are also called white kidney beans and *haricots blancs* in French. They are excellent in salads because their thin skins allow them to absorb flavors well. Cook cannellini gently and slowly, preferably in the oven so they keep their shape.

Borlotti or Dried Cranberry Bean Recipes

Florentine Borlotti Bean and Tuna Salad
Pasta and Beans from the Villa Cipriani
Toto's Pasta "Fazool"
Sardinian-Style Cranberry Beans with Fennel and Savoy Cabbage

Suggested Uses

• Add cooked beans to a tomato-based sauce for pasta.
• Cook until soft and creamy inside and toss while still warm with a vinaigrette dressing that's heavy on the vinegar. Balsamic vinegar will darken their color; sherry vinegar, which has a higher level of acidity than wine vinegar, is ideal.
• Purée cooked beans, adding garlic, olive oil, hot pepper flakes, and lemon juice or vinegar for a quick dip.

Coco (French Navy Bean): The elegant, rounded French navy bean is smaller than the American navy bean. It is ivory white with a tinge of green and is especially creamy and tender. Coco beans cook quickly and are excellent for salads, where their small shape is noticeably attractive, and in French Navy Bean and Shrimp Salad.

Cranberry Bean (Roman Bean): These medium-sized, oval, creamy white beans have crimson speckles and streaks and are most frequently used in Italian dishes and soups. These New World beans were enthusiastically adopted in Europe, especially Italy and North Africa.

Savory Cannellini Bean Recipes

White Bean Salad Contadina
Crostini with Cannellini Bean Spread and Oven-Roasted Plum Tomatoes
Chicory and Cannellini Bean Soup
Creamy White Bean Soup with Hazelnut-Sage Pesto
Haricot Bean and Oven-Roasted Tomato Soup with Pimentòn
Tuscan Winter Minestrone

Sweet Cannellini Bean Recipes

Creamy White Bean Ice Cream with Molasses Caramel Sauce
Viennese White Bean and Hazelnut Torte

Old World farmers took the American beans and bred them, producing many new regional varieties. The cranberry bean was brought back to the New World by Italian immigrants and is now grown mostly on the California coast.

Fresh Cranberry Bean: These gorgeous beans in their long, flattened, crimson and cream-streaked pods are often found fresh in season in late summer in Asian, Italian, and farmers markets and are well worth seeking out. To prepare fresh shell cranberry beans, split open the pods on the slightly curved inner sides and remove the beans. These creamy, mild beans are such a treat when fresh that it's best to prepare them as simply as possible. Freshly shelled beans do not need soaking, will keep about 1 week if refrigerated, and can also be frozen, either raw or cooked, for later use. Simply cook them in simmering stock or water until tender and plump, generally for about half an hour. Cranberry beans are closely related to tongues of fire beans and Italian borlotti.

> ### Fresh Cranberry Bean Recipes
>
> Maccheroni Rustica
> Adriatic Grilled Shrimp with Cranberry Beans, Broccoli
>   Rabe, and Sweet Red Pepper Sauce
> Mustard-Crusted Rack of Lamb with Spinach and
>   Cranberry Bean Ragout
> Bolognese Bean Soup
> Tuscan Beans Cooked in a Flask

Flageolet de Chevrier: These highly prized small, elongated immature bean seeds are usually light green or sometimes red, resembling the inner seeds of a common green bean, and are unusual in that they are picked and dried before being fully ripened. A yellow variety is sometimes found. They may be cooked fresh or dried. In the United States flageolets are only available dried.

A variety of *haricot* bean, flageolets were first developed by Gabriel Chevrier in Brittany, France, in 1872 and were a particular favorite of the great French chef Auguste Escoffier. In France they are also called *chevrier* or *flageolets de chevrier*.

Flageolets do not need soaking. They have very delicate, thin skin so cook them gently and slowly, with salt, until tender but not mushy. Place the flageolets in a medium heavy-bottomed saucepan. Cover with cold water and bring to the boil. Skim off and discard the white foam that rises to the top. Reduce the heat to a bare sim-

mer and cook slowly for about 1 hour or until the beans are close to tender without stirring, which breaks open the skins. Remove from the heat and pour off any remaining water.

> ### Flageolet Recipes
>
> Roasted Gigot of Lamb with Flageolet Gratin
> Ragout of Flageolets, Chicken-Basil Sausage, and Spinach
> Flageolets with Fennel, Tomato, and Green Olives

Haricot Lingot: These large, flattened, oval white beans are grown in northern France in their place of origin, Lingot. They are higher in cost because of the care with which they are grown. These beans cook up to a creamy plumpness that makes them perfect to use in cassoulet.

Fagioli Sorana: These rare Italian heirloom beans have been grown for centuries in a small valley along the stream of Pescia in the province of Pistoia. Sorana beans are milky white with pearly veins or wine red with more intensely colored veins. The white beans have a squashed shape, while the red ones are cylindrical with a harder seed coat. Both kinds have a rich but delicate taste and tender skin. They were said to be a favorite of the great Italian composer Gioacchino Rossini.

Fagioli Scritti: This heirloom Italian bean in the cranberry bean family has a tender skin and delicate flavor that make it much sought after by gourmets. A round, off-white bean with red striations, the scritti bean is grown exclusively on family farms in the province of Piedmont in northern Italy. The taste is both earthy and meaty with notes of light chestnut. Fresh, shelled scritti beans are outstanding and may be found in Italy in the summer months.

Fagioli Pavoni: Heirloom beans from Italy, *fagioli pavoni* (peacock beans) are plump and kidney-shaped, with a creamy, smooth texture. They have a dark brown background and deep purple speckles, and will maintain their plump oval shape and much of their color during cooking. They are so named because their coloring is as flashy as a peacock's tail feathers. Both earthy and meaty, pavoni have a sweet, chestnutlike flavor with a mineral taste on the finish. They are good in soups and salads.

Tolosana Bean: A variety introduced in the 1920s, these beans, also known as prince beans, are well loved in Spain. With distinctive cinnamon and burgundy markings, they have a creamy texture and are especially suited to cooking with seafood, such as clams and shrimp.

Tarbais Bean: This famous large, white bean is cultivated in southwestern France and named for the city of Tarbes in the foothills of the French Pyrénées. In the early 1700s the bishop of Tarbes learned about the cultivation of beans while on a stay in Spain and introduced them to the valley of the Adour, the beautiful river that flows through Tarbes. The bean variety now known as Tarbais resembles a cross between lima and cannellini—flatter and shorter than cannellini and not as wide as lima. It holds its shape extremely well and has a mild flavor and a smooth texture. Because of their large size, Tarbais beans must be thoroughly soaked and cooked for a long time. They are the preferred beans in the region for cassoulet.

Zolfino Pratomagno: This small, round, yellow Italian heirloom bean is also called the *burrino*, because it melts in the mouth like butter (*burro* in Italian), and sometimes *fagiolo del Cento* (one hundred bean), because it is sown on the hundredth day of the year, in April. They are thin-skinned and delicate, but maintain their texture very well during cooking. Harvesting zolfini is labor-intensive, and they are quite expensive, but they are well worth it. They are best boiled, drizzled with fine olive oil, and served on slices of toasted Tuscan bread, or as a side dish to the classic Bistecca alla Fiorentina, a rare-grilled double-thick T-bone steak.

Limas
Phaseolus limensis or lunatus

The lima bean is a large, flattish bean with a creamy texture and sweet flavor that originated in Peru. Limas form one of the two main branches of the *Phaseolus* bean family; common beans are the other. When young, limas are pale green, but as they ripen they develop the pale yellow color that gives them their common name in Britain (and in older American cookbooks), the butter bean. Very large dried butter beans are also called potato beans. The name "lima" refers to its origin in Lima, Peru. The fact that it is now pronounced LYE-MA rather than LEE-MA comes from earlier carelessness in adopting foreign words. Another name is the Madagascar bean, because it's extensively cultivated on this island off the east coast of Africa. The Italian name *fagioli di Spagna,* meaning "Spanish bean," refers to the fact that it was originally brought to Italy by Spanish colonists. Burpee's Fordhook lima, also known as the potato lima, is a famous American variety with excellent yield and flavor developed by Atlee Burpee and named after his experimental farm, Fordhook.

Fresh Green Lima Bean: Young, green limas in their large, flat, tough green pods are in season in late summer. Sometimes markets will sell fresh-shelled limas, saving the cook the effort of shelling. To shell, break the tips of the pods and pull down along the sides to remove the strings and expose the insides. Remove the limas and store in a plastic bag in the refrigerator for 3 to 4 days. If young and pale green, they will cook quickly, almost like green beans. When older and creamy yellow in color, they are starchier and will need to simmer for about 30 minutes. Frozen baby limas are an excellent product and can be added to chowders and other vegetable-laden soups or used to make succotash. They make a good substitute for the more elusive fresh fava.

Note: No lima beans should be eaten raw as they can contain poisonous cyanogenic glucosides. These substances have mostly been reduced to safe levels by seed selection. Proper preparation, including changing the soaking and cooking water, eliminates any poisons contained in the limas. Darker varieties of limas have the greatest tendency to contain toxins, so it's best to cook limas with the lid off so any toxins can boil away.

Dried limas come in many forms. The larger (and older) the bean, the longer it will need to soak. Soak large limas for at least 24 hours, changing the water at least once to discourage fermentation if the weather is warm. Their tough skins can make them difficult to digest, so be sure to blanch the beans, bringing them to a boil, discarding the water, and then starting with fresh water for the final cooking.

Large White Lima Bean (*Phaseolus lunatus,* Madagascar, Burma Bean, Rangoon Bean, Habas Grandes-Spanish, Fagioli della Nonna, Fagioli di Spagna, Italian Grandma's Bean, Duffin Bean): These large limas are native to the altiplano in Peru. Nearly an inch long and creamy white in color with a pale greenish tint, it has a buttery flavor and creamy texture but tends to become mushy if overcooked. This type of lima grows well in cooler climates.

Baby White Lima Bean (*Phaseolus limensis,* Small Lima Bean, Butter Bean, Sieva Bean, Civet Bean, Dixie Speckled Butter Bean, Calico Bean, Florida Speckled Pole Bean): These small, flat, off-white limas are probably of Guatemalan or Mexican origin. More delicate than large limas, they are in a different botanical category. They are about one-half inch in length, flatter and thinner than the large ones with a buttery texture, and their thinner skin allow them to cook faster. They are more tender, fruity, and sweet than large limas and less mealy. They were introduced to Africa with the slave trade, where they are still popular because they do well in tropical and subtropical climates. The Dixie is a bit larger and plumper, with a calico pattern of black and cream, and is resistant to heat and humidity so that it grows well in the hot weather of the southern United States.

Christmas Lima Bean: Also called chestnut lima, this beautifully marked, large heirloom lima is dark red with deep brown streaks. Very popular 75 years ago, it has a chestnut flavor and nutty texture. The striking markings are retained when cooked.

Hopi Orange Lima Bean: This heirloom lima has been preserved as a dry bean by the Hopi Indians, who also grind it for flour. It is very close in appearance to an ancient orange bean with dark markings found in pre-Columbian graves in Peru.

Red Lima Bean: Also known as the Worcester Indian red pole lima, red limas were originally ground for flour by Native Americans, or served with red corn. In the South, slaves first cooked this bean with brown goober peas (close relatives of the peanut) and red sweet potatoes to make a variation of *fufu*, the African mashed dumplings also made of mashed plantains and other roots. They are also known as Peruvian limas.

Lima Bean Recipes

Crab Chowder with Limas, Green Beans, and Corn
Gratin of Summer Succotash with Crabmeat
Cholent (Sabbath Beef, Bean, and Barley Casserole)
Tricolor Succotash
Pennsylvania Dutch Chow-Chow
Seven-Vegetable and Chicken Couscous

Runner Beans
Phaseolus coccineus

Runner beans originated in Mexico, where 6,000-year-old pods of this bean have been found in caves. A close cousin of the lima bean, these beautiful beans have both ceremonial and decorative uses in the native cultures of the American Southwest and Mexico. Their Latin name, *Phaseolus coccineus,* which most likely refers to the scarlet runner variety, comes from the Greek word for the brilliant red dye called cochineal, which is extracted from the shells of a variety of ladybug.

Because runner beans can be successfully grown in cooler climates, they are a popular garden vegetable in England, where many varieties have been developed. The beans grow on long runners that can produce huge pods of one foot or longer. They have large showy blossoms and are commonly grown as ornamental plants, especially in England. Consequently, runner beans are often listed in the ornamental section of garden catalogs, especially in England. White Dutch runner beans are pure white, painted lady runners have scarlet and white bicolored flowers, and scarlet runners have brilliant red blooms and magenta seeds veined with black. If you grow your own runner beans, note that the blossoms are also edible and can be added to salads and stir-fries.

Black Runner Bean: Black runners have long been prized both in the United States and in Great Britain for their beautiful blossoms. The beans are large with a shiny, deep black skin and a slightly sweet flavor. They hold their shape well when cooked. Serve as a side dish or marinate for a salad.

Fabada Bean: This sought-after, large, runner-type bean of the variety called *granja* is exclusively grown in the province of Asturias, Spain, and packaged in beautiful hand-tied burlap bags in the city of Léon. Beans grown in this region cost twice as much as fabada beans grown elsewhere in Spain, but they are quite in demand.

Giant White Coco Bean: These large, flat French white beans are highly prized by French chefs as a side dish. They are similar in size and texture to the Emergo bean sold by specialty bean suppliers and to the gigandes or gigante bean.

Haricot Blanc de Soisson: These large white beans, grown in the Soissons region of France, are shaped like oversized limas and taste especially meaty. In Italy they are known as *Bianchi di Spagna* (Spanish whites), *corona*, or *bianco grande* (crown or large white). They are similar in size and shape, though with a different texture and flavor, to the gigante, a type of white runner bean.

Judiós Bean (Judias): These huge, white, runner-type beans come packed in hand-tied burlap bags from Spain. After soaking, each bean may be up to two inches across. They are used for hearty bean stews and soups. It is certainly possible, if not proven, that these beans were either brought to Spain by Jewish colonists from the New World or that they were particularly used by them. According to Clifford Wright, author of the incredible and fascinating book *A Mediterranean Feast,* the name for these beans "derives either from the Latin word for Jews, which was also the word used on occasion for Palestine, or it is an Arabism unrelated to *judio* and deriving from *ghudiya,* a word meaning *al-lubiya* in Arabic, namely 'beans.' The derivation and meaning is, in short, controversial." Whatever their history, they are wonderful beans.

Gigante Bean (Gigandas or Hija): These huge, sweet-tasting, creamy colored white beans are from the white runner bean family. They are excellent marinated in salads like Turkish White Bean Salad because they hold their shape so well. This bean was brought to the United States from Spain and Greece, places where they are still quite common.

Scarlet Runner Bean: First described in 1750, scarlet runners were introduced to England by Tradescant, the gardener of King Charles I, and are still a favorite for decorative gardens, especially in Britain. Also called stick beans, these dramatic red beans come from a plant that is often grown for its gorgeous scarlet blossoms. The beans themselves are deep magenta and black in color.

Tocomares (Chocolate Runner): This magnificent but hard-to-find heirloom bean is large and chocolate brown in color with a rich and starchy flavor. It is grown by the people at Sacramento's Bean Bag and sold until they are out of stock. (See Sources, page 341).

White Emergo Bean (Sweet White, White Runner): Larger than a standard lima, emergos are white and plump with a shape close to a half moon though slightly irregular. They make a good substitute for the hard-to-find gigante beans grown in Europe. They have a very fine texture and hold their shape well in marinated bean salads and absorb flavors well.

Runner Bean Recipes

Scarlet Runner Beans in Brown Butter and Shallots
Green Gigandas Bean Salad with Grilled Octopus
Turkish White Bean Salad
White Bean Salad with Moroccan Charmoula Dressing

Suggested Use

• Cook and serve as a snack with a flavorful mayonnaise-based dipping sauce such as Preserved Lemon Aïoli.

Tepary Bean
Phaseolus acutifolius

Tepary Bean: The Tepary bean is a New World variety (*Phaseolus acutifolius*) used dried that is especially adapted to desert conditions. It is quick growing with long roots that can reach any moisture in the ground. Tepary beans have long been grown in the Arizona desert by Native Americans. Because of its ability to produce a quick high protein crop in the desert, there has been recent interest in growing this bean. However, they are difficult to harvest because the pods tend to split open,

scattering the beans, which are quite small. The Indians of the Southwest associated a plentiful harvest of white Tepary beans with the abundant white stars of the Milky Way. Tepary beans are also known as *tepari, yori mui, pavi,* and *moth dal.*

THE PEANUT FAMILY
ARACHIS HYPOGAEA

Peanuts originated several thousand years ago in South America. Spanish and Portuguese traders disseminated peanuts around the world, especially to Asia and Africa. African slaves brought peanuts with them to North America, which explains why some of the first names used for it were of African (Congo) origin, including *pindar* and *goober*. Unlike any other legume, after its flower is fertilized, the peanut buries itself in the soil, where the fruit or pod develops underground, hence its other common name, groundnut.

Many types of peanuts are raised in the United States, where about one-tenth of the world's crop is grown. Nearly half the United States crop is grown in Georgia. The number of kernels in a pod ranges from two or three in some varieties to as much as five to seven in others. Peanuts are nutritious, containing 40 to 50 percent oil and 20 to 30 percent protein. Larger peanuts like Virginias are used for candies and roasted for snacks. Salted, roasted peanuts have become a universally popular snack, second only to potato chips in this country. About half the peanuts grown in the United States are made into peanut

---

PEANUT RESEARCH

George Washington Carver (1864–1943) was an outstanding innovator in the agricultural sciences whose name is forever associated with peanuts. Born to slave parents in Missouri, he left the farm and settled in Kansas, where he worked his way through high school. Following his graduation in 1894 from the Iowa State College of Agriculture and Mechanic Arts (now Iowa State University), he became director of the Department of Agricultural Research at Tuskegee Normal and Industrial Institute (now Tuskegee University). There he experimented with peanuts, developing more than 300 industrial uses for them and urging cotton farmers to switch to growing peanuts as a cash crop.

butter and one-quarter more are sold roasted. Many chefs, including myself, insist on peanut oil for deep-frying because of its high smoke point and nutty flavor.

Peanut butter was first concocted in the early 1900s, and quickly became an American staple. Other cultures, particularly Indonesian and Thai, have long used ground peanuts as a key ingredient to enrich and thicken their sauces.

Buy raw, shelled peanuts in bags at a natural foods store. Use these peanuts when you're going to further toast or fry the nuts. If you live in a part of the country that grows peanuts, you might be able to buy green peanuts in their shell. They may also be available in season at Asian markets. They are boiled for a long time in salted water and eaten as a snack in the Low Country regions of South Carolina and Georgia, as the Japanese do with the salted green soybeans called edamame.

Spanish Peanut: These smaller peanuts, also known as Valencias, are red-skinned and rich tasting. They are better known in Europe and are used in the United States to make peanut butter and oil. Because of their small size, they are the peanuts found in many candy bars and inside boxes of Cracker Jacks.

Virginia Peanut: The Virginia peanut, also called the Virginia bunch peanut, provides most of the peanuts eaten whole in the United States, both shelled and in the shell as "ballpark peanuts" and as the green or boiled peanuts especially popular in the American South. They are quite large and elongated with a dense, crunchy texture and thin skin.

ASIAN AND AFRICAN LEGUMES

ASIAN BEANS

Asian Beans
Vigna unguiculata
(formerly *Sinensis,* meaning Chinese)

The small fruit of an annual plant, Asian beans include a group of very small, slightly oblong beans with a prominent small eye. China is probably the original home of the red adzuki bean though it was introduced into Japan about 1,500 years ago. They are eaten whole in their skins, though quite often, especially in India, they are sold already shelled as *dal*. The major varieties of these mung type beans are the green mung, black mung (or black gram), and red bean or adzuki.

Adzuki beans may be popped like corn. Green mung beans are familiar to us as bean sprouts. In China, these sprouts are called "pea" sprouts as opposed to "bean" sprouts made from soybeans. Red adzuki beans are served in many forms for holidays in both China and Japan, such as Chinese New Year dumplings and mooncakes and steamed rice and red beans served in Japan.

Green mung beans probably originated in India though they are grown throughout Asia, the Caribbean, and in Africa. Because mung beans grow quickly, several crops a year are possible. Mung bean starch is used to make the Chinese cellophane noodles.

The black gram is the most important member of this family in India, where it has ceremonial significance in Hindu birth and death rites. However, there is much confusion over different varieties in the mung family because some black gram beans may be green. The green ones are smaller and ripen later than the black ones. The best way to tell the difference is to split them open; the urud (or black gram) is white inside, while the mung (or green gram) is yellow inside. Black gram beans need a long time to cook and they are difficult for some people to digest.

Adzuki Bean (Azuki, Aduki): Called red beans in China and Japan, these small, burgundy red oval beans are especially popular in China and Japan for desserts because of their sweet, nutty flavor. Inside their rather tough skins, adzuki are velvety in texture without any discernable grain. Though not essential, I prefer to soak these beans overnight to soften them before cooking for a more even texture.

Green Mung Bean: This small, rounded, olive green mung bean, from the plant *Phaseolus vigna radiata*, probably originated in India. It has a slightly sweet flavor and soft texture. When skinned and split they are yellow inside, very tender, and cook quickly. In India, this is the most widely used form of the mung bean and is known as moong dal. Dals and the *moong dal* in particular are very easy to digest and take well to seasonings and spices.

Black Gram Bean: Also called urad or urd beans, these small, black-skinned, oval beans are pale yellow inside. Their texture is glutinous. When split and cooked, they have a slightly viscous texture. They are also used as a seasoning in south India, where beans are thrown into hot oil to give it a red color and nutty flavor.

A member of the mung bean family, black gram beans are especially popular in northern India, where they are cooked with ginger, onions, and butter to make a rich creamy purée called *kali dal*. When split with their skins removed, they are white inside. This white variety, called split white lentil (*urud dal* in India), is easy to digest and delicious in stuffing or served with curries and sautéed vegetables. Toasted and ground, they are used as an Indian spice.

Rice Bean: The seeds of this small bean of tropical Asian origin are a bit larger than rice grains, and are eaten, when dried, with or instead of rice. Ranging in color from yellow to red to brown and black, rice beans have a delicate flavor, soft texture, and are highly nutritious. These beans have been grown in the northeast of India and adjoining regions to the east, although they are difficult to harvest because they grow like vines and the seed pods open on their own, scattering the seeds. Rice beans are quick cooking, tender and slightly sweet. Their thin skins make them easy to digest.

Soybeans
Glycine max

The soybean has been called "the meat of the soil," "the cow of China," and "the miracle bean." It probably originated in China and is of huge economic importance worldwide. There are more than 1,000 varieties of the extraordinarily nutritious and protein-rich soybean, ranging in color from yellow, green, and red to black, white, and mottled. Soybeans generally taste quite bland, although fresh green soybeans have a pleasingly delicate flavor and creamy texture. Unlike other legumes, soybeans are low in carbohydrates and high in protein and oil. Mild-tasting soybean oil, low in saturated fats, has long been the favored cooking fat in Chinese cuisine. Look at the label on a container labeled "vegetable oil": normally the only ingredient is soybean oil.

The soybean has been used for thousands of years in its native eastern Asia in a wide variety of forms. Its young, fresh sprouts with yellowish bean ends are eaten as a crunchy vegetable; soybeans are soaked in water to produce soy milk, from which bean curd is prepared (known as tofu). Soybeans are fermented to produce soy sauce and other condiments like miso and tamari, are ground to make flour, and are even made into a sweet dessert paste. Transformed into textured vegetable protein (seitan or tempeh), soybean products are commonly used as a fillers for ground meat products (see Soybean-Related Products, page 42).

Edamame: Fresh young soybeans in their fuzzy green pods appear in the market in the summer months and are a seasonal treat, much like fresh favas. Delicious and fun to eat, fresh soybeans are a well-loved snack in China and Japan, cooked in heavily salted water and then sucked out of their pods. Green soybeans are often sold shelled and frozen (much like baby limas) in Asian markets and natural food stores.

Soybean-Related Products

Since I would need to write a whole book to even begin to cover the incredibly diverse family of soybean-based products, I will give only a very simple, basic introduction to these ingredients here.

SOY SAUCE

Soy sauce has been known in the West since the 17th century when Dutch traders in Nagasaki exported it to Europe. It was the secret seasoning served at the court banquets of Louis XIV in France. The word "soy" or *soya* comes to us via the Dutch *soja* originally from the Japanese word *shoyu*. Shoyu was borrowed from the Chinese *shiyau—shi*, meaning salted beans, *yau* meaning oil.

Soy sauce was used to prevent foods from spoiling in the summer heat and to preserve foods for the winter months. In the 15th century, Japan started to produce its own type of soy sauce. By the 16th century, soy sauce was commercially manufactured instead of being made by farm families for their own or local use.

This culinary bedrock of Asian cooking is a dark, salty sauce made by fermenting boiled soybeans and roasted wheat or barley with salt. A mixture of carefully selected and roasted soybeans is inoculated with a mold and then mixed with brine to make a liquidy mash (much like a wort for beer). The mash is placed in fermentation tanks to brew for 1 year. After brewing, the raw soy sauce is separated from any solids.

China and Japan produce all different kinds of soy sauces including light, medium, dark, thin to very thick, black soy, and mushroom soy. Chinese soy sauce is generally quite salty with a dense flavor. Japanese soy sauces have a relatively bright taste and aroma. Far more wheat is used in Japanese soy sauces, so they are sweeter and less salty than the Chinese. Japanese sauces are generally lighter and thinner than the dark, thick Chinese type.

Be sure to check that the soy sauce you buy is naturally brewed. Inexpensive but artificially brewed soy sauces with Chinese-sounding names are sold at lower prices in many supermarkets. They are brewed by chemical rather than natural fermentation in as little as 3 or 4 days rather than the 1-year period necessary for natural fermentation. It's certainly worthwhile to seek out a good brand, as even the best is relatively inexpensive and it lasts indefinitely.

Artificially fermented brands list water, then salt, hydrolyzed soy protein, corn syrup, caramel color, and potassium sorbate (with no quantity given) as a preservative. A naturally brewed brand lists water, then wheat and soybeans before salt, and less than one-tenth of a percent of sodium benzoate as a preservative.

There's a huge variety among soy sauce brands. For Chinese soy sauce, a recommended brand is Pearl River Bridge from China with a label that reads "Superior Soy," for its large, round well-balanced flavor. For Japanese-style dark soy sauce, I like to buy the dark Kikkoman that is widely available and of excellent quality. Now made in Walworth, Wisconsin, using American soy, wheat, and salt, Kikkoman originally began producing soy sauce in Japan in 1630.

Black soy sauce is a concentrated soy sauce made with molasses. It's perfect when you want a lot of color and flavor with less liquid, as in a cold noodle dish where the sauce should cling to the noodles. It is aged for an extra-long time and lasts indefinitely. Mushroom soy is a seasoned black sauce flavored with dried Chinese black mushrooms. It has a rounded, almost meaty flavor. I love the Pearl River Bridge brand for its smooth, deep flavor and the extra dimension of the strong mushroom taste.

Japanese light soy sauce is amber in color, thinner and saltier than the dark. It does not darken the color of the food and is salty enough to season it without heavy application. Kikkoman's light soy sauce is still produced in Japan and has a different label. Dark soy sauce has deeper color and more body, is less salty, and may be used in relatively greater quantities as a basting sauce, a marinade, or in simmered dishes.

TAMARI

This is a Japanese cousin of soy sauce, often sold in health food stores. It is a thick, very dark liquid with a stronger flavor than soy sauce and a clear soy aroma. It is made mainly of soybeans and is cultured and fermented like miso. Even in Japan, it is hard to find good-quality tamari. It is generally used in Japanese cooking as a dipping sauce or a foundation for a basting sauce. I recommend the San-J brand. I have used it extensively from the five-gallon containers in food-service dishes and it was consistently excellent.

MISO

Miso is a Japanese fermented soybean paste that has been important in the Japanese diet for centuries. It is used in a wide variety of dishes, such as a dressing for vegetables and a pickling medium. It is also spread on grilled foods as a seasoning. It is most commonly eaten in the form of miso-shiru or soup, the ubiquitous Japanese breakfast that is often served for lunch and dinner as well.

All of the many types of miso, each with its own aroma and flavor, color and texture, are made essentially by the same method. First boiled soybeans are crushed, and then wheat, barley, or rice is added. The mixture is injected with a yeastlike mold and allowed to mature for several months or up to 3 years. Light, yellow miso, injected with rice mold, is relatively sweet and very good for dressings. Red miso, made with barley, is quite savory and good for winter soups. A third, fudge brown and thick type of miso, made mainly from soybeans, is very rich and salty and can be cut with a knife. Miso will keep refrigerated for up to 1 year.

CHINESE YELLOW AND BROWN BEAN PASTE

Bean pastes are a family of condiments made from fermented soybeans and are available in many different names and types throughout China. Hot bean paste is a frankly hot, lumpy mixture that is stirred into sauces. Sweet bean paste is a smoother, sweeter variation used in both marinades and sauces.

FERMENTED BLACK BEANS

These beans are a Chinese specialty made of small soybeans (not black turtle beans) that have been preserved in salt before packing. Because they have a pungent, salty flavor, some people rinse them before using. I normally give them a quick rinse that removes the surface salt without diluting the intense flavor that I crave. Look for Pearl River Bridge brand packed in a yellow, round cardboard box. I also like Koon Chun brand in plastic bags from Hong Kong, which is spiced with orange rind, ginger, and garlic. If I can only find plain salted beans, I add finely chopped garlic, ginger, and orange rind to them.

BEAN CURD (TOFU)

Bean curd originated in China between A.D. 200 and 900. During this long period of time its use spread completely throughout the Far East so that today, from Indonesia to Korea to Mongolia, it is essential to the national cuisine. Bean curd's Japanese name is tofu, and it was probably introduced to Japan around 1,200 years ago. Japanese tofu is softer and more delicately flavored than the firmer Chinese-type of bean curd.

Like cheese, bean curd is made from curdled or coagulated liquid. It is extremely high in protein and low in cost, though quite perishable. Like fresh white cheese, it will only keep a few days. Intrinsically quite bland, bean curd absorbs flavors well. There are now modified atmosphere packages of bean curd available that have a longer shelf life as long as they are not opened. A 6-ounce portion of fresh bean curd contains a mere 100 calories. More concentrated types of drained bean curd may contain over 50 percent protein.

Bean curd is made from dry soybeans that are soaked in water until softened, then crushed and boiled. The crushed mash is separated into pulp and milk. Just as in cheese-making, a coagulant is added to make the milk separate into curds and whey. The curds are poured into molds and left to settle and take shape. The molded curds are then soaked in water to firm and to keep cool and fresh. In Japan, small cakes of tofu are cut from large blocks (just like butter used to be cut from large blocks at the grocery). In this country we usually buy it already cut and packaged, except in Asian supermarkets where the fresh blocks are often available.

Chinese bean curd cakes tend to be smaller, like little pillows. Excess moisture is often pressed out beforehand, so you will see Chinese-style bean curd cakes sold dry in plastic bags in the refrigerator case. Japanese-style, water-packed tofu is the most common form found in American supermarkets. It cannot be frozen successfully without becoming somewhat chewy.

There are three main types of Japanese tofu. "Regular" tofu is known in Japan as *momen* or cotton tofu. It is drained in cloth and has a slightly coarser texture than silken tofu. Silken, or *kinu*, tofu is a soft tofu that has not been drained. It is quite delicate and can't be pressed. Its fine texture is enjoyed in elegant, clear soups, especially in Japan. *Yakidotu* is tofu that has been lightly broiled. It has a light-brown mottling on its skin and a firm texture. Though it has been grilled, this tofu is packed in water. It is most often used in one-pot dishes such as *sukiyaki*.

For deep-frying or use in salads, tofu is pressed to remove water. Wrap the drained bean curd cakes in clean towels. Weight with two plates for about 30 minutes. You can also purchase already deep-fried bean curd called *agé*. It is golden brown in color and sold dry, like a pastry, in the refrigerator case. This type of bean curd is also cut into thin sheets and commercially deep-fried, forming pockets. These pockets can be split open along one end and stuffed with vegetables or rice.

Soybean, Bean Curd, and Miso Recipes

Asian Wrap Sandwich with Shiitakes, Bean Sprouts, and Hoisin Sauce
Chinese Shanxi Vinegar Dressing
Chinese Steamed Clams with Fermented Black Bean Sauce
Edamame (Steamed Japanese Green Soybeans in the Pod)
Hot and Sour Soup with Duck, Pea Shoots, and Tofu
Indonesian Salad
Miso-Marinated Glazed Halibut
Chinese Noodle Salad with Snow Peas, Bean Sprouts, and Shanxi Dressing
Salmon Scaloppine with Chinese Black Bean Sauce
Spinach and Beef Filet Tip Salad with Fermented Black Beans

This is a large group of eyed peas mostly grown in the American South. The Southern peas came to the United States and to the Caribbean from Africa with the slave trade. They are thought to have first been cultivated in Ethiopia about 5,000 years ago. They are still an important crop in Africa, where the seeds, leaves, and sprouts are eaten. The Southern peas, also called cowpeas, include black-eyed peas, field peas, crowder peas, and cream peas. There are many colorful names for specific varieties of Southern peas, including Mississippi silver, whippoorwill, knucklehull purple, and zipper cream.

Cowpeas

Vigna unguiculata

"Cowpeas" and "field peas" are generic terms for the varieties of Southern peas grown for cow fodder or soil enrichment rather than for human consumption. They are in the same family of African beans as black-eyed peas. They are one of the main food crops of Haiti. Cowpeas need a hot climate to grow, and in the United States, they will only grow in the South, where they were first cultivated. Cowpeas can be divided into those grown for their seeds, which are usually dried, and those grown for their immature pods. These seed plants are most often grown in Africa, India, and the United States. The pod peas are tall climbers with exceptionally long pods called yard-long beans. In Nigeria, the dried peas are a staple legume. Some tribes in West Africa eat the young shoots and leaves as a vegetable.

Black-Eyed Pea: These medium-size, light cream-colored oblong beans with a small but very noticeable black circular "eye" on the curved inner side have a distinct, savory flavor and light, crunchy texture. Black-eyed peas were brought into this country by slaves from Africa and are, therefore, still most popular in the southern part of the country. Black-eyed peas hold up well to strong-tasting ingredients such as chiles, garlic, and smoked pork products. They may be found under the name *Lobiya* or *Chawli* in Indian groceries, or *Fagioli di Spagna* in Italian markets.

Black-eyed peas are sold in many forms, including fresh in the pod, frozen, and dried. To prepare fresh black-eyed peas, break back the tips of the pods; then pull down to remove the strings, exposing the beans inside. Remove the beans and store, refrigerated, in a plastic bag for 3 to 4 days. They can also be frozen for later use. Fresh-shelled peas do not need soaking. Simply cook in simmering stock or water until tender and plump, generally for about 30 minutes. Cook frozen black-eyed peas the same as fresh shelled. Dried black-eyed peas should be soaked overnight before rinsing, par-cooking, and proceeding with the recipe.

Black-Eyed Pea Recipes

Bahian Acarajé Fritters with Ajili Mojili
African Black-Eyed Pea and Okra Salad with Corn
Skillet-Roasted Chicken with Black-Eyed Peas, Country Ham, and Savory
Smoked Turkey Chili with Black-Eyed Peas
Hoppin' John
Texas Stuffed Tomatoes with Black-Eyed Pea Salad
Individual Chicken Potpies with Assorted Legumes

Cream Pea: Closely related to black-eyed peas, cream peas are creamy white in color. They are most commonly found in the South. Black-eyed peas may be substituted.

Crowder Pea: Crowder peas get their name from being very crowded in their pods. All of these legumes can be cooked like black-eyed peas and substituted for them in these recipes.

Lady Pea: This smaller, more delicate black-eyed pea is from South Carolina. It has a very thin skin and cooks quickly to a creamy, smooth texture. Lady peas are often served with rice and green tomato relish in the style of Charleston. They may be found fresh in season at farmers markets, especially in the South.

Southern Checker Pea: A distant relative of black-eyed peas, Southern checker peas are small, flat, and angular. It's easy to see why they were named after a checkerboard. These half white and half black beans have a subtle flavor and good texture. They cook without soaking in about 35 minutes.

Yard-Long Bean: Yard-long beans *(Vigna unguiculata, sesquipedalis)* are hearty-tasting fresh beans that grow between one and three feet long. They are closely related to the black-eyed pea and are also known as long beans, *dau gok,* and, with winged beans, they share the nickname asparagus beans. All long beans are on the starchy side rather than being juicy like a fresh green bean. Choose thin, blemish-free beans with small seeds and plan to cook them within 1 or 2 days. Prepare for cooking by cutting off both ends. The most common variety is thin, dark green, and pliable, although there are also purple and pale green varieties.

Yard-long beans are mild tasting, but firm enough to keep their texture during braising or in stir-fries. Their chewy and slightly slippery texture lends itself well to stir-fries with strong tasting sauces, such as black bean and garlic or chili sauce. Their alternate name, asparagus bean, is misleading because they resemble asparagus only in their length and shape. The two vegetables require very different cooking methods. Yard-long beans should be blanched before adding to a stir-fry where they will finish cooking in a strongly flavored sauce.

Yard-Long Bean Recipes

Chinese Yard-Long Beans with Black Bean and Garlic Sauce
Gado Gado (Indonesian Salad)

Pigeon Peas
Cajanus cajan

Widely believed to be native to tropical Africa, pigeon pea remains were discovered in tombs in ancient Egypt between 2200 and 2400 B.C. It is assumed they were carried by traders to India or Ceylon and were later brought by Indian immigrants to the Caribbean. Pigeon peas are popular in the Caribbean and India because they grow well in hot climates. They are an important food staple in India, where 95 percent of the world's crop is grown, and are especially high in protein.

Piegon peas' scientific name comes from a Malay word meaning "pea," *kacang;* they got their common name because they were used to feed pigeons. They are called yellow lentils, *toor dal* or *toovar dal* in India, *gandules* in Puerto Rico, *Congo pea* or *pois* Angola (most likely because of their African origin) and *googoo beans* in Jamaica. The immature green seeds are sometimes eaten like peas or the whole young pods cooked like green beans. Some Indian groceries carry split pigeon peas that have been coated with oil as a preservative. These must be rinsed in hot water before cooking. Pigeon peas are reputed to have slightly narcotic effects. They come in colors that range from red to white and brown to black, and also come in mottled shades. They have a small "eye" on the inner ridge, an earthy flavor, and a soft, somewhat mealy texture. Dal made from split pigeon peas is the most popular lentil in India and is thick and gelatinous or even meaty when cooked.

Toor and Anhar Pea: In India, the two main varieties are the relatively small and light-colored annual *toor* and the larger perennial with dark seeds called *arhar* and

anhar. In the West Indies, *toor* (*toovar* or *tur*) is known as the *gunga,* or Congo pea, and *arhar* is called the no-eye pea (presumably as compared to the "eyed" peas popular in the Caribbean). They are best used in Indian and Caribbean dishes and soups.

Split Yellow Lentils: The split yellow lentil is the seed of the plant *Cajanus cajan,* the Latin name for the pigeon pea, so yellow lentils are actually hulled split pigeon peas. In India, the classification of legumes is much looser and legumes of different families that are closely related in culinary uses are considered the same. For example, red lentils *(Lens culinaris)* and these yellow "lentils" are both considered lentils.

Unusual Legumes

Aside from the members of the main families of legumes—beans, peas, and lentils—there are a number of members of the legume family that have special properties. All of the unusual legumes in this section are tropical in origin. They include the winged bean (Goa bean or asparagus pea), the yam bean (jicama or Mexican water chestnut), the purple hyacinth (lablab) bean, and the goober pea (Bambarra pea).

Goober Pea: Goober peas are a legume related to fava beans that originated in West Africa. The dry beans can be ground for flour. They are similar to peanuts. At one time they were extensively cultivated by slaves along the South Carolina coast. Other names include Congo goober, groundnut, and Bambarra. They must be cooked before being eaten and have a flavor similar to lima beans. In West Africa, they are often boiled, crushed and formed into cakes, and then fried to make a long-keeping food. A closely related species is the Hausa groundnut, which is grown in many parts of West Africa. It has seeds that are somewhat flattened, kidney-shaped, and dark brown or black. Goobers are less common now because peanuts have mostly supplanted them.

Purple Hyacinth Bean: The purple hyacinth bean originated in tropical Asia or Africa and it thrives on heat. It has been cultivated in India since early times. Like runner beans, the hyacinth bean is cultivated for both its ornamental purple flowers and its seedpods. It has high protein content, a high yield, and the ability to stay green during droughts. It is also easy to harvest. The beans are usually black, or close to black, but some varieties are white. Note that the dry bean seeds contain toxic amounts of cyanogenic glucosides and must be boiled to become edible. Children are especially vulnerable to this toxin. The beans also need a long time to cook because of their thick skin. This same bean goes under many names including its Latin name *dolichos labla*, *moneghine* (a Venetian name meaning "little nuns"), lablab (its North African common name), Egyptian bean, bonavist bean, and *frijoles caballeros* (or cowboy bean).

Winged Bean: Also known as goa beans, asparagus beans, four-angled beans, Manila beans, and princess peas, winged beans are four-sided tropical legumes with flared ridges. A legume originally grown in limited areas of New Guinea and Southeast Asia, it is now being raised all over Southeast Asia and India. The plant produces edible shoots, leaves, flowers, tubers, pods, seeds, and cooking oil extracted from the seeds and is comparatively high in protein. The pods are usually deep green, but may be red, pink, or purple. Each bean has four slightly ruffled wings or fins that run its length. The pods are larger than green beans but very lightweight. When cooked, they are meatier, blander, and starchier than a green bean but crunchier than a shell bean. Choose small pods with undeveloped seeds and plan to cook them within 1 or 2 days, as they don't store well. To prepare, cut off and discard the tips and then slice crosswise or on the diagonal. Wing beans are good sliced and added to stir-fries, braised and tossed in a strong-tasting sauce, or pickled.

Yam Bean: The yam bean (or jícama) is a name applied to the large, edible tubers of a leguminous plant native to Central and South America. This large, papery, brown-skinned root has a crisp, crunchy texture and can be eaten raw or cooked; however, the skin must be peeled before eating. Chinese cooks add yam bean to stir-fried vegetables as an easy-to-prepare alternative to fresh water chestnuts. The young pods of this plant may be eaten, but mature pods and their seeds are toxic. The enlarged root is the part of the plant sold in most supermarkets and ethnic markets. Interestingly, the tubers of leguminous plants are generally more nutritious than other tubers (such as potatoes). In the last few hundred years, yam beans have been introduced to most tropical and subtropical regions of the world. In Hawaii, it is called the "chop sui potato."

Where Do Our Beans Come From?

Today, America is by far the world leader in dry bean production, due largely to climate: long, mild summers and average rainfall of about eleven to twelve inches dur-

GROWING HEIRLOOM BEANS IN IDAHO

The Zürsun Company in Twin Falls, Idaho, started out in 1985 wholesaling twelve different beans. Its list has since grown to thirty varieties of beans, including many heirlooms, and six varieties of lentils, many organic. It's a great source for heirloom beans and specialty lentils. Zürsun's products can now be found at retail under the name "Cassoulets U.S.A." and "Good Taste of Idaho." The company continues to expand its selection through research and hybridization with unusual beans like the blue Azure; Amethyst, named for its color (also known as Zebra bean); and Provence Bean, originally from Africa, improved and renamed in Provence in southern France. The legumes are grown under contract by Zürsun in the high altitude Snake River Plain of Idaho. Large varieties needing a longer growing season are grown in California. Lentils are grown in the Palouse area of Idaho and the high plains of Montana. Zürsun's beans are dried in the field, rather than in ovens, making them easier to cook. Once harvested, the beans are sorted electronically, hand inspected, and placed in controlled low-humidity storage until shipped.

ing the growing season represent nearly perfect bean-growing conditions. Each year, U.S. farmers plant from 1.5 to 1.7 million acres of edible dry beans. And while Americans are the chief consumers of these beans, 40 percent are shipped to international markets in more than 100 different countries around the globe. The sale of these bean products to international venues generates about $275 million for the American economy annually.

Dry bean production is centered in fourteen states and includes fifteen different classes of beans. A number of states specialize in the growing of a particular bean. For instance, Michigan is one of the largest producers of navy beans. California grows the greatest portion of large and baby lima beans and black-eyed peas in the United States, in addition to light and dark kidneys, pink beans, small whites, and chickpeas. Idaho is the country's largest grower of beans for export. In Idaho, pinto, pink, great Northern, and small red beans are referred to by farmers and economists as the "Big 4"; Nebraska is well-known as a producer of Great Northern beans while Colorado is known for its pintos. The volume produced by each state varies, primarily due to weather conditions, but Michigan, North Dakota, Nebraska, and California usually produce the largest volume of beans.

AMERICAN-GROWN GOURMET LEGUMES

As European growers have long known, raising high-quality beans, peas, lentils, and chickpeas requires a unique combination of soil, moisture, and climate. Many people believe that the world's best overall area for growing dry legumes is in the Pacific Northwest corner of the United States (on the borders of Idaho, Oregon, and Washington) in a region called the "Palouse." In the rain shadow of the Cascade Mountains, the Palouse region's warm, dry summer days, cool nights, and nutrient-rich volcanic soils form the ideal combination to produce high yields of top-quality dry peas, lentils, and chickpeas. The high altitude means there is less chance of fungus growth in the soil, and the rich volcanic ash is excellent for growing quality beans. The four corners area of Colorado is similarly high in altitude and renowned for the high quality of its beans, especially pinto and Anasazi. It's especially important to recognize the work that specialty bean growers are doing in this country because they will help raise the status of legumes to the high position they deserve.

ANASAZI BEANS: AN ANCIENT VARIETY BROUGHT BACK TO LIFE

Dove Creek, Colorado, in the four corners area where Adobe Milling is located, is known as the "Pinto Bean Capital of the World." It is a beautiful agricultural plateau at over 7,000 feet, once the home to thousands of Anasazi who cultivated corn, squash, and beans, and built spectacular cities at Chaco Canyon, Mesa Verde, and other cliff dwellings. Ernie Waller, who founded Adobe Milling in 1983, popularized this heirloom bean now trademarked as Anasazi and first grown 1,000 years ago. These beans were found in the ruins by settlers in the early 1900s. Adobe Milling now takes in over 1 million pounds of Anasazi beans along with 2 million pounds of other heirloom beans such as bolita, Rio Zape, scarlet runner, and Zuni gold from local farmers.

IMPORTING ITALIAN REGIONAL HEIRLOOM BEANS

Chef Cesare Casella, of Beppe Restaurant in New York City, grew up in the restaurant his parents ran in the Tuscan city of Lucca. "When I opened Beppe, I wanted to re-create some of the dishes for which I was known in Tuscany," he says. "However, I found the quality of the beans that were readily available was not up to my standard. I missed the densely flavored heirloom beans which I had used in my signature dishes. For that reason, I decided to import beans from Tuscany for use at the restaurant." Among many other dishes, he uses these beans for his signature dish Sette: Warm Seven-Bean Salad from "Republic of Beans."

PURCHASING LEGUMES

DRIED LEGUMES

If you're accustomed to using canned, cooked legumes, you may not know how much of the dried type you'll need when a recipe calls for a certain amount of cooked legumes. Here's an easy general rule: When soaked and cooked, most varieties of small dried legumes, such as lentils, will at least double in size; medium- to large-size dried beans will triple in size.

BEAN AND BELUGA?

"American households have finally emerged from their anti-bean prejudice, and today we join the world in prizing dried legumes . . . the interest in dried legumes among American consumers has created a massive increase of imports and availability, resulting in a dizzying variety of dried bean, pea and lentil types on American grocery shelves today. We are proud to have pioneered in this country many of the currently available types (though it's not true that we are considering a name change to Bean and Beluga)."
—David Rosengarten, *The Dean & DeLuca Cookbook*

When shopping for dried legumes, it pays to buy them from reputable sources. Dried legumes from the current year's crop take less time to cook and cook more evenly. They are also easier to digest. It's certainly worthwhile spending the extra money on "gourmet" beans. Even a pound bag of fancy beans works out to an inexpensive meal. If you buy dried beans from a place that doesn't turn over stock quickly, you may get beans that are up to 10 years old. If you buy beans from a specialty store that really moves its stock, you'll be more likely to get fresher beans. The older the bean, the more problems you're likely to experience, both in cooking and in digesting. See the many companies selling high-quality heirloom and specialty beans, most sold through the Internet (see Sources, page 341).

Look for harvest dates that may be included on bean bags and boxes. I've seen this done with a very special kind of large white bean from Spain, *faves de Huelga,* which are packed in their own numbered cloth bag, with controlled origin (like Cognac or Champagne) and dated. In Spain there are many highly respected regional dry beans, as opposed to the United States, where beans have until recently been treated as a commodity, with the lowest price prevailing. Fortunately, stores such as Dean & DeLuca and companies like Indian Harvest have been an influential proponent of heirloom and specialty beans for more than 20 years. Simple but effective packaging in clear cellophane bags and a large variety of new harvest beans have won them many customers who are committed to the cause of great bean cookery.

USING FROZEN LEGUMES

The next best thing to freezing your own beans is buying them already frozen. Most supermarkets carry baby Fordhook limas and petits pois. Markets with a large southern or African-American clientele will often carry frozen black-eyed peas. I can find frozen pigeon peas *(gandules),* favas, and cannellini beans at Latino and Portuguese markets. Frozen green soybeans (edamame), which make a great addition to stir-fries, and frozen fava beans are sold at many Asian markets.

I often cook a large batch of beans and freeze them in 1-quart freezer bags. Opening a bag of my homemade precooked beans is as easy as opening, rinsing, and draining canned beans. To freeze your own beans, cool them to room temperature and divide among labeled quart-size "zipper-style" freezer bags. Squeeze out the excess air and seal well. I often double-bag my beans to protect them from extraneous smells and freezer burn. Beans may be frozen for 2 to 3 months. It's important to label frozen legumes (and other foods) with the name and the date. Use an indelible marker that won't rub off. Believe me, you'll never remember what was in those bags a month later.

USING CANNED LEGUMES

What about using dried beans that have been canned, such as pinto, kidney, and black beans? By all means use them for their convenience, but be sure to try cooking your own and see if you don't prefer their texture and flavor. In a dish where beans are going to be cooked further, such as baked beans or beans and rice, canned will work fine. In soups it's hard to get a rich multileveled flavor of beans if they have not been cooked all the way from dried.

I highly recommend the glass jars of cooked beans imported from Spain that are of excellent quality and are sold by the Whole Foods stores under their private label, 365. They are firm, plump and hold their shape with excellent flavor. I also recommend the large selection of canned and dried beans sold by Goya. Natural and organic food companies are a good choice for canned beans. Avoid low-priced store brands, which might not be of the best quality. I think it's worth buying the best, especially since beans are a good value, no matter how you buy them.

Legume Cooking Basics

WHY COOK DRIED BEANS?

To me there are good reasons for taking the trouble to cook your own dried legumes, rather than settling for canned. While cooking, you impart flavor and texture by the ingredients that go into the pot. A prosciutto bone, a country ham bone, smoked turkey legs, a head of garlic, an onion stuck with cloves, the rind of a lemon, fragrant bay leaves, a chunk of pastrami, fennel, coriander, cumin, and caraway seeds each gives its own taste. By following my directions for soaking and cooking, you can also diminish, if not eliminate, any digestive problems, something you can't do with canned beans.

GENERAL LEGUME COOKING TIPS

Use Soft Water

When cooking beans, the most important ingredient may be water! Always use cold water; hot water can pick up lead and other undesirable minerals from the pipes. If you live in an area that has very hard, mineral-laden water, you may not ever have been able to cook the beans until soft. The solution is to add a pinch of baking soda to the water to neutralize the acid. Don't overdo it as this will cause the skins to separate and fly off the beans. In hard water areas, use ⅛ teaspoon baking soda per pound of beans. The beans will actually absorb more liquid if cooked in a smaller, rather than larger, amount of water. Give the beans enough water to soak up and swell, but don't drown them.

Get the Dirt Out

Many bean recipes start with the admonition to pick through and rinse the beans. In most cases this isn't necessary. I have noticed, however, that black turtle beans and certain imported beans often contain small lumps of dirt, small stones, or debris. So picking over your beans and rinsing them is probably still a good idea, just to be on the safe side.

Prevent Fermentation

When cooking beans, keep in mind that they are prone to ferment. I would basically skip cooking beans on very hot humid days because they are more likely to spoil. If you do make a large pot of beans, place the pot of beans in a sink half-filled with ice water to chill them quickly. Once cold, beans can either be refrigerated in an airtight container for up to 4 days or frozen. Do not leave the cooked beans at room temperature because they ferment easily. I have found this out the hard way; be especially attentive in hot humid weather or during low-pressure weather patterns, such as before a thunderstorm, when spoilage seems to happen more quickly.

Blanch Beans for Increased Digestibility

In the most isolated and tradition-bound areas of the Mediterranean, beans, known as "the poor man's meat," are cooked by a time-honored method: they are blanched or par-cooked (placed in an earthenware pot or heavy pan with plenty of cold water and a pinch of baking soda, brought to a boil and cooked for 5 minutes, then drained and rinsed under cold water). In her book *Honey from a Weed*, Patience Gray notes that "This preliminary blanching is a definite ritual with regard to any bean of the species *Phaseolus vulgaris* (all the kidney bean varieties) fresh or dried, in Italy, Spain, and Greece."

In Tunisia, a country whose cuisine is rich in legumes like chickpeas, favas, and lentils, this preliminary blanching is done as a matter of course. My Portuguese friend, Maria Mata, never fails to blanch beans for dishes like Salad of Salt Cod and Red Beans. While testing bean recipes, I and my testers have found that blanching is an effective way to make dried beans more easily digestible. If I skip this step, I often have trouble, especially with black beans and chickpeas. However, this step can safely be eliminated if the beans are from the current year's harvest.

Add Hardening Ingredients Last

Beware of cooking legumes with salt, sugar, or acid (such as vinegar, tomato, or molasses), all of which harden the skin of the beans and prevent them from softening. This is why, to make good Boston baked beans, you must first cook the beans at least halfway *before* adding the sweet and salt ingredients. I've included three baked bean recipes that contain sweeteners. It is especially important in these dishes that the beans be softened, though not mushy, before the final baking step. If the beans are too hard to begin with, they'll never absorb enough liquid to get tender, no matter how long you cook them.

Shake—Don't Stir—Beans

If you carefully shake the pot rather than stir it, especially near the end of cooking, you'll avoid breaking up the soft beans. The fewer the broken beans, the better the texture. Newer beans, from this or last year's harvest, will hold their shape better without breaking up; older beans break up and get mushy when they're finally cooked.

Bean Cookery Controversy

According to former *Los Angeles Times* food editor Russ Parsons, in his book of kitchen science, *How to Read a French Fry*, "One comon myth is that beans should never be salted before cooking because that toughens their skins. Not only is there no scientific evidence for this, but practical experience says otherwise as well. Actually, salting before cooking has no effect on cooking time or digestibility." He also declares, "It is said that cooking beans with certain herbs—epazote, fenugreek, asafetida or seeweed, depending on the culture—can help reduce gas. This too is false; while these additions may taste good, there is no demonstrated benefit to either cooking or digestion."

Know When to Salt

I like to salt beans halfway through their cooking, after the skins have softened but when there is enough liquid left in the pot to dissolve the salt. You can, of course, salt after cooking, but there's no substitute for the mellow flavor you get when the salt is evenly distributed throughout the beans rather than sprinkled over the top. If you pressure-cook your beans, salt them *before* cooking to prevent them from becoming mushy under high pressure. Also, if you soak beans for a full 12 hours, you can add salt to the soaking liquid to help keep them whole. It is especially helpful to add salt both to the soaking liquid and to the cooking water of beans with fragile skins such as flageolets, soybeans, and limas to help keep their skins intact. If your beans are relatively fresh, you may salt from the beginning of cooking.

ANTI-FLATULENCE COOKING TIPS

Some of us have trouble digesting beans. To minimize the gas-producing effects of certain legumes, try the following tips:

• Purchase the most recent crop of dried beans. The older the bean, the more gastrointestinal problems you're likely to experience. Buy dried beans from a specialty store that turns over its stock quickly.

• Soak and drain your beans first. Soak the beans for at least 4 hours in a bowl of cold water, changing to fresh water once or twice, especially in hot and humid weather (to prevent fermentation). The longer you soak, the more of the offending oligosaccharides are leached out into the soaking water. Drain and rinse the beans thoroughly before cooking, discarding the soaking water.

• Blanch or precook beans of the common bean family, such as kidney, black beans, cannellini, and pinto. To precook beans, bring a large pot of unsalted fresh water to a boil. Add the beans and cook 5 minutes, skimming off and discarding any white foam impurities that rise to the surface. Drain and rinse, discarding the cooking water. Continue cooking the beans as the recipe directs; otherwise freeze the beans for later use.

• Remove the skin from beans or eat skinless legumes, such as split peas, split mung beans, and split chickpeas. When making a puréed soup, especially from beans with tougher skins, such as black beans, white beans, limas, and red kidney beans, strain the soup through a food mill or a sieve to remove the skins. When preparing chickpeas, rub off the skins before using them.

• Cook southwestern-style beans, such as pintos, red kidney beans, and especially black beans, with epazote, a strong-tasting leaf called wormseed in English that has anti-carminative properties.

• Cook Indian-style legumes with seasonings such as ginger, turmeric, tiny quantities of *asafetida* (dried plant resin), fennel seed, and *ajwain* seeds (lovage or carom seeds), all of which taste great and aid in digestion.

• Cook Mediterranean-style bean dishes with alkaline-rich greens such as wild chicory, dandelion, spinach, or chard to balance the acidity of the beans. To do this, simply add the blanched, drained, and chopped greens during the last 15 minutes of cooking. Alternatively, you can add a small amount of baking soda (also an alkaline) to the water when cooking legumes. Although this method does leach some of the nutrients into the water, it solves the problem.

• When using a pressure cooker to cook beans, add a strip of dried kombu (a type of alkaline seaweed sold at natural food stores), which makes the beans more digestible.

• If all else fails, try a commercial natural enzyme product, such as Beano, which breaks down the oligosaccharides before they are acted upon by gas-producing bacteria. In its powdered form, this product is sprinkled on food. Note that the enzyme is destroyed by heat, so it must be added directly to the finished dish. In its pill form, it is taken by mouth just before eating.

TO SOAK OR NOT TO SOAK?

The purpose of soaking is to rehydrate dried legumes, ensure even cooking, and shorten the cooking time. Another benefit of soaking beans is to remove indigestible oligosaccharides that can cause gas. These oligosaccharides are soluble in water. For even better results in removing them, change the water up to three times over the soaking period. Be sure to drain and thoroughly rinse the beans before covering with cold water and cooking. Remember to never cook the beans in the same soaking liquid.

Because legumes vary so much in size, texture, and shape, the soaking and cooking methods aren't uniform. Many kinds of small legumes, such as lentils, peas, and mung beans, don't require soaking because they are small

enough to cook through without this preliminary step. Whole beans and peas must be soaked in water because their skins are impermeable. Water can only enter beans through the "hilum" (the eye or point at which each bean was attached to its pod). Therefore, rehydrating the flesh inside the skin is a slow process. However, if you know the beans are freshly picked from the current year's crop, it is *not* necessary to presoak them.

Generally, beans are soaked in cold water for at least 8 hours. Small, thin-skinned beans can take as few as 4 hours. I prefer to soak all large beans up to 12 hours in a bowl of cold water to cover. The larger (and older) the bean, the longer it will need to soak. Thus, I soak large, thick-skinned dried favas and limas for at least 24 hours, changing the water frequently to discourage fermentation if the weather is warm. To save time, you can also quick-soak beans (see Soaking Chart, page 57). To check if the beans have been soaked long enough, cut a bean cross-wise in half. If the bean has no opaque center it is ready to cook.

If you plan to soak beans for the full overnight period (8 to 10 hours), add salt to the beans while soaking. The salt helps keep the skins firm and intact and promotes more even cooking, resulting in a better shaped bean. Add 1 teaspoon table salt (2 teaspoons kosher salt) to the soaking water per pound of beans.

On the Other Hand . . .

Interestingly, not every authority recommends soaking beans. I remember working with Chef Bradley Ogden for a special event. He asked me not to soak the black beans because their color would lighten from jet black to a deep purple. While I have to agree that unsoaked black beans are definitely darker and more dramatic in color, I am willing to forgo a bit of color to ease the digestion of my meal. Cooks in Mexico don't generally soak their beans. They depend on the nutritious cooking liquid as a kind of soupy sauce. Mediterranean cooks do soak, a habit learned from cooking Old World legumes like chickpeas and favas.

Diana Kennedy, a culinary authority I've admired greatly ever since her seminal book, *The Cuisines of Mexico,* also has strong opinions about preparing beans. She recommends not soaking beans to avoid the unpleasant odor the skins can produce. However, if the beans are soaked, she recommends not throwing out the soaking water because it contains all the minerals and flavor.

In *How to Read a French Fry,* Russ Parsons notes: "At the most, presoaking beans shortens their cooking time and provides for a more even softening of the starch granules (since beans are dried ingredients, part of the cooking process is simply add the water that was lost in drying). . . soaking also removes a marginal amounts of nutrients and, in the case of beans, a noticeable amount of flavor. In fact, in the cultures that best love beans, they are rarely soaked."

Personally, I find it hard to throw away so much accumulated folk knowledge of bean cooking rituals, traditions, and customs. My advice is to experiment and find out what works best for you: the Mediterranean method, in which beans are soaked and blanched, or the Mexican method, in which beans are cooked without this preliminary step but with plenty of liquid to make rich, soupy "pot liquor." In other words, there's more than one good way to cook a bean.

COOKING METHODS FOR LEGUMES

Here is some general information on cooking all types of beans by all types of methods. Although some methods allow for deeper, richer flavors because they involve longer, slower cooking times, you can use any method you choose to cook legumes and still get terrific results—especially if you season your beans while they cook. So, if you're lucky enough to own a pressure cooker, why not use it to cook all your legumes? On the other hand, if you're a fan of ovenware, like those pieces made in wonderful colors by the French company Le Creuset, by all means use them. And never fear—if all you have is a big pot, you can still boil up a great dish of beans.

LEGUMES AND CHILDREN'S STORIES

Two of the most famous children's stories involving riches also involve legumes. In *The Princess and the Pea,* the princess's rank was determined by testing her sensitivity. If she was a true princess, she would be able to feel a single pea while sleeping on a stack of pea-stalk hay mattresses. In *Jack and the Beanstalk,* Jack exchanges his poor, widowed mother's cow for some magic beans. Learning of her son's foolishness, she throws the beans out the window. The next day, they discover that the beans have grown into an enormous beanstalk reaching far up into the clouds—and into a giant's lair that contains riches, including a goose that lays golden eggs. Jack manages to steal the goose from the giant, who meets his fate chasing Jack back down the beanstalk.

Using a Pot

Cooking dried legumes in a pot on the stovetop (see Basic Cooking chart, page 58) is one of the fastest methods and the easiest alternative to using canned beans. In general, dried legumes take 1 to 2 hours to cook. Avoid using a pot made from a reactive metal, such as aluminum, as the beans can pick up an unpleasant metallic taste. Choose a heavy-bottomed pot for best results.

For simple boiled beans, place the soaked, rinsed, and drained beans in a large pot with fresh cold water. If you use this method, be sure to add plenty of liquid; you can always pour off the excess later, although some people say that beans will plump more if cooked in less water. This way, you'll never have to worry about the beans sticking and burning—a disaster in the making. The water level should come to about one inch above the beans. For each pound (2 cups) of dried legumes, you can add 1 tablespoon cooking oil to reduce foaming, which should be skimmed off and discarded. (Save the nutritious cooking liquid for your next soup.)

Boil beans for 10 minutes; then cover the pot, reduce the heat to low, and simmer until tender (about 1 to 2 hours, depending on the variety), checking the beans occasionally. Add seasonings (see chart, page 58) during the cooking time, if desired. Never add anything acidic, such as tomatoes, vinegar, wine, or citrus juices, while the beans are cooking. Add acidic ingredients only after the beans are almost tender. Stir occasionally to prevent heavy beans from sinking to the bottom. The beans will keep their shape much better if you stir them gently with a rubber spatula or wooden spoon. Salt the beans halfway through cooking. Their skins should be soft enough to absorb the salt. Allow the beans to cool at least partially in their cooking liquid before draining them, long enough to begin firming up without drying out.

Using a Dutch Oven

A fail-safe way of cooking legumes is to combine the flavorings, legumes, and liquid in a heatproof casserole with a lid. Bring it to a boil on the stove top; then place in a preheated moderate (300°F) oven and cook until the liquid has been absorbed and the beans are soft but not mushy.

Using an Earthenware Bean Pot or Slow-Cooker

Like many rustic-style cooks in the Mediterranean, Diana Kennedy prefers to cook dried beans in the Mexican style—in an earthenware pot that retains all the bean flavors. Since care must be taken that the beans do not scorch, Mexican cooks place a small *cazuela* (a shallow-sided earthenware casserole) filled with water over the top of the bean pot. This cuts down on the evaporation and keeps steaming hot water handy for adding to the beans, if necessary.

Kennedy also recommends using an electric slow-cooker with a ceramic liner. (These once ubiquitous cookers can often be found at yard sales for a couple of dollars.) She leaves her beans cooking on medium heat overnight. Look for a slow-cooker with a glass, rather than plastic, top. Kennedy prefers the slow-cooker over the pressure cooker because she believes beans taste better if they're not cooked in metal. I would agree with that and I avoid any reactive metals, especially aluminum. However, to my mind, a stainless-steel pressure cooker or pot doesn't adversely affect the beans.

Using a Pressure Cooker

While testing the recipes for this book, I convinced Linda Gellman, my intrepid recipe tester, to try out my pressure cooker. When she returned it, Linda told me, "I fell in love with a pot today," and immediately went out to buy her own. Though not inexpensive, a good stainless steel pressure cooker is a lifetime investment in good results. Once you've tried a modern pressure cooker (newly popularized because of improved features) you'll be convinced. Nothing is faster and more reliable. There

are many excellent brands for sale now, most imported from Europe, where they've been standard kitchen equipment for years. Mine is a large, 7½-quart model called a Duromatic, made by the Kuhn-Rikon Company of Switzerland.

The exception to the "rule" of not adding salt until the beans are soft is when you're using a pressure cooker. The directions on my box of imported French *haricots lingots* instructed me to add the salt from the beginning of cooking. Because of the great buildup of pressure in the pot, the salt doesn't prevent the beans from softening as it would in standard cooking methods. Instead, it helps them keep their shape by making them a bit more firm. They will also retain their shape because you won't break them up when stirring in salt near the end of cooking.

A good way to prevent foaming and tenderize beans is to add a strip of kombu (a type of seaweed sold in dehydrated strips at health food stores). Rinse the kombu quickly before placing a strip on top of the beans. Discard the kombu after cooking.

Pressure cookers produce dramatic time savings when cooking beans. Most beans can be cooked in one-third to one-half the time of conventional cooking methods. Exact times are impossible to give because of variables such as the age and dryness of the beans.

BEAN LANGUAGE

Because of how long they've been around and how important they are to the cuisines of many cultures, beans and legumes appear in many colorful ways in our language. For example:
- Someone who is "full of beans" is not credible; on the other hand, someone who is "full of beans" is also energetic and cheerful.
- Something that is "not worth a hill of beans" is pretty worthless.
- Someone who is said to be "a bean counter" is a corporate penny-pincher.
- Someone who has been "beaned" has most certainly been hit on the head.
- "Pulse" is an old term for edible seeds derived from leguminous plants. Though not common anymore, the word originally derived from the Latin *puls*, which meant a sort of thick porridge almost identical to the British pease pudding. The words "poultice" (a soft mixture of grains and other ingredients used to spread on an injured area), "polenta" (also a kind of porridge made originally from Old World buckwheat and later New World corn), and "pollen" are closely related to pulse.

Once the pressure builds up in your pressure cooker, reduce the heat to medium pressure—about 15 p.s.i. (pounds per square inch). Lentils, split peas, and lima beans should be cooked at low pressure—about 8 p.s.i. Don't fill the pressure cooker more than halfway with beans, as they will need enough room to expand. Adding about 1 teaspoon vegetable oil to the pressure cooker will reduce the foaming, especially for chickpeas. Because the foam can cause the steam vent to clog, you may need to press the vent occasionally to let off steam, which unclogs it.

KNOWING WHEN DRIED BEANS ARE FINISHED

According to food maven Paula Wolfert in her book *Mediterranean Grains and Greens,* "You can tell when the beans are almost done by removing one or two beans with a spoon and blowing gently on them—the skins will burst." New England cooks have long used the same method when making baked beans to tell if the beans are sufficiently soft to absorb hardening ingredients like sweet molasses and salt pork. The American Dried Bean Board recommends tasting a few beans to see if they are done: they should be tender, but not mushy. When cooling cooked legumes, keep them in their cooking liquid to prevent them from drying out. When reheating them, add a tablespoon or two of water.

Storing Cooked Legumes

When cooking dried legumes, why not make more than you need for immediate use? Extras are very easy to store—especially if packaged in moisture-proof containers. Cooked legumes may be kept in the freezer for up to 3 months. Bean dishes may be kept 4 or 5 days in the refrigerator.

Basic Cooking Chart for Fresh Legumes

Beans that are fresh-shelled and not dried for storage are sometimes sold in season, especially in farmers markets and at roadside stands. These beans should be treated like fresh vegetables and cooked in salted, boiling water until tender. They do not need any soaking. Keep in mind that green beans will lose their bright, attractive color if cooked with anything acidic in the water, such as lemon or vinegar. They keep the best color and flavor if cooked as quickly as possible over the highest heat with salt added to the water, or by using steam, which is hotter than boiling water. If precooking the beans, drain and rinse them under cold running water to set their color. Otherwise, drain and serve immediately. There is no better way than tasting to judge their doneness, because beans vary so much in maturity and tenderness.

Types of Legumes	Three Methods of Cooking
Green Beans Fresh Limas Green Romano Beans Fresh Favas All "shell" beans, such as fresh cranberry beans or black-eyed peas sold in their pods	**I. Steaming** Steam the beans in a basket steamer over a pot of boiling water until tender and brightly colored. **II. Boiling** Bring a large pot of salted water to a boil and add the beans. Bring the water back to a boil as quickly as possible, making sure to stir the beans so they will cook evenly. Cook until tender and brightly colored. Be sure to rinse under cold water to stop the cooking and set the color, unless serving immediately. **III. Pan Cooking** In a large skillet, bring one to two inches of salted water to a boil. Add the beans, stirring them occasionally and bringing the water back to the boil as quickly as possible. Cook until tender and brightly colored. (If seasoning the beans with acidic ingredients, such as lemon, vinegar, wine, or tomatoes, toss with the beans at the last minute to preserve their bright green color.)

Quick-Soaking Dried Legumes

Quick-soaking can be done in about 1½ hours from start to finish. The advantage of this method is that you do not need to blanch or par-cook and drain the beans before their final cooking in order for them to be digestible. However, the beans tend to break up more as they cook when quick-soaked, so it's better to use this method for dishes where the beans don't need to keep their shape, such as in soups where broken-up beans act as a thickener.

Basic Quick-Soak Method

For every pound (2 cups) of dried legumes, add 10 cups cold water. Heat to boiling; let boil 2 to 5 minutes, depending on the size of the bean (the larger the bean, the longer the cooking time). Remove from heat, cover, and set aside for at least 1 but no more than 4 hours. Drain and discard the water and rinse the beans. Proceed with any recipe that calls for soaked beans. *Note:* The longer the soaking time, the greater the amount of gas-causing properties that will dissolve in the water, thus helping to improve digestion of beans. Whether you soak the beans for an hour or several hours, remember to discard the soak water.

Soaking Chart for Dried Legumes

When soaking beans for recipes, figure that most dried beans will double in size when soaked and triple in size when cooked. For example, 1 cup dried beans will yield at least 2 cups soaked and 3 cups cooked.

Soaking is highly recommended for the following legumes:

Type of Dried Beans	Slow-Soak Times in Cold Water	Quick-Soak Times
Large, thick-skinned beans: *brown favas, large lima beans, white emergo beans, gigandes, giant white cocos, Christmas limas, scarlet runners*	12 hours at room temperature; change the water once to prevent fermentation in hot humid weather	Bring to a boil and cook 5 minutes; remove from heat and let soak 1 hour.
Whole chickpeas, whole starchy peas	10 hours at room temperature; change the water once to prevent fermentation in hot humid weather	Bring to a boil and cook 3 minutes (add a pinch of baking soda to cooking water for chickpeas); remove from heat and let soak 1 hour.
Medium-sized thick-skinned beans: *black beans, cannellini, red kidney, pinto, navy*	6 hours at room temperature (*Note:* Soak in lightly salted water if you plan to cook these beans in a pressure cooker so that their skins will stay intact under pressure.)	Bring to a boil and cook 2 minutes; remove from heat and let soak 1 hour.
Small thin-skinned beans: *French navy beans, pea beans, rice beans, red chile beans*	4 hours at room temperature	Bring to a boil and cook 1 minute; remove from heat and let soak 1 hour.
Small thick-skinned beans: *azuki, mung*	8 hours at room temperature	Bring to a boil and cook 1 minute; remove from heat and let soak 1 hour.

Soaking is not necessary for the following legumes:

Skinned split beans: *split favas, split yellow and green peas, split chickpeas*

Flageolets (dried seeds are immature and not starchy)

Shell beans or fresh-shelled pod beans: *limas, cranberry, roman, black-eyed peas*

Lentils (with and without skins)

Field-dried beans from current year's crop (rather than oven-dried)

Frozen shelled beans: *black-eyed peas and limas*

All fresh green beans and peas: *garden peas, green favas, green limas, green beans, yard-long beans, green romanos*

Legume Volumes: Dried vs. Cooked

Most dried legumes triple in volume when soaked and cooked. Here is an easy reference for measuring:
1 pound dried beans = 2 cups dry = 6 cups cooked
1 cup dried beans = 3 cups cooked

Basic Cooking Chart for Dried Legumes

Here is an easy guide to the simplest method of cooking dried legumes—in a pot of water on a stove top.

Type of Dried Beans	Water Amounts and General Cooking Times	Flavoring Suggestions (For All Legumes)
Large thick-skinned beans: *brown favas, butter beans, emergo beans, gigandes, giant white cocos, Christmas limas, scarlet runners, red kidney beans*	Use 3 parts water to 1 part beans. Boil 10 minutes (remove skins of favas); simmer covered on low heat 2½ hours.	Ham or smoked turkey bones Goose or duck legs and wings Bacon rind or *la cotenna* (the skin of prosciutto) whole unpeeled onion stuck with 3 or 4 whole cloves (peel onion for white beans) head of garlic with the top ½ inch sliced off bay leaves and/or small bunch of fresh thyme, marjoram, sage, rosemary, or savory tied up with string; several whole carrots dried and fresh hot chile pepper pods: green jalapeños, smoky dried chipotles, dark and rich ancho chiles, or salty-strong Korean red pepper strips of lemon and orange peel or a wedge of orange toasted, ground seeds: coriander, fennel, cumin, caraway, dill, and anise
Whole chickpeas Whole, starchy green peas	Use 3 parts water to 1 part beans. Boil 10 minutes (add a pinch of baking soda to cooking water for chickpeas); simmer covered on low heat 2½ hours.	
Soaked medium-sized thick-skinned beans: *black turtle beans, cannellini, black-eyed peas, pinto, navy*	Use 2 parts water to 1 part beans. Boil 10 minutes; simmer covered on low heat 1½ hours.	
Small thick-skinned beans: *adzuki, mung*	Use 3 parts water to 1 part beans. Bring to a boil; then simmer covered on low heat 1 hour.	
Small thin-skinned beans: *French navy beans, pea beans, rice beans, red chile beans*	Use 3 parts water to 1 part beans. Bring to a boil; then simmer covered on low heat 45 minutes to 1 hour.	

Times for Pressure Cooking

It is difficult to give exact times for cooking beans in a pressure cooker, but here are some approximate ones. Start timing after the pressure cooker has reached its full pressure level. Use 3 cups liquid for every cup of dried beans and never fill more than halfway. Once you've tested the beans, you'll be able to judge how long is needed the next time.

Black-eyed peas (soaked)	15 minutes
Chickpeas (soaked)	25 minutes
Kidney beans (soaked)	15 minutes
Pinto beans (soaked)	12 to 15 minutes
Large lima beans (soaked)	25 minutes
Black beans (soaked)	10 to 12 minutes
Lentils (not soaked)	12 minutes on lowest pressure
Split peas (not soaked)	12 minutes on lowest pressure
French green lentils (not soaked)	12 minutes on lowest pressure
Flageolets (not soaked)	15 to 20 minutes on lowest pressure

CHAPTER FOUR

Snacks and Dips

Chile-Spiced Fried Chickpeas

(VEGETARIAN)

As a young teen, I was lucky enough to spend two summers in Mexico. I lived first in Mexico City and then in the colonial university city of Puebla. Our apartment, complete with maid's quarters, was up in a luxury high-rise building with only four apartments on each floor. Downstairs was a wonderful supermarket where I would go every day to get a package of these chile-spiced chickpeas along with an exotic mango or passion fruit paleta, *or frozen fruit bar. You could vary this vegetarian recipe by tossing the fried chickpeas with a good curry powder, such as Madras style from India or S & B brand from Japan. Serve as a snack with a pitcher of frosty margaritas or chilled Cuban* mojitos.

—— *Advance preparation required. Serves 8 (Makes 6 cups)* ——

2 tablespoons ancho chile powder

2 tablespoons ground oregano

1 tablespoon garlic powder

1 teaspoon ground allspice

1 tablespoon popcorn salt or fine sea salt

1 pound (2 cups) dried chickpeas, soaked for 24 hours (see Soaking Chart, page 57)

3 cups canola, soybean, or peanut oil, for frying

1. Combine the ancho chile powder, oregano, garlic powder, allspice, and salt and set aside. Drain the soaked chickpeas. Bring a large pot of unsalted water to a boil. Add the chickpeas and cook for 10 minutes; then drain. Spread out on paper towels or a kitchen towel to dry completely.

2. In a large, heavy skillet or a wok, heat the oil until shimmering hot but not smoking, about 340°F on a deep-frying thermometer. Fry the chickpeas, in batches of about 1 cup, for 8 to10 minutes, or until golden brown and crunchy. Using a slotted spoon or wire skimmer, scoop out the chickpeas and drain on paper towels. Repeat until all the chickpeas have been fried. While still warm, toss them with the spice mixture. Store in an airtight container for up to 2 weeks.

The ancient Romans regarded chickpeas as food for peasants and the poor. When sickened by city life, the Roman poet Horace purportedly longed for a simple dish of chickpeas.

Spicy Homemade Beer Nuts

(VEGETARIAN)

In 1970, just out of high school, I spent three months hiking and camping in Jasper National Park, in the middle of the Canadian Rockies. My funds were extremely limited, but the local lager at the village tavern was cheap. I learned to enjoy it as the Canadians did, with a tomato juice chaser and several packages of beer nuts to round out my "meal." Needless to say, I spent many an evening in convivial company. This is my crunchy, spicy version of the packaged beer nuts I used to eat. The raw peanuts are available at natural food stores and Asian markets.

Serves 6 (Makes 3 cups)

1 pound raw, shelled Virginia peanuts (about 2½ cups)

1 cup sugar

1 cup water

1 tablespoon ground coriander

2 teaspoons Korean red pepper flakes (see below) or cayenne

1 teaspoon freshly ground black pepper

1 tablespoon paprika

Popcorn salt or fine sea salt, for seasoning

1. Preheat the oven to 350°F. Spread the peanuts on a baking sheet and toast for 10 minutes, or until just starting to brown. Remove from the oven and reserve, keeping the oven on.

2. In a large saucepan, make a syrup by bringing the sugar and water to a boil. When the syrup is clear, remove from the heat and stir in the coriander, red pepper flakes, black pepper, and paprika. Stir in the peanuts and return to the heat. Cook on medium heat for about 10 minutes, or until the syrup has thickened, shaking often.

3. Spray a baking sheet with nonstick vegetable spray or line with parchment paper. Spread the nuts along with their syrup on the prepared baking sheet. Bake, stirring once or twice, for about 15 minutes, or until the peanuts are evenly browned and the syrup has crystallized on the nuts. Remove from the oven and cool slightly. Season to taste with salt and cool completely before serving. Store in an airtight container, such as a cookie tin, for up to 2 weeks.

KOREAN RED PEPPER FLAKES

I've become a rabid fan of these salted hot red pepper flakes. There is one aisle in my local Korean market that shelves nothing but different brands, grades, and package sizes of this spice. The brilliant red, seedless flakes are spicy hot, but also have a full vegetable taste of the chile. Keep this spice refrigerated to maintain its color and potency.

Crunchy Fried Favas with Pimentón

(VEGETARIAN)

You will need to start this dish 2 days before serving it, to allow the favas sufficient time to soak. Similar preparations of fried favas, eaten as a snack, are found everywhere from Portugal, Spain, and the South of France to Morocco, Egypt, and Lebanon, and as far away as Mexico, South America, and even Korea. After frying, sprinkle the favas with pimentón, *the smoky Spanish paprika, or substitute cayenne, Korean red pepper flakes, Italian hot red pepper flakes, or Middle Eastern ground Aleppo pepper. Serve as a snack with a pitcher of drinks, such as margaritas or sangria.*

Advance preparation required. Serves 8 to 12 (Makes about 4 cups)

1 pound (2 cups) large split golden fava beans (without skins)

1 cup extra-virgin olive oil, for frying

3 cups canola, peanut, or soybean oil, for frying

1 teaspoon *pimentón,* or ½ teaspoon cayenne or hot red pepper flakes

½ teaspoon garlic powder

Fine sea salt or popcorn salt, for seasoning

1. Soak the favas overnight in 4 quarts water. The next day, drain, rinse, and cover again with cold water. Repeat two more times, changing the water every 12 hours or so, for a total of 36 hours. The beans should expand greatly and soften somewhat. Remove and discard any remaining pieces of skin. Bring a large pot of unsalted water to a boil. Add the beans and cook for 5 minutes, or until crispy. Drain and spread out on paper towels or kitchen towels to dry completely.

2. In a large, heavy skillet, combine the olive oil and canola or other oil and heat until shimmering hot but not smoking, about 340°F on a deep-frying thermometer. Add the dry favas, in batches of about 1 cup, for 10 to 12 minutes, or until crunchy and golden in color. Scoop out with a slotted spoon or skimmer and drain on paper towels. Repeat until all the favas have been fried; then toss with the *pimentón,* garlic powder, and salt to taste. Store in an airtight container for up to 2 weeks

Edamame
(Steamed Japanese Green Soybeans in the Pod)

(V E G E T A R I A N)

Young soybeans in their fuzzy green pods appear in the market in the spring and summer months. Delicious with drinks and fun to eat, they are a well-loved seasonal snack in China and Japan. The Japanese call green soybeans edamame or "branch beans." In Asian markets, they are sold as bunches of stalks with the pods attached. When the pods are shelled, the soybeans inside are green, smooth, sweet, and crunchy. In the springtime, fresh green soybeans, salted and cooked in their pods, are a traditional Chinese and Japanese snack served with drinks.

Serves 4

1 bunch young green soybeans on the stalks (about 1 pound)
2 tablespoons salt

1. Separate the soybean pods from the stalks. Using scissors, snip off a bit of the stem end of each pod to allow the beans to be easily squeezed from their pods after cooking. Place the bean pods in a bowl and sprinkle with the salt. Rub with the salt until evenly coated. Let them rest for 15 minutes to absorb the salt. (This enhances the color of the beans and accents their sweet flavor.)

2. Bring 4 quarts of water to a boil. Add the beans and boil over high heat for 7 to 10 minutes. Test for doneness after 7 minutes (the bean should be crisp-tender) and continue cooking for the remaining time if you prefer a softer bean.

3. Drain well in a colander. Serve the soybeans in baskets or bowls with drinks, along with a bowl for the discarded pods. To eat them, squeeze the pods between your lips, pressing the beans into your mouth. For best flavor, eat the beans the same day they are cooked.

SNACKING ON LEGUMES

In the southern Mediterranean region, lupine beans are a favorite snack. These Old World beans, related to flowering lupines, are mustard yellow with a distinctive small round hole at one end. Cooked and lightly pickled, the southern Italians call these beans *lupini* while the Portuguese refer to them as *tremoços*. In Lebanon, lupine beans are wrapped in a newspaper cone and eaten as street food.

In the Low Country of South Carolina, summertime roadside stands sell a regional favorite legume as a snack: boiled green peanuts. These are freshly dug peanuts boiled in salted water for up to 12 hours until soft and tasty. Green peanuts are sometimes seasonally available in Asian markets.

Pappadums
(Crispy Lentil Wafers) with Coconut–Cilantro Chutney
(VEGETARIAN)

In the early nineties, I had the chance to plan the initial menu for a landmark project, the Dock Street Brewing Company and Restaurant in Philadelphia. Owner and founder Jeff Ware started his company by contract, producing an extremely well-received microbrew called Dock Street Amber. After petitioning for a change in legislation in the state capital, Ware received the permits to open his own microbrewery and restaurant. These thin lentil wafers, called pappadums, *flavored with fenugreek, garlic, nigella seeds, cumin, and chile, were a popular snack food served at the bar.*

———————————— *Serves 10 to 12* ————————————

4 cups peanut or vegetable oil
1 (12-ounce) package plain or flavored
    lentil *pappadums*
2 cups Fresh Coconut–Cilantro Chutney
    (see page 311), for dipping

1. In an electric skillet or deep, heavy-bottomed pot, heat the oil to 365°F on a deep-frying thermometer. One at a time, carefully place the *pappadums* in the oil, cooking four or five in a batch. Fry for about 1 minute, or until small bubbles form over the surface of the *pappadums*. Using tongs, turn the *pappadums* over and continue to fry until bubbles form again. The *pappadums* should not brown, but should be crispy and light in color.

2. Remove *pappadums* from the oil and drain on paper towels. Keep them warm in a 200°F oven while frying the remaining *pappadums*. Serve with the Coconut-Cilantro Chutney.

COOK'S NOTE

Pappadums, poppdoms, poppadums, papdoms—whatever way you spell them (the *Oxford English Dictionary* lists eleven spellings)—are crisp, thin, savory lentil pancakes served in Indian restaurants in the West as a nibble before the first course. Don't be tempted to overcook them while frying. Once they begin to brown, they develop an unpleasant bitter aftertaste. Purchase dried *pappadum* wafers at Indian groceries or specialty food markets.

Crostini with Cannellini Bean Spread
and Oven-Roasted Plum Tomatoes
(VEGETARIAN)

Crostini or bruschetta are a frugal Italian peasant's way of using up day-old bread by brushing it with olive oil, then toasting it. Endlessly versatile, crostini can be topped with anything from Tuscan-style chicken liver spread to an elegant seasonal Piedmontese specialty of anchovy-garlic butter topped with thin slices of fresh white truffle. In this recipe, the crostini are brushed with rosemary-infused oil before being toasted and spread with white beans. Plump, herb-marinated roasted tomatoes contrast beautifully with the creamy bean topping. You can prepare the bean spread up to 2 days ahead and the tomatoes up to 1 week in advance.

——————————— *Serves 10 to 12 (Makes about 36 pieces)* ———————————

Cannellini Bean Spread

2 tablespoons extra-virgin olive oil

2 cloves garlic

½ cup chopped fresh sage
    (about ½ bunch)

¼ cup chopped fresh marjoram
    (about ¼ bunch)

½ teaspoon hot red pepper flakes

3 cups canned cannellini beans, rinsed
    and drained, or 1 cup dried cannellini
    beans, cooked and drained (see
    Basic Cooking Chart, page 58)

Salt and freshly ground black pepper

Crostini

2 tablespoons finely chopped rosemary
    (about ¼ bunch)

6 tablespoons extra-virgin olive oil

1 round or oblong loaf fresh Italian
    country bread (preferably day-old),
    cut into ½-inch slices

36 (approximately) Oven-Roasted Plum
    Tomatoes (see page 309), drained

1. Prepare the Cannellini Bean Spread: In a medium sauté pan, cook the olive oil, garlic, sage, marjoram, and red pepper flakes until the aromas are released. Add the beans and cook until the mixture thickens and starts to come away from the side of the pan.

2. In a food processor, purée the bean mixture to a paste, or put through a food mill. Season to taste with salt and black pepper. Reserve.

3. Prepare the Crostini: Preheat the oven to 350°F. Combine the rosemary and olive oil in a small bowl. Cut the bread slices into 2 x 3-inch pieces. Arrange the pieces in a single layer on a baking sheet. Brush the rosemary oil lightly on each side. Toast for 5 minutes; then turn the pieces and toast for 5 minutes longer, or until the crostini are golden.

4. Reduce the oven temperature to 325°F. Spread the crostini with a ¼- to ½-inch layer of the bean mixture. Top each with one drained Oven-Roasted Plum Tomato half. Arrange on a baking sheet and bake for 10 minutes, or until heated through. Serve immediately.

Spicy Hummus Dip

(VEGETARIAN)

My favorite, although untraditional, version of the Lebanese chickpea spread hummus gets its piquancy from Mexican chipotle chiles (smoke-dried jalapeños), enriched with a splash of good-quality fruity green olive oil. I'm also a big believer in the value of toasting spice seeds like coriander and particularly cumin—and I can't resist the garnish of pungent cilantro, though you can certainly omit it if you don't care for its forthright flavor. Yes, it's more work to start with dried chickpeas, and if you use canned, your hummus will still taste great. But if you go the extra mile here, the results will be worth it. Every time I make this recipe with dried chickpeas, my friends can't get over how good it tastes.

—————————— *Serves 12 to 16 (Makes 8 cups)* ——————————

3 cups (½ recipe) Basic Cooked Chickpeas
    (see page 299), or 3 cups drained
    cooked chickpeas
¼ cup fresh lemon juice (about 1 lemon)
2 cloves garlic
1 cup sesame tahini, preferably Lebanese
1 tablespoon chopped chipotle chiles
    in adobo sauce, or pimentón
    (smoked Spanish paprika) → 1 tsp *[handwritten]*
1 tablespoon salt *[handwritten: 1 tsp.]*
3 teaspoons ground toasted cumin seeds *[handwritten: 2 tsp.]*
    (see Toasting Seeds, page 225)
1 teaspoon paprika, for garnish
1 tablespoon extra-virgin olive oil,
    for garnish
2 tablespoons chopped fresh cilantro,
    for garnish
Pita bread, for serving

[handwritten: added ¼ c water]

1. In the bowl of a food processor, purée most of the chickpeas with the lemon juice and garlic, reserving a few whole beans for garnish. Add a little water to the chickpea purée—only as much as necessary to blend. Add the tahini, chipotles in adobo sauce, salt, and 2 teaspoons of the cumin, and process again until the mixture is smooth, creamy, and thick enough to hold its shape.

2. To serve, mound the hummus in the center of a large, flat serving dish. Using the back of a spoon, smooth the hummus outward to create a slight hollow in the center. Decorate the hummus in a star pattern with sprinkles of paprika and the remaining 1 teaspoon cumin. Drizzle the olive oil into the center hollow. Garnish with chopped cilantro and the reserved whole chickpeas. Heat the pita bread and cut into wedges. Serve the hummus with the pita wedges for dipping.

Black Bean Nachos with Salsa and Guacamole

(VEGETARIAN OPTION)

So many restaurants serve nachos these days, and their versions are usually decent. But homemade is so much better. These colorful nachos are always a satisfying snack while watching "the game"—especially when served with Mexican beer. For a crunchier, crusty texture, make these nachos in a paella pan, a shallow slope-sided stainless steel pan with a flat bottom. For a vegetarian version, simply omit the sausage.

— *Serves 4 to 6* —

1 (21-ounce) bag restaurant-style (thick) tortilla chips
2 cups Black Turtle Beans with Epazote (see page 250)
1 recipe (1½ cups) Spicy Guacamole (see page 314)
1 cup Pico de Gallo Salsa (see page 319)
½ cup sour cream
¼ pound chorizo sausage, cooked and thinly sliced, or thinly sliced pepperoni
¼ pound sharp Cheddar cheese, shredded

1. Preheat the oven to 450°F. Spray a 15 x 10-inch, metal jelly roll pan with nonstick vegetable spray, or use a 15-inch paella pan.

2. Spread the tortilla chips out in a reasonably even layer on the pan. Spoon dollops of the Black Turtle Beans with Epazote onto the chips. Spoon dollops of Spicy Guacamole, Pico de Gallo Salsa, and sour cream in between. Sprinkle with the chorizo or pepperoni. Cover the entire top of the nachos with the shredded cheese. Bake on the top shelf of the oven for about 15 minutes, or until the cheese is browned and bubbling. Allow to cool slightly before serving directly from the pan.

A "beanery" is a small, inexpensive restaurant such as a diner. A life-size sculpture entitled "The Beanery" is permanently installed in Amsterdam's Stedlijk Museum. Inside the 3-D sculpture, artist Edward Keinholtz has re-created every authentic detail of a beanery restaurant, a surreal combination of the ultra-realistic and the nonsensical, based on the famous Barney's Beanery in West Hollywood.

Chile Ancho Empanadas with Frijoles and Chorizo

(VEGETARIAN OPTION)

Empanadas are savory, single-serving pastry turnovers stuffed full of meat, vegetables, or cheese. They originated in Spain, but have become ubiquitous throughout South America. The key to an empanada is to stuff as much well-seasoned filling into the dough as possible, and then seal it so that none of the good juices leak out in the baking or frying. The simplest method is to use a fork to press down and crimp the edges, forming a pattern just as you would crimp a double piecrust. Latin American cooks often use a rolled "rope" edge; see the Cook's Note at right for instructions. These empanadas are perfect for a Mexican-themed cocktail party. If you're a meat eater, add the crumbled cooked chorizo sausage for extra flavor and richness. If desired, serve with Pico de Gallo Salsa (see page 319), Mexican Tomato Sauce with Allspice (see page 330), or sour cream mixed with lime juice and cilantro. For a vegetarian version, prepare the Refried Beans using olive oil and omit the sausage.

―――――― *Serves 12 (Makes 24 empanadas)* ――――――

3 cups Refried Beans (see page 301), chilled
½ pound fresh chorizo sausage, cooked, crumbled, and cooled

Chile Ancho Dough

3½ cups unbleached all-purpose flour
½ cup whole-grain cornmeal
2 tablespoons ancho chile powder or commercial chili powder
1 teaspoon salt
1 cup vegetable shortening or lard
¼ cup butter, chilled and cut into bits
3 eggs
¾ cup ice water
¼ cup milk or light cream, for sealing

1. Mix the Refried Beans with the cooked chorizo. Reserve in the refrigerator to keep cold.

2. Prepare the Chile Ancho Dough: Into the bowl of a food processor, measure the flour, cornmeal, ancho chile powder, and salt. Pulse until combined. Add the shortening and butter, and pulse until the mixture resembles oatmeal. In a small bowl, lightly beat 1 egg with the ice water. With the machine running, pour in the egg-water mixture, processing just until the dough comes together in a dryish, but not crumbly, ball. Do not overprocess. Remove the dough from the processor, place in a plastic bag, seal, and chill for 1 hour.

3. Roll out the dough on a floured surface until between ⅛ and ¼ inch in thickness. Using a large jar lid (such as the lid of a mayonnaise jar) or a 4- to 5-inch cookie cutter, cut out circles. Gather all the dough scraps together and reroll them once. Discard any remaining dough scraps as a third rolling might result in tough pastry.

4. In a small bowl, beat the remaining 2 eggs with the milk and reserve. Place a tablespoonful of the filling in the center of each dough circle. Using a pastry brush, apply the egg wash around the edges of the circles and fold over to form half-moons. Press or crimp the edges with a fork to seal tightly. When all the empanadas have been filled, brush them with the remaining egg wash. Poke each pastry with a fork to form steam holes. (Empanadas may be frozen at this point, as directed in the Cook's Note.)

5. Preheat the oven to 350°F. Arrange the empanadas on a parchment-lined baking sheet, leaving about 1 inch between them. Bake for 25 to 30 minutes, or until the filling starts to bubble up through the fork holes. Cool slightly before serving.

Cook's Note

To form a rope edge on the empanada, start at one end and pull out a piece of the edge with your thumb and forefinger to form a petal shape. Moving forward, fold this edge over and then press it together where it meets the dough. Pull out the pressed, folded corner of the dough to form another petal; then fold over and press again. Continue in this manner, making a regular pattern until you've crimped the entire empanada.

To freeze, arrange the prepared, unbaked empanadas in a single layer on a baking sheet and freeze. Once the empanadas are frozen solid, transfer them to a plastic bag, sealing well. Proceed with the directions for baking, adding about 15 minutes if they're frozen.

Red Bean Dip
with Crunchy Pita Chips and Vegetables
(VEGETARIAN)

During the years that I worked as a food stylist for cookbook authors at QVC, I prepared hundreds of dishes, many of them low in fat because these books always sold well. This spread, adapted from my original inspiration, which was a lower-fat chickpea spread in Lighter, Quicker, Better *by Marie Simmons and the late Richard Sax, is a real winner. Bring it to your next potluck buffet and watch it disappear. Use dark red kidney beans for a richer color.*

Serves 12 to 16 (Makes 3 cups)

3 cups cooked red kidney beans, rinsed and drained (see Basic Cooking Chart, page 58)

½ cup fresh lemon juice (about 3 lemons)

2 tablespoons extra-virgin olive oil

2 tablespoons roasted Japanese sesame oil

1 head roasted garlic, cloves peeled and puréed

1 chipotle chile in adobo sauce, chopped

Salt and freshly ground pepper

½ cup chopped fresh cilantro (about ½ bunch)

½ cup chopped fresh Italian parsley (about ½ bunch)

Crunchy Pita Chips

2 tablespoons extra-virgin olive oil

1 tablespoon chopped garlic

1 tablespoon ground cumin

½ teaspoon hot red pepper flakes (optional)

1 package pita breads, each cut into 6 wedges

Paprika, for garnish

1 English (seedless) cucumber, half-peeled in stripes and cut diagonally into rounds, for serving

½ pound carrots, peeled and cut diagonally into long slices, for serving

2 heads Belgian endive, separated into leaves, for serving

1. In a food processor, purée the beans with the lemon juice, olive oil, sesame oil, garlic, and chile; season to taste with salt and black pepper. Strain through a food mill or sieve to remove skin pieces if desired (this step will make the beans more digestible). Combine the cilantro and parsley. Fold three-fourths of the herbs into the bean mixture. Spoon the bean mixture into the serving dish; then sprinkle the remaining herbs over the top.

2. Prepare the Crunchy Pita Chips: Preheat the oven to 350°F. In a small bowl, combine the olive oil, garlic, cumin, and red pepper flakes. Brush each pita wedge with the oil mixture. Arrange in a single layer on a baking sheet. Bake 6 to 8 minutes; then turn over and bake for 2 to 4 minutes longer, or until lightly and evenly toasted. Reserve.

3. Serve the dip sprinkled with the paprika and accompanied by the cucumber, carrots, endive leaves, and pita chips.

Chickpea Fries Riviera Style *(Paniccia Rivierasca)*

(VEGETARIAN OPTION)

In the early eighties, I immersed myself in studying Italian and even proposed translating the great classic (still never translated) Le Ricette Regionali d'Italia *(The Regional Recipes of Italy), now in its thirteenth edition. According to author Anna Gosetti della Salda, if you go to the seaside city of Savona from April to September and visit the frying places* (friggitorie), *you can taste this superb rustic specialty. Many dishes cross the border, with some modifications, from France to Italy. After all, Nice was part of the Italian principality of Savoy for many years, which is why you will find* raioules *in Nice (ravioli) and* paniccia *(panisse) in Italy. Alice Waters's Berkeley restaurant, Chez Panisse, commemorates this dish in its name. A character named Panisse, after the eponymous Niçoise dish, was immortalized by the great Provençal writer and director Marcel Pagnol in his "Marseilles Trilogy,"* Marius, Fanny, *and* César.

--- Serves 6 ---

2 tablespoons olive oil
1½ cups chickpea flour
4 cups cold water
4 cups canola, peanut, or soybean oil,
    for frying
Salt and freshly ground black pepper
½ cup freshly shredded Parmigiano-
    Reggiano or other strong-flavored
    hard grating cheese, such as Asiago
    or Pecorino romano

1. Generously brush an 8-inch, square cake pan with the olive oil. Place the chickpea flour into a bowl and vigorously whisk in the cold water. Keep whisking until you have a smooth paste. Pour the batter into a heavy-bottomed pot and bring to a boil over medium heat, stirring constantly with a wooden spoon. Cook for 5 to 10 minutes, or until the mixture thickens and comes away from the side of the pan, as with polenta. Remove from the heat and beat until very smooth. Using a rubber spatula, scrape the batter into the oiled pan and cool; then place a sheet of waxed paper or plastic wrap on top and chill in the refrigerator.

2. When ready to finish the dish, cut the cold batter into 2½-inch-long matchsticks, the size of French fries. In a large pot, heat the canola or other oil to 365°F on a deep-frying thermometer. Fry about one-fourth of the sticks at a time. When they are crispy, golden, and covered with blisters, after about 8 minutes remove them carefully using a wire skimmer or slotted spoon and drain on paper towels. Sprinkle with salt and pepper to taste.

3. Preheat the broiler. Arrange the chickpea fries in a single layer on a shallow baking pan and sprinkle generously with salt, pepper, and the cheese. Broil for 5 to 10 minutes, or until the cheese is lightly browned and crusty. Serve immediately.

Dosa
(Yellow Split Pea Pancakes) with Cucumber-Yogurt Raita
(VEGETARIAN)

This large, lacy pancake from India's vast repertoire of vegetarian dishes is flavored with onions, cilantro, and fresh ginger. You'll need to start the naturally fermented batter of split pea and rice purée a day ahead. Unusual but delicious, dosa is related to other Indian flatbreads made with lentils, or dals such as pappadum and dohkla. Serve the dosa with Green and Yellow Bean Curry with Cauliflower (see page 159) for an Indian vegetarian meal. Indian-style toasted clarified butter, or ghee, is used as a cooking fat here and gives further dimension to these simple pancakes. The raita is a simple, refreshing, and nutritious salad/relish made from thick yogurt, cucumber, and mint, similar to Greek tzatziki.

—————————— *Advance preparation required. Serves 6* ——————————

½ cup dried yellow split peas

1½ cups raw long-grain rice, preferably basmati

1¼ cups cold water

½ cup finely chopped onion

¼ cup finely chopped cilantro leaves (about ¼ bunch)

2 tablespoons grated fresh ginger

1 jalapeño pepper, halved, seeded, and thinly sliced

2 teaspoons salt

3 tablespoons ghee (see Making Ghee, below) or vegetable oil, for frying

2 cups Cucumber-Yogurt Raita (see page 308)

1. Rinse the yellow split peas and rice separately in cold water. Place in separate bowls and cover each with cold water. Soak at room temperature for 12 hours or overnight.

2. Drain the split peas and purée in a blender with ½ cup of the cold water. The mixture should be as smooth as pancake batter. Transfer the pea purée to a large bowl. Drain the rice and purée with ½ cup of the cold water; then combine with the split pea purée. Stir well, cover with a damp towel, and set aside at room temperature to ferment for at least 24 hours and up to 2 days, or until the mixture is bubbly and slightly sour tasting.

3. When ready to cook, stir the onion, cilantro, ginger, jalapeño, salt, and the remaining ¼ cup cold water into the fermented batter to make a soupy mixture.

4. In an 8- or 9-inch, nonstick skillet, melt 1 teaspoon of the ghee. Pour in ¾ cup of the batter, tilting the pan so the batter spreads out evenly, as if you were making a crepe. Cook for 2 to 3 minutes, or until bubbles form across the surface. Drizzle ½ teaspoon ghee over the top. Cover the pan with a large heatproof plate; then flip over. Slide the uncooked side of the pancake back into the pan and cook for 2 minutes longer, or until lightly browned. Continue until all the batter has been used. Keep the *dosa* warm in a 200°F oven. Serve with the Cucumber-Yogurt Raita on the side for dipping.

MAKING GHEE

Place at least 1 pound cut-up butter into a small heavy pot and melt over very low heat. Cook slowly until the white butter solids foam up and then turn nutty brown in color. Be careful not to burn the ghee, especially when it's almost ready. Skim off and discard all solids floating on the surface. Strain the hot ghee through a paper towel- or cheesecloth-lined sieve to remove any remaining particles. It should be completely clear; any remaining solids could cause it to spoil or burn. Ghee will keep indefinitely in the refrigerator.

Tex-Mex Seven-Layer Salad
with Homemade Tortilla Chips
(VEGETARIAN OPTION)

It seems like seven is the magic number for this super-popular party dish. Of course, you could leave out a layer, but it might be missing a bit of magic. To get the full effect of this salad, you will need a large, footed glass trifle dish or glass salad bowl with straight sides. Layer the ingredients in the order given for the best color contrast. You can make the salad early in the day it is served, but no sooner or the colors will start to run together. For a vegetarian version, prepare the Basic Black Turtle Beans without the ham hocks, using Liquid Smoke for flavor, if desired.

--- *Serves 10 to 12* ---

1 head romaine lettuce, rinsed, dried, and shredded
1 recipe (2 cups) Pico de Gallo Salsa (see page 319)
2 cups Basic Black Turtle Beans (see page 297)
1 recipe (2 cups) Avocado Mousse (see page 315)
½ pound sharp Cheddar cheese (preferably orange colored), shredded
1 pint (2 cups) sour cream
½ cup pimiento-stuffed green olives, cut into halves or slices, depending on the size
½ cup pitted Kalamata olives, cut into halves or slices, depending on the size
12 ounces Homemade Tortilla Chips (recipe follows)

Arrange the following layers in a large, clear glass trifle dish or straight-sided bowl, making sure to spread out each layer evenly to the edges so it can be seen from the side: romaine lettuce, Pico de Gallo Salsa, Basic Black Turtle Beans, Avocado Mousse, shredded cheese, and sour cream. Decorate the top with the green and Kalamata olives. Serve with the Homemade Tortilla Chips.

HOMEMADE TORTILLA CHIPS

1 (12-ounce) package fresh 6-inch corn tortillas
3 cups canola, peanut, or soybean oil, for frying
1 container popcorn salt or fine sea salt, for seasoning

Cut each tortilla into six to eight wedges. In a deep, heavy-bottomed pan or fryer, heat the oil to 365°F on a deep-frying thermometer. Place the tortilla wedges into the oil one at a time so they won't stick together, adding as many as will fit in a single layer. Stir with a pair of metal tongs or a spoon so they cook evenly. When the chips start to brown and stiffen, remove from the oil using a wire skimmer or metal tongs. Drain on paper towels, sprinkle lightly with salt, and keep warm in a low oven, if desired. To crisp the tortilla chips later, place in a 200°F oven for 10 minutes. Store in a cookie tin if possible.

Falafel with Yemenite Fenugreek (Hilbeh) Sauce

(VEGETARIAN)

I never get tired of eating falafel. Don't ask me why. Perhaps it's the seasoning or the combination of fried crunchy bean cakes with juicy vegetables and creamy, sour yogurt-cucumber dressing. I haven't been in Israel for too many years, but I still remember the beautiful hillside seaport of Haifa. On one steep street, falafel stands abounded, each with an elaborate assortment of condiments, relishes, sauces, and toppings with which to embellish the basic falafel in pita. The traditional Yemenite Fenugreek Sauce, made with lots of fenugreek and served with the falafel, is very popular in Israel. You must use raw, soaked dried chickpeas to make this dish because canned beans are already cooked.

—————————— *Serves 6* ——————————

1 pound (2 cups) dried chickpeas, soaked
    (see Soaking Chart, page 57)
1 egg, lightly beaten
3 tablespoons salt
1 teaspoon freshly ground black pepper
1 teaspoon turmeric
½ cup chopped fresh cilantro leaves
    (about ½ bunch)
1 teaspoon ground coriander seeds
½ teaspoon ground cardamom
½ teaspoon cayenne
3 cloves garlic
2 tablespoons sesame tahini
½ cup fresh white bread crumbs
½ cup sesame seeds, preferably natural,
    or unhulled
4 cups canola, peanut or soybean oil,
    for frying
1 (8-ounce) package pita bread
1 cup Yemenite Fenugreek Sauce
    (see page 312)

1. Drain the soaked chickpeas. Using a meat grinder or food processor, grind the chickpeas to a paste. Add the egg, salt, pepper, turmeric, cilantro, coriander, cardamom, cayenne, garlic, tahini, and bread crumbs and process again until well combined. The mixture should be soft, but firm enough to hold its shape. Using a small ice cream scoop or tablespoon, form the falafel mixture into 1-inch balls with the tops slightly flattened. Dip the tops of the falafel into the sesame seeds, pressing them in lightly. Cover and chill in the refrigerator until ready to cook.

2. In a large, heavy-bottomed pot, heat the oil to 365°F on a deep-frying thermometer. Gently place the falafel into the oil, one at a time, until about one-fourth are added. Fry until crisp and evenly browned, about 5 minutes. Using a slotted spoon, remove the falafel and drain on paper towels. Continue frying the remaining falafel in batches. Serve with pita bread and Yemenite Fenugreek Sauce.

TRADITIONAL CONDIMENTS FOR FALAFEL

For a traditional spread, serve the falafel with small bowls of yogurt tahini sauce; *torshi*, or magenta, beet-pickled turnips (available from Middle Eastern groceries); Yemenite Fenugreek Sauce; and a larger bowl of Israeli salad with diced cucumber, red onion, and tomato in lemon juice and olive oil. Other garnishes might include marinated hot peppers, marinated olives, small pickled gherkins from Israel or kosher-style pickles, and hot grilled pita bread, along with *za'atar* pita bread if you have a Lebanese bakery in your area.

Black Bean Quesadillas
with Pepita-Tomatillo Sauce
(VEGETARIAN)

While I was staying at the lovely high-style Camino Real Hotel in Cancun, the black beans I ate every morning at the fabulous buffet were sprinkled with salty, strong aged cotija cheese. In this dish, charred poblano chiles and onions are layered with tasty black beans on tortillas. The creamy, tangy Pepita-Tomatillo Sauce lightens the dish while giving it another dimension of flavor. For a crunchy garnish, toast green pumpkin seeds (pepitas) in a 300°F oven for about 10 minutes and then sprinkle on top just before serving.

———— *Serves 6* ————

4 poblano chiles

2 large onions, unpeeled and quartered

1 tablespoon vegetable oil

2 cups Basic Black Turtle Beans
(see page 297), or Black Turtle Beans
with Epazote (see page 250)

1 (12-ounce) package corn tortillas

2 cups Pepita-Tomatillo Sauce
(see page 305)

¼ pound cotija cheese, French feta, or
ricotta salata, crumbled

1. Preheat a grill or grill pan until hot. Rub the poblano chiles and onions with the oil and grill until the skins are blackened but the flesh is still firm, about 10 minutes. When cool enough to handle, peel both the poblanos and the onions. Seed the poblanos and remove the stems. Cut into strips. Peel the onions, cut into strips, and combine with the chiles in a bowl.

2. Preheat the broiler. Spread about a ¼-inch-thick layer of the Basic Black Turtle Beans over half of the tortillas. Top with a portion of the poblano mixture and cover with a second tortilla. Repeat with the remaining beans, poblano mixture, and tortillas. Grill the quesadillas on both sides until browned and scattered with bubbles. Arrange the grilled quesadillas in a shallow, broiler-proof baking dish. (I would use a steel paella pan here.) Ladle the Pepita-Tomatillo Sauce on top and sprinkle with the cheese. Place under the broiler long enough for the sauce to get bubbling hot; then serve.

Bitar's Pan-Grilled Falafel

(VEGETARIAN)

Amin and Jude Bitar run one of Philadelphia's culinary treasures, Bitar's Grocery and Pita Hut. The two brothers have carried on the business started by their father when he brought his family here from Beirut in 1974. Lebanese Christians, the Bitar brothers reach out to the city's entire food community: Christians, Muslims, Jews, and everyone else. As Philadelphia's Arabic-speaking population has grown, so has the demand for sometimes hard-to-find foods like pomegranate molasses, fava beans, labni yogurt, Aleppo pepper, sumac, apricot leather, and za'atar spice, all found at Bitar's. Amin developed this popular recipe for his customers who were looking for a lighter version of falafel. You must start with dried beans.

--------- *Serves 6* ---------

Falafel

¼ pound (½ cup) dried split fava beans, soaked (see Soaking Chart, page 57)

¼ pound (½ cup) dried chickpeas, soaked (see Soaking Chart, page 57)

½ cup diced, seeded green bell pepper

½ cup chopped Italian parsley leaves (about 1 bunch)

1½ teaspoons garlic powder

1½ teaspoons onion powder

1 teaspoon salt

¼ teaspoon freshly ground black pepper

½ teaspoon ground cumin

¼ teaspoon baking soda

½ teaspoon olive oil, for cooking

Garlic Dressing and Salad

½ cup fresh lemon juice (about 4 lemons)

2 tablespoons extra-virgin olive oil

1 teaspoon minced fresh garlic

1 head lettuce (romaine, iceberg, or green leaf), shredded

2 large ripe tomatoes, seeded and diced

1 cup chopped Italian parsley leaves (about 2 bunches)

2 sour dill pickles, diced

6 white, whole wheat, or *za'atar*-spiced pita breads

1. Prepare the Falafel: Drain the favas and chickpeas. Place in a food processor and blend to a pasty texture. Add the bell pepper, parsley, garlic powder, onion powder, salt, black pepper, cumin, and baking soda. Process until well mixed. Transfer the mixture to a bowl. Form into balls about 1 inch in diameter and arrange on a waxed paper–lined tray. Cover and chill thoroughly in the refrigerator for at least 1 hour.

2. Prepare the Garlic Dressing and Salad: Using a hand-held blender, or in a blender, mix the lemon juice, extra-virgin olive oil, and garlic to create a creamy liquid. Reserve.

3. Preheat a nonstick skillet over medium heat, and add the olive oil for cooking. Pat the falafel balls into thin patties and add to the pan. Cook falafel patties on both sides as you would pancakes. When browned on both sides, remove from the pan.

4. Toss the lettuce, tomatoes, parsley, and pickles with the dressing, and divide among plates. Serve the falafel on top of the salad, accompanied by heated or grilled pita breads.

FALAFEL'S ORIGIN

These small fried cakes originated in Egypt with the Coptic Christians, who refrained from eating meat on certain holidays. Made with fava beans in Egypt, they are known as falafel in Alexandria and *ta'amia* in Cairo. Because Alexandria was a port city, it most likely exported this dish and its name to Syria, Lebanon, and Israel, where it is made with either all chickpeas or chickpeas mixed with favas, as in this Lebanese recipe for Pan-Grilled Falafel.

Black Bean Pâté with Tequila

The strong flavors in this modern pâté, inspired by a recipe in Joyce LaFray's Cocina Cubana, *make it a natural to serve with cocktails such as margaritas. You will need to start the pâté a day in advance, but you can also make it up to 3 days before serving. I've added the classic Mexican liquor, tequila, made from the fermented and distilled sap of the agave, called* maguey *in Spanish. In Mexico, there are many specially distilled and aged tequilas that are sought and sampled with the same dedication displayed by aficionados of single-malt Scotch whiskey. Tequila's strong, unmistakable punch reinforces the flavor of the black beans. You will need a 6-cup metal cake pan or ring mold to shape the pâté.*

———————— *Advance preparation required. Serves 12* ————————

3 (¼ ounce) packages unflavored gelatin
½ cup cold water
½ cup tequila
1 recipe (6 cups) Black Turtle Beans with Epazote (see page 250)
1 tablespoon chopped garlic
2 tablespoons ancho chile powder or commercial chili powder
2 tablespoons Worcestershire sauce
2 tablespoons salt
1 tablespoon ground cumin, preferably toasted (see Toasting Seeds, page 225)
2 teaspoons ground allspice
1 cup sour cream
1 medium red onion, finely diced
½ cup chopped pimiento-stuffed green olives
½ cup sliced dry-pack sun-dried tomatoes (see page 89)
1 bunch cilantro leaves, chopped (about 1 cup)
1 cup Mexican *crema* or sour cream, preferably in a plastic squeeze bottle
Homemade Tortilla Chips (see page 73)
4 limes, sliced and halved

1. In a small bowl, soften the gelatin in the cold water for 5 minutes, or until it "blooms" and absorbs some of the liquid. Place the bowl over a pan of hot water and heat until the mixture become thin and clear. Stir in the tequila and remove the gelatin mixture from the heat.

2. Place 4 cups of the Black Turtle Beans with Epazote in the bowl of a food processor with the garlic, chile powder, Worcestershire sauce, salt, cumin, and allspice. Purée until smooth. Add the sour cream and reserved gelatin mixture and process again to combine. (For a smoother pâté, strain the mixture through a food mill or sieve.) Transfer to a bowl and fold in the red onion, green olives, sun-dried tomatoes, and chopped cilantro. Spray a 6-cup mold, preferably ring-shaped, with nonstick spray and use a rubber spatula to fill it with the mixture. Bang the mold on the counter to remove any air pockets. Cover with plastic wrap and chill until firm, 4 hours or overnight.

3. To serve, dip the mold briefly into a bowl of very hot water; then unmold onto a large platter. Decorate with swirls of *crema* or sour cream from the plastic squeeze bottle. Fill the center of the mold with the Homemade Tortilla Chips and surround with small slices of lime. Chill again until ready to serve.

CHAPTER FIVE

Salads, Hearty and Light

Spinach and Beef Filet Tip Salad
with Fermented Black Beans

This dish of roasted beef filet in a dark Korean-style marinade features fermented black beans and is served over fresh spinach, making it a perfect main-dish salad. The beef tastes best if served hot or at room temperature rather than cold, which dulls the flavors. The fermented beans are actually soybeans that turn black from fermentation—not to be confused with black turtle beans, which are more common and closely related to pinto and kidney beans.

Look for relatively inexpensive filet tips in your local supermarket. These conical ends of the filet are too small to serve whole, but they work well here because they are sliced. Of course, you may substitute center-cut filet of beef.

—————— *Advance preparation required. Serves 6* ——————

Marinade

¼ cup molasses (not blackstrap)
¼ cup peanut oil
2 tablespoons roasted Japanese
    sesame oil
¼ cup grated fresh ginger
¼ cup mushroom soy sauce
¼ cup Shanxi or Chinese black vinegar
¼ cup hoisin sauce
¼ cup fermented black beans, rinsed,
    drained, and chopped
4 beef filet tips (about 1 pound total),
    trimmed, silverskin removed

Dressing

2 tablespoons soy sauce
2 tablespoons rice wine vinegar
2 tablespoons Shanxi or balsamic vinegar
1 tablespoon grated fresh ginger
½ teaspoon freshly ground black pepper
1 tablespoon Dijon mustard
2 tablespoons roasted Japanese
    sesame oil
6 tablespoons peanut oil

1 medium white onion, thinly sliced,
    soaked in salted ice water for
    10 minutes, then drained
1 (10-ounce) bag salad spinach, stems
    removed

1. Prepare the Marinade: In a large shallow bowl, blend the molasses, peanut and sesame oils, ginger, soy sauce, vinegar, hoisin sauce, and black beans. Add the beef tips, turning to coat well. Cover and refrigerate overnight.

2. Preheat the oven to 450°F. Drain off and discard the marinade from the beef tips. Place the beef in a small roasting pan and roast until rare, about 135°F on a meat thermometer. Cool to room temperature; then thinly slice with a sharp knife, preferably an electric knife. Reserve.

3. Prepare the Dressing: Combine the soy sauce, rice wine and shanxi vinegars, ginger, black pepper, and mustard into a blender. Blend until well combined. Slowly pour in the sesame and peanut oils, continuing to blend until the mixture is creamy. Reserving a few onion slices, toss about half the dressing with the spinach and remaining onions.

4. Divide the spinach mixture among six large salad plates. Arrange the beef slices over the top and sprinkle with the reserved onion slices. Drizzle the remaining dressing over the beef.

Marinated Bean Sprouts and Jícama

(VEGETARIAN)

This simple relish makes a good snack on its own, or a nice garnish for your next green salad. Mung bean sprouts are about 2 inches long, with a tiny head. In China, the root end is removed. For extra-special occasions, the yellowish head end is also removed, and then they're called "silver sprouts." You may also see larger, 3- to 4-inch-long sprouts with a larger yellow head. These are soybean sprouts, which are not as tender. You must remove the head end of the soybean sprout before using. In both kinds, look for fresh-smelling, firm, and silvery white sprouts.

Serves 6

1 (8-ounce) package fresh mung bean sprouts (about 2 cups)

1 jícama (about 8 ounces), peeled and cut into matchsticks

¼ cup rice wine vinegar

2 tablespoons roasted Japanese sesame oil

2 tablespoons soybean oil

2 tablespoons light soy sauce

1 clove garlic, crushed

½ teaspoon hot red chile paste, cayenne, or hot pepper sauce

1. Bring a medium pot of water to a boil. Add the bean sprouts and boil for 2 to 3 minutes. Drain and lightly squeeze out the water.

2. In a medium bowl, combine the sprouts, jícama, vinegar, sesame and soybean oils, soy sauce, garlic, and chile paste. Marinate in the refrigerator for at least 1 hour and up to 3 days before serving.

Haricots Verts and Beet Salad
with White Balsamic–Truffle Vinaigrette, Goat Cheese, and Olivada Crostini

(VEGETARIAN)

This colorful salad is full of surprises. The crunchy baby green beans, sweet but earthy beets, and tantalizingly perfumed truffles are all accented with tangy fresh goat cheese. The white balsamic vinegar called for here was developed in Italy for chefs who wanted the sweet, rounded flavor of traditional balsamic vinegar without the dark color. I use truffle oil as a relatively inexpensive way of imparting the indescribable taste and aroma of truffle to the dressing. Substitute fresh young green beans, combined with wax beans if desired, when they're in season.

--- *Serves 6* ---

1 pound *haricots verts,* tails trimmed, pointed tips left on

1 pound young beets, trimmed to 1 inch of greens

White Balsamic–Truffle Vinaigrette (recipe follows)

6 ounces goat cheese, crumbled

6 tablespoons pine nuts, lightly toasted (optional)

Olivada Crostini (recipe follows)

1. Have ready a bowl of ice water. Bring a large pot of salted water to a boil. Add the *haricots verts* and boil 2 to 3 minutes, or until brilliant green and firm but tender. Scoop the beans from the water using a wire skimmer and immediately plunge them into the ice water to shock and set the color.

2. Add the beets to the same pot and bring the water back to a boil. Simmer about 20 minutes, or until the beets are tender when pierced with a fork. Note that smaller beets will cook more quickly and should be removed first. Drain and rinse under cold water until cool enough to handle. Rub off the outer skin and beet tops; then trim any remaining skin and root ends. Cut the beets into 6 to 8 wedges each.

3. To finish the salad, toss the *haricots verts* with enough White Balsamic–Truffle Vinaigrette to coat lightly. Separately, toss the beets with enough vinaigrette to coat lightly. Form the *haricots verts* into a pyramid shape in the center of each of six salad plates. Arrange the beets around the pyramid. Sprinkle with goat cheese and pine nuts, if desired. Serve one Olivada Crostini with each portion of salad.

COOK'S NOTE

I love goat cheese, both fresh and aged. Fresh, mild goat cheeses are usually best for crumbling on salad. Among my favorite brands are Madame Chèvre from Canada, Silver Goat from Israel, Coach Farm from New York State, and Laura Chenel from California.

WHITE BALSAMIC–TRUFFLE VINAIGRETTE

— *Makes 1 cup* —

1 tablespoon coarse-grain mustard
2 tablespoons minced shallots
2 teaspoons chopped fresh thyme leaves
2 teaspoons kosher salt
¼ cup white balsamic vinegar
¾ cup canola oil
¼ cup white truffle oil
Freshly ground black pepper to taste

Using a hand-held blender or a blender jar, combine the mustard, shallots, thyme, salt, vinegar, oils, and pepper. Purée until smooth and reserve.

OLIVADA CROSTINI

½ baguette, preferably stale
¼ cup plus 2 tablespoons extra-virgin
    olive oil
Generous ½ cup Kalamata olives, pitted
Generous ½ cup oil-cured black olives,
    pitted
1 teaspoon ground fennel seeds
Juice of 1 orange and grated zest
    of ½ orange
Juice of 1 lemon
Freshly ground black pepper (no salt)

Preheat the oven to 400°F. Cut the baguette on the diagonal into slices 1 inch thick. Using a pastry brush, brush slices on both sides with ¼ cup of the olive oil. Arrange in a single layer on a baking sheet and toast for about 10 minutes on one side, or until browned on the edges. In a food processor, purée the olives, fennel seeds, orange juice and zest, lemon juice, and the remaining 2 tablespoons olive oil. To serve, spread on the crostini.

Greek Gigandas Bean Salad with Grilled Octopus

(VEGETARIAN OPTION)

Recently I traveled to Greece with a group of food writers on a wonderful trip sponsored by the International Olive Oil Council. We visited the Kalamata region, home of both the famed purple brine-cured olives and superb olive oil, some of it organic. Greeks are known, justifiably, for their skill in cooking octopus. If you've never cooked octopus—or even if you have—try this method in which I first poach it in a red wine broth, then grill it and combine it with the large white runner beans known as gigandas in Greece and emergo beans in the United States. For best flavor, grill the octopus over natural hardwood charcoal (available in Whole Foods Markets and at Trader Joe's; see Sources, page 341). To make this dish vegetarian, eliminate the octopus and top the bean salad with colorful grilled pepper wedges, fennel wedges, and red onion slices.

Serves 6 to 8

Red Wine–Poached Octopus

2 carrots, peeled and cut into large chunks

2 ribs celery, cut into large chunks

1 medium onion, peeled and cut into quarters

3 bay leaves

3 sprigs fresh thyme

3 sprigs fresh oregano

3 cups dry red wine

6 cups water

2 tablespoons kosher salt

2 teaspoons whole black peppercorns

2 teaspoons whole coriander seeds

3 pounds young octopus, cleaned and defrosted if necessary

2 cups Lemon-Garlic Vinaigrette (see page 307)

2 cups Oven-Cooked Vegetarian Beans (see page 296), made with gigandas beans, preferably warm

½ cup chopped Italian parsley

½ cup Kalamata pitted olive halves

Extra-virgin olive oil, for drizzling

1. Prepare the Red Wine–Poached Octopus: In a large pot, combine the carrots celery, onion, bay leaves, thyme, oregano, dry red wine, water, salt, peppercorns, and coriander seeds. Bring to a boil, then reduce the heat and simmer for 30 minutes. Add the octopus and poach at lowest heat for 45 minutes to 1 hour, or until tender. Allow the octopus to cool in the poaching liquid, then drain. Peel the octopus, cutting off and discarding any hard parts.

2. Preheat a charcoal or gas grill, or the broiler. Leave the octopus tentacles whole, discarding the tougher body section if preferred. Marinate the tentacles in ½ cup Lemon-Garlic Vinaigrette. Grill the octopus until it curls and browns along the edges, 5 to 8 minutes. Slice the octopus tentacles on the diagonal into 1- to 2-inch sections.

3. Toss the Cooked Vegetarian Beans with the remaining dressing and the chopped parsley. Arrange on plates, top with the octopus, sprinkle with the olives, and drizzle with a thin stream of olive oil just before serving.

Gado Gado (Indonesian Salad)

(VEGETARIAN OPTION)

An impressive and decorative party dish, the salad really can't be made in small quantities because of the number of ingredients used. The legume family contributes five members to this dish: tofu, Chinese long beans, bean sprouts, peanuts, and soybean oil for frying. Gado gado has a rich, spicy sauce based on peanuts and coconut milk. The pungent undertone of the dressing comes from trassi or blanchan, a paste made from dried, salted, fermented shrimp. The special ingredients called for here are all dried, and so will keep well in your pantry. For a vegetarian version, omit the shrimp wafer garnish and the blanchan or trassi from the dressing.

—————————————— *Serves 12 to 15* ——————————————

Tofu

¼ cup tamarind liquid (see Preparing
　　Tamarind, page 310)
1 teaspoon salt
1 pound fresh firm tofu, cut into 2-inch
　　cubes, drained (see page 43)
Canola, peanut, or soybean oil, for frying
1 package Asian shrimp wafers (optional)

Dressing

¼ cup soybean oil
1 medium onion, chopped
1 tablespoon chopped garlic
1 tablespoon chopped fresh ginger
2 teaspoons *trassi* or fresh *blanchan*
2 cups chunky peanut butter
2 (12-ounce) cans unsweetened
　　coconut milk
¼ cup dark brown sugar
¼ cup tamarind liquid
1 stalk lemongrass, tender inner heart
　　only, thinly sliced
1 tablespoon hot chile paste

Salad

1 pound fresh Chinese long beans or
　　green beans, trimmed and cut into
　　4-inch lengths
1 pound carrots, thinly sliced
1 pound golden potatoes, sliced ½ inch thick
1 small head cabbage, cored and shredded
1 pint mung bean sprouts
4 to 6 hard-cooked eggs, sliced
　　(see Hard-Cooking Eggs, page 183)
1 seedless English cucumber, halved
　　lengthwise and sliced

1. Prepare the Tofu: Combine the tamarind liquid and salt in a bowl. Add the drained tofu cubes and marinate for 10 to 15 minutes, turning once or twice.

2. In a large, heavy-bottomed pot, heat a 2-inch depth of canola or other oil to 365°F on a deep-frying thermometer, or until a haze forms on the oil, just before it starts to smoke. If using the optional shrimp wafers, fry them first until they puff up and get crisp, about 2 minutes; then drain on paper towels. Then fry the tofu for 2 to 3 minutes, or until golden brown. Drain on paper towels. Cut into ½-inch-wide strips. Reserve.

3. Prepare the Dressing: Combine the oil, onion, garlic, and ginger in a medium, heavy pot. Cook for about 2 minutes, until softened but not browned. Add the *trassi* and mash until well blended with the other ingredients. Stir in the peanut butter, coconut milk, brown sugar, tamarind liquid, lemongrass, and chile paste. Simmer for 15 minutes, or until just thick enough to hold its shape on a spoon. Add water, if necessary, to thin the sauce. Cool and reserve.

4. Prepare the Salad: Bring a pot of salted water to a boil. Add the long beans and cook until bright green and crisp-tender, about 10 minutes. Scoop from the water and refresh under cold running water to set the color. If desired, cook the carrots for 1 minute and rinse under cold water, or serve them raw. Add the potatoes to the boiling water and cook until still firm but tender in the center, about 10 minutes. Drain and reserve.

5. Cover a large serving platter with the shredded cabbage; then arrange the potatoes, long beans, bean sprouts, tofu, carrots, and egg slices over it in sections. Surround the salad with the cucumber slices. Serve the dressing on the side with a bowl of the fried shrimp wafers to garnish each portion.

Turkish White Bean Salad

(VEGETARIAN)

In 1974, I spent two weeks exploring Istanbul and some of the surrounding areas, including its fascinating old Jewish neighborhood. Passing an impressive building, which turned out to be the city's largest synagogue, I entered and spoke with the caretaker, who invited me back that evening for the start of Passover. After the lovely services, conducted in both Ladino (the ancient Spanish dialect still spoken there more than 500 years after the ancestors of these Jews were expelled from Spain) and Hebrew, I was invited to a marvelous Seder at the home of a prominent Turkish Jewish family. I remember eating tiny, crisp, deep-fried whitebait and a version of this salad. I only wish I had known enough then to write down everything I ate.

——————————————— *Serves 8* ———————————————

1 pound (2 cups) dried large white beans, such as gigandas or emergo beans, or *haricots lingots,* soaked (see Soaking Chart, page 57)
½ cup lemon juice (about 2 lemons)
½ cup extra-virgin olive oil
½ teaspoon hot red pepper flakes
Salt and freshly ground black pepper
½ cup chopped Italian parsley leaves (about ½ bunch)
1 bunch scallions, thinly sliced
Seeds of 1 pomegranate, for garnish

1. Drain and rinse the soaked beans. Place in a large pot with 6 cups of cold water and bring to a boil. Simmer, partially covered, for 1½ to 2 hours, or until the beans are tender. Drain the beans, reserving about ¼ cup of the cooking liquid.

2. Whisk together the lemon juice, olive oil, red pepper flakes, salt, and black pepper to taste. Place the hot cooked beans, reserved cooking liquid, parsley, and scallions in a bowl. Toss gently with the dressing. Taste for seasoning and serve immediately or refrigerate until needed. (The salad may be made up to 2 days in advance but will need a little extra lemon juice and salt before serving.) Garnish with the pomegranate seeds just before serving.

African Black-Eyed Pea and Okra Salad
with Corn

(VEGETARIAN)

In this colorful dish, I combine three native African foods: black-eyed peas, okra, and peanuts. African slaves brought these foods to America, where the vegetables became incorporated into our cuisine through the skillful cooks who worked in the "big houses" of southern plantations. Black-eyed peas have a crunchy texture and lively look. Fresh okra can be delicious and won't get slimy if you cook it quickly. Choose smaller okra pods for less gumminess. If you grow your own okra, their large, beautiful, edible blossoms (related to the hibiscus) will reward you. Make this salad in summer when fresh okra and corn are both in season.

Serves 8

1 cup (½ pound) dried black-eyed peas, or 3 cups frozen black-eyed peas

1 head garlic, outer skin rubbed off and 1 inch cut off the top

1 whole dried chile

2 cups fresh corn kernels (about 4 ears), or 2 (10-ounce) packages frozen corn kernels

1 pound fresh young okra, sliced ½ inch thick, or 1 (10-ounce) package frozen sliced okra

2 tablespoons peanut oil

3 or 4 ribs celery, thinly sliced

1 medium red onion, diced

2 bell peppers (red, yellow, and/or orange), seeded and diced

1½ cups Barley Malt Vinaigrette (see page 305)

Salt and freshly ground black pepper

¼ pound roasted Virginia peanuts, coarsely chopped (about 1 cup), for garnish

2 tablespoons chopped fresh parsley, for garnish

1. Place the dried black-eyed peas in a medium, heavy-bottomed pot with 6 cups cold water. Bring to a boil, skimming off and discarding any white foam that rises to the surface. Drain and rinse the peas. Refill the pot with 6 cups cold water and add the peas, garlic, and the chile. Bring to a boil, reduce the heat, and simmer until quite soft, about 2 hours. (If using frozen black-eyed peas, combine 3 cups cold water with the garlic and hot pepper pod. Bring to a boil; then reduce heat and simmer for 30 minutes. Add the frozen black-eyed peas and cook for 10 to 15 minutes, or until the beans are tender.) Remove from the heat, discard the garlic and chile, and allow the beans to cool slightly in the liquid. Drain off any excess liquid and rinse the beans. Reserve.

2. In a medium pan, quickly sauté the corn and okra in the peanut oil until crisp-tender. Remove from the heat and stir in the celery, onion, and bell peppers. Transfer to a bowl, and stir in the black-eyed peas. Pour on the Barley Malt Vinaigrette and toss gently. Season generously to taste with salt and black pepper. Sprinkle with peanuts and parsley. Serve.

Chinese Noodle Salad with Snow Peas,
Bean Sprouts, and Shanxi Dressing
(VEGETARIAN)

Noodle salads are crowd pleasers and make a great hot-weather entrée or buffet dish. This version includes a few of my favorite Asian ingredients: fresh ginger, Shanxi vinegar, mushroom soy sauce, and fermented black beans. Shanxi vinegar is a wonderful product fermented from barley, sorghum, and peas. Made in a remote northern province of China, the vinegar has been brewed in the traditional way for thousands of years. With a mellow, sweet taste reminiscent of balsamic vinegar, it is drunk in small quantities as a pick-me-up and also used as a versatile seasoning. If you have a food processor with a slicing blade, use it to cut the carrots and radishes.

―――――― *Serves 8* ――――――

¼ pound snow peas, trimmed
  (see Cook's Note)
1 pound whole wheat spaghetti
1 bunch scallions, white and green part,
  thinly sliced on the diagonal
2 cups bean sprouts, rinsed and drained
½ pound carrots, thinly sliced
1 small bunch radishes, trimmed and
  thinly sliced
½ cup fermented black beans, rinsed
  under cold water and drained
½ cup chopped fresh cilantro leaves
  (about ½ bunch)
1½ cups Chinese Shanxi Vinegar Dressing
  (see page 307)
½ cup toasted sesame seeds, for garnish

1. Bring a large pot of salted water to a boil. Add the snow peas and cook just until they turn bright green, 1 to 2 minutes. Scoop out and rinse under cold water to set the color and stop the cooking.

2. Bring the water back to a boil and add the spaghetti. Cook until almost done, about 6 minutes; you should still be able to see a small white pearly heart in the center of a noodle. Don't overcook or the noodles will become mushy when dressed. Rinse under cold water, drain, and reserve. (Recipe may be prepared 1 day in advance up to this point.)

3. To serve, toss the scallions, bean sprouts, carrots, radishes, black beans, cilantro, snow peas, and noodles with the Chinese Shanxi Vinegar Dressing in a large bowl, reserving a little bit of each ingredient to garnish the salad. Divide the salad among large serving bowls and garnish with the reserved ingredients and toasted sesame seeds.

COOK'S NOTE

To trim snow peas, hold the pod just below the stem, between the thumb and forefinger, and break back the stem end. Grasp the tip of the stem and pull it down parallel to the pod to remove the stem and string.

White Bean Salad Contadina

This hearty, country-style main-course salad tastes great when made a day or so in advance. Serve it as part of a buffet dinner, or arrange individual servings on a bed of salad greens. Caperberries, the fruit of a caper bush, have a flavor similar to that of regular capers, but they are larger, oval in shape, and pickled complete with stems. Nonpareil capers will work fine, but they won't be as noticeable in the salad because they're so much smaller. For a quicker dish, you could substitute rinsed and drained white beans from a can or jar, though they won't contribute the gelatinous richness of the Oven-Cooked Italian Style Beans.

Serves 8

Salad

1 cup sliced Oven-Roasted Plum Tomatoes (see page 309), or 1 cup dry-pack sun-dried tomatoes (see Cook's Note)

¼ pound Genoa salami, cut into small dice

½ cup oil-cured black olives, pitted and halved (about ¼ pound)

½ cup caperberries or capers, drained and rinsed

1 cup coarsely chopped Italian parsley leaves (about 1 bunch)

6 cups (1 recipe) Oven-Cooked Italian-Style Beans (see page 294), prepared with cannellini beans and cooled

Dressing

¾ cup balsamic vinegar

¾ cup extra-virgin olive oil

1 tablespoon Dijon mustard

1 tablespoon finely chopped fresh thyme

1 teaspoon hot red pepper flakes

Freshly ground black pepper

1. Prepare the Salad: Place the Oven-Roasted Plum Tomatoes, salami, olives, caperberries, and parsley in a large mixing bowl, reserving a bit of each to sprinkle on top for garnish. Add the cooled Oven-Cooked Italian-Style Beans, which should be soft and creamy but still hold their shape, and stir to combine.

2. Prepare the Dressing: In a medium bowl, whisk together the vinegar, oil, mustard, thyme, red pepper flakes, and black pepper to taste. Toss the salad with enough dressing to coat well. If making ahead, taste again just before serving, as bean salads absorb liquids. The flavor is best if served at room temperature. Just before serving, sprinkle with the reserved garnishes.

COOK'S NOTE

If you want a quick substitute for the Oven-Roasted Plum Tomatoes, bring 1 cup water and 1 cup red wine to a boil in a small pan. Turn off the heat and add 1 cup dry-pack sun-dried tomatoes. Allow the tomatoes to cool and plump in the liquid for about 1 hour. Use or store in the refrigerator in the liquid for up to 1 week.

Provençal Chickpea Salad with Tuna Caviar

(VEGETARIAN OPTION)

This salad uses a dried fish roe preparation that is a specialty of both the French and Italian Rivieras. Called bottarga *in Italian and* poutargue *in French, this strong-flavored, pressed mullet or tuna roe was known to the people of Crete and imported to Marseilles and the rest of Provence by Phoenician sailors. Related to the Greek* tarama *(also made from mullet roe), it is used as an accent flavor, like anchovies or capers.*

You'll have extra Herb Mayonnaise because it's difficult to make a mayonnaise using the blender in smaller quantities. Use it to dress chicken, tuna, or turkey salad, or to spread on sandwiches. The Niçoise olives called for here are very small, dark purplish brown, delicious, and quite mild in flavor, though rather pricy. Substitute other black olives like Italian Gaeta or Greek Kalamata. For a vegetarian version, omit the bottarga and the anchovy garnish. Increase the quantity of olives, if desired.

--- *Serves 6* ---

Herb Mayonnaise

2 cloves garlic, peeled

¼ cup fresh lemon juice (about 2 lemons)

2 teaspoons salt

½ teaspoon freshly ground black pepper

2 tablespoons Dijon mustard

½ cup chopped fresh herbs (a mixture
    of parsley, chives, thyme, chervil,
    and tarragon)

2 cups light olive oil

1 small red onion, diced

Chickpea Salad

3 cups (½ recipe) Basic Cooked Chickpeas
    (see page 299), or 3 cups drained
    cooked chickpeas

1 green bell pepper, cut into julienne
    strips

1 red bell pepper, cut into julienne strips

1 cup Lemon-Garlic Vinaigrette
    (see page 307)

½ ounce *bottarga* or Greek *tarama*

2 ounces whole anchovy fillets packed in
    olive oil, well drained, for garnish

½ cup Niçoise olives, for garnish

Freshly grated nutmeg, for garnish

½ cup chopped fresh Italian parsley
    (about ½ bunch), for garnish

1. Prepare the Herb Mayonnaise: Using a garlic press, squeeze the garlic into a blender jar. Add the lemon juice, salt, pepper, mustard, and herbs. Blend for 1 minute; then gradually blend in 1 cup of the olive oil. Continue to add the remaining 1 cup oil slowly, waiting until it is absorbed before adding more. Stir in the onion and taste for seasoning.

2. Prepare the Chickpea Salad: Toss the Basic Cooked Chickpeas and bell peppers in a bowl with the Lemon-Garlic Vinaigrette. Arrange in a mound in a large salad bowl. Grate the *bottarga* over the chickpeas (or sprinkle with the *tarama*); reserve.

3. Place a large mound of the Herb Mayonnaise in the center of the chickpeas; then garnish with the anchovy fillets and olives. Sprinkle with the nutmeg and parsley.

Curry Noodle Salad
with Sugar Snap Peas and Peanuts
(VEGETARIAN)

This colorful noodle salad is full of mouth-pleasing flavor, from the fragrant curry dressing to the red cabbage cooked with ginger and garlic. It makes a terrific party dish to bring to a potluck buffet and is inexpensive to prepare. You could use either Japanese curry or a Madras-type curry powder. Use a French mandoline or a Japanese Benriner cutter to make perfect julienne vegetables. If you have an old-fashioned cabbage slicer, cut thin even rounds of cabbage; then cut the rounds into matchsticks with a knife. You can also shred the vegetables with a box grater or a food processor shredder blade. Both of these will work but won't produce the same neat look.

--- *Serves 8* ---

Dressing

2 tablespoons roasted Japanese sesame oil

1 tablespoon dry mustard

1 tablespoon curry powder (see Cook's Note)

2 tablespoons soy sauce

¼ cup Dijon mustard

¼ cup peanut oil

¼ cup rice wine vinegar

Salad

1 pound linguine

1 tablespoon roasted Japanese sesame oil

3 tablespoons peanut oil

2 tablespoons chopped fresh ginger

2 teaspoons chopped garlic

1 small head red cabbage, cut into 1-inch squares

2 tablespoons rice wine vinegar

1 rutabaga or butternut squash, peeled and cut into matchsticks

½ pound sugar snap peas, strings removed

2 red bell peppers, cut into matchsticks

1 bunch scallions, white and green parts, cut diagonally into 1-inch slices

1 cup chopped toasted peanuts

1. Prepare the Dressing: Whisk together the sesame oil, dry mustard, curry powder, soy sauce, Dijon mustard, peanut oil, and vinegar. Reserve.

2. Prepare the Salad: Bring a large pot of salted water to a boil. Add the linguine and cook for about 8 minutes, or until firm to the bite. Drain and rinse under cold water; then mix with the sesame oil. Reserve.

3. Place the 2 tablespoons peanut oil, ginger, and garlic in a sauté pan, and heat until sizzling. Add the cabbage and vinegar, and cook until the cabbage is wilted and the liquid has been absorbed. Remove from pan and reserve.

4. In the same pan, add the remaining 1 tablespoon peanut oil and quickly stir-fry the rutabaga and then the sugar snaps. Combine with the linguine, the cabbage mixture, most of the scallions, most of the peanuts, and the dressing. Garnish with the remaining scallions and peanuts.

COOK'S NOTE

I've become enamored of S & B (Sun Bird brand) curry powder from Japan. Available in most Asian markets, it comes in a small, round, red-and-yellow tin. Its flavors are sweetly aromatic, fresh, and well balanced, without too much inexpensive, acrid-tasting turmeric.

Florentine Borlotti Bean and Tuna Salad

(VEGETARIAN OPTION)

As a young, ambitious chef at Philadelphia's fine northern Italian restaurant DiLullo's, I was determined to learn Italian so that I could travel and converse, and read Italian cookbooks in their original language. After studying intensely for six months, I went off on my own to Italy. During my stay in Florence, I enjoyed this classic Tuscan salad at the wine bar Cantina Antinori, where the gracious waitstaff complimented my questionable Italian. You might not immediately think of combining beans and tuna, but trust me—they're naturally compatible. The borlotti beans called for here are the Tuscan bean of choice. Available in Italian groceries, borlotti look like fat, rounded cranberry beans with a tan background. If fresh cranberry beans are in season, by all means use this close cousin of borlottis instead. They cook quickly, have a firm yet creamy texture, and keep their shape without splitting open. Omit the tuna for a vegetarian version.

--- *Serves 6* ---

½ cup red wine vinegar

1 cup extra-virgin olive oil

2 teaspoons hot red pepper flakes

¼ cup Dijon mustard

Salt and freshly ground black pepper

6 cups (1 recipe) Oven-Cooked
  Vegetarian Beans (see page 296)
  prepared with borlotti, or Cooked
  Fresh Cranberry Beans (see page
  294), warm

1 cup chopped Italian parsley leaves
  (about 1 bunch)

2 tablespoons finely chopped fresh
  rosemary

1 (9-ounce) can tuna packed in olive oil,
  well drained

¼ cup pitted cured black olives

½ cup radishes, quartered or sliced

Lemon wedges, for garnish

1. Whisk together the vinegar, olive oil, red pepper flakes, and mustard. Season to taste with salt and black pepper. Reserve.

2. In a large bowl, gently toss the warm Oven-Cooked Vegetarian Beans with the parsley, rosemary, and reserved dressing. (Dressing the beans while they're still warm helps them absorb the flavors.) Mound the beans into the centers of six large salad plates. Top each mound of beans with a portion of tuna and garnish with black olives, radishes, and lemon wedges.

French Navy Bean and Shrimp Salad

(VEGETARIAN OPTION)

This is a French variation on the Tuscan custom of serving white beans with tuna, which has expanded to serving white bean salad garnished with all sorts of seafood and even caviar. Here I garnish a salad of tiny French navy beans tossed in a tarragon-shallot vinaigrette with vermouth-poached shrimp. A sprinkling of delicate chives completes the dish. If you happen to grow chives, make this salad when they blossom. Remove the lavender-colored flower heads, separate them into small florets, and then sprinkle the salad with these sweet, onion-perfumed blossoms. For a vegetarian version, simply serve the salad without the shrimp.

Serves 6

4 cups water

½ cup dry white vermouth

2 bay leaves

6 sprigs fresh thyme

¼ cup fresh lemon juice (about 1 lemon)

1½ pounds large shrimp (16 to 20 per pound), peeled and deveined

6 cups (1 recipe) Oven-Cooked Vegetarian Beans (see page 296) prepared with French navy beans

1½ cups French Tarragon–Shallot Vinaigrette (see page 308)

Sea salt and freshly ground black pepper

Grated zest of 1 lemon

¼ cup snipped fresh chives (about 1 bunch)

1. Combine the water, vermouth, bay leaves, thyme, and lemon juice in a medium stainless-steel or enameled pot with a lid. Bring to a boil and simmer for 15 to 20 minutes. Bring the liquid to a rolling boil, add the shrimp, and stir to distribute evenly. Cover and turn off the heat. Allow the shrimp to sit in the steaming water for 3 to 4 minutes, or until they are curled and opaque. (Cut a shrimp in half through the thickest part if you need to check.) Drain and reserve the shrimp, discarding the bay leaves and thyme.

2. To assemble the salad, cut the shrimp into 1-inch lengths, reserving 1 whole shrimp (for each portion) for garnish. Toss the Oven-Cooked Vegetarian beans, preferably while still warm, with the shrimp and French Tarragon–Shallot Vinaigrette. Season to taste with salt and pepper. Serve immediately, garnished with the lemon zest, whole shrimp, and chives.

French Green Lentil Salad
with Bacon and Tomato

This appetizing salad of French green lentils marinated in a classic French Tarragon–Shallot Vinaigrette is colorful because of the red and gold tomatoes and green chives. It not only got the most raves at my tastings, it was also a favorite with Linda Gellman, my tireless recipe tester. Turn this salad into a main dish by topping each portion with a crisp, oven-roasted Confit of Duck Leg (see page 329) or pan-seared oily fish, such as tuna, salmon, mahi-mahi, or black cod. You could also make a lentil BLT salad by serving each portion on a nest of tender Boston lettuce.

Serves 4 to 6

½ pound thickly sliced bacon, cut into matchsticks
½ cup French Tarragon–Shallot Vinaigrette (see page 308)
2 cups Basic Cooked French Green Lentils (see page 298)
2 ripe red and/or yellow tomatoes, diced
Salt and freshly ground black pepper
¼ cup snipped fresh chives (about ½ bunch)

1. Cook the bacon until crisp and browned; then drain on paper towels.

2. Pour the French Tarragon–Shallot Vinaigrette over the Basic Cooked French Green Lentils while they're still warm, tossing to coat well.

3. Add most of the bacon and most of the tomatoes to the lentils, reserving some for garnish. Season the salad with salt and pepper to taste and serve warm, garnished with the reserved bacon and tomato, and the chives.

Niçoise Pasta Shell Salad
with Green Beans, Chickpeas, and Tuna
(VEGETARIAN OPTION)

One of the great American contributions to the salad bar and deli counter in the last fifteen years has been pasta salad. Although unknown and unappreciated in Italy, these salads are popular because they are inexpensive and relatively easy to make. Often I find them bland and mushy, because pasta is starchy and continues to absorb flavors and liquid after it's cooked. To prevent limp pasta, I use an imported Italian brand and take care to remove it from the cooking water while it is still firm and resilient. For best flavor and texture, serve this salad the day you make it. I especially enjoy it as a summertime meal. If you can find the imported canned tuna fish packed in olive oil, this is a great way to enjoy it. Vegetarians can simply omit the tuna.

—————————————— *Serves 8* ——————————————

½ pound fresh green beans, cut diagonally into 1-inch pieces

2 cups Basic Cooked Chickpeas (see page 299)

2 large ripe beefsteak tomatoes, seeded and diced

½ cup pimiento-stuffed green olives, sliced

1 large red onion, thinly sliced

1 (9-ounce) can tuna packed in olive oil, well drained

1 pound medium pasta shells, cooked and drained

1 cup fresh basil leaves, cut into thin strips (about ½ bunch)

1½ cups Lemon-Garlic Vinaigrette (see page 307)

1 head escarole, washed and shredded

2 tablespoons caperberries or tiny capers (optional)

1. Bring a small pot of lightly salted water to a boil. Add the green beans and cook for 3 minutes. Drain and run under cold water to stop the cooking and set the color.

2. In a large bowl, combine the Basic Cooked Chickpeas with the green beans, tomatoes, olives, red onion, tuna, pasta shells, and basil. Add the vinaigrette and toss to coat evenly. Serve the salad on a bed of shredded escarole and sprinkle with caperberries.

Portuguese Salt Cod and Kidney Bean Salad
(Salada de Bacalhau e Feijãos)

(VEGETARIAN OPTION)

My friend Maria Mata is a wonderful Portuguese cook who makes the rustic but extremely tasty dishes her country is known for. Here, she combines poached and grilled salt cod, or bacalhau, *with kidney beans in red wine vinaigrette. With its garnish of sliced eggs and black olives, this makes a colorful and satisfying main-dish salad. Start at least 1 day ahead to allow time for soaking the salt cod. For the most striking color, look for dark red kidney beans, sold in many specialty markets and in Indian groceries, where they are known as* badi rajma. *Ordinary kidney beans will cook up paler. For a vegetarian version, omit the salt cod and increase the quantity of eggs and olives, if desired. Whole salt cod on the bone will cook up firm and gelatinious.*

———————— *Advance preparation recommended. Serves 6* ————————

2 pounds whole salt cold on the bone
2 red bell peppers
2 green bell peppers
3 cups canned red kidney beans,
    preferably dark red, rinsed and
    drained, or ½ pound (1 cup) dried
    dark red kidney beans, cooked and
    drained (see Basic Cooking Chart,
    page 58)
½ cup chopped Italian parsley leaves
    (about 1 bunch)
1 cup extra-virgin olive oil
½ cup red wine vinegar
Freshly ground black pepper
6 hard-cooked eggs, sliced (see Hard-
    Cooking Eggs, page 183)
½ cup cured black olives, pitted

1. Place the salt cod in a large bowl of cold water. Soak for 24 hours, changing the water several times. In hot weather, cover and refrigerate; in cold weather, it can be soaked at room temperature.

2. Drain the soaked cod; then rinse and drain again. When it has soaked sufficiently, it should be white, pliable, and plump. Bring a large pot of unsalted water to a boil. Add the cod and poach gently for about 5 minutes. It will be partially cooked. Drain and cool.

3. Brush a grill lightly with oil and preheat. Grill the bell peppers, charring the skins on all sides. Remove and cool. Peel and discard the blackened skins; then seed, and cut the peppers into thin strips. Clean the grill with a wire brush if necessary and grill the cod until completely cooked, about 5 minutes per side. Remove from the grill and cool. Remove and discard the skin and bones; then use your fingers to flake the fish into large chunks.

4. In a large bowl, combine the kidney beans, cod, roasted pepper strips, and most of the parsley. Add the olive oil, vinegar, and black pepper and toss gently but thoroughly. You probably won't need salt because the cod is salty, but adjust the seasoning as necessary. Arrange the salad on a large platter. Decorate with the egg slices and olives, and sprinkle with the reserved parsley. Serve at room temperature for best flavor.

CODFISH AND THE PORTUGUESE

Not long after the discovery of the New World, intrepid Portuguese fishermen were combing Newfoundland's Grand Banks for cod. By 1506, codfish, or *bacalhau,* was already a significant part of their catch, and the Portuguese, who learned to salt the cod while still at sea to preserve it, are said to know 365 ways to cook it. Whole *bacalhau* can be found in Italian and Spanish markets.

Romano Bean and Navel Orange Salad

(VEGETARIAN)

Fresh romano beans are in season in late summer. They do require a little more cooking than the usual green beans unless they are extremely young, but they have a wonderful "beany" flavor and chewy texture. Here, I combine them with orange slices trimmed until only the flesh is left, in a technique called à vif, or "to the quick," in French. By all means, if dramatic red-streaked blood oranges are in season, substitute them for the navel oranges. Be sure to wash the orange under hot water to remove excess pesticides, unless your orange is organic.

--- *Serves 6* ---

Orange-Honey Dressing

¾ cup olive oil

¼ cup sherry vinegar

Grated zest of 1 orange

2 tablespoons whole-grain mustard

2 tablespoons honey

1 tablespoon finely chopped fresh
    rosemary leaves

1 tablespoon finely chopped garlic

1 tablespoon salt

¼ teaspoon freshly ground black pepper

Salad

2 pounds romano beans, ends trimmed
    and diagonally cut into 1½-inch
    pieces, or 2 (12-ounce) boxes frozen
    romano beans, rinsed

4 navel or blood oranges

1 red onion, cut into thin slices

1. Prepare the Orange-Honey Dressing: Whisk together the olive oil, vinegar, orange zest, mustard, honey, rosemary, garlic, salt, and pepper. Reserve.

2. Prepare the Salad: Bring a large pot of salted water to a boil. Add the fresh romano beans and cook for 5 minutes. Drain and rinse under cold water and reserve. (Skip this step if using frozen beans.)

3. Using a sharp paring knife, cut away the skin and the white pith of the oranges, exposing all the flesh inside. Cut the oranges into halves from end to end, and then cut half moon–shaped slices from each half. Only bright orange slices, with no pith or membrane, should be left.

4. Combine the romano beans, orange slices, red onion, and dressing in a large bowl along with any juices from the cut oranges, tossing together gently to avoid breaking up the orange sections.

Southwest Black Bean Salad
with Baked Spiced Goat Cheese

(VEGETARIAN)

This hearty, spicy black bean salad is a good example of the modern salads popularized by Texas and Santa Fe chefs. These chefs have been exploring local culinary traditions while updating flavors and presentations. Purple-black, red, yellow, orange, white, and green—these are the eye-appealing colors of this salad. The tangy spiced goat cheese rounds are an addition popularized by influential chefs from the Southwest, such as Mark Miller and Stephan Pyles. This salad is another example of the palate-awakening properties of combining hot and cold elements in one dish.

————————— *Serves 8* —————————

Spiced Goat Cheese Rounds

½-pound log mild goat cheese

2 tablespoons black sesame seeds or
    poppy seeds

2 tablespoons ancho chile powder or
    New Mexican red chile powder

¼ cup snipped fresh chives
    (about 1 bunch)

Black Bean Salad

2 bell peppers (red, yellow, green, and/or
    orange), seeded and diced

1 red onion, diced

2 bunches scallions, white and green
    parts, cut into ½-inch slices

8 whole ripe plum tomatoes, seeded
    and diced

1 or 2 poblano chiles, seeded and diced

1 recipe (6 cups) Black Turtle Beans
    with Epazote (see page 250)

1 recipe (2 cups) Cumin-Lime Citronette
    Dressing (see page 315)

Salt and freshly ground black pepper

1. Prepare the Spiced Goat Cheese Rounds: Using a sharp knife dipped into hot water, cut eight rounds from the goat cheese. Place the sesame seeds, chile powder, and chives in three small bowls. Dip 1 edge of the goat cheese rounds into the black sesame seeds, and then dip the opposite edge into the red chile. Sprinkle the centers with the chives. Place the rounds, chive sides up, on a foil pie plate, small baking pan, or folded-over piece of heavy-duty foil coated with nonstick spray. Reserve in the refrigerator.

2. Assemble the Salad: Combine the bell peppers, red onion, scallions, tomatoes, chiles, and Black Turtle Beans with Epazote in a large bowl. Pour in the Cumin-Lime Citronette Dressing and toss to coat lightly and evenly. Season to taste with salt and pepper.

3. When ready to serve, preheat the oven to 400°F. Place the goat cheese rounds in the oven. Bake for 10 minutes, or until the cheese begins to crack through the spice coating. Remove from the oven and cool slightly. Arrange the bean salad on individual plates. Using a spatula, lift up one baked goat cheese round at a time and place in the center of each salad portion.

Three-Bean Salad Ring
with Avocado Mousse

I always knew that jellied salads and desserts, popular in the 1950s, were ripe for a big comeback. Recently, I've noticed prize-winning dessert jellies and the growing popularity of the Italian jellied cream dessert, panna cotta. It's only a matter of time before colorful, refreshing, natural-tasting jellied dishes, like this variation on the classic American three-bean salad picnic dish, regain their popularity. Here the beans are suspended in a clear jelly with a vegetable juice base. For a winning combination, serve this dish with a bowl of cool Avocado Mousse on the hottest summer day.

——————— *Advance preparation recommended. Serves 8* ———————

4 cups (1 quart) Light Chicken Stock (see page 320)

1 large (46-ounce) can vegetable juice

¼ cup egg whites (about 2 eggs)

½ pound fresh ground beef

1 tablespoon salt

½ teaspoon freshly ground black pepper

½ cup red wine vinegar

½ cup water

¼ cup (8 envelopes) unflavored gelatin

2 cups canned red kidney beans, rinsed and drained, or ¾ cup dried red kidney beans, cooked and drained (see Basic Cooking Chart, page 58)

2 cups canned black turtle beans, rinsed and drained, or ¾ cup dried black turtle beans, cooked and drained (see Basic Cooking Chart, page 58)

1 (12-ounce) package frozen baby lima beans, rinsed and drained

½ cup diced roasted red peppers (use a good commercially prepared brand)

3 ribs celery, diced

1 red onion, finely diced

½ cup chopped fresh cilantro leaves (about ½ bunch)

1 tablespoon cayenne pepper hot sauce

1 recipe (2 cups) Avocado Mousse (see page 315), for serving

1. Have ready a 2-quart decorative mold, preferably ring-shaped.

2. In a large stockpot, combine the Light Chicken Stock, juice, egg whites, ground beef, salt, and black pepper. Slowly bring to a boil, whisking until the mixture begins to get hot. Allow a "raft" of egg white and beef to coagulate on top, which will take about 20 minutes. Remove and discard using a slotted spoon or skimmer. Strain the broth through a sieve lined with a double layer of cheesecloth. Reserve the strained broth.

3. In a large saucepan, mix the wine vinegar and water. Sprinkle in the gelatin and stir gently to mix. Allow the gelatin to "bloom" (absorb the liquid and soften), about 5 minutes. Add the reserved broth to the bloomed gelatin and place over low heat. Cook until clear, about 3 minutes.

4. Pour the gelatin mixture into a large bowl. Cool it by placing over a larger bowl filled with ice water. Stir frequently to cool evenly, using a spoon (rather than a whisk, which will stir up unwanted bubbles). When the mixture is syrupy and starts to gel, remove from the ice water bath. Pour a thin layer of the gelatin mixture into the mold and let it set in the refrigerator for about 15 minutes. Fold the kidney beans, black beans, lima beans, roasted peppers, celery, red onion, cilantro, and hot sauce into the remaining gelatin mixture. Pour into the mold and chill until set, about 3 to 4 hours, or overnight.

5. Unmold the salad by dipping the mold for about 10 seconds in a deep bowl of hot water, then shaking to loosen it. Turn the mold out onto a decorative platter and serve with the Avocado Mousse.

Texas Stuffed Tomatoes with Black-Eyed Pea Salad

(VEGETARIAN)

I got the idea for this lovely summertime dish from a recipe in The Junior League Centennial Cookbook, *a compilation of the best of this country's many Junior League cookbooks, which I had the pleasure of food styling for QVC. I make it in late summer when the sweetest locally grown tomatoes and corn are in season. It's a tasty, inexpensive first course with a dramatic presentation. Frozen black-eyed peas are found in some supermarkets and many ethnic markets, especially those with a large African American clientele. Be sure to make this salad when vine-ripened local tomatoes are in season because you'll need big, bright, juicy tomatoes here. If you can find them, any of the colorful heirloom tomatoes sold at many farmers markets would be wonderful.*

Serves 6

1 cup dried black-eyed peas, cooked (see Basic Cooking Chart, page 58), or 2 (12-ounce) packages frozen black-eyed peas, rinsed

2 cups white corn kernels (about 4 ears), or 1 (12- to 15-ounce) package frozen white corn

2 large ripe beefsteak tomatoes, seeded, diced, and drained

2 red, yellow, or orange bell peppers, roasted (see page 332), seeded, and diced

1 bunch scallions, thinly sliced

1 to 2 red or green jalapeño peppers, seeded and minced

1 cup Cumin-Lime Citronette Dressing (see page 315)

6 large ripe beefsteak tomatoes, for serving

1 teaspoon salt

½ cup sour cream, for serving

2 limes, cut into wedges, for serving

1. In a medium bowl, combine the black-eyed peas, corn, tomatoes, roasted peppers, scallions, and jalapeños. Add the Cumin-Lime Citronette Dressing and toss lightly. Reserve.

2. Cut a 1-inch slice off the top of the tomatoes. Using a tablespoon, scoop out the insides, leaving the outside wall about ½ inch thick. Sprinkle the insides of the tomatoes with salt and turn them upside down on a double-thick layer of paper towels to drain for about 15 minutes.

3. Fill the tomato shells with the salad. Garnish each tomato with a spoonful of sour cream and a lime wedge. Serve cold or at room temperature.

Kidney Bean Salad in Mustard Vinaigrette

(VEGETARIAN)

Before smooth-style Dijon mustard was made, the oldest types of prepared mustard had large, visible grains of mustard seeds. One of the most venerable brands is Moutarde de Meaux, which has been made in the town of Meaux, France, since 1632. It gives a crunchy texture to the beans, and its milder flavor means you can use it generously without making the salad too "hot." Mustard and tarragon have a long-standing relationship in France, where rabbit in mustard sauce with tarragon is a Sunday standard. As much as I'm a fiend for fresh herbs, dried tarragon is one of the few herbs that maintains a reasonably close resemblance to its fresh counterpart.

Serves 6

½ cup extra-virgin olive oil

¼ cup sherry or balsamic vinegar

¼ cup coarse-grain mustard

2 tablespoons chopped fresh tarragon (about ¼ bunch), or 2 teaspoons dried

Salt and freshly ground black pepper

6 cups cooked red kidney beans, preferably dark red, or small red beans (*pequeños,* see page 31) drained and rinsed

3 or 4 ribs from a celery heart, sliced

¼ cup finely chopped shallots

1. Whisk together the olive oil, vinegar, mustard, tarragon, salt, and pepper to taste. Pour the mixture over the beans and toss well to combine. Marinate the beans for at least 2 hours at room temperature, or preferably overnight in the refrigerator.

2. Stir the celery and shallots into the bean mixture and serve.

Emergo Bean Salad
with Moroccan Charmoula Dressing
(VEGETARIAN)

Bean salads taste best when made with highly flavored condiments. This paprika-colored salad includes bold accents from Morocco like hot paprika, preserved lemon, cumin, and nigella seeds. I tested this delicious, unusual salad by bringing it to an annual picnic of the Philadelphia chapter of Chef's Collaborative 2000. It was a big hit, especially among the many vegetarians who attended. I've since made the salad for numerous cooking demonstrations, where it always gets rave reviews. Substitute cannellini beans if you can't find the emergo beans.

Serves 8

2 tablespoon nigella seeds (see Nigella Seeds, page 148)
½ cup extra-virgin olive oil
¼ cup red wine vinegar
¼ cup fresh lemon juice (about 2 lemons)
1 tablespoon finely chopped garlic
2 tablespoons sweet Spanish paprika
2 teaspoons hot paprika
2 teaspoons ground toasted cumin seeds (see Toasting Seeds, page 225)
2 teaspoons salt
½ teaspoon freshly ground black pepper
1 preserved lemon (see Sources, page 341)
1 pound (2 cups) dried white emergo or gigandas beans, cooked and drained (see Basic Cooking Chart, page 58)
¼ cup chopped fresh cilantro leaves (about ¼ bunch)

1. In a heated dry skillet, toast the nigella seeds over medium heat, shaking constantly until their aroma is released. Remove from the heat and cool.

2. Using a hand-held or standard blender, blend the olive oil, vinegar, lemon juice, and garlic. When smooth and creamy, blend in the sweet and hot paprika, cumin, salt, and pepper.

3. Scrape off and discard the pulp and white pith from the preserved lemon; finely dice the rind. Pour the dressing over the beans and toss with most of the nigella seeds, most of the cilantro, and most of the diced lemon. Serve the salad garnished with the remaining nigella seeds, cilantro, and lemon.

Pinto Bean Salad
with Smoked Turkey Sausage

This simple but flavorful pinto bean salad is hearty enough to serve as a main course. There are many tasty sausages at the market these days. For a wonderful flavor, try using Southwest-style turkey sausage from Aidell's Sausage Company (see Sources, page 341). Chorizo, chipotle chicken sausage, or kielbasa all make excellent substitutions.

Serves 8

1 pound smoked turkey sausage

½ cup vegetable oil

1 chipotle chile in adobo sauce, chopped, with about 2 tablespoons of liquid

½ cup balsamic vinegar

2 teaspoons ground toasted cumin seeds (see Toasting Seeds, page 225)

Salt and freshly ground black pepper

2 teaspoons dried oregano

6 cups cooked pinto beans, rinsed and drained, or 1 pound (2 cups) dried pinto beans, cooked and drained (see Basic Cooking Chart, page 58)

2 bunches scallions, thinly sliced

2 green bell peppers, seeded, and diced

½ cup coarsely chopped Italian parsley leaves (about ½ bunch)

1. Remove and discard the sausage skin. Cut the sausage into small cubes. Heat the oil in a large pan over medium heat. Add the sausage and cook, shaking the pan occasionally, for about 10 minutes, or until the sausage is nicely browned on all sides. Remove from the heat and reserve both the oil and sausage.

2. Whisk together the reserved oil, chipotle, vinegar, cumin, salt, pepper, and oregano. Pour over the beans. Stir in the sausage, scallions, green peppers, and parsley, reserving a little of the scallions, green pepper, and parsley to sprinkle on top.

Spanish Lentil Salad
with Salt Cod *(Bacala)* Fritters and Preserved Lemon Aïoli
(VEGETARIAN OPTION)

Spanish pardina *lentils are small, prized lentils that cook quickly and keep their shape well. Here I've combined them in a salad seasoned with Spanish sherry vinegar. Fritters of* bacala, *or salt cod—a favorite on the little tapas plates customary with drinks during the long, leisurely cocktail hour in Spain—accompany the salad. Note that the salt cod requires 24 hours of soaking. The preserved lemon aïoli is a variation on the classic olive-oil mayonnaise served in Spain with fried fish. Preserved lemon, actually cured in salt, gives the salad a zesty flavor with a slight sharp-bitter aftertaste that awakens the palate. While the dish has several components, everything can be done ahead of time except for frying the* bacala *fritters. This is another example of the Iberian habit of combining legumes and salt cod, because* bacala's *potent flavor is balanced by the creamy yet starchy lentils. For a vegetarian version, omit the salt cod fritters, or serve topped with vegetable fritters.*

——————— *Advanced preparation required. Serves 6 to 8* ———————

1 pound salt cod fillet

Preserved Lemon Aïoli
2 egg yolks
1 egg
¼ cup lemon juice (about 2 lemons)
1 cup light olive oil
2 tablespoons finely chopped shallots
Finely diced rind of 1 preserved lemon
    (see Sources, page 341), or grated
    zest of 1 lemon
Freshly ground black pepper

1. Soak the salt cod fillet in a large bowl of cold water for 24 hours, changing the water after 12 hours. In hot weather, cover and refrigerate; in cold weather it can be soaked at room temperature.

2. Prepare the Preserved Lemon Aïoli: Place the egg yolks, whole egg, and lemon juice in the bowl of a food processor. Process for 1 minute, or until creamy. With the machine running, slowly pour the oil through the feed tube, waiting until each increment of oil has been absorbed before adding more. Continue until all the oil is completely absorbed and the aïoli is thick.

3. Transfer the aïoli to a bowl and stir in the shallots, preserved lemon, and black pepper to taste. Taste for seasoning. Because the lemons are cured in salt, you probably won't need any additional salt. If you substitute lemon zest, add salt to taste. Those who are immune-sensitive or wish to avoid raw eggs may combine a good-quality purchased mayonnaise with the fresh lemon juice, chopped shallots, and preserved lemon or lemon zest.

4. Prepare the Lentil Salad: In a large bowl, combine the Basic Cooked French Green Lentils, sherry vinegar, olive oil, red onion, salt, and black pepper in a large bowl; toss to combine and reserve.

5. Combine the flour and baking powder in a large bowl. Whisk in the buttermilk, egg yolks, and red pepper flakes. Allow the batter to rest in the refrigerator, covered, for 30 minutes.

Lentil Salad

3 cups Basic Cooked French Green Lentils
  (see page 298) made with Spanish
  pardina lentils

¼ cup sherry vinegar

½ cup extra-virgin olive oil

1 red onion, diced

1 teaspoon salt

¼ teaspoon freshly ground black pepper

2½ cups unbleached all-purpose flour

1 teaspoon baking powder

1½ cups buttermilk

3 eggs, separated

1 teaspoon hot red pepper flakes

1 white onion, finely chopped

1 teaspoon chopped garlic

¼ cup chopped fresh cilantro leaves
  (about ¼ bunch)

Olive or vegetable oil, for deep-frying

6. Drain the soaked cod and rinse under cold fresh water. Place the cod in a pot and cover with cold water. Bring to a boil. Reduce the heat to a simmer and poach for about 10 minutes, or until the fish flakes easily. Remove from the water and flake. You should have about 2 cups of flaked cod.

7. Stir the cod, onion, garlic, and cilantro into the batter. In a separate bowl, beat the egg whites until they form soft peaks. Fold the egg whites into the batter. In a deep-fryer or deep, heavy-bottomed pot no more than one-third full of oil, heat the olive oil to 365°F. Carefully drop the batter by tablespoonfuls into the hot oil, frying until browned on all sides. Drain on paper towels and repeat until all the batter has been fried.

8. Place a mound of the Lentil Salad in the center of each serving plate and surround the salad with the hot fritters. Top each fritter with a dollop of Preserved Lemon Aïoli. For a more stylish presentation, fill a small round mold or clean tuna can with top and bottom removed with the lentil salad and press down to create a molded vertical salad on each plate when you remove the ring.

Tabbouli Salad
with Lentils, Lemon, and Mint
(VEGETARIAN)

Tabbouli is a type of cracked wheat that is cooked and then dried. It is popular in Turkey, Lebanon, Syria, and Israel. Contrary to common American practice, tabbouli salad is not really a grain salad, but rather a parsley and vegetable salad that contains cracked wheat. In this recipe, the addition of lentils makes the dish into a hearty main-course salad. I prefer to use Kirby cucumbers, the small, firm cucumbers used to make sour dill pickles, or the European variety of cucumbers that don't need to be peeled. These "burpless" cukes, so called because of their small seeds, are generally hothouse grown and often come from Canada. They're sometimes known as English cucumbers.

Serves 6 to 8

1 cup bulgur wheat

1 cup extra-virgin olive oil

½ cup fresh lemon juice (about 2 lemons)

1 tablespoon chopped garlic

2 teaspoons ground cumin, preferably
toasted

Salt, freshly ground black pepper, and
cayenne to taste

2 cups Basic Cooked French Green Lentils
(see page 298), well drained

4 plum tomatoes, seeded and diced

1 bunch scallions, white and green parts,
thinly sliced

1 European cucumber, diced (or 4 or 5
Kirby cucumbers, diced)

1 small bag red radishes, diced

3 cups coarsely chopped Italian parsley
(about 2 bunches)

½ cup coarsely chopped fresh mint
(about ½ bunch)

1. Soak the bulgur in boiling water to cover for 10 minutes, or until the grains become soft and plump. Drain off any excess water.

2. In a small bowl, whisk together the olive oil, lemon juice, garlic, cumin, salt, black pepper, and cayenne. Combine the dressing with the bulgur and Basic Cooked French Green Lentils. Stir in the tomatoes, scallions, cucumber, radishes, parsley, and mint. Taste for seasoning and serve.

Crunchy Sprouting Bean Salad

(VEGETARIAN)

If you can find packages of mixed sprouting beans (not bean sprouts) that are sold in many supermarkets, especially those with a large natural food selection, this salad is a cinch to make. Follow the directions for Home-Grown Bean Sprouts (see page 326) if you'd like to make your own bean sprouts. Children greatly enjoy the process, though they might not necessarily be willing to eat them. This salad tastes best when made a day in advance. That's a plus when you're entertaining or planning to bring it to a potluck dinner.

Serves 6

---

3 cups mixed fresh sprouted beans
    (about 2 pints)
3 carrots, cut into small dice
2 red, yellow, or orange bell peppers,
    seeded and cut into small dice
1 bunch scallions, green and white parts,
    thinly sliced
¼ cup chopped Italian parsley leaves
    (about ¼ bunch)
1 teaspoon finely chopped garlic
1 small red onion, diced
3 tablespoons balsamic vinegar
6 tablespoons olive oil
Salt and freshly ground black pepper
1 pint ripe red cherry tomatoes

1. Bring a pot of salted water to a boil. Add the sprouted beans and cook for 30 minutes, or until crisp-tender and still brightly colored. Drain and rinse under cold water to set the color and stop the cooking.

2. In a large bowl, combine the sprouted beans, carrots, bell peppers, scallions, and parsley.

3. In a small bowl, combine the garlic, red onion, and vinegar. Slowly pour in the oil while whisking. Season to taste with salt and pepper. Pour the oil mixture over the vegetables and toss to combine. Cover and refrigerate overnight to give the flavors a chance to meld.

4. When ready to serve, garnish the salad with cherry tomatoes.

LENTILS

The Latin word for lentil, *lens*, gives us our word for a lentil-shaped piece of glass, a term that has been in use since the seventh century.

Tennessee Pickled Yellow Wax Beans
in Sour Cream Dressing
(VEGETARIAN)

Prepare this country-style dish 1 or 2 days before you want to serve it, to allow the wax beans time to pick up the flavors of the pickling liquid. The great thing about using wax beans here is that the pickling mixture won't discolor them. These make a worthy addition to a summer buffet table, barbecue, or potluck dinner. The Sour Cream Dressing is also delicious mixed with steamed golden potatoes.

———————— *Advance preparation required. Serves 6 to 8* ————————

Pickled Wax Beans

2 cups water

3 cloves garlic, slightly crushed

¼ cup sugar

1 cup cider vinegar

¼ cup vegetable oil

2 tablespoons salt

1 tablespoon mixed pickling spices, wrapped in cheesecloth or enclosed in a tea ball

2 pounds yellow wax beans, trimmed, blanched, and refreshed in ice water

1 large sweet onion (such as Vidalia or Texas Sweet 100), thinly sliced

Sour Cream Dressing

½ cup sour cream

¼ cup mayonnaise

2 tablespoons fresh lemon juice (about 1 lemon)

2 teaspoons dry mustard

1 tablespoon prepared horseradish

¼ cup snipped chives (about 1 bunch)

1. Prepare the Pickled Wax Beans: Combine the water, garlic, sugar, vinegar, oil, salt, and pickling spices in a 2- to 3-quart stainless-steel or enameled pot. Bring to a boil and boil for 5 minutes; then turn off the heat and allow the mixture to cool to room temperature.

2. Layer the wax beans, onion, and cooked garlic cloves in a large, deep stainless-steel, glass, or ceramic bowl or jar. Strain the pickling liquid over the beans and onion. Cover and refrigerate for at least 12 hours. (The beans may be stored in the liquid for up to 3 days before proceeding with the dish.)

3. Prepare the Sour Cream Dressing: In a medium bowl, whisk the sour cream, mayonnaise, lemon juice, dry mustard, horseradish, and most of the chives.

4. Drain the pickled beans well. Toss with enough of the dressing to coat thoroughly. Serve as a side dish or relish with the reserved chives sprinkled on top.

CHAPTER SIX

Soups

Senate Navy Bean Soup

This white bean soup, flavored with smoked ham hocks, has been served for almost 100 years in the United States Senate's restaurant, operated for senators and their guests. Credit for creating the soup—or at least for introducing it to the Senate restaurant—has gone to Senator Fred Dubois of Idaho in the 1890s and to Senator Knute Nelson of Minnesota in the early part of the twentieth century. The soup couldn't be simpler, but don't be tempted to leave out the cloves, which provide its characteristic flavor. Do remember, however, that a little clove goes a very long way, and too much produces an unpleasantly medicinal taste.

Serves 6 to 8

1 pound (2 cups) dried navy beans, soaked (see Soaking Chart, page 57)
2 quarts cold water
1 ham hock
1 cup diced onion
1 cup diced celery, including leaves
1 cup peeled and finely diced potato
2 teaspoons chopped garlic
¼ teaspoon ground cloves
Salt and freshly ground black pepper
¼ cup chopped Italian parsley leaves (about ¼ bunch)

1. Drain the soaked navy beans. Combine with the water and ham hock in a stockpot and bring to a boil. Reduce the heat and simmer about 1½ hours, or until the beans are tender.

2. Remove the ham hock from the pot. Cool, pick the meat from the bone, and discard the bone. Add the meat to the pot, along with the onion, celery, potato, garlic, and cloves. Bring the soup back to a boil. Reduce the heat and simmer until the potato is soft, about 20 minutes.

3. Remove the soup from the heat. Remove a cupful or so of beans and reserve. Using a potato masher or a heavy whisk, mash the remaining soup until creamy. Add the whole beans for texture. Season to taste with salt and pepper, and stir in the parsley. Serve hot.

Bolognese Bean Soup
(Minestra di Fagioli Bolognese)

(VEGETARIAN)

In Italian, a minestra *is a thick soup made from a few simple ingredients, as opposed to a* minestrone, *which is more of a meal in a bowl, or a* zuppa, *which is based on a clear broth. Pink-streaked cranberry beans grown in the southern United States are commonly sold fresh in the pod during the summer months. These creamy, smooth, mild-tasting beans are such a treat in season that it's best to prepare them as simply as possible, topped with the nutty, sweet flavor of freshly grated, imported Parmigiano-Reggiano, as in this vegetarian soup from Bologna, one of the gastronomic capitals of Italy. Bolognese cooks are renowned for their skill in making fresh pasta, called* pasta sfogliata, *or sheet pasta, of the type used here.*

You may substitute less expensive and slightly coarser Grana Padano cheese, made in the same region as Parmigiano-Reggiano, though aged for only about 6 months instead of a minimum of 14 months, as for the Parmigiano. Though not considered as splendid a table cheese as Parmigiano and with much less strict production guidelines, Grana makes a high-quality, less expensive substitute for use as a grating cheese. If using cooked borlotti beans, start with Step 2.

—————————— *Serves 6 to 8* ——————————

1½ pounds fresh cranberry beans, shelled; or 3 cups Oven-Cooked Italian-Style Beans, made with borlotti beans (see page 294)

4 to 6 cloves garlic

½ cup extra-virgin olive oil

¼ cup chopped Italian parsley leaves (about ½ bunch)

2 cups tomato purée

Salt and freshly ground black pepper

½ Durum Pasta Dough (see page 325) sheets, cut into maltagliati (roughly square shapes; see directions on page 325)

Freshly grated Parmigiano-Reggiano or Grana Padano cheese, for serving

1. If using fresh beans, in a large pot, cover the shelled cranberry beans with 8 cups cold water and bring to a boil. Cover and simmer for 30 minutes, or until tender to the bite. Remove from the heat and reserve. Do not drain.

2. In another large pot, cook the garlic in the olive oil until golden. Add 3 tablespoons of the parsley and the tomato purée. Simmer together for 5 minutes; then add the reserved beans and their cooking liquid, which should equal about 8 cups. Bring the soup to a boil; then scoop out 2 to 3 cups of the beans and purée in a blender. Stir the puréed beans back into the soup, season to taste with the salt and pepper, and bring back to a boil.

3. Add the pasta squares and simmer for 3 to 4 minutes, or until the pasta is tender. Ladle the soup into serving bowls. Garnish each portion with some of the remaining 1 tablespoon parsley and serve with a separate bowl of grated cheese to sprinkle on top.

Mung Bean Dal with Spiced Tadka

(VEGETARIAN)

The moong dal, *or mung beans, used here are actually the tiny, golden yellow, oval split seeds that remain after the green skins of the mung bean (the same one used for bean sprouts) have been removed. Tadka is an ancient Indian topping used to give bright, fresh flavor to relatively bland foods like legumes. It is made by briefly cooking ghee (the nutty-tasting browned and clarified butter) with fragrant spices and seasonings at high heat to release the aromatic oils. This simplest of poor people's vegetarian dishes is surprisingly flavorful and satisfying.*

Serves 6

Dal

1 pound (2 cups) dried yellow split
    mung beans (*moong* or *mung dal*),
    picked over and rinsed
1 teaspoon turmeric
1 tablespoon grated fresh ginger
8 cups (2 quarts) cold water
1 tablespoon salt
2 tablespoons fresh lemon juice
    (about 1 lemon)

Tadka

¼ cup ghee or clarified butter (see
    Making Ghee, page 72)
2 teaspoons black mustard seeds
1 to 2 small green chiles (such as
    jalapeño or serrano), seeded and
    thinly sliced
¼ cup chopped cilantro (about ¼ bunch),
    for serving

1. Prepare the Dal: Combine the beans, turmeric, and ginger in a large, heavy-bottomed saucepan with a lid. Add the cold water and bring to a boil, stirring occasionally (these beans stick easily). Reduce the heat, partially cover the pan, and simmer for about 30 minutes, or until the beans are soft when pressed between your fingers. Continue to stir occasionally, especially near the end of the cooking time when the beans are starting to thicken. The beans should disintegrate to form a thick, soupy purée. Reserve.

2. Prepare the *Tadka*: Heat the ghee in a small pan with a lid over high heat until it shimmers but is not yet smoking. Add the black mustard seeds and cover the pan immediately because the seeds will pop and jump like popcorn. When the seeds have all popped and turned gray, stir in the chiles. Cook for about 1 minute; then remove from the heat.

3. Just before serving, stir the salt and lemon juice into the Dal, and reheat if necessary. Pour the hot *Tadka* over the Dal and sprinkle each portion generously with the cilantro.

ABOUT DAL

Dal is often made from the pealike seeds of the tropical mung bean that is widely eaten in Africa, India, and the Caribbean. The Hindu name *dal* is a derivative of the Sanskrit word *dal*, meaning "split." This is because the seeds in India are commonly split and dried for storage. *Dal* has come to refer to all kinds of dried and split legumes, as well as porridge-like dishes made with mung beans, onions, and spices.

Chicory and Cannellini Bean Soup
(Minestra di Cicoria e Cannellini)
(VEGETARIAN OPTION)

A dish of la cucina povera (the Italian cuisine of frugality), this simple soup makes a satisfying meal on its own with a glass of country-style red wine. Even the bread used here is leftover crostini, so that nothing good goes to waste. This soup is traditionally made with wild chicory, or cicoria, though here I call for curly endive, our closest substitute. If you can find catalogna, a spiky leafed green often sold as dandelion, it's excellent in this soup and a close relative of wild chicory. This recipe comes from my friend, restaurateur Toto Schiavone, who grew up in Calabria (the instep of Italy's "boot"). Close to Greece both geographically and culturally, the region is filled with fig, olive, and hazelnut trees, bitter wild onions, and homemade sun-dried tomatoes that resemble prunes, hanging in bunches and wreaths from the whitewashed walls. This soup is a good example of the Mediterranean habit of combining alkaline greens with beans, both because they're so nutritious and because the combination helps makes the beans more digestible by neutralizing their acidity. For a vegetarian version, substitute Vegetable Stock (see page 323) for the chicken stock.

—————————— *Serves 4* ——————————

2 large bunches curly endive, cut into
    2- to 3-inch pieces
¼ cup finest extra-virgin olive oil
1 tablespoon chopped garlic
1 cup broken Crostini (see page 65)
3 cups cooked cannellini beans, drained,
    or 1 cup dried cannellini beans,
    cooked and drained (see Basic
    Cooking Chart, page 58)
1 cup Light Chicken Stock (see page 320)
Salt and hot red pepper flakes
½ cup grated Pecorino Romano cheese

1. Fill a large bowl with cold water and add the endive pieces. Swish the water around to release any dirt. Let the dirt settle; then scoop out the endive. Bring a pot of salted water to a boil. Add the endive and cook for about 5 minutes, or until completely wilted. Drain and rinse under cold water. Gently squeeze out the excess water. Reserve.

2. In a large, heavy-bottomed saucepan, combine the olive oil and garlic. Cook together over medium heat for 3 to 4 minutes, or until the garlic releases its fragrance but isn't browned. Reduce the heat, add the endive, and cook slowly for 8 to 10 minutes.

3. Stir in the Crostini and beans. Add the Light Chicken Stock little by little and cook until most of the stock has been absorbed. Season to taste with the salt and red pepper flakes. Let the soup rest for a few minutes before serving. Serve with the grated cheese.

Haricot Bean and Oven-Roasted Tomato Soup
with Pimentón
(VEGETARIAN OPTION)

This soup gets its wonderful flavor from fabulous oven-roasted tomatoes, which I first tasted when I worked at a special dinner with Michael Romano of Union Square Café in New York City. For the paprika flavor in this recipe, you can use any one of a number of items, including pimentón, *smoked Spanish paprika from the Extremadura (my first choice), smoked chipotles, good-quality sweet Hungarian paprika, or Spanish paprika. The* pimentón *and chipotles are both smoke-dried, for extra flavor. Either the Hungarian or the Spanish paprika will give you a good soup with a lovely pinkish orange color, but without the extra smokiness. The smoked turkey stock makes a wonderful soup base, but you may substitute Vegetable Stock (see page 323) for a vegetarian version.*

--------------------------------- *Serves 8* ---------------------------------

1 pound (2 cups) dried Great Northern beans, soaked (see Soaking Chart, page 57)

2 medium onions, peeled and quartered

6 cloves garlic, peeled

2 tablespoons olive oil

1 teaspoon dried oregano

2 teaspoons ground cumin

2 cups Oven-Roasted Plum Tomatoes (see page 309)

2 tablespoons *pimentón* (see About *Pimentón*, page 339) or minced chipotle chile

4 quarts Smoked Turkey Stock (see page 321)

¼ cup fresh cilantro leaves (about ½ bunch), chopped

1. Drain the soaked beans. Place them in a large pot and cover with cold water. Bring to a boil; then drain the beans, discarding the liquid. Reserve.

2. Preheat the oven to 400°F. Combine the onions, garlic, olive oil, oregano, and cumin in a small roasting pan. Cook for 1 hour, turning once or twice, or until the onions are roasted and well browned.

3. In a large soup pot, combine the roasted onion and garlic mixture, Oven-Roasted Plum Tomatoes, soaked beans, *pimentón*, and Smoked Turkey Stock. Bring to a boil, reduce the heat to a simmer, and cook for 2 hours, or until the beans are tender. Allow the soup to cool somewhat, drain off and reserve the soup liquid, and purée half the solids in a food processor or blender until smooth. Strain through a sieve, if desired, to remove any skin pieces and combine with the remaining soup liquid and whole beans. Garnish with chopped cilantro.

ABOUT HARICOT BEANS

"Haricot bean" is an antiquated term for any member of the New World bean family. Old New England cookbooks refer to what are now known as Great Northern, navy, Boston, and pea beans as "haricots." In France, an *haricot lingot* is a large white bean perhaps most famous in cassoulet. The Aztec name for these beans was *ayacotl*, which was eventually transformed into *haricot.*

Quebeçois Yellow Split Pea Soup

At age eighteen, I spent a month in Montreal, where I first sampled this hearty, satisfying soup at a traditional Quebeçois restaurant in the city's Old Quarter. It was a rare treat for me to eat in an actual restaurant, so maybe that's why this soup tasted so good and was so memorable. Serve it piping hot in large bowls accompanied by thick slices of buttered multigrain bread, preferably in front of a roaring fire, and end with a creamy, sweet maple sugar pie. The yellow split peas used here are nuttier and richer tasting than the more common green split peas.

Serves 6 to 8

3 pounds smoked ham hocks

3 bay leaves

4 quarts water

2 teaspoons celery seeds, or
   1 tablespoon celery salt

1 pound (2 cups) dried yellow split peas

2 large onions, diced

4 ribs celery, sliced

Salt

1. Combine the ham hocks, bay leaves, water, and celery seeds in a large soup pot. Bring to a boil. Cover, reduce the heat, and simmer for 2 hours.

2. Add the yellow split peas, onions, and celery and bring back to a boil. Reduce the heat and cook, covered, for 1 hour, or until the yellow split peas are very soft. Remove the ham hocks, cool, and pick the meat from the bones. Stir the meat back into the soup, remove and discard the bay leaves, and season to taste with salt. Serve immediately or cool and freeze.

COOK'S NOTE

The versatile bean has even been used to describe weather conditions. Herman Melville wrote, in his *Journal of a Visit to London and the Continent 1849,* "Upon sallying out this morning, [I] encountered the old-fashioned pea soup London fog."

Summer Minestrone with Pesto alla Genovese

(VEGETARIAN OPTION)

My garnish for this summer minestrone is an all-too-short-lived delicacy: female zucchini blossoms, the sweetest, most succulent vegetable you can imagine. If you grow your own zucchini, the females are the blossoms from which the zucchini grow. These blossoms have a thick, fleshy center and won't last much longer than a day or two after picking. The male blossoms, which grow along the stem of the plant, don't produce fruits. These are also good, though, to my taste, are not nearly as desirable as the females. Serve this soup as they do in the summer in Milan, at cool room temperature. For a vegetarian version, substitute Vegetable Stock (see page 323) for the chicken stock.

Serves 8

Pesto alla Genovese

½ cup extra-virgin olive oil

8 to 10 cloves fresh young garlic

1 cup pine nuts

Leaves from 1 large bunch basil, washed and dried, about 3 cups

Soup

1 pound shelled fresh cranberry beans

1 pound fresh plum tomatoes, blanched, peeled, and seeded

2 leeks, white and light green parts, sliced and washed

2 quarts Light Chicken Stock (see page 320)

½ pound fresh romano beans, diagonally sliced, or 1 (10-ounce) package frozen romano beans

½ pound yellow squash, sliced into half-moons

½ pound small zucchini, sliced into half-moons

½ pound ditalini, or short-cut penne

12 female zucchini blossoms, for garnish (optional)

Salt and freshly ground black pepper

½ cup grated Parmigiano-Reggiano cheese

½ cup grated Pecorino Romano cheese

1. Prepare the Pesto alla Genovese: Have ready about ¼ cup ice cubes, crushed if possible. Combine the olive oil, garlic, and pine nuts in a food processor or blender and process to a paste. A handful at a time, add the basil leaves and the ice cubes and process again to produce a bright green paste.

2. Prepare the Soup: In a large soup pot, combine the cranberry beans, tomatoes, leeks, and Light Chicken Stock. Bring to a boil, reduce the heat, and simmer for 15 to 20 minutes, or until the beans are almost tender. Skim off any white foam that rises to the surface. Add the romano beans, yellow squash, zucchini, and ditalini and bring back to a boil. Reduce the heat and simmer for 5 to 8 minutes, or until the pasta is cooked through and the romano beans are tender.

3. Just before serving, stir in the zucchini blossoms; then remove the pot from the heat. Season to taste with salt and pepper. Divide the soup among serving bowls. Top each with a generous spoonful of the pesto. Combine the grated Parmigiano and Pecorino cheeses in a small bowl and serve with the soup.

KEEPING PESTO EMERALD GREEN

When making Pesto alla Genovese, it is most important to first sharpen your food processor blade or bring it to a knife sharpening service. A dull blade will bruise and blacken rather than cut the basil. Then add the ingredients in the proper order: fats first (oil and cheeses), greens last. In addition to basil, other herbs make great pesto (an Italian word simply meaning "paste"). I like to make a Southwest version using cilantro, pumpkin seeds, garlic, aged Monterey Jack or Asiago cheese, and a little fresh green chile. I also make a sage pesto with hazelnuts to stir into hearty white bean soup (see Hazelnut-Sage Pesto, page 120). Adding ice cubes along with the basil keeps the mixture cold and green.

Hot and Sour Soup
with Duck, Pea Shoots, and Tofu

Just about every time I eat in a Chinese restaurant, I have to order hot and sour soup. Sometimes it is quite wonderful, with a heat that makes my eyes tear and my nose run, but too often it is overly thickened with cornstarch. I just had to include a recipe for this soup, though it's not at all traditional. Here, inspired by a soup I tasted at the late Barbara Tropp's China Moon Restaurant in San Francisco, I've made a lighter version using her suggestion of duck breast instead of the traditional shredded pork. I also added tender fresh pea shoots, fresh shiitakes, and tofu.

——————— *Advance preparation recommended. Serves 6 to 8* ———————

½ pound boneless, skinless duck breast

¼ cup plus 1 tablespoon mushroom soy sauce

2 teaspoons ground Szechuan peppercorns (optional)

1 tablespoon saké or dry sherry

1 teaspoon minced fresh ginger

1 teaspoon minced garlic

1 tablespoon finely chopped cilantro leaves

3 tablespoons cornstarch

¼ cup rice wine

2 teaspoons roasted Japanese sesame oil

2 quarts Rich Chicken Stock (see page 322)

½ pound shiitake mushrooms, stems removed and caps sliced

½ pound fresh firm tofu, drained on paper towels and cut into ½-inch cubes

1 bunch fresh pea shoots, washed and trimmed

1 bunch scallions, green and white parts, sliced into thin rings

¼ cup rice wine vinegar

2 teaspoons hot red pepper flakes

1. Chill the duck meat in the freezer for 30 minutes; then cut into matchsticks. Reserve.

2. In a large bowl, combine 1 tablespoon mushroom soy sauce, the peppercorns, saké, ginger, garlic, cilantro, and 1 tablespoon cornstarch; stir until mixed. Add the duck and toss to coat in the marinade. Cover and refrigerate for at least 2 hours or up to overnight.

3. Place the duck and marinade in a small pot and bring to a boil, stirring constantly. Cook for about 3 minutes, until lightly cooked. Drain the duck, discarding the marinade, and spread the meat on a plate to cool.

4. Combine the remaining ¼ cup mushroom soy sauce and the rice wine, sesame oil, and remaining 2 tablespoons cornstarch in a small bowl and reserve.

5. Place the Rich Chicken Stock in a large soup pot and bring to a boil. Add the shiitake mushroom slices and the cooled duck meat, stirring to combine. Pour in the reserved cornstarch-soy mixture. Bring back to a boil, stirring occasionally so the cornstarch is evenly distributed. Just before serving, stir in the tofu, pea shoots, and scallions. Add the rice wine vinegar and red pepper flakes. Serve immediately in large soup bowls.

ABOUT PEA SHOOTS AND PEA SPROUTS

Pea shoots, the topmost tiny leaves and curly tendrils of snow pea vines, are a great delicacy in Chinese cooking and often the most expensive vegetable on the market. Add them to a soup just before serving, or as a last-minute addition to a vegetable stir-fry. They add a fresh, sweet, springtime flavor to dishes and make an outstanding garnish for any light dish. Companies that specialize in sprouts are now selling pea sprouts. These pea sprouts are less expensive than pea shoots, and though not as sweet and spring-green—only the leaf portion is green—they make a good substitute. Use pea sprouts in salads and as a crunchy sandwich green instead of lettuce.

Tuscan Winter Minestrone

This Tuscan-style soup is a hearty but simple white bean and savoy cabbage minestrone flavored with pancetta. It is infused with the herb flavors of Italian parsley, thyme, rosemary, and basil. Savoy cabbage, called la verza *in Italian, is a mild-flavored, tender cabbage with beautiful "savoyed," or curly, dark and light green leaves. It has much less of the strong aroma associated with common green cabbage, and balances well with the beans here. You can substitute a small white cabbage if you can't find the savoy, but it's really worth looking for. This soup is served without cheese in Tuscany, but because many Americans enjoy cheese in their soup and this minestrone has a hearty flavor and full body, I recommend serving it with shredded aged Pecorino Romano cheese, either domestic or imported.*

--- *Serves 8 to 10* ---

1 cup dried cannellini beans, soaked
    (see Soaking Chart, page 57), or
    3 cups cooked cannellini beans
    (see Basic Cooking Chart, page 58)
Salt
¼ pound pancetta, frozen until firm and
    cut into cubes
2 carrots, trimmed and peeled
1 rib celery
3 cloves fresh young garlic
1 large sprig fresh basil
1 large sprig fresh rosemary
½ cup extra-virgin olive oil (preferably
    Tuscan)
1 medium onion, thinly sliced
2 cups chopped plum tomatoes, fresh
    or canned
1 small savoy cabbage, cored and
    shredded
1 cup pearl barley, cooked in boiling
    salted water until tender but firm
1 tablespoon chopped fresh thyme
Salt and freshly ground black pepper
1 bunch Italian parsley, chopped for
    garnish
¼ pound aged Pecorino Romano cheese,
    shredded for serving (optional)

1. If using the dried beans, place them in a large pot, cover with cold water, and bring to a boil. Simmer until the beans are tender to the bite. Transfer half the beans to the bowl of a food processor or blender, purée, and strain through a food mill or sieve to remove the skin pieces. Stir the purée back into the whole beans and their cooking liquid, and reserve.

2. Chop together (either by hand or using the food processor) the cubed pancetta, carrots, celery, garlic, basil, and rosemary to form a chunky paste. Place the mixture in a large Dutch oven and add the olive oil and onion. Cook over medium heat for several minutes, or until the aromas are released. Stir in the tomatoes, cabbage, barley, thyme, and the cooked beans with their liquid. Bring to a boil, stirring occasionally; then season to taste with salt and pepper. (The soup can be cooled, covered, and refrigerated for up to 2 days at this point before serving.)

3. When ready to serve the soup, bring it back to a boil, sprinkle with parsley, and serve immediately, accompanied by a bowl of the cheese.

Spring Green Pea and Snow Pea Soup

(VEGETARIAN OPTION)

There's nothing quite like enjoying a lovely lunch at Takashimaya's stylish tea room in New York City to celebrate spring. The store, operated by the top Japanese department store chain, appeals to all the senses. As you walk in, there is a fragrant flower shop filled with blossoming branches of Japanese cherry and tall stems of Japanese irises, as well as pots of white lacecap hydrangeas. Downstairs is the tea emporium, filled with big boxes of fine loose teas and all the exquisite paraphernalia for tea preparation. The adjoining tea room serves light, exquisitely presented foods, including this delicate green spring soup. I loved it so much I had to adapt it for this book. For a vegetarian version, substitute Vegetable Stock (see page 323) for the chicken stock.

Serves 6 to 8

2 pounds fresh young green peas, shelled, or 1 (12-ounce) package frozen petits pois

1 pound snow peas, tipped

2 bunches scallions, sliced

1 quart Light Chicken Stock (see page 320)

2 tablespoons cornstarch

½ cup saké

1 (2-inch) length fresh ginger, grated

¼ cup light soy sauce

½ bunch fresh pea shoots or pea pod sprouts, for garnish

¼ cup Chinese flat chives, thinly sliced (about ½ bunch), for garnish

1. In a stainless steel or enameled soup pot, place the fresh or frozen peas, snow peas, scallions, and Light Chicken Stock. Bring to a boil, reduce the heat, and simmer for 15 to 20 minutes. Purée the mixture using a hand-held blender or in batches in a blender. Strain through a sieve or food mill.

2. Wash out the pot and place the strained soup mixture back into it. Bring to a boil. In a small bowl, combine the cornstarch, saké, ginger, and soy sauce. Slowly pour into the boiling soup while whisking constantly until well combined. Bring back to a boil; then remove from the heat. Divide the soup among serving bowls and sprinkle each bowl with pea shoots and chives.

Creamy White Bean Soup
with Hazelnut-Sage Pesto

Though we usually think of pesto as a basil sauce, the word just means "paste" in Italian and can be made with many kinds of herbs. Here, I use hazelnuts and fresh sage to make a woodsy-scented pesto to liven up this creamy white bean soup recipe. Hazelnuts are so much more common in Europe than here, but I happen to adore the bittersweet flavor they add. For the pesto, I combine the hazelnuts with a wonderful French hazelnut oil. Though more expensive than walnut oil, it's worth trying. Store the oil in the refrigerator, as nut oils quickly become rancid at room temperature. Be sure to bring the oil to room temperature before making the pesto.

Serves 8

Soup

1 pound (2 cups) dried cannellini beans, soaked (see Soaking Chart, page 57)
2 quarts Light Chicken Stock (see page 320)
2 bay leaves
1 small dried hot red chile
½ pound pancetta or bacon, cut into small pieces and finely chopped in a food processor
1 large onion, diced
2 leeks, white and light green parts only, sliced and washed
½ rib celery, sliced
Salt and freshly ground black pepper

Hazelnut-Sage Pesto

½ cup hazelnut or walnut oil
10 cloves fresh young garlic
¼ pound hazelnuts, preferably without skins
1 bunch fresh sage leaves
1 bunch Italian parsley leaves
½ cup grated Parmigiano-Reggiano cheese
½ cup grated Pecorino Romano cheese

1. Prepare the Soup: Drain the soaked beans. Combine in a large pot with the Light Chicken Stock, bay leaves, and chile. Bring to a boil, reduce the heat, and simmer for 2½ hours, or until nearly soft all the way through.

2. In a medium saucepan, cook the chopped pancetta or bacon, onion, leeks, and celery until softened but not browned. After the beans have cooked for about 2½ hours, add the pancetta-onion mixture to them. Continue cooking for 30 minutes, or until the beans are very soft.

3. Prepare the Hazelnut-Sage Pesto: Combine the hazelnut oil, garlic, and hazelnuts in a food processor and process to a paste. A handful at a time, add the sage and parsley leaves and process again until the mixture becomes a chunky green paste. Stir in the cheeses and reserve.

4. Purée the soup in a food processor or blender; then strain through a food mill to remove the bean skins. Season to taste with salt and black pepper. Divide the soup among soup bowls and top each with a dollop of pesto.

Broad Bean and Nasturtium Soup

(VEGETARIAN OPTION)

This recipe is adapted from a dish served in season at the Sooke Harbour House, a small but world-renowned thirteen-room inn on the west coast of Vancouver Island. The menu changes daily and focuses on fresh local organic seafood, often caught right off the shore. The inn's gardens have about 400 varieties of organic herbs, greens, vegetables, edible flowers, and trees that inspire the chefs' culinary creations. According to my friends who've visited there, the place is as dreamy as it sounds, and the food is spectacular. Here, the blossoms of nasturtium, a member of the watercress family, are used to add a special flavor and lovely color to a soup of fresh green fava beans; like watercress, they have a spicy heat. Watercress, though it won't be as colorful, makes a good substitute. For a vegetarian version, substitute Vegetable Stock (see page 323) for the chicken stock. It is not necessary to remove the inner hull of the fava beans.

Serves 6 to 8

6 tablespoons (¾ stick) unsalted butter
1 medium onion, diced
4 cloves garlic, finely minced
¼ cup cider vinegar
½ cup dry white wine
2 pounds fresh fava beans, hulled,
    or 1 (12-ounce) package frozen
    green favas
1 quart Light Chicken Stock (see page
    320)
Pinch of freshly grated nutmeg
Salt and freshly ground black pepper
1 cup heavy cream, whipped
12 to 16 nasturtium flowers and 12 to 16
    small nasturtium leaves, for garnish
    (optional)

1. Melt the butter in a large heavy-bottomed soup pot. Add the onion and cook until translucent. Stir in the garlic and cook for about 30 seconds. Add the cider vinegar and white wine and bring to a boil. Cook until almost all the liquid has evaporated. Add the fresh or frozen favas and Light Chicken Stock and bring to a boil. Season with nutmeg and salt and pepper to taste. Reduce the heat and simmer for 3 to 5 minutes, or until the beans are tender. Stir in the whipped cream.

2. Purée the soup in a food processor or blender, and strain through a sieve to remove the bean skins. Garnish with the nasturtium flowers and leaves.

Fresh Tomato and White Bean Soup

(VEGETARIAN OPTION)

Cookbook authors Linda and Fred Griffith tell me that their garden usually includes twenty varieties of heirloom tomatoes, so they have developed many fresh tomato recipes, including their original version of this soup. I have adapted it to include more onion and garlic, along with an underlying flavor of lovage, a potent, celery-like herb that grows with abandon in my garden. I finish the soup with shredded aged Gouda cheese because it has a rich nutty flavor and it doesn't turn grainy or stringy in the hot soup. You could use Chinese celery, cutting celery, or the leaves of celery root tops, or simply substitute the ever-adaptable thyme. Be sure to make this soup when locally grown tomatoes are in season. While one usually expects a bean soup to be rather sturdy, this one is light, smooth, and refreshing because of the vine-ripened tomatoes. If there's any left over, freeze it and you'll be able to enjoy the pleasure of garden-fresh flavors in the middle of winter. For a vegetarian version, substitute Vegetable Stock (see page 323) for the chicken stock

---

Serves 8

---

1 pound (2 cups) dried Great Northern beans, soaked (see Soaking Chart, page 57)

¼ cup olive oil

1 sweet onion, diced

4 large cloves garlic, sliced

2 bay leaves

¼ teaspoon ground cloves

5 pounds vine-ripened beefsteak tomatoes, cored and coarsely chopped

4 to 5 large sprigs lovage (substitute thyme sprigs)

1 tablespoon kosher salt

½ teaspoon freshly ground white pepper

4 quarts Light or Rich Chicken Stock (see page 320 or 322)

1 cup shredded aged Gouda cheese, or sharp Cheddar

1 cup thinly sliced fresh chives, for garnish

1. Drain the soaked beans. Heat the olive oil over low heat in a 6-quart, heavy-bottomed pot. Add the onion, garlic, bay leaves, and ground cloves. Cover and cook over very low heat until the onion becomes transparent, 5 to 8 minutes. Stir in the tomatoes and lovage. Cook, covered, for 20 minutes. Stir in the salt and white pepper. Cook, uncovered, over low heat for 30 minutes, or until the tomatoes are soft and the juices have thickened.

2. While the tomatoes cook, place the drained beans and Light or Rich Chicken Stock in a 6-quart soup pot. Bring to a boil over medium heat. Reduce the heat; simmer for 2 hours, or until the beans are tender.

3. When the tomatoes are cooked, combine them with the cooked beans. Simmer together, partially covered, for 10 to 20 minutes, or until the soup thickens. Adjust seasonings to taste. Purée the soup in a blender and (for smoothest texture) strain through a food mill, discarding the skins and seeds.

4. To serve, ladle into flat soup plates and garnish with the shredded cheese, chives, and additional freshly ground white pepper.

Curried Red Lentil Soup

(VEGETARIAN)

This is an easy-to-make vegetarian soup of quick-cooking split red lentils from the southern part of India. You could also substitute split yellow mung beans, split yellow chickpeas, or yellow split peas. The key to many Indian dishes is the warm, nutty flavor of popped black mustard seeds. They pop just like popcorn, so you'll need to use a pot with a lid when making them.

Serves 8

2 tablespoons vegetable oil

2 tablespoons whole black mustard seeds

1 large white onion, chopped

¼ cup chopped fresh ginger

1 tablespoon chopped garlic

2 jalapeño peppers, seeded and finely chopped

¼ cup ghee or melted butter (see Making Ghee, page 72)

2 tablespoons Madras-type curry powder

1 pound (2 cups) red lentils

3 quarts Vegetable Stock (see page 323)

1 teaspoon salt

¼ teaspoon freshly ground black pepper

2 tablespoons fresh lime juice (about 1 lime)

¼ cup chopped fresh cilantro

1 cup plain yogurt, preferably full fat

1. In a small saucepan with a lid, heat the vegetable oil with the black mustard seeds. Be sure to cover the pot, or the seeds will start popping out of it. Cook for about 4 minutes, or until the popping sound stops.

2. In a large soup pot, cook the onion, ginger, garlic, and jalapeño in the ghee or butter. Add the curry powder and cook for 2 minutes longer. Stir in the lentils, Vegetable Stock, salt, and black pepper. Bring to a boil, reduce the heat, and simmer until soft, about 1 hour, stirring occasionally. Using a potato masher, partially mash the lentils to thicken the soup.

3. Just before serving, stir in the mustard seeds with their cooking oil, the lime juice, and the cilantro. Garnish each serving with a dollop of yogurt and sprinkle with cilantro.

REHEATING THICK SOUPS

Most thick soup will thicken even more when refrigerated overnight. When reheating, cover the bottom of the pot with ½ inch water and bring to a boil. Then add the cold soup. Reduce the heat to low and bring back to a boil, stirring often to prevent burning and heat thoroughly.

Crab Chowder
with Limas, Green Beans, and Corn

This lovely summer soup is elegant enough to serve for your next dinner party. Those of us who live on the East Coast usually prefer the tender, succulent meat of Chesapeake blue crabs. In other parts of the country, peekytoe or Dungeness crabmeat may be substituted. While fresh-picked crabmeat is the sweetest, for this soup the more easily found pasteurized crabmeat makes a good substitute. For the most elegant presentation, do as the fancy restaurants do and place the corn, crab, and tomatoes in the bottom of each hot bowl and ladle the hot creamy soup over the top at the table.

Serves 8

4 ears sweet white corn, husked

2 quarts milk

1 peeled onion, stuck with 3 or 4 whole cloves

2 teaspoons ground allspice

1 tablespoon coriander seeds

3 bay leaves

1 pound yellow potatoes, peeled and diced

¼ pound bacon, cut into small strips

1 medium onion, diced

½ pound fresh green beans, cut into ¼-inch slices

1 (12-ounce) package frozen baby limas, thawed and drained

3 tablespoons unbleached all-purpose flour

1 cup light cream

Salt and freshly ground black pepper

Freshly grated nutmeg

1 pound jumbo lump crabmeat, cartilage removed, for serving

1 pound ripe beefsteak tomatoes, peeled, seeded, and diced, for serving

¼ cup chopped fresh chervil (1 bunch), for serving

2 tablespoons chopped fresh thyme leaves (¼ bunch), for serving

Pinch of cayenne

1. Cut the corn kernels off the cobs. Reserve. Place the cobs in a large soup pot with the milk, whole onion, allspice, coriander seeds, and bay leaves. Bring to a boil over moderate heat. Reduce the heat and simmer for about 30 minutes, stirring occasionally to prevent the milk from scorching. Strain through a sieve, reserving the aromatic milk and discarding the solids.

2. Return the milk to the pot and add the potatoes. Simmer over medium heat until the potatoes are tender when pierced with a fork, about 15 minutes. Reserve.

3. In a medium pan, cook the bacon until crisp. Transfer the bacon to a paper towel, reserving the bacon drippings. Sauté the diced onion in the bacon drippings until transparent. Add the green beans and limas. Stir in the flour and cook together for 3 minutes, continuing to stir until thickened.

4. Transfer the beans to the potato mixture and bring to a boil. Add the cream and remove the soup from the heat. (If you want to serve the soup the next day, cool it quickly by placing the pot in an ice water bath; then remove and refrigerate. The next day, slowly heat the soup, just until it boils.)

5. When ready to serve, season the soup to taste with salt, black pepper, and nutmeg. Divide the reserved corn kernels, crabmeat, and diced tomato among the individual soup bowls. Ladle the soup into the bowls. Sprinkle each portion with the remaining herbs, the cayenne, and the reserved bacon bits. Serve immediately.

Velouté of White Coco Beans and Black Truffles

This marvelous soup is served at Le Bec-Fin, the world-class restaurant run by Philadelphia's magnificent chef Georges Perrier. Inspired by an unforgettable meal he enjoyed at Joël Robuchon's former restaurant in Paris, he re-created the dish for his own menu using fresh truffles. In this version of the soup, I have substituted less expensive and more accessible black truffle paste from France, although if you happen to come by a stash of fresh truffles, use them as generously as you can bear. For the most delicate soup, use small white beans such as the French coco or American navy beans.

Serves 8

1½ cups dried white coco beans, soaked (see Soaking Chart, page 57)

1 smoked ham hock

4 quarts Rich Chicken Stock (see page 322)

4 bay leaves

2 tablespoons chopped fresh thyme leaves (about ¼ bunch)

½ pound bacon, diced

3 leeks, white part only, well washed and sliced

1 white onion, diced

3 ribs celery, sliced

2 teaspoons chopped garlic

2 cups heavy cream

Sea salt and finely ground white pepper

1 (3.5-ounce) jar black truffle paste

1 bunch fresh chives, finely chopped, for garnish

1. Drain the soaked beans. Combine the beans, ham hock, Rich Chicken Stock, bay leaves, and thyme in a large soup pot. Bring to a boil. Reduce the heat, cover, and simmer for 1½ hours.

2. Cook the bacon in a medium skillet until lightly browned. Add the leeks, onion, celery, and garlic and cook for 10 minutes, or until softened but not browned.

3. After cooking the beans for 1½ hours, scrape the leek mixture into the soup. Simmer for 30 minutes, or until the beans are soft but not mushy. Remove and discard the ham hock and bay leaves.

4. Using a hand-held blender (or working in small batches in a blender), purée the soup. Strain through a fine sieve or food mill. Return to the pot. Stir in the heavy cream. Bring the soup to a simmer and season to taste with salt and white pepper. Reserve until ready to serve.

5. Reheat the soup if necessary, stirring constantly; then ladle into heated soup plates. Spoon a generous teaspoonful of black truffle paste into the center of each bowl. Sprinkle with the chives and serve immediately.

Moroccan Golden Split Pea and Pumpkin Soup

(VEGETARIAN OPTION)

There is a rich culinary tradition among Moroccan Jews, who at one time made up fully 10 percent of that country's population. Each city in Morocco has its own special dishes. In Marrakesh, Jews typically served this symbolically golden soup on the first night of Rosh Hashanah, the Jewish New Year. The use of precious saffron and other spices shows that the dish was hardly for everyday use. This soup is also made with chickpeas, so you could substitute the split golden chickpeas, called channa dal, *if you are fortunate enough to find these little beauties. For a vegetarian version, substitute Vegetable Stock (see page 323) for the chicken stock.*

--- *Serves 8* ---

3 quarts Rich Chicken Stock
   (see page 322)
1 quart cold water
1 pound (2 cups) dried yellow split peas
3 bay leaves
½ cup olive oil
2 large onions, chopped
1 tablespoon ground cinnamon
1 tablespoon ground ginger
2 large pinches of saffron threads,
   crumbled
2 pounds peeled and diced red pumpkin,
   butternut squash, or calabaza
Salt and freshly ground black pepper

1. In a large soup pot, combine the Rich Chicken Stock, water, yellow split peas, and bay leaves and bring to a boil. Skim off and discard any white foam that forms on the surface. Reduce the heat and simmer for about 1 hour, or until the split peas become tender.

2. In a separate pan, heat the olive oil over medium heat. Add the onions, cinnamon, ginger, and saffron. Cook until the onions are softened but not browned. Add this mixture to the soup along with the pumpkin cubes. Simmer for 30 minutes longer, or until the pumpkin is quite soft. Remove and discard the bay leaves. Season to taste with salt and pepper and serve.

ABOUT FRENCH RED PUMPKINS

The firm, red-fleshed pumpkin called for in this recipe is similar to the French *potiron rouge*. Grown in the United States by a few specialty growers, it is sometimes known as a Cinderella pumpkin and has a flattened shape and strikingly beautiful brick red skin. A favorite of chefs in 19th-century Paris, this pumpkin is considered especially good for soup because of its mild flavor and pleasing color. The closest easily available substitute is butternut squash, sometimes sold already peeled and cut into chunks in the supermarket produce section. Calabaza, a squash that is greenish on the outside and orange on the inside, is also a good substitute. Our jack-o'-lantern pumpkins are too stringy to use here.

Creamy Lentil Soup
with Celery Root

This simple soup, which I developed for the Omni Hotel at Independence Park in Philadelphia when it first opened, is a regional Pennsylvania specialty that combines homely brown lentils with the sweet, earthy taste of celery root. Substitute smoked turkey legs if you don't want to use the ham hocks. If you like making your own soup stock, save the washed trimmings of the celery root in the freezer for your next batch. They'll give your stock a deep, almost haunting flavor of celery.

Serves 8

2 smoked ham hocks

4 quarts cold water

4 bay leaves

½ bunch fresh thyme, wrapped and tied with kitchen twine

1 pound (2 cups) dried brown lentils

1 large celery root, pared and finely diced

½ cup chopped fresh sage leaves (about ½ bunch)

2 tablespoons chopped garlic

2 teaspoons ground coriander seeds

½ teaspoon cayenne

4 tablespoons (½ stick) unsalted butter

Salt and black pepper to taste

1. In a large pot, combine the ham hocks, water, bay leaves, and thyme. Bring to a boil, reduce the heat, and simmer for 2 hours. Add the lentils and cook for 45 minutes, or until the lentils are very soft. Remove the ham hocks and, if desired, pick the meat from the bones when cool enough to handle. Reserve the meat and discard the bone. Remove and discard the bay leaves.

2. Let the soup cool slightly; then purée half the soup in a blender (or with a hand-held blender) and strain through a sieve or food mill. Stir in the reserved meat, if using, and return to the same pot along with the remaining half of the soup.

3. Meanwhile, in a medium pan, cook the celery root, sage, garlic, coriander, and cayenne in the butter until softened but not browned. Add this vegetable mixture to the lentil soup and simmer for 10 minutes, or until the celery root is tender when pierced with a fork. Season to taste with salt and pepper.

Cuban Black Bean Soup
with Sofrito and Smoked Turkey

Cuban cookery often includes a flavorful sofrito, *aromatic vegetables slowly cooked in annatto oil. Annatto, or achiote, is an extremely hard red seed used for its beautiful deep red color and delicate flavor. I make this soup with smoked turkey legs instead of the traditional, higher-fat smoked ham hocks. A piping-hot bowl of this smoky dark soup followed by a green salad and a loaf of whole-grain bread makes a delicious, filling meal. Black turtle beans are very popular for soup because they make an exceptionally smooth, velvety purée.*

Serves 8

1 pound (2 cups) dried black turtle beans, soaked (see Soaking Chart, page 57)

1 peeled medium onion, stuck with 8 whole cloves

3 bay leaves

1 pound smoked turkey legs

2 quarts Light Chicken Stock (see page 320)

2 quarts cold water

1 large white onion, diced

1 tablespoon chopped garlic

1 tablespoon ground toasted cumin seeds (see Toasting Seeds, page 225)

2 tablespoons annatto oil, or peanut oil, plus 1 tablespoon paprika

1 (15-ounce) can plum tomatoes, chopped

2 tablespoons malt or sherry vinegar

Salt and freshly ground black pepper

1. Drain and rinse the soaked black turtle beans. In a large soup pot, add the beans and enough water to cover. Bring the water to a boil, reduce the heat, and simmer for 5 minutes. Drain the beans, discarding the water.

2. Place the beans back in the pot along with the whole onion, bay leaves, and turkey legs. Cover with the Light Chicken Stock and cold water. Bring to a boil, skim off any white foam impurities that rise to the surface, and reduce the heat to a simmer. Cook very slowly until the beans are quite soft, about 2 hours. (Alternatively, cook the beans in a pressure cooker for 25 minutes, starting the timer after the steam has built up pressure in the pot.) Remove the onion and bay leaves and discard. Remove the turkey legs, and when cool enough to handle, dice the meat and reserve.

3. Purée three-fourths of the beans, along with their liquid, in a blender or a food processor. Leave the remaining beans whole. To make the soup easier to digest, strain the bean purée through a sieve or food mill to remove the skins. Return to the pot with the whole beans.

4. In a skillet, sauté the diced onion, garlic, reserved diced turkey meat, and cumin in the oil until softened. Add the tomatoes and vinegar. Add the sautéed vegetable mixture to the beans. Bring the soup back to a boil and season to taste with salt and pepper.

1. *French green lentils*; 2. *Castelluccio lentils*; 3. *Black beluga lentils*; 4. *Split red lentils*; 5. *Pardina lentils*; 6. *Green lentils*; 7. *Red mung beans*; 8. *Split yellow "lentils" (pigeon peas)*; 9. *Split yellow fava beans*; 10. *Fava beans with skins*; 11. *Lamon beans (borlotti type)*; 12. *Lupini beans*; 13. *Split black gram beans (white color)*; 14. *Green mung beans*; 15. *Black soybeans*; 16. *Black-eyed peas*; 17. *Persian lima beans*; 18. *Black turtle beans*; 19. *Anasazi® beans*; 20. *Toscanelli beans*; 21. *Saluggia beans*; 22. *Dark red kidney beans*; 23. *Bolita beans*; 24. *Alubia beans*; 25. *Pavoni (peacock) beans*; 26. *Split peas (green)*; 27. *Split peas (yellow)*; 28. *Christmas lima beans*; 29. *Ceci (chickpeas)*; 30. *Cicerchie (heirloom chickpeas)*

An elegant Viennese flourless White Bean and Hazelnut Torte is delicious when served alone or with a scoop of Creamy White Bean Ice Cream, lavished with Molasses Caramel Sauce.

Hot and Sour Soup with Duck, Pea Shoots, and Tofu is a soul-warming dish with plenty of spicy character. Tender pea shoots and shiitake mushrooms add a bright, fresh touch.

Maccheroni Rustica, with browned sausage, caramelized garlic, roasted tomatoes, and cranberry beans, is a satisfying, boldly flavored dish and a definite crowd-pleaser.

Bean salads taste best when made with highly flavored ingredients, such as hot paprika, cumin, and preserved lemon in Emergo Bean Salad with Moroccan Charmoula Dressing.

Using a naturally raised chicken, strong cured ham, and fresh herbs will make Skillet Roasted Chicken with Black-Eyed Peas, Country Ham, and Savory as good as it can be.

Spicy Homemade Beer Nuts (foreground), Crunchy Fried Favas with Pimenton, and Chile-Spiced Fried Chickpeas are wholesome snacks with lots of forthright flavor.

Rustic and colorful, Portuguese Salt Cod and Kidney Bean Salad combines poached and grilled bacalhau *with kidney beans, red wine vinaigrette, sliced eggs, and black olives.*

In Pan-Seared Scallops with Beluga Lentils, black lentils with bits of fennel, squash, and corn are accented by the striking color and creamy texture of corn-saffron vinaigrette.

This colorful Bean Pebbled Paella features chickpeas, red kidney beans, and black beans along with ham, chard, piquillo peppers, and short-grain rice tinted with saffron.

Chickpea Fries Riviera Style are fried until crispy, then lightly crusted with grated Parmigiano-Reggiano. A drizzle of Tunisian Harissa Sauce adds peppery contrast.

Frittata with Romano Beans, Prosciutto, and Fontina makes an ideal lunch or light supper dish. It can be prepared a few hours earlier, then reheated or served at room temperature.

Green Soybeans with Cantonese Bacon is an unexpectedly delicious side dish. Cantonese bacon is cured, but not smoked--much like pancetta, which makes a worthy substitute.

For Chinese Yard-Long Beans with Black Bean and Garlic Sauce, Asian long beans are stir-fried in a pungent fermented black bean sauce with tangerine zest, ginger, and garlic.

Brazilian Feijoada Completa is a great party dish, with black beans, spiced short ribs, smoked chorizo, rice, and braised greens, accompanied by spicy lemon-pepper mojo.

This Chow-Chow is a vibrantly colored, prominently spiced version of the traditional sweet-and-sour bean relish that's a favorite condiment on the Pennsylvania Dutch table.

1. Mung bean sprouts; 2. Sugar snap peas; 3. Yard-long beans; 4. Fava beans in pod; 5. Dragon tongue beans; 6. Purple wax beans; 7. Haricots verts; 8. Freshly shelled black-eyed peas; 9. Green beans; 10. Wax beans; 11. Edamame in pod

Diner-Style Split Pea Soup

Every old-fashioned diner should serve a rib-sticking split pea soup, so thick that a spoon inserted in the middle of a bowl can stand upright. This version has a unique depth of flavor because of the three aromatic, resinous herbs: winter savory, thyme, and sage. For a mouth-pleasing contrast of texture, serve the soup topped with garlic croutons. This soup freezes and reheats so well, why not make a big batch and have it ready for a cold drizzly day or unexpected company?

Serves 8
---

1 pound (2 cups) green split peas

1 pound ham hocks

2 quarts water

3 leeks, white and light green parts, sliced and washed

2 large onions, diced

¼ cup bacon fat or chicken fat, or unsalted butter

1 tablespoon chopped garlic

2 tablespoons chopped fresh summer or winter savory leaves (about ¼ bunch), or 1½ teaspoons dried

2 tablespoons chopped fresh thyme leaves (about ½ bunch), or 2 teaspoons dried

¼ cup chopped fresh sage (about ½ bunch), or 1 tablespoon dried

2 quarts Light Chicken Stock (see page 320)

Salt, freshly ground black pepper, and cayenne

1. Bring the split peas, ham hocks, and water to a boil in a large pot. Cover and reduce the heat and simmer for 2 hours, or until the split peas are soft. Remove the ham hocks and pick the meat from the bones when cool enough to handle, discarding the bones. Place the meat back in the pot.

2. Cook the leeks and onions in the bacon fat until softened. Add the garlic, savory, thyme, and sage and cook for 5 minutes longer. Add the vegetable mixture to the peas. Add the Light Chicken Stock, return to a boil, and remove from heat. Season to taste with salt, black pepper, and cayenne.

ABOUT PEA AND PEASE

"Pease" was the Old English name for the pea and is actually a singular, not plural, form. In what must be the ancestor of split pea soup, the English staple back then was a rib-sticking thick pease soup. Its enduring importance is shown in the nursery rhyme: "Pease porridge hot, pease porridge cold, pease porridge in my pot, nine days old." The word "pea" itself is a very old term, and the Greek, Italian, Old Irish, French, and English share variations on the same word.

Egyptian Fava Bean Soup *(Ful Medames)*

(VEGETARIAN)

The national dish of Egypt, ful medames, *is so basic to the local diet that it is more than a dish; it's a way of life. There, small brown fava beans, called* ful, *are cooked in a special pot that tapers to a narrow neck. As the steam from the cooking beans condenses on the sloping sides, it drops back into the pot, keeping all the flavorful juices in the beans. It is yet another member of the family of narrow-necked, usually earthenware, bean pots, including the Italian* fiasco, *the Spanish and Mexican* olla, *and the good old American Boston bean pot.*

--- *Serves 8* ---

1 pound dried brown fava beans, soaked
   (see Soaking Chart, page 57)
4 quarts water
3 cloves garlic, finely chopped
2 tablespoons extra-virgin olive oil
¼ cup fresh lemon juice (about 2 lemons)
1 tablespoon salt
½ teaspoon freshly ground black pepper
4 hard-cooked eggs, sliced, for garnish
   (see Hard-Cooking Eggs, page 183)
2 tablespoons finely chopped Italian
   parsley leaves, for garnish

1. Preheat the oven to 300°F. Drain the fava beans, place in a heavy, ovenproof Dutch oven, and cover with the cold water. Bring to a boil on top of the stove; then cover and place in the oven. Bake for 3 to 4 hours, or until the beans are soft but still mostly whole. Remove from the oven.

2. Stir in the garlic, olive oil, lemon juice, salt, and pepper. Ladle into large soup bowls, garnish with the sliced eggs, and sprinkle with the parsley.

Irish Bean and Smoky Bacon Soup

On a long-ago trip hitchhiking, camping, and hosteling throughout Ireland, I learned to love that emerald-green country and its warm people, and I ate inexpensive, filling soups very much like this one. Years later Jack Downey, the owner of Downey's, a Philadelphia pub at the corner of Front and South Streets, asked me to help develop recipes for his high-end line of canned soups. This Irish Bean and Smoky Bacon Soup sold quite well, though not quite as well as his star soup, Lobster Bisque.

Serves 8

1 pound (2 cups) dried navy beans
4 bay leaves
1 large white onion, peeled and left whole
4 sprigs fresh thyme
4 tablespoons chopped fresh sage leaves
2 quarts Light Chicken Stock (see page 320)
2 quarts cold water
¼ pound smoky bacon, cut into strips
1 large white onion, diced
½ pound good-quality ham, cut into small dice
2 leeks, white and light green parts, washed and diced into ½-inch pieces
2 cloves garlic, chopped
2 cups light cream
Salt and freshly ground black pepper

1. Place the beans in a large pot, cover with cold water, and bring to a boil. Simmer for 5 minutes; then drain.

2. Return the beans to the pot; add the bay leaves, whole onion, thyme, 2 tablespoons of the sage, the Light Chicken Stock, and water, and bring to a boil. Cover, reduce the heat, and simmer until tender, about 1½ hours. Remove and discard the whole onion, thyme sprigs, and bay leaves. Purée half of the beans in a blender or food processor, leaving the remaining beans whole. Strain the purée through a food mill, if desired, and return to the pot.

3. Cook the bacon in a pan until lightly browned. Add the diced onion, ham, leeks, garlic, and the remaining 2 tablespoons sage. Cook for 3 minutes, or until softened but not browned.

4. Add the bacon mixture to the beans and bring to a boil. Stir in the cream and return to a boil. Season to taste with salt and pepper. Serve immediately.

Mulligatawny Soup
with Chicken, Rice, and Lime

My trusty Oxford Diner's Dictionary tells me that employees of the great East India Company originally brought this soup to England. The soup as it has evolved in England bears little resemblance to its aromatic South Indian original. The name comes from the Tamil word milakutanni, *which means "pepper water." I admit that I've taken liberty in naming this soup "mulligatawny." I just loved the name, and when I worked as a restaurant chef and wanted to entice customers to order this delicious, hot and spicy red lentil soup with chicken, I called it mulligatawny.*

—— *Serves 8 to 10* ——

3 quarts Light Chicken Stock (see page 320)
1 quart water
2 pounds skinless chicken thighs
2 medium onions, diced
½ cup chopped fresh ginger
½ cup chopped garlic
2 jalapeño peppers, seeded and chopped
6 tablespoons (¾ stick) unsalted butter
3 tablespoons ground toasted cumin seeds (see Toasting Seeds, page 225)
3 tablespoons ground toasted coriander seeds (see Toasting Seeds, page 225)
2 tablespoons turmeric
2 tablespoons black mustard seeds
1 pound (2 cups) split red lentils
Salt
Juice of 3 limes
3 cups cooked basmati rice, for serving
2 tablespoons nigella seeds, for garnish

1. In a large soup pot, bring the Light Chicken Stock and water to a boil. Add the chicken thighs, and return to a boil. Reduce the heat, cover, and poach the chicken for 20 minutes, or until the large bone jiggles freely in its joint. Remove the thighs from the stock reserving both chicken and stock. When cool enough to handle, remove the meat from the bones. Shred the meat, being careful to remove and discard any fat and connective tissue. Cover the chicken meat and refrigerate until ready to use.

2. In a medium pan, cook the onions, ginger, garlic, and jalapeños in the butter until softened. Add the cumin, coriander, turmeric, and mustard seeds, and cook for 5 minutes. Add the mixture to the soup pot with the lentils and reserved stock. Bring to a boil. Reduce the heat and simmer for 1 hour, or until the lentils are soft.

3. Cool the soup slightly; then purée using a food processor or blender, and season to taste with salt. When ready to serve, stir in the lime juice, cooked rice, and reserved chicken meat. Sprinkle each portion with nigella seeds and serve piping hot.

NIGELLA SEEDS

The angular black seeds—called variously *nigella, kalonji,* or *charnushka*—used as a garnish in this recipe have a distinctive aroma and mild flavor. Acrid and nutty at the same time, they taste a bit like a pungent poppy seed. Irresistible to me, they are the seed of choice on the Russian-style black and rye breads baked in New York City, where they are called *charnushka*. The same seed is also mixed with bread dough to make an addictively delicious Indian nan bread, and is often combined with legumes as in the nigella-studded lentil *pappadum* wafers. In India, there are two common names for this seed that is used extensively to flavor legumes. In the north, it is known as *kala jeera* (also the name for black cumin, a totally different plant); elsewhere in India, it is called *kalonji*.

Lentil Soup with Hot Dogs

I grew up in a kosher home, and my mother often used garlicky kosher hot dogs in dishes like this lentil soup. It's easy to make and a real kid-pleaser. This soup freezes extremely well, so serve half and freeze the other half for a quick cold-weather meal. While it's not necessary to use kosher hot dogs, I happen to believe their quality is outstanding because by law only beef muscle meat can be used. They are also more highly flavored with garlic than standard dogs.

Serves 8

¼ cup vegetable oil

1 large onion, diced

2 carrots, diced

2 leeks, white and light green parts, sliced and washed

2 ribs celery, sliced

2 teaspoons chopped fresh thyme leaves, or 1 teaspoon dried

1 teaspoon chopped fresh sage leaves, or ½ teaspoon dried

2 quarts Rich Chicken Stock (see page 322)

2 quarts cold water

1 pound (2 cups) dried brown lentils

1 pound kosher high-quality hot dogs, cut into ½-inch slices

Salt and freshly ground black pepper

1. Heat the oil and add the onion and carrots. Sauté until well browned, stirring often, and then add the leeks, celery, thyme, and sage. Cook for about 5 minutes, stirring often, until softened but not browned.

2. Add the Rich Chicken Stock, water, and lentils and bring to a boil. Reduce the heat to very low and simmer for 1 hour. Add the hot dog slices and continue cooking until the lentils are quite soft, about 15 minutes longer. Season to taste with salt and pepper.

Pasta and Beans *(Pasta e Fagioli)*
from the Villa Cipriani

When I turned forty-five, I promised myself a birthday present: a trip to France and Italy with my daughter, Ginevra, who was then eight years old. One of the high points was a day trip to the beautiful artist's colony of Asolo in the foothills of the Italian Dolomites. The Cipriani family runs a lovely country inn along one of the narrow, steep, stony streets of the town. We enjoyed a totally sybaritic lunch in the dining room with its spectacular view of the countryside on the plains below. After demolishing my bowl of Pasta e Fagioli, *I asked our gracious waiter if I might have the recipe. Perhaps because my daughter was charming him, he introduced me to the chef, Secondo Ceccato, who gladly dictated his recipe to me as I scrawled it onto a scrap of paper. He wouldn't let me leave without a bagful of* fagioli di lamon belluno, *the special heirloom beans he uses in this unctuous soup.*

Serves 8
---

1 pound (2 cups) dried cranberry beans, soaked (see Soaking Chart, page 57)

½ pound ditalini pasta

1 (6-ounce) piece pancetta

1 (6-ounce) piece *cotenna* (the skin of a prosciutto) or pork rind

2 cloves garlic

4 quarts cold water

2 tablespoons beef concentrate (such as Marmite or Knorr brands) or fresh beef drippings

6 ounces Parmigiano-Reggiano or Grana Padano cheese, grated

Sea salt and freshly ground black pepper

½ cup finest quality extra-virgin olive oil, for garnish

1. Drain the soaked cranberry beans.

2. Bring a pot of salted water to a boil. Add the pasta and cook for 3 minutes. Drain and rinse well under cold running water.

3. In a large pot, combine the beans, pancetta, *cotenna*, garlic, and water. Bring to a boil, skim off any white foam, and reduce the heat. Cover and cook very slowly for 4 hours. Remove from the heat; discard the pancetta and *cotenna*.

4. Purée half of the soup in a blender or food processor, and then pass through a food mill to remove the bean skins. Combine the purée with the remaining beans. Stir in the beef concentrate and cheese. Season to taste with salt and pepper.

5. Just before serving, reheat the soup and add the reserved pasta. Serve in wide shallow bowls and, at the table, drizzle each serving with about 1 tablespoon extra-virgin olive oil.

COOK'S NOTE

The *fagioli di lamon* I try to use for this soup are grown in the high plains of Lamon, a mountainous region in the Veneto in the province of Belluno. The beans have been cultivated there since 1530, thanks to a locally born brother and assistant to Pope Clemente VII, who brought them back from the Court of Spain soon after Spanish explorers had introduced the first common beans to Europe. *Fagioli di lamon* have been highly prized ever since and are now protected by an I.G.T. (Protected Geographical Indication), an Italian government rating that recognizes their particular regional character. A consortium of about 100 producers holds a Festa del Fagiolo (Festival of the Bean) every September. Similar varieties of Italian heirloom beans are available from Republic of Beans (see Sources, page 341).

Queen Victoria's Favorite Green Pea Soup
with Buttered Croutons
(VEGETARIAN OPTION)

This recipe for green pea soup, flavored with mint and scallions and enriched with butter, is adapted from Lafcadio Hearn's 1885 cookbook, La Cuisine Creole: A Collection of Culinary Recipes. *His name alone is enough to inspire thoughts of romance and exotic locales. Hearn was a journalist, restaurateur, cartoonist, and novelist in New Orleans in the 1880s and later traveled to Japan. His cookbook, now considered a classic, is filled with recipes Hearn collected from the many New Orleans homes he visited. For a vegetarian version, substitute Vegetable Stock (see page 323) for the chicken stock.*

Serves 8 to 10

Buttered Croutons

1 (1-pound) loaf dense white sandwich bread, sliced

¼ pound (1 stick) unsalted butter, melted

Soup

2 quarts Rich Chicken Stock (see page 322)

3 (12-ounce) packages frozen green peas, thawed under cold running water

½ cup coarsely chopped Italian parsley leaves (about 1 bunch)

½ cup coarsely chopped fresh mint leaves (about 1 bunch)

3 bunches scallions, white and green parts, sliced

2 tablespoons cornstarch mixed with ¼ cup water

½ pound (2 sticks) unsalted butter, cut up

2 tablespoons sugar

Salt and freshly ground black pepper

Freshly grated nutmeg

1. Prepare the Buttered Croutons: Preheat the oven to 300°F. Cut the crusts from the bread slices and discard. Cut the bread slices into small cubes. Toss with the melted butter and spread out onto a shallow baking pan. Bake for 15 minutes. Stir and bake again for 10 minutes longer, or until the croutons are golden brown.

2. Prepare the Soup: In a large soup pot, bring the Rich Chicken Stock to a boil. Add the thawed peas, parsley, mint, and scallions and return to a boil. Reduce the heat to low. Add the cornstarch-water slurry to the soup and simmer for 5 minutes, stirring occasionally, until thickened.

3. Using a hand-held or traditional blender, purée the soup until smooth. Strain through a sieve or food mill to remove the pea skins and then transfer back to the pot. Stir in the butter one piece at a time, along with the sugar, heating until the butter is melted. Season to taste with salt, black pepper, and nutmeg. Serve each portion of soup topped with a small handful of the Buttered Croutons.

Black Turtle Bean Purée
with Madeira, Lemon, and Egg Mimosa

This subtly flavored soup originated in a 19th-century marketing campaign to make black beans more acceptable to Americans, who were scared off by their dark color. Renamed "turtle" beans, they were promoted as a poor man's substitute for turtle soup, a highly appreciated delicacy enjoyed by the upper classes at the time. Turtle soup was usually laced with Madeira, the fortified wine made on the Portuguese island of Madeira and imported into our coastal cities since precolonial times. The chopped egg mimosa garnish—named for its resemblance to the small, round yellow blossoms of the mimosa tree—the ground mace, and the sliced lemon are all traditional flavorings for turtle soup.

make ½ recipe

Serves 8

1 pound (2 cups) dried black turtle beans, soaked (see Soaking Chart, page 57)

2 smoked ham hocks

4 quarts Light Chicken Stock (see page 320)

2 bay leaves

2 large yellow onions, coarsely chopped

½ pound carrots, peeled and chopped

3 or 4 ribs celery, sliced

1 tablespoon chopped garlic

¼ cup (½ stick) unsalted butter

2 tablespoons cider vinegar

½ cup dry Madeira

Grated zest of 1 lemon

2 tablespoons fresh lemon juice (about 1 lemon)

1 teaspoon ground mace or nutmeg

Salt and freshly ground black pepper

1 lemon, thinly sliced, for garnish

2 hard-cooked eggs (see Hard-Cooking Eggs, page 183), chopped, for garnish

2 tablespoons chopped Italian parsley leaves, for garnish

1. Drain and rinse the soaked black turtle beans. In a large soup pot, combine the beans, ham hocks, Light Chicken Stock, and bay leaves. Bring to a boil and skim off any white foam impurities that rise to the surface. Reduce the heat and simmer for 2 hours.

2. In a separate pan, cook the onions, carrots, celery, and garlic in the butter over medium heat until softened but not browned, 5 to 10 minutes. Transfer the mixture to the soup pot and continue simmering until the beans are soft enough to be easily mashed with a fork against the side of the pot, about 30 minutes. Remove and discard the bay leaves and ham hocks.

3. In a blender or food processor, purée the soup. Strain through a food mill or sieve to remove any bean skins. Return the purée to the soup pot and stir in the vinegar, Madeira, lemon zest, lemon juice, and mace. Season to taste with salt and pepper; then pour into individual bowls. Garnish each portion with a lemon slice, chopped egg, and parsley.

Dutch Green Split Pea Soup *(Erwtensoep)*

I spent a year in Holland as a young child and even learned to speak Dutch. I don't remember much about that time, though I have a clear recollection of gorging myself on rich butter cookies. I ate so many that I couldn't stand the smell of butter cookies for years afterward. Holland has a simple, hearty cuisine with dishes like apple pannekoecken *(thick apple pancakes), herring in all forms (including the delicacy of raw, live herring eaten whole), tasty aged Gouda and Edam cheeses, and this soup. It's perfect for a cold, rainy day, and you can make a meal of it with buttered whole-grain bread, sliced aged Gouda, and a good Dutch apple cake for dessert.*

Serves 8

2 ham hocks
½ pound piece salt pork, rinsed (optional)
4 quarts water
1 pound (2 cups) green split peas
1 pound potatoes (yellow varieties, russets, or all-purpose), peeled and cut into small dice
1 bunch leeks, white and light green parts, sliced and washed
1 celery root, peeled and cut into small dice
Heart of 1 rib celery (including the leaves), cut into thin slices
1 tablespoon chopped fresh summer savory, or 1 teaspoon dried
½ pound cooked smoked sausage (such as kielbasa), sliced into rounds
Salt and freshly ground black pepper

1. Place ham hocks, salt pork, and water in a large soup pot and bring to a boil. Skim off and discard any white foam impurities that rise to the surface. Reduce the heat and simmer, covered, for 1 hour. Add the green split peas and return to a boil. Reduce the heat and simmer for 2 hours. Remove the salt pork and ham hocks; reserve until cool.

2. Add the potatoes, leeks, celery root, celery heart, and savory. Simmer for 30 minutes longer. Cut the salt pork into small dice and remove the meat from the cooled ham hock. Add the salt pork, ham hock meat, and sausage to the pot and season to taste with salt and black pepper. Simmer for 5 to 10 minutes to thoroughly heat the meat. Serve the soup in large bowls.

In upper New England, a French-Canadian person is often referred to as a "pea soup."

Faki
(Greek Lentil Soup)
(VEGETARIAN OPTION)

This delicious lentil soup is called faki *in Greek. It is a popular dish during the Lenten season, when meat is not eaten. Simple to make, with few ingredients—though each one is essential—it has full-bodied flavor and texture. Soups similar to this have long been part of the Greek diet. Imported Greek oregano, sold dried on the branch, is highly resinous, with a powerful aroma obtained by plants that have struggled to grow in rocky soil under the rays of a blazing sun. Like wine grapes, the more they struggle, the more flavor they develop. Though not traditional, French green lentils are excellent used in this soup, because they maintain their shape and nutty texture so well. For a vegetarian version, substitute Vegetable Stock (see page 323) for the chicken stock*

--- *Serves 6 to 8* ---

1 pound (2 cups) dried brown lentils

4 quarts Light Chicken Stock (see page 320)

2 cups chopped onions

1 cup diced carrots

1 cup sliced celery

1 tablespoon chopped garlic

½ cup tomato sauce, purchased or homemade

½ cup extra-virgin olive oil

1 tablespoon crumbled dried oregano, preferably Greek

Salt and freshly ground black pepper

¼ cup fresh lemon juice (from 1 to 2 lemons) or red wine vinegar

1. Place the lentils in a large soup pot with the Light Chicken Stock and bring to a boil. Reduce the heat and simmer for 1 hour or until tender.

2. Add the onions, carrots, celery, garlic, tomato sauce, olive oil, oregano, and salt and pepper to taste. Cook for 30 minutes longer, or until the soup is slightly thickened.

3. Just before serving, stir in the lemon juice or vinegar. Divide among soup bowls.

Spanish Chickpea Soup with Garlic-Mint Pesto

(VEGETARIAN OPTION)

This simple Spanish peasant soup is an example of how a few inexpensive ingredients can be transformed into a hearty and satisfying meal. The use of chickpeas shows the Arabic origin of the soup because the Arabs brought chickpeas along with many other foods to Spanish cuisine. The pesto is yet another variation on the theme of crushing fresh herbs with garlic and olive oil. Stirring in the pesto releases a heady aroma and infuses the soup with the bright flavor of uncooked herbs, garlic, and olive oil. For a vegetarian version, substitute Vegetable Stock (see page 323) for the chicken stock.

Serves 8

¾ cup extra-virgin olive oil
½ loaf country-style white bread (about ½ pound), crust trimmed, cut into small cubes
2 tablespoons chopped garlic
2 teaspoons salt
½ cup chopped Italian parsley leaves
½ cup chopped fresh mint leaves
4 cups cooked chickpeas with their cooking liquid (see Basic Cooking Chart, page 58)
2 quarts Rich Chicken Stock (see page 322)

1. Preheat the oven to 350°F. Make the croutons by tossing ½ cup of the olive oil with the bread cubes. Spread out on a baking pan and toast in the oven for 15 minutes, stirring after about 10 minutes for even browning. Remove from the oven and reserve.

2. In a food processor or blender, process the remaining ¼ cup olive oil with the garlic, salt, parsley, and mint to a thick green paste. Remove and reserve.

3. Bring the Rich Chicken Stock to a boil in a large soup pot, and add the chickpeas. Reduce the heat and simmer for 15 minutes. To serve the soup, ladle the chickpeas and broth into individual bowls. Let each person add a spoonful of the mint pesto to their bowl, stirring to release the aroma. Then top with the croutons.

CHICKPEA TALK

In Italy, a *cicerone* (meaning a large chickpea) is a guide who leads and informs sightseers. The name derives from that of the famed Roman orator Cicero because these guides are typically glib and loquacious. Cicero is said to have had a large wart on his face, and the Italian word for wart is *ceco* (chickpea).

CHAPTER SEVEN

Appetizers and Light Meals

Golden Risotto
with Baby Limas and Red Pepper
(VEGETARIAN)

The saffron called for here is the world's most expensive spice, costing about $45 when purchased by the ounce and much more if purchased in smaller quantities. In this case, more is not better because a little goes a long way—adding too much can produce a medicinal taste. Saffron's powerful, slightly acrid flavor permeates this risotto and tints it an unmistakably rich, warm, golden color. To maintain freshness, store saffron threads in a well-sealed plastic bag or glass jar in the freezer.

This is a variation on the classic Milanese risotto, which is simmered with saffron and traditionally served with braised veal shanks, or osso buco. Baby limas are a lovely pale green with a creamy texture and mild flavor. If you've never cared for limas, try baby limas and you might change your mind. You may substitute double-shelled baby favas (with inner skin removed) or frozen shelled edamame here, with excellent results.

Serves 4

Large pinch of saffron threads
½ cup dry white vermouth
2 tablespoons unsalted butter
½ cup chopped onion (about 1 medium)
2 tablespoons chopped shallot
  (about 1 large)
1 red bell pepper, seeded and diced
1 teaspoon chopped garlic
1 cup raw arborio or other short-grain
  rice
3½ cups Vegetable Stock (see page 323)
  or Rich Chicken Stock (see page 323),
  simmering
1 (10-ounce) package frozen baby lima
  beans, green favas, or edamame
¼ cup freshly grated Parmigiano-
  Reggiano cheese
2 tablespoons chopped Italian parsley
  leaves
Salt and freshly ground black pepper

1. Add the saffron to the dry white vermouth and reserve.

2. In a large saucepan over medium heat, melt the butter. Add the onion, shallot, and red pepper and cook, stirring frequently, for about 5 minutes, or until the onion is tender. Stir in the garlic and rice. Cook 2 minutes, stirring constantly. Stir in the vermouth-saffron mixture and bring to a boil. When the vermouth has been absorbed, add about 1½ cups of the hot stock. Heat to boiling, then reduce the heat. Simmer, uncovered, stirring occasionally, until most of the liquid is absorbed. Stir in 1¼ cups of the remaining stock and the lima beans. Simmer, uncovered, stirring occasionally, until most of the liquid is absorbed. Add the remaining 1¼ cups stock and continue cooking until the liquid has been absorbed and the rice is tender, about 15 minutes. Stir in the cheese and parsley, and season to taste with salt and black pepper. Sprinkle each portion with additional black pepper as desired.

Green and Yellow Bean Curry with Cauliflower

(VEGETARIAN)

This colorful, aromatic vegetable curry calls for a panoply of pungent Indian spices. Indian groceries are the best places to buy fresh and inexpensive spices, although many of these spices or substitutes are available in supermarkets, too. The black mustard seeds put a sharp edge on the flavor of the dish, but yellow mustard seeds can be substituted. The acrid aroma of fenugreek says "curry," but is optional. Garam masala, the traditional Indian spice mix, which typically includes black pepper and fragrant sweet spices such as cinnamon, clove, and allspice, is also available in specialty stores and Indian groceries, but I have included a recipe. Recipes for garam masala vary according to regional styles and personal tastes.

--- *Serves 6* ---

Seasoning Paste

1 (2-inch) piece fresh ginger, peeled and chopped

3 cloves garlic

1 jalapeño pepper, seeded and chopped

1 teaspoon turmeric

½ teaspoon ground fenugreek

½ teaspoon Garam Masala (see page 313), or purchased

1 teaspoon ground cumin

¼ cup fresh lime juice (about 2 limes)

Vegetables

2 tablespoons peanut oil

2 teaspoons black mustard seeds

1 white onion, sliced into strips

1 head cauliflower or broccoflower, cut into florets

½ pound fresh green beans, cut into 2-inch lengths

½ pound fresh wax beans, cut into 2-inch lengths

2 red or yellow peppers, cut into 1-inch squares

½ pound sugar snap peas, trimmed

1 cup diced plum tomatoes (fresh or canned)

Salt, to taste

1. Prepare the Seasoning Paste: In a blender or food processor, process the ginger, garlic, jalapeño, turmeric, fenugreek, Garam Masala, cumin, and lime juice until smooth. Reserve.

2. Prepare the Vegetables: Heat the peanut oil in a large skillet over medium heat. Add the mustard seeds and cover the pan to prevent the seeds from popping out. As the seeds start to pop, add the onion and cook for 3 minutes more. Add the cauliflower, green beans, and wax beans. Cook for 3 minutes more. Add the peppers and sugar snaps.

3. Stir the seasoning paste into the vegetables and cook for 5 minutes. Stir in the tomatoes, season with salt, and serve immediately.

Socca (Chickpea Flour Tart Niçoise)
with Roasted Peppers and Goat Cheese
(VEGETARIAN)

This delicious, crispy, thin chickpea flour tart, called socca *in Provençal dialect, is commonly served hot as a snack in Nice, France, and along the French and Italian Rivieras. Chickpea flour is available at most Indian groceries and health food stores. Be sure to keep the flour in the freezer to prevent spoilage.*

Serves 6

Chickpea Flour Tart
8 tablespoons olive oil
2 cups chickpea flour
3 cups water
Salt and freshly ground black pepper

Roasted Bell Pepper Topping
1 tablespoon chopped fresh herbs, such
    as marjoram, thyme, or savory
4 cloves garlic, peeled
2 teaspoons salt
¼ cup extra-virgin olive oil
½ teaspoon freshly ground black pepper
4 red or orange bell peppers, cut into
    quarters and seeded
¼ pound fresh mild goat cheese,
    crumbled, for serving

1. Prepare the Chickpea Flour Tart: Generously brush a 12-inch round pizza pan with 1 tablespoon of the olive oil. Mix the chickpea flour, 6 tablespoons oil, water, and salt and pepper to taste in a bowl. Stir well to create a batter and let stand at room temperature for 1 hour.

2. Prepare the Roasted Bell Pepper Topping: Preheat the oven to 400°F. Chop together the herbs, garlic, and salt until mixture is chunky. Mix with the olive oil and black pepper in a large bowl. Add the quartered pepper and toss. Spread the peppers in a single layer on a baking sheet. Roast for 15 to 20 minutes, or until the peppers are well-browned at the edges. Cool.

3. Preheat the broiler. Pour a thin layer (about ⅛ inch) of the reserved tart batter into the prepared pizza pan. Place the pan under the broiler, as close to the heat source as possible. Broil for 3 minutes or until bubbling. Remove from the oven and sprinkle with the remaining 1 tablespoon olive oil. Broil for 5 to 10 minutes longer, or until the tart is crispy and golden watching carefully so the tart doesn't burn. Sprinkle with salt and pepper to taste. Slide onto a serving platter and cut into 2-inch squares. Top each square with a few of the roasted peppers and sprinkle with the crumbled goat cheese. Serve immediately.

SOCCA AND TORTA DI CECI

According to the great Italian culinary authority Anna Gosetti della Salda, *torta di ceci*, the Italian version of *socca*, should be baked in a wood-burning bread oven because of the smoky flavor it imparts. This dish is not served at the table, but is tasted and savored throughout the day as a snack. To serve it Italian style, cut the *torta* into diamond shapes and accompany it with apéritifs like Martini & Rossi, half sweet and half dry; Lillet with orange; Dubonnet; or a glass of Italian *spumante* or *prosecco* (sparkling wine).

Oaxacan Corn Tortillas in Black Bean Sauce (*Enfrijoladas*)

Oaxaca is one of the gastronomic capitals of Mexico and home to wonderful open-air markets. This typical Oaxacan dish is ideally served at a light brunch. It is unusual because the tortillas are fried and then dipped in a bean sauce, which results in a texture that is crunchy on the inside and soft on the outside. Because many of our larger cities now have large Mexican populations, you can often find specialty cheeses like the queso fresco *(fresh white cheese) used here.*

—————————— *Serves 6 to 8* ——————————

½ head garlic

4 tablespoons lard or vegetable oil

1 small onion, sliced

1 or 2 small dried red chiles (optional)

1 tablespoon crumbled dried epazote, or avocado leaves (see Cook's Note)

About 1 cup water

1 recipe (6 cups) Earthenware-Cooked Beans (see page 300), prepared with black turtle beans

Kosher salt

¼ cup vegetable oil

1 package 6-inch corn tortillas (about 12)

1 white onion, sliced into thin rings, for serving

½ cup crumbled Mexican *queso fresco* (or mild French feta, ricotta salata, or fresh farmer cheese)

¼ cup sliced pickled jalapeños, for serving

1. Char the head of garlic on a hot grill, over a gas flame, or on an electric coil until the skin is blackened. Cool, peel, and reserve.

2. In a large skillet, heat 2 tablespoons of the lard. Add the sliced onion and dried chiles and fry until lightly browned. Transfer the mixture to a blender (with or without the chiles, depending on how hot you'd like the dish) or use a hand-held blender. Add the epazote, garlic cloves, and about ½ cup water. Purée until smooth. Working in batches, if necessary, add the Earthenware-Cooked Beans and their liquid and blend until smooth. If necessary, add about ½ cup more water to blend.

3. Heat the remaining 2 tablespoons lard in a skillet; stir in the bean purée. Cook about 10 minutes over medium heat, stirring up from the bottom to prevent sticking. Season to taste with salt. Partially cover, so the bean sauce doesn't form a crust but has enough air circulation to prevent fermentation, and reserve.

4. Just before serving the dish, reheat the bean sauce, adding a little water if it has thickened. It should be thin enough to lightly coat the tortillas.

5. In a skillet, heat the oil, add the tortillas one at a time, and fry just until they begin to get crispy and are thoroughly heated. Drain on paper towels. Immerse the tortillas, one at a time, in the warm bean sauce and then fold into quarters. Sprinkle each serving of 1 to 2 tortillas with onion rings, crumbled cheese, and several slices of pickled jalapeños.

COOK'S NOTE

In Oaxaca, charred avocado leaves are used for flavoring. To prepare, hold a sprig of the tender avocado leaves or half a dozen larger leaves over a flame to singe them slightly and just bring out their aroma. Cool and crumble the leaves, discarding the stems. Use in place of the epazote in this recipe.

Chinese Steamed Clams
with Fermented Black Bean Sauce

These steamed clams are served in a sauce made from pungent fermented black beans accented with chopped ginger and garlic. Steamed clams seem to cry out for wine, garlic, and hot pepper, as in the classic Italian preparation. Here the wine is rice wine instead of the white wine favored in Italy. The garlic and hot red pepper remain, but the ginger and the two derivatives of the soybean family (soy sauce and fermented black beans) give it a Chinese flavor. Although it's not traditional, serve these clams with a crusty French baguette to mop up the delicious sauce, and there won't be any left. You won't need to add any salt here, as the clam juices, soy sauce, and fermented black beans are all salty.

Serves 6

½ cup bottled clam juice or Light Chicken Stock (see page 320)

2 tablespoons soy sauce

2 teaspoons sugar

¼ cup rice wine

2 teaspoons cornstarch

2 tablespoons soybean oil

2 tablespoons fermented black beans, lightly rinsed and coarsely chopped

1 bunch scallions, white and green parts sliced separately

1½ tablespoons chopped garlic

1½ tablespoons chopped fresh ginger

1 teaspoon Korean red pepper flakes or hot red pepper flakes

48 littleneck clams, scrubbed (see Cleaning Clams, below)

1. In a small bowl, combine the clam juice, soy sauce, and sugar. In a separate bowl, combine the rice wine and cornstarch.

2. Heat a wok or a large skillet over high heat; then add the oil and swirl around until coated. Add the black beans, white parts of the scallions, garlic, ginger, and pepper flakes. Stir-fry for about 30 seconds, or until the mixture releases its fragrance. Add the clam juice mixture and heat until boiling, stirring constantly.

3. Add the clams, cover, and cook, shaking the wok occasionally, until most of the clams have opened. (So as not to overcook the clams, pry open the last few partially opened clams using the edge of a pair of tongs, a clam knife, or the edge of an icing spatula.) Discard any clams that have sand inside or that do not open.

4. Scoop the clams out of the wok, placing them in a deep bowl to keep warm. Slowly, while stirring constantly, add the rice wine mixture to the wok and bring to a boil. Spoon the sauce over the clams and sprinkle with the sliced scallion greens. Serve immediately.

CLEANING CLAMS

To clean fresh clams, first place them in a sinkful or large pot of cold water. Scrub the clams well, using a scrub brush or a clean scouring pad and lots of cold water. Discard the water, place the clams in fresh salted water, and soak for 20 to 30 minutes to purge them of any sand inside. Remove from the water and keep cold until ready to cook.

Chickpea Flour Pizza
with Arugula and Roasted Tomatoes

(VEGETARIAN)

Chickpea flour gives a nutty flavor to this pizza topped with all sorts of intensely flavored ingredients from the Riviera. If you like really funky flavors, substitute shriveled, shiny, black oil-cured olives for the pointed purple Kalamatas. Make this pizza in summertime when local arugula is available. Because the arugula is cooked, which tones down its flavor, local field-grown arugula (instead of the more expensive hydroponically grown type) is best. Just be sure to wash it thoroughly and vigorously because it tends to be quite sandy.

—————————————— *Serves 4 to 6* ——————————————

Dough

2¾ cups all-purpose flour

¾ cup chickpea flour (see Sources, page 341)

1 teaspoon salt

1 package active dry yeast (about 1 tablespoon)

1 to 1½ cups warm water

2 tablespoons olive oil

Topping

1 tablespoon chopped garlic

4 tablespoons olive oil

2 bunches arugula, trimmed of large stems and washed thoroughly

12 Oven-Roasted Plum Tomatoes, cut into strips (see recipe, page 309)

½ pound goat cheese, crumbled

½ pound fresh mozzarella, cut into small cubes

1 cup Kalamata olives, halved and pitted

1. Prepare the Dough: In a food processor or a mixer fitted with the dough hook, combine flours, salt, and yeast. Combine 1 cup warm water with the olive oil. With the motor on low speed, slowly add just enough water to form a soft dough that sticks to your fingers but can be pulled away cleanly and easily from the sides of the mixing bowl. Add the remaining water, if necessary. When the dough is smooth and elastic, set it aside to rise in an oiled bowl in a warm place, covered tightly with plastic wrap, until doubled in volume, about 2 hours.

2. Meanwhile, prepare the Topping: In a large skillet, heat the garlic in 2 tablespoons olive oil until sizzling. Add the arugula leaves and cook until wilted. Remove from the heat and cool to room temperature.

3. About 20 minutes before you want to make the pizza, preheat the oven to 475°F, using a pizza stone, if available. Punch down the dough, divide into two balls, and roll into two round pizza shells. If using pans, transfer to two lightly oiled baking sheets. If using a pizza stone, roll the dough balls out into circles and transfer to a floured wooden peel.

4. Brush each pizza round lightly with the remaining 2 tablespoons of olive oil, especially on the edges. Arrange the cooked arugula, tomato halves, goat cheese, mozzarella, and olives in an attractive pattern on each pizza round. Bake until well browned, about 8 minutes, and then cut into eight wedges.

Bahian Acarajé Fritters with Ajili Mojili

(VEGETARIAN OPTION)

Several years ago, I visited Brazil with a group of chefs from the restaurant Sushi Samba, of which there are now four—two in New York City, one in Chicago, and one in Miami. We set out to explore the intriguing cuisine of this multiethnic, multiracial country. One highlight was our visit to Salvador, the capital of Bahia province, the first Portuguese settlement in Brazil in 1500 and a center of Afro-Brazilian culture and cuisine. There, acarajé *fritters, often split and stuffed with the dried shrimp cream called* vatapá, *are prepared in small fry pots along the narrow, winding cobblestone streets by adherents of Condomblé, who revere these fritters as the ritual food preferred by the goddess Yansâ, ruler of tempests and winds.*

Serve the fritters, either plain or split and stuffed with the vatapá, *with Brazilian Lemon-Pepper Mojo (see page 304) or with this Puerto Rican sauce that complements fried foods. For authentic Afro-Brazilian flavor, fry the fritters in 3 cups canola oil mixed with 1 cup Brazilian* dendê *oil or palm oil. For a vegetarian version, just leave out the* vatapá.

Serves 8

1 pound (2 cups) black-eyed peas, soaked for 4 to 6 hours, drained, and rinsed (see Soaking Chart, page 57)
½ cup water
1 cup minced onion
¼ cup chopped cilantro
1 teaspoon hot sauce or chopped pickled *malagueta* chile
Salt and freshly ground black pepper
1 quart canola oil, for frying
Ajili Mojili Sauce (recipe follows)
Vatapá (recipe follows) (optional)

1. Loosen the outer skins of the peas by rubbing them between your hands. Transfer the peas to a large bowl of water; the skins will float to the top. Skim off and discard the skins. Drain the peas and transfer to the bowl of a food processor. Process the peas, adding the water gradually until you have a thick smooth paste. Fold in the onion, cilantro, and hot sauce, and season generously with salt and pepper.

2. In a large pot, heat the oil to 365°F. Drop in the bean paste, 1 rounded tablespoon at a time, without crowding. Fry the fritters on both sides until browned and crispy, about 5 minutes. Skim from the oil and drain on paper towels. Serve with Ajili Mojili Sauce. If desired, split open the fritters and fill with Vatapá.

Ajili Mojili Sauce

2 red bell peppers, roasted, peeled, and
    seeded
1 canned chipotle chile in adobo, seeded,
    liquid reserved
2 teaspoons chopped garlic
2 tablespoons cider vinegar
Juice of 1 lime
1 teaspoon crushed black peppercorns
1 tablespoon kosher salt
¼ cup extra-virgin olive oil
½ cup finely diced red onion

In a food processor, combine the peppers, seeded chipotle and its liquid, garlic, cider vinegar, lime juice, crushed peppercorns, and salt to form a chunky paste. Whisk in the olive oil, stir in the red onion, and refrigerate. Store, refrigerated, for up to 1 week.

Vatapá (Spicy Shrimp Purée)

— 3 cups —

½ loaf stale French or Italian bread
2 cups milk
1 cup dried shrimp
½ cup roasted peanuts
½ cup roasted cashews
¼ cup cilantro leaves
1 small onion, peeled and quartered
1 clove garlic
1 (1-inch) section peeled fresh ginger
½ teaspoon grated nutmeg
Juice of 1 lime
1 teaspoon hot sauce
1 cup unsweetened coconut cream
½ cup *dendê* oil (see Sources, page 341)
½ pound cooked shrimp, finely chopped
Salt

Soak the bread in the milk until soft. Squeeze out and discard liquid. In a food processor, combine the bread, dried shrimp, peanuts, cashews, cilantro, onion, garlic and ginger, and process to a fine paste. Transfer to a large nonreactive skillet and simmer, stirring constantly, for 10 minutes. Add the nutmeg, lime juice, hot sauce, coconut cream, and *dendê* oil, and simmer 10 minutes longer. Just before serving, stir in the cooked shrimp and salt to taste (note that the dried shrimp can be quite salty).

Black Bean Burgers
on Garlic Toasted Buns
(VEGETARIAN)

These tasty burgers are a welcome and satisfying alternative to beef burgers. Even my meat-loving daughter came back for seconds. Because these cakes tend to absorb oil and stick to the pan, it's best to brown them in a nonstick skillet. Top them with fresh Pico de Gallo Salsa and sliced avocado, and even die-hard meat eaters will be clamoring for more. The hazelnuts have a bittersweet flavor that I really like here, but you could substitute sweeter, buttery pecans.

--- *Serves 8* ---

1 recipe Black Bean and Hazelnut Cakes, prepared through Step 1 (see page 171)
2 tablespoons (¼ stick) butter, softened
2 teaspoons minced garlic
8 hamburger buns
¼ cup canola oil
1 firm but ripe avocado, cut into thin slices
1½ cups Pico de Gallo Salsa (see page 319)
1 head Boston lettuce, leaves separated, washed and patted dry

1. Preheat the oven to 375°F. Shape the bean mixture into eight burgers and reserve in the refrigerator. Place the butter and garlic in a small bowl and beat with a spoon until well combined. Split the buns and spread the garlic butter over the inside halves. Wrap the buns in foil and bake for 6 to 8 minutes, or until lightly browned but still soft inside.

2. Meanwhile, heat the oil in a nonstick skillet. Add the burgers and brown on both sides over medium heat, about 6 minutes per side. Transfer the burgers to a baking pan and bake for 10 minutes, or until somewhat firm. Place the browned burgers on the bottom halves of the toasted buns, and top each burger with a few lettuce leaves, 3 or 4 slices of avocado, and ¼ cup Pico de Gallo. Serve immediately.

Pan-Seared Scallops over Autumn Beluga Lentil Ragout
with Corn-Saffron Vinaigrette

I first prepared this dish with its warm palette of autumn colors for a special fall dinner featuring the superb wines of California's Far Niente Vineyards. This course was served with their Nickel & Nickel Suscol Ranch Merlot 1999. The elegant black beluga lentils studded with bits of fennel, squash, and corn are accented by the creamy, strikingly yellow vinaigrette made with corn and saffron. Saffron is actually the three threadlike filaments inside the autumn-flowering Crocus sativus. More than 225,000 stigmas must be hand-picked to produce one pound of saffron. Although saffron is expensive, a little goes a long way; 1 gram is enough to flavor and color about ten recipes. I recommend Penzeys or Kalustyan's (see Sources, page 341) for Internet and mail-order purchase of saffron. Both places sell it in different grades, along with every other exotic spice you can think of.

--- *Serves 4 to 6* ---

Marinated Scallops
¼ cup olive oil
1 tablespoon chopped fresh thyme
Grated zest of 1 lemon
Salt and black pepper to taste
2 pounds large natural (or dry-pack) sea
  scallops, with hard adductor muscle
  on the side trimmed off

Corn-Saffron Vinaigrette
½ teaspoon saffron threads
¼ cup champagne vinegar
2 tablespoons butter
2 cups white or yellow corn kernels
  (about 2 ears fresh corn)
Salt and black pepper to taste
½ cup plus 2 tablespoons mild olive oil
  or grapeseed oil
2 tablespoons vegetable oil

Lentil Ragout
2 tablespoons butter
1 bunch scallions, sliced on the bias
1 small fennel bulb, finely diced
1 cup finely diced butternut squash or
  other dense winter squash
1 cup white or yellow corn kernels
2 cups Basic Cooked French Green Lentils,
  made with beluga lentils (see page 298)
2 tablespoons chopped mixed tender
  herbs, such as thyme, basil, tarragon,
  chervil, and/or Italian parsley
Kosher salt and black pepper

1. Prepare the Marinated Scallops: In a medium, nonreactive, glass or stainless-steel bowl, combine the olive oil, thyme, lemon zest, salt, and pepper. Toss with the scallops and marinate, refrigerated, for at least 2 hours or up to overnight.

2. Prepare the Corn-Saffron Vinaigrette: Crumble the saffron in the vinegar and allow it to steep for at least 10 minutes. In a medium skillet, melt the butter over moderate heat. Add the corn kernels and cook for about 5 minutes, or until thoroughly cooked but not browned. Scrape the corn into the container of a blender and add the saffron-vinegar mixture, salt, and pepper. Blend until smooth, add the olive oil, and blend again. Strain the vinaigrette through a sieve to remove the corn skins. Cover and refrigerate until ready to use. (Vinaigrette keeps for up to 3 days.)

3. Prepare the Lentil Ragout: In a large skillet, melt the butter and add the scallions. Sauté briefly and add the fennel, squash, and corn. Cook for 3 to 4 minutes, until the squash is cooked through but still firm. Add the Basic Cooked French Green Lentils and cook for several minutes, until the mixture is hot and somewhat thickened. Keep warm.

4. In a large skillet, preferably nonstick, heat the vegetable oil until shimmering hot, but not quite smoking. Add the scallops and sear until well browned on both sides but still rare in the middle, about 3 minutes per side. Transfer the scallops to a plate and keep warm.

5. At the last minute, stir the chopped herbs into the lentils and season with salt and pepper to taste. Place a mound of lentils on each of four dinner plates. Arrange the scallops around the lentils and drizzle with the vinaigrette and any scallop cooking juices.

Portuguese Green Peas
with Chorizo and Eggs

Here is a simple, filling dish from Portugal's southern Algarve coastal country that is perfect for a brunch menu. If you live near a Portuguese neighborhood, look for linguiça, *a long, thin, tongue-shaped sausage flavored with lots of garlic and paprika. Otherwise, a Spanish-style* chourico, chorizo, *or even Italian pepperoni will do. Poaching is one cooking technique that reveals if an egg is fresh. A fresh egg will poach into a neat, firm oval; an older egg will be runny and hard to form. I use jumbo eggs here because they are easier to poach so that the whites are firm and the yolk is still liquid.*

—————————— *Serves 6* ——————————

2 tablespoons olive oil

1 medium onion, chopped

2 red bell peppers, seeded, cored, and cut into thin strips

½ pound *linguiça, chourico,* chorizo, or pepperoni, thinly sliced

2 pounds fresh green peas, shelled, or 2 (12-ounce) packages frozen green peas, rinsed

4½ cups water

Salt and freshly ground black pepper

2 tablespoons white vinegar

1 tablespoon salt

6 very fresh jumbo eggs, preferably organic

2 tablespoons chopped fresh cilantro leaves

1. In a medium heavy pot with a lid, heat the olive oil and sauté the onion, bell peppers, and *linguiça* until the onion is softened but not browned. Reduce the heat as low as possible, cover, and cook for 15 to 20 minutes, or until thickened. Add the fresh or frozen peas and ½ cup water and continue cooking until the peas are tender. Season with salt and pepper to taste.

2. In a medium, shallow saucepan, bring the remaining 4 cups water to a simmer. Stir in the vinegar and salt. Break open each egg and drop carefully, one at a time, into the simmering water. Cook for 3 to 4 minutes, depending on how you prefer the yolks cooked. The whites should be firm and opaque and the yolks still liquid in the center. Remove the eggs, using a slotted spoon, and gently place on a clean kitchen towel or paper towels to drain.

3. To serve, divide the pea mixture among six shallow serving bowls. Form a hollow in the center of each bowl and place a poached egg in it. Sprinkle with the chopped cilantro and serve immediately.

Asian Wrap Sandwich
with Shiitakes, Bean Sprouts, and Hoisin Sauce

(VEGETARIAN)

In the nineties, every restaurant trade magazine was filled with stories about wraps, the purported "sandwich of the future." For a while, it seemed as though they were everywhere. Though the publicity has waned, wrap sandwiches are still good, especially when they're stuffed with full-flavored ingredients cooked to order for best texture. This Asian vegetarian wrap combines crunchy bok choy cabbage and bean sprouts with the smoky, earthy flavor of shiitake mushrooms, in a dressing of assertive Chinese seasonings: hoisin sauce, roasted sesame oil, and mushroom soy sauce.

Serves 6

1 cup water
½ cup long-grain rice
½ cup hoisin sauce
¼ cup mushroom soy sauce
2 tablespoons roasted Japanese sesame oil
2 tablespoons grated fresh ginger
4 tablespoons peanut oil
1 head bok choy cabbage, sliced into 1-inch shreds
1 pound shiitake mushrooms, stems removed, caps sliced
2 cups fresh bean sprouts, rinsed and drained
½ cup chopped fresh cilantro leaves (about 1 bunch)
1 bunch scallions, white and green parts, thinly sliced
6 (10-inch) whole wheat tortillas

1. In a small saucepan with a lid, bring the water to a boil. Add the rice. Cover and cook for 15 minutes over very low heat until tender and fluffy. Remove from heat and cool. Reserve.

2. In a small bowl, combine the hoisin, soy sauce, sesame oil, and ginger.

3. In a wok or large skillet, heat 2 tablespoons of the peanut oil. Add the bok choy and stir-fry until bright green and slightly softened, about 3 minutes. Remove from the wok and reserve in a bowl. Wipe out the wok with paper towels.

4. Heat the remaining 2 tablespoons peanut oil in the wok. Add the mushrooms and stir-fry until softened and lightly browned. Pour in the reserved hoisin sauce mixture and bring to a boil. Transfer the mushroom mixture to the bowl with the bok choy. Add the cooked rice, bean sprouts, cilantro, and scallions, mixing well.

5. Lightly heat the tortillas for 15 seconds in the microwave (or wrap in foil and bake at 350°F for 5 to 10 minutes). Spread the tortillas out on a flat surface. Place one-sixth of the filling (about 1¼ cups) on the bottom half of each tortilla, forming it into a 6 by 2-inch rectangle. Fold in the right and left sides of the tortilla to the center over the filling. Fold the bottom edge over the filling; then fold and continue to roll up like an egg roll. Place seam side down on a baking pan. (If desired, refrigerate the wraps, covered with plastic wrap, for up to 1 day.)

6. Preheat the oven to 350°F. Wrap each sandwich individually in foil and place on a baking sheet. Bake for 10 to 15 minutes, or until the wrap steams when pricked through the foil with a fork.

French Green Lentils
with Black Truffles and Caramelized Shallots

We think of lentils as earthy, even plebeian, but not in this dish, adapted from the cookbook I coauthored with the great chef Georges Perrier. At Le Bec-Fin, his Philadelphia "restaurant classique," he serves the lentils with glazed pearl onions. Here I've substituted shallots—I prefer their taste and they're easier to peel. The truffles' loamy earthiness and pungency are perfectly complemented by the nutty, slightly granular quality of the lentils, while caramelized shallots make the whole dish very appealing.

Serves 6

1 quart Rich Chicken Stock (see page 322)

1 (12-ounce) package dried French green lentils

1 whole fresh black winter truffle, scrubbed and peeled, or 1 canned winter truffle plus 2 tablespoons truffle juice

2 tablespoons (¼ stick) unsalted butter

½ cup rendered duck fat (see About Duck Fat, page 329), or 4 tablespoons (½ stick) unsalted butter

½ pound firm fresh shallots, peeled and quartered

1 tablespoon sugar

Salt and freshly ground black pepper

1 bunch fresh chives, thinly sliced

1. Combine the lentils and the Rich Chicken Stock in a heavy-bottomed pot and bring to a boil. Reduce the heat to very low and simmer for about 45 minutes, or until the lentils are cooked through but still firm—the skins shouldn't split open. (You can also cook the lentils in a 300°F oven, covered, until they're tender but still firm.) Drain off and reserve any cooking juices and keep the lentils warm in their cooking pot.

2. Cut the truffle into tiny dice. In a small saucepan, reduce the lentil cooking juices (and the juices from the canned truffle, if using) to ¼ cup and mix in the diced truffles. Whisk in the butter, and reserve.

3. Preheat the oven to 300°F. In an ovenproof pan over medium heat, heat the duck fat until sizzling, and add the shallots. When they begin to brown, add the sugar and cover with a lid or aluminum foil. Place the pan in the oven and roast the shallots until tender, about 15 minutes. Drain off and discard the duck fat.

4. Have ready six shallow soup plates, preferably heated. Season the lentils to taste with salt and pepper. Ladle each portion into a soup plate. Cover each portion of lentils with the reserved truffle sauce, making sure each serving has its portion of truffle. Divide the caramelized shallots among the six plates and sprinkle with chives.

Black Bean and Hazelnut Cakes
with Steamed Clams

Derek Davis, chef-owner of the Main Street Restaurants Group in Philadelphia, has made a name for himself as the kingpin of the city's revitalized Manayunk neighborhood. An old and proud working-class neighborhood, in recent years it has become a magnet for boutiques and restaurants. This recipe is from Derek's California restaurant, Sonoma. I love the combination of flavors. These cakes are quite versatile: you can double the recipe and freeze half the mixture, then defrost it in the microwave, form into larger "bean burgers," and prepare them following the recipes for Black Bean Burgers on Garlic Toasted Buns (see page 166).

—————————— *Serves 12 as an appetizer; 6 to 8 as an entrée* ——————————

Black Bean Cakes

6 cups cooked black beans, drained (reserving some of the liquid separately; see Basic Cooking Chart, page 58) and rinsed

1 small white onion, roughly chopped

1 poblano chile, trimmed, seeded, and roughly chopped

2 jalapeño peppers, trimmed, seeded, and roughly chopped

6 cloves garlic

1 cup hazelnuts, toasted, skinned, and coarsely chopped

Salt

½ to 1 cup bread crumbs

½ cup vegetable oil

Clams

6 dozen littleneck clams, cleaned (see Cleaning Clams, page 162)

2 cups chopped plum tomatoes

2 cups diced tomatillos

2 tablespoons chopped garlic

1 cup dry white wine

¼ pound (1 stick) unsalted butter

3 tablespoons chopped fresh cilantro leaves

12 fresh cilantro sprigs, for garnish

1. Prepare the Black Bean Cakes: Combine the black beans, onion, poblano, and jalapeños in the bowl of a food processor and pulse until smooth, adding a little of the reserved cooking liquid, if necessary. (*Note:* The drier the bean mixture is, the fewer bread crumbs it will need to make a proper texture.) Fold in the hazelnuts. Season to taste with salt. Cool and then add enough bread crumbs so the mixture holds its shape.

2. Using about ½ cup of the mixture for each, form into cakes shaped like hockey pucks. (The cakes may be prepared several days ahead and refrigerated, or even frozen.) Just before serving, heat the oil in a skillet, preferably nonstick, over medium heat. Add the cakes and cook for 5 minutes on each side, until browned.

3. Prepare the Clams: Combine the clams, tomatoes, tomatillos, garlic, and wine in a large pot with a lid. Steam over high heat for about 8 minutes, discarding any clams that don't open. When the clams are open, stir in the butter and chopped cilantro.

4. To serve, place each black bean cake in the center of a large plate. Surround each cake with 6 clams. Spoon the butter sauce over the clams. Garnish with fresh cilantro sprigs.

COOK'S NOTE

If you have a meat grinder, use it to grind the black bean mixture. The texture will be somewhat chunky and you won't need to add any liquid, so the cakes will hold together with less, if any, bread crumbs.

Bouillabaisse of Little Peas Escudier

(VEGETARIAN)

When Jean-Noël Escudier (also known as Monsieur Provence) published his classic cookbook La Véritable Cuisine Provençale *in France in 1953, it was the first anthology of authentic Provençal recipes. As an inveterate flea-market treasure hunter, I picked up Peta Fuller's English version, titled* The Wonderful Food of Provence, *for a mere $2 and proceeded to fall in love. According to Escudier, this simple dish of tiny peas is actually considered a bouillabaisse. It is an ancient Provençal way of dressing peas with wild fennel, potatoes, poached eggs, and bread. American domesticated Florence fennel or sweet anise is much sweeter and more delicate. To intensify its licorice-like flavor, I add ground fennel seed.*

Serves 4

2 medium onions, diced

¼ cup extra-virgin olive oil

1 large (28-ounce) can chopped plum tomatoes

½ pound potatoes (preferably yellow), peeled and cut into thick slices

2 quarts boiling water

1 bouquet garni, Provençal style (1 sprig thyme, 2 sprigs Italian parsley, 1 bay leaf, 1 strip orange peel, and 1 tablespoon fennel seeds tied together or placed in a cheesecloth bag)

3 cloves garlic

1 small fennel bulb, diced

1 teaspoon ground fennel seed

Salt and freshly ground black pepper

6 cups shelled fresh little peas, or 2 (12-ounce) boxes frozen petits pois rinsed in cold water

4 cups water

2 tablespoons white vinegar

1 tablespoon salt, for poaching

4 eggs

½ loaf country-style bread (about ½ pound), sliced about ½ inch thick and toasted

1. In a large pan, cook the onions in the oil until transparent. Add the tomatoes and potatoes, and toss. Pour in the boiling water and add the bouquet garni, garlic, diced fennel, fennel seed, salt, and pepper to taste. Cover and boil over high heat until the potatoes are almost tender, about 5 minutes. Add the fresh or frozen peas and cook for 2 to 3 minutes longer.

2. In a medium, shallow pan, bring the 4 cups water to a simmer. Stir in the vinegar and salt. Break open each egg and drop carefully, one at a time, into the simmering water. Cook for 3 to 4 minutes, depending on how you prefer the yolks cooked. (The whites should be firm and opaque and the yolks still liquid in the middle.) Remove the eggs using a slotted spoon and gently place on a clean towel or paper towels to drain.

3. To serve, lay a toasted bread slice in each of four large soup plates. Top with a poached egg; then ladle some of the bouillabaisse over the top.

Frittata with Romano Beans,
Prosciutto, and Fontina

Why is a frittata different from other egg dishes? Similar to a Spanish tortilla, it's more of an egg cake than an omelet. Frittata is an ideal lunch or light supper dish. It can easily be made an hour or two ahead, then briefly reheated in the microwave or simply served at room temperature, as is common in Italy. Growing up, I loved the bias-cut "Italian beans" my mother would buy in boxes from the freezer case. It took a trip to Italy to discover the real thing: fresh romano beans. They have a distinct beany flavor, a chewy texture, and when they're young, a lovely, velvety skin that begs to be caressed. They work wonderfully with prosciutto. It's worthwhile to seek out genuine Fontina cheese made in the Val d'Aosta of northern Italy. It's full flavored with rich nuttiness and melts beautifully. There are many imitations with similar names, such as Fontinella and Fontal. Fontina-type cheeses are also made in Scandinavia and the United States. I have not found these imitations to compare with the real thing.

Serves 6

1 pound fresh romano beans, cut into
  ½-inch lengths
4 tablespoons extra-virgin olive oil
1 large onion, diced
¼ to ½ pound prosciutto in one piece,
  trimmed of excess fat, frozen until
  firm, and cut into small dice
12 eggs, lightly beaten
½ pound imported Italian Fontina cheese,
  shredded
Salt and freshly ground black pepper

1. In a medium pan, precook the beans in boiling water for 4 minutes, or until crisp-tender. Drain and rinse under cold running water.

2. In a large (12-inch) ovenproof skillet, heat 2 tablespoons of the olive oil. Add the onion and prosciutto and cook over medium heat until lightly browned. Add the reserved beans; then remove the skillet from the heat. In a large bowl, combine the bean mixture with the eggs, along with half of the cheese, and salt and pepper to taste.

3. Preheat the broiler to high. Wipe out the skillet with a paper towel. Add the remaining 2 tablespoons olive oil and warm over medium heat. Pour in the egg mixture and cook for about 6 minutes, shaking occasionally, until most of the egg sets (the top should be soft and somewhat liquid). Sprinkle the frittata with the remaining ¼ pound cheese and place the skillet under the broiler for 2 to 3 minutes, or until the cheese is bubbling and browned and the eggs are set on top.

4. Cool slightly and then cut into wedges. Serve accompanied by roasted potatoes, if desired.

Haricots Verts and Fried Quail Eggs
in Black Truffle Vinaigrette

(VEGETARIAN)

Haricots verts, *which simply mean "green beans" in French, are fashionably pencil-thin green beans hand-picked at just the right size. Commercial ones from Central America come all lined up like a box of green pencils, but are often somewhat shriveled.* Look for haricots verts *from local growers at farmers markets in midsummer, or substitute young, slender green beans. The sweetest, plumpest ones I've ever eaten came from Bucks County's Branch Creek Farm, organic growers of fine vegetables, herbs, and greens.* Haricots verts *retain their brilliant emerald green color best if they're steamed rather than boiled.*

Quail eggs are tiny with artistically speckled brown and ivory colored shells. They make perfect miniature fried eggs. I find the best, most reasonably priced quail eggs not in a fancy gourmet supermarket, but at my local Korean grocery store.

Serves 6

Black Truffle Vinaigrette

1 tablespoon (or more) minced black truffle, fresh or canned

2 large shallots, minced

¼ cup champagne vinegar

½ cup hazelnut or walnut oil

Salt and freshly ground black pepper

Salad

1½ pounds *haricots verts,* stem ends trimmed

2 tablespoons (¼ stick) unsalted butter

6 to 8 quail eggs (allow a few extra in case any break)

Salt and freshly ground pepper

1 ripe tomato, cut into small dice

¼ cup snipped fresh chives (about 1 bunch)

1. Prepare the Black Truffle Vinaigrette: In a small bowl, whisk together the truffle, shallots, vinegar, oil, and salt and pepper to taste. (If using canned truffles, add a little of their liquid to the dressing.)

2. Prepare the Salad: Have ready a bowl of ice water. Place the *haricots verts* in a steamer basket over a pot of rapidly boiling water. Steam for 3 to 4 minutes, or until bright green. Drain and refresh in the bowl of ice water. Drain and reserve.

3. In a small nonstick skillet, heat the butter over medium heat until sizzling. Using a serrated knife, gently slice through the rather tough inner membrane of the quail eggs without breaking the yolks. Add the quail eggs one at a time to the skillet as if making miniature sunnyside-up eggs. Sprinkle each fried egg with salt and pepper to taste. Cover and cook for about 1 minute; then remove the pan from the heat.

4. To serve the salad, toss the *haricots verts* with the vinaigrette. Divide among six serving plates. Top each serving with a fried quail egg; then sprinkle with the tomato and chives. Serve immediately.

Huevos Rancheros y Frijoles Refritos
(Ranch-Style Eggs with Refried Beans)
(VEGETARIAN OPTION)

This dish has been a personal favorite since I lived in Mexico as a teenager. There's something about the warm spiced flavor of Mexican Tomato Sauce with Allspice soaked into corn tortillas and topped with runny, rich fried eggs and dense, concentrated refried beans that I crave on a regular basis. Maybe it's just because the whole thing evokes good memories. For whatever reason, this dish is a classic and suitable for either brunch or supper. To make a vegetarian version, prepare the refried beans using olive oil.

— *Serves 4* —

2 tablespoons corn or peanut oil

1 (12-ounce) package medium corn tortillas

2 cups Mexican Tomato Sauce with Allspice (see page 330), heated thoroughly

8 eggs

¼ pound shredded Monterey Jack or Cheddar cheese

2 cups Refried Beans (see page 301), heated thoroughly

½ cup chopped fresh cilantro leaves (about ½ bunch), for garnish

1. Heat a thin film of corn oil in a heavy cast-iron skillet. Add the tortillas, one at a time, and cook for 30 seconds on each side, or until toasted, adding a bit more oil for each tortilla. Place two overlapping tortillas per portion on the bottom of a shallow, ovenproof baking dish, or in individual baking dishes.

2. Preheat the broiler. Spread the Mexican Tomato Sauce with Allspice over the tortillas, using a spoon to form two rounded hollows on the surface. Carefully break two eggs per person into the hollows in the sauce. Sprinkle with the cheese.

3. Broil for 8 to 10 minutes, or until the cheese is bubbling and the egg whites are set. Serve accompanied by a generous dollop of hot Refried Beans. Garnish with cilantro.

Bombay-Style Split Chickpea Cakes
(Khaman Dhokla)
with Date-Tamarind Chutney

(V E G E T A R I A N)

This unusual spongy steamed lentil cake served with a dark, sweet-tart chutney is a specialty of the city of Bombay, now known as Mumbai. Tamarind is a common ingredient in many countries, used for its sour, pruny flavor and the thickening power of its pulp. Tamarind is most often sold dried and pressed into blocks, which must be rehydrated in water and then strained to remove the large seeds. Tamarind concentrate is also available, but it tends to be salty, so you may need to adjust the seasoning. The channa dal *called for here are tiny skinned, split chickpeas, which are available from Indian groceries or from www.Kalustyans.com.*

——————— *Advance preparation recommended. Serves 8* ———————

1 pound (2 cups) dried yellow split chickpeas (*chana* or *channa dal*), soaked for 12 hours (see Soaking Chart, page 57)

½ cup plain yogurt

1 teaspoon salt

1 teaspoon finely chopped fresh green chile (such as jalapeño)

1 teaspoon grated fresh ginger

3 tablespoons corn oil

½ teaspoon black mustard seeds

½ teaspoon sesame seeds

2 tablespoons chopped fresh cilantro leaves

1 recipe (1½ cups) Date-Tamarind Chutney (see page 310)

1. Drain the soaked split chickpeas, discarding the water. Combine with the yogurt and salt, place in a blender, and purée until smooth. (The mixture should be thick enough to hold its shape without running.) Place the mixture in a bowl and cover. Let it stand overnight at room temperature to ferment. The next day, it should be bubbling and light. Stir the batter well to remove excess bubbles. Stir in the chile and ginger.

2. Lightly oil a Chinese bamboo steamer or the perforated insert of a pasta pot. Bring a pot of water to a boil. Pour the batter into the steamer to a thickness of ¼ inch. Cover and steam the thin cake for 15 minutes, or until a knife stuck in the middle comes out clean. Cool for 10 minutes; then, using a sharp knife, cut the cake into 1-inch diamond shapes.

3. In a small pan with a lid, heat the oil with the mustard seeds. Cook, covered, until the seeds pop, like popcorn. Add the sesame seeds and remove from the heat.

4. Drizzle the hot mustard–sesame oil over the chickpea cakes and leave for 5 minutes to absorb the flavors. Garnish with the cilantro and serve with the Date-Tamarind Chutney.

Indian Vegetable Tempura in Chickpea Batter

(VEGETARIAN)

I prepared this fragrant, flavorful vegetable tempura for the first legume cooking class I taught. Everyone loved it. The nutty chickpea flour, the toasted seeds, and the tangy yogurt combine to make a frying batter with considerable intrinsic flavor. By choosing an imaginative variety of vegetables for frying, you can make a memorable dish from simple ingredients. I've listed fifteen vegetables that all cook up firm and tasty without becoming too watery. Serve these crunchy fried vegetables with Cucumber-Yogurt Raita, a tangy cucumber and yogurt relish.

————— *Makes 4 cups batter, enough for 3 to 4 vegetables* —————

2 cups chickpea flour

1 cup cold water

2 teaspoons salt

1 teaspoon ground toasted cumin seed
   (see Toasting Seeds, page 225)

1 teaspoon ground toasted coriander seed

1 teaspoon ground toasted fennel seed

2 teaspoons ground fenugreek

½ teaspoon cayenne

2 teaspoons turmeric

1 cup plain yogurt

6 cups canola or soybean oil, for
   deep-frying

6 cups assorted vegetables

2 cups Cucumber-Yogurt Raita
   (see page 308)

1. In a medium bowl, whisk together the chickpea flour, water, salt, cumin, coriander, fennel, fenugreek, cayenne, turmeric, and yogurt to make a thick batter. Cover and let the batter rest in the refrigerator for 30 minutes.

2. Preheat the oven to 200°F. Fill a large, heavy-bottomed pot or wok no more than one-third full with oil. Preheat the oil to 365°F on a deep-frying thermometer. Dip bite-size chunks of vegetables, one at a time, into the chickpea batter. (If the batter is too thick, gradually add more water. The batter should be just thick enough to coat the vegetables.) Gently lay each vegetable onto the surface of the hot oil, making sure not to crowd the pan. For best results, each vegetable should be surrounded by oil. Deep-fry in batches until light brown and crispy, about 6 minutes. Drain vegetables on paper towels. Spread out in a single layer on a baking sheet, wire rack, or ovenproof platter and keep warm in the oven while continuing to fry. Serve with Cucumber-Yogurt Raita.

Vegetables for Tempura

Butternut squash, peeled and cut into ½-inch half-slices

Carrots, cut into 2- to 3-inch sticks, or whole baby carrots

Cauliflower, cut into small florets

Daikon radish rounds, peeled and cut into ½-inch coins

Fennel, trimmed with outer layer removed, cut into wedges, and rubbed with a little lemon juice

Japanese eggplant, cut lengthwise into ½-inch slices

Romano beans, blanched 3 minutes in boiling salted water if fresh (or use frozen)

Salsify, peeled and cut into 2- to 3-inch sticks, rubbed with a little lemon juice

Spinach leaves, stems removed

Sweet potatoes, pared and cut into ½-inch half-moons

Sweet white or red onions, roots trimmed but not removed, each cut into 6 to 8 wedges

Taro root, peeled and cut into ½-inch slices

White mushrooms, wiped clean, quartered if large

White or yellow turnip, peeled and cut into thin wedges

Yellow squash, scrubbed and cut on the diagonal into ½-inch slices

Spring Greens Ravioli
with Creamy White Bean Sauce
(VEGETARIAN OPTION)

As a young chef, I spent several weeks working in Bologna. There I had the great pleasure of watching pasta being prepared by the women in the kitchen of the restaurant Diana. These expert craftswomen would take a huge wooden rolling pin, as long as a table, and use it to stretch and roll out a thin but textured sheet of pasta dough. After filling the ravioli with a simple ricotta and spinach stuffing, or pumpkin and chopped amaretti cookie, or this spring greens stuffing, they would arrange them one by one on wood-framed wire trays to keep air circulating and prevent the ravioli from sticking. I admit that it's a formidable task to make your own ravioli, but otherwise you'll never get to taste these tender, plump pillows hand-stuffed with fresh greens. You could, however, serve purchased ravioli filled with spinach or other greens and ricotta cheese, topped with the creamy white bean sauce. Vegetarians may substitute Vegetable Stock (see page 323) for the chicken stock.

Serves 6 to 8

Creamy White Bean and Sage Sauce

2 tablespoons olive oil

¼ cup chopped garlic

3 cups cooked cannellini beans, drained (see Basic Cooking Chart, page 58)

2 cups Light Chicken Stock (see page 320)

1 cup shredded sage leaves (about 1 bunch)

½ cup heavy cream

Salt and freshly ground black pepper

Filling

1 bunch sorrel, stems trimmed, leaves cut into narrow shreds

1 bunch spinach, stems trimmed, leaves cut into shreds

1 bunch young mustard greens, stems trimmed, leaves cut into shreds

1 head curly endive, stalks trimmed, leaves cut into shreds

¼ pound (½ cup) whole-milk ricotta cheese

¼ pound Parmigiano-Reggiano cheese, grated

1. Prepare the Creamy White Bean and Sage Sauce: Heat the olive oil in a medium pot, add the garlic, and cook for 3 to 4 minutes. Do not brown. Add the beans, Light Chicken Stock, and sage. Bring to a boil, reduce the heat, and simmer for 20 minutes.

2. In the blender or food processor, purée half the beans; then stir the purée into the remaining beans. Add the heavy cream and cook over low heat until hot. Season to taste with salt and pepper. Keep warm, or refrigerate if preparing ahead.

3. Prepare the Filling: Bring a large pot of water to a boil. Add the sorrel, spinach, mustard greens, and endive and cook just until wilted and soft. Drain and run under cold water. Squeeze out the greens in your hands, removing as much water as possible. In a large bowl, combine the squeezed greens with the ricotta, Parmigiano, eggs, nutmeg, salt, and pepper. Cover and refrigerate until ready to fill the ravioli.

4. To assemble the ravioli, use a ravioli plaque, or see the Cook's Note. Lay 1 sheet of Durum Pasta Dough on the bottom of the plaque, pressing to make indentations for the filling. (If the dough is dry, brush the edges with water; if it's moist enough to stick together well, this won't be necessary.) Fill each indentation with 1 tablespoon of the filling, being careful not to smear any on the edges. (The dough will only stick to dough, not to the filling.) Cover with a second sheet of dough; then roll over the top with a rolling pin to seal. Use your fingers to press down on all the edges to strengthen the seal. Arrange the filled ravioli on a clean, flour-dusted

4 eggs
1 teaspoon freshly ground nutmeg
2 teaspoons salt
1 teaspoon freshly ground black pepper
1 recipe Durum Pasta Dough (see page 325)
2 tablespoons chopped Italian parsley leaves, for garnish

window screen (reserved for this purpose), or on a perforated pan or flour-dusted waxed paper. Repeat with the remaining dough and filling. Reserve until ready to cook. Cook within 1 hour to prevent the ravioli from sticking to the pan.

5. Bring a large pot of salted water to a boil. Drop in the filled ravioli one at a time. Bring the water back to a boil, stirring the ravioli gently with a wooden spoon. When all the ravioli have floated to the surface, cook for 2 to 3 minutes longer. Scoop out using a skimmer or a wire sieve. Drain by shaking off the water; then gently toss with the Creamy White Bean and Sage Sauce (reheat if necessary). Sprinkle with parsley and serve immediately.

COOK'S NOTE

If you don't have a ravioli plaque you can shape the ravioli by hand. I actually prefer this method, which I learned from Italian *pastaioli*, or pasta makers: Roll out 1 sheet of the pasta dough as wide as the machine will allow. Fold the sheet in half lengthwise and then unfold it, to make a crease. Starting from the left side, place 1 tablespoon of the filling 1 inch from the edge of the dough, just below the crease. Repeat, making sure to leave 1 inch between each mound of filling. When the dough has been filled, brush around all of the mounds with cold water. Fold the top half of the dough over the bottom half. Press firmly between and around all of the mounds of filling to seal the edges, pressing out excess air pockets. Using a knife or ravioli cutter, cut between each of the ravioli to make half-moon or square shapes.

Provençal Artichokes with Fava Beans *(Barbouiado)*

(V E G E T A R I A N)

This old-time Provençal dish, called barbouiado *in the regional dialect, combines two vegetables I can never get enough of—fresh favas and artichokes. Naturally, they both take a seemingly inordinate amount of time to prepare. You have the choice of making the dish from scratch to serve to highly discriminating guests, or taking the easy way out and using frozen green favas (sold in Asian and Mediterranean markets) and frozen artichoke hearts. I recommend Birdseye brand, available in some supermarkets, and the frozen artichokes sold by the Trader Joe's stores. Cara Mia brand is more common but has too much citric acid for my taste.*

—————————————————— *Serves 6* ——————————————————

1 pound fresh shelled green favas, or
   1 (1-pound) bag frozen green fava
   beans
4 large fresh artichokes, trimmed (see
   Preparing Fresh Artichokes, below), or
   1 (12-ounce) box frozen artichokes
¼ cup extra-virgin olive oil
1 large sweet onion, sliced into strips
½ cup dry white vermouth
½ teaspoon freshly grated nutmeg
Salt and freshly ground black pepper

1. Bring a large pot of salted water to a boil and add the fresh or frozen favas. Cook for 2 minutes; then drain and rinse. Remove and discard the skins. Refill the pot with water and bring to a boil. Cook the skinned favas for 5 to 10 minutes, or until nearly tender. Drain and reserve.

2. In a medium pan, brown the artichoke slices (or frozen wedges) in the olive oil over high heat. Add the onion and cook for 3 minutes, or until the onion is softened. Pour in the vermouth. Bring the mixture to a boil, add the favas and nutmeg, and season to taste with salt and pepper. Toss to combine well. Serve immediately.

PREPARING FRESH ARTICHOKES

Have ready a bowl of cold water mixed with 2 tablespoons lemon juice (about 1 lemon). Using a stainless-steel knife, slice off the stems of the artichokes so they sit upright. Slice off the tops of the artichokes, leaving about 1½ inches of leaves on them. Turn the artichokes upside down. Working in a spiral, grasp one leaf at a time, first bending it back at the point where the leaf meets the artichoke bottom and then breaking it off. Keep breaking off leaves, going in order around the artichoke until all the leaves have been removed except the inner light-green section. Now, using a sharp paring knife, pare away all the tough dark green outer skin from the artichoke bottom. You should have only light green flesh left. As you finish trimming each artichoke, place it in the lemon water. Using a melon baller or a heavy stainless-steel teaspoon, scrape out and discard the inedible hairy choke in the center of each artichoke. Cut the trimmed artichoke bottoms into ¼-inch slices and reserve in the lemon water until ready to cook. (*Note:* Do not attempt to grind the artichoke trimmings in a sink disposal. They are much too fibrous and should be discarded in the trash.)

French Lentil and Foie Gras–Stuffed Won Ton Ravioli

with Tomato and Truffle Oil

I've had the pleasure of tasting this dish several times as prepared by my friend, chef Philippe Chin, now at Bambu on Hickman at The Partridge Inn in Augusta, Georgia. Chin specializes in French-Asian fusion cuisine with an emphasis on the French techniques he learned in school in his native Paris. From his Chinese grandfather, he learned about Asian ingredients and methods, and incorporates them into his own stylish cuisine. Here, Chin fills won ton skins with firm, almost meaty green lentils and ultra-rich fresh foie gras. This extraordinarily good filling could be properly set off only by the light tomato sauce drizzled with truffle oil. The aroma that wafts over the table when the waiters remove the silver cloches from the dishes is indescribably intoxicating.

—————————————— *Serves 6* ——————————————

Filling

6 (1-ounce) slices fresh foie gras
    (see Sources, page 341)
Salt and freshly ground black pepper
¼ cup well-washed chopped leek, white
    and light green parts
1 tablespoon chopped carrot
1 teaspoon olive oil
1 cup Basic Cooked French Green Lentils
    (see page 298)
12 round, thin won ton wrappers
1 egg yolk mixed with 1 tablespoon water

Sauce

1 tomato, peeled, seeded, and diced
3 teaspoons extra-virgin olive oil
½ cup tomato juice
1½ cups Light Chicken Stock (see page
    320)
Salt and freshly ground black pepper
2 tablespoons (or more) truffle oil, for
    serving
6 fresh basil leaves, for garnish

1. Prepare the Filling: Preheat a large nonstick skillet over high heat. Season the foie gras with salt and pepper. Add in two batches to the hot pan, and sear on each side, cooking just long enough to brown the outside. Transfer the foie gras slices to a platter, cover, and refrigerate, reserving the fat from the pan separately.

2. In a saucepan, cook the leek and carrot in the olive oil for about 3 minutes, or until the leek is translucent. Add the lentils and foie gras fat. Season generously to taste with salt and pepper, as some of the seasoning will be absorbed by the won ton skins. Cover and refrigerate the filling. (Steps 1 and 2 can be done up to 1 day ahead.)

3. Place 6 won ton wrappers on a clean surface. Brush around the edges with the egg yolk mixture. Place about 1 tablespoon of the chilled filling in the center of each wrapper. Top each with a slice of the foie gras. Cover with the remaining 6 wrappers. Seal the ravioli by pressing lightly all around the edges. Let dry for a few minutes before cooking.

4. Prepare the Sauce: Cook the diced tomatoes in 1 teaspoon of the olive oil in a small saucepan. Add the tomato juice and Light Chicken Stock. Bring to a boil, reduce the heat, and simmer for 10 minutes. Purée the tomato mixture in a blender or with a hand-held blender, slowly adding the remaining 2 teaspoons olive oil. Season to taste with salt and pepper.

5. When ready to serve, bring a large, wide pot of salted water to a boil. Add the ravioli, dropping them in one at a time so they don't stick together. Cook for about 4 minutes, then scoop out using a slotted spoon or wire skimmer. Shake off the excess water and immediately place in 6 heated large shallow soup bowls. Top with the tomato sauce and a drizzle of truffle oil. Garnish each won ton with a basil leaf.

Golden Garlic Aïoli
with Romano Beans and Sugar Snaps
(V E G E T A R I A N)

This variation on a traditional Niçoise specialty makes a lovely dish to serve on a hot summer night. Everything can be made ahead of time, though the vegetables and eggs will taste best if they're cool but not icy cold. Serve with a chilled carafe of rosé wine preferably from Provence, such as Bandol. I happen to love the flavor of the caramelized garlic in the aïoli. It also makes this dish a little more user-friendly because the cooked garlic doesn't leave a strong aftertaste.

—————————————— *Serves 6 (Makes 3 cups sauce)* ——————————————

Roasted Garlic Aïoli

1 cup peeled garlic cloves

½ cup olive oil

2 tablespoons finely chopped fresh
     thyme leaves (about ½ bunch)

2 tablespoons Spanish or sweet
     Hungarian paprika

¼ cup red wine vinegar

2 cups high-quality mayonnaise,
     homemade or purchased

2 teaspoons salt

1 teaspoon hot pepper sauce

Salad

½ pound fresh romano beans or green
     beans, stems trimmed

½ pound sugar snap peas, tops trimmed
     and strings removed

1 pound young beets, preferably gold
     and red

½ pound fresh artichoke wedges (see
     Preparing Fresh Artichokes, page
     180), or frozen artichoke hearts,
     thawed and drained on paper towels

1 fennel bulb, trimmed, cut into thin
     wedges, and soaked in ice water
     with lemon juice

12 hard-cooked eggs, quartered (see
     Hard-Cooking Eggs, page 183)

1. Prepare the Roasted Garlic Aïoli: Combine the garlic cloves, olive oil, and thyme in a small pot and cook over medium heat, shaking often, until the garlic begins to turn golden. Remove from the heat and cool to room temperature. Transfer the mixture to a food processor and purée to a fine paste. Add the paprika, vinegar, mayonnaise, salt, and hot sauce. Purée again until smooth. Taste for seasoning. (The aïoli will keep well for 2 weeks if tightly covered and refrigerated.)

2. Make the Salad: In a vegetable steamer basket over boiling water, steam the romano beans for 5 to 7 minutes, or until tender but still brightly colored. Lift out the steamer basket and rinse the beans under cold running water. If you like, briefly steam the sugar snap peas for about 1 minute, or until they turn a light, bright green. Rinse under cold running water. (The sugar snaps are delicious raw or cooked. They are fresher and crunchier when raw, and more tender and bright when cooked.)

3. Set the steamer up again, adding enough water to the pot to reach a depth of at least 1 inch. Trim off the beet greens, if any, leaving about 1 inch of stems attached to the tops. Be careful not to cut into the root end of the beets or they will bleed and lose much of their bright magenta color. Steam the whole beets for 20 to 30 minutes, or until tender when pierced with a fork. When cool enough to handle, rub the skins off the warm beets and trim off the root ends. (To prevent staining, wear rubber gloves and cut the beets on a nonporous surface.) Cut into wedges.

4. In a medium pot, bring the fresh artichoke wedges and their soaking liquid to a boil over high heat. Reduce the heat and cook for about 8 minutes, or until the artichokes are tender when pierced with a fork. Drain, cool, and reserve. If using frozen artichoke hearts, cook for 2 to 3 minutes, or until tender.

5. Transfer the aïoli to a small bowl. On a large platter, arrange the romano beans, sugar snaps, artichokes, beets, raw fennel, and eggs in a decorative pattern, with the bowl of aïoli in the center for dipping.

Hard-Cooking Eggs

To avoid rubbery, overcooked eggs with a green halo around the yolk, don't boil them. Instead, place the eggs in a medium pot and add 1 tablespoon salt and enough cold water to cover them by about 2 inches. (Adding salt to the cold water helps to cleanly separate the shells from the eggs.) Cover, bring to a boil, and allow the water to a boil for 1 minute. Turn off the heat and let the eggs continue to cook in the hot water for 6 minutes for European-style eggs (soft in the center), or 8 minutes for firm eggs. Check the eggs by cracking the shell of one: the eggs should feel moderately firm, but still slightly yielding toward the center for firm eggs. Place the eggs in a large bowl of cold water to chill, changing the water once or twice, until the eggs are cold. Peel immediately and cut into quarters, as desired.

Shrimp and Bean Thread Spring Rolls
with Spicy Peanut Dipping Sauce
(VEGETARIAN OPTION)

Is it really worth making your own spring rolls? I believe it is because I find most spring roll fillings to be overcooked and heavy. Here, the filling is light because of the slippery bean thread noodles and crunchy with napa cabbage shreds. You can certainly serve the rolls without the sauce, but if you have time, give it a try. The sauce can be made several days ahead of time. The spring rolls can be filled and rolled up to 1 day ahead of time. Be sure to use fresh oil for frying. The lightest results come from the first frying in clear, fresh, bubbling oil. Good choices for frying oil are soy, canola, or peanut. For a vegetarian version, substitute firm tofu, cut into small cubes and well drained, for the shrimp.

—————— *Makes 12 spring rolls* ——————

2 ounces bean thread (cellophane) noodles

1 tablespoon peanut oil

1 tablespoon roasted Japanese sesame oil

2 teaspoons chopped garlic

1 tablespoon chopped fresh ginger

½ pound small shrimp, peeled

¼ head napa cabbage, shredded

2 carrots, shredded

1 tablespoon mushroom soy sauce

½ teaspoon hot red pepper flakes

1 tablespoon cornstarch

¼ cup rice wine, saké, or dry sherry

¼ bunch scallions, white and green parts, sliced

¼ cup chopped fresh cilantro leaves (about ½ bunch)

12 egg roll wrappers

1 egg white mixed with 1 tablespoon cold water

Canola, peanut, or soybean oil, for frying

2 cups Spicy Peanut Dipping Sauce (see page 317)

1. Soak the bean thread noodles in cold water to cover until softened, about 15 minutes. Drain and reserve.

2. In a medium pan over medium heat, combine the peanut and sesame oils. Add the garlic and ginger and cook for 2 minutes. Add the shrimp and sauté until just cooked through. Remove from heat and reserve.

3. In another pan over medium heat, cook the cabbage until wilted. Remove from the heat and stir in the carrots. Add the shrimp and noodles to the cabbage mixture and toss to combine. Transfer to a colander set over a bowl. Drain and reserve the excess liquid; then transfer the mixure to a bowl.

4. In a small pot, over medium heat, cook the reserved liquid, reducing until syrupy. Stir in the soy sauce and pepper flakes. In a small bowl, combine the cornstarch and wine. Whisk into the reduced liquid and bring to a boil, stirring constantly. Remove from the heat and stir into the reserved shrimp-vegetable mixture. Add the scallions and cilantro. Cover and refrigerate for about 1 hour, until well chilled.

5. Arrange the egg roll wrappers on a large, clean surface. Divide the filling into 12 equal portions. Place one portion of filling on each wrapper, forming it into an oblong shape and leaving a 1-inch border on all sides. Brush the egg white mixture all around the edges of the wrappers. Roll up, envelope style, pressing to seal the packets well. Refrigerate until ready to cook.

6. When ready to serve, preheat the oven to 200°F. Fill a large, heavy-bottomed pot, deep-fryer, or wok no more than one-third with oil. Heat to 365°F on a deep-frying thermometer. Fry a few spring rolls at a time, leaving plenty of room in the pot, until brown, about 4 minutes. Drain well on paper towels and then transfer to a baking sheet topped with a wire rack, lined with paper towels. Place in the oven to keep warm while cooking the remaining spring rolls. Serve with the Spicy Peanut Dipping Sauce.

Gratin of Summer Succotash with Crabmeat

(VEGETARIAN OPTION)

The word "gratin" refers to the crunchy crumb topping of this dish, which is a lovely seasonal variation on the classic succotash. The basic combination of limas and sweet corn is preserved, but I've enhanced it with crabmeat in a creamy sauce. I love sweet blue crabmeat, but the top-quality jumbo lump crabmeat is quite expensive. Here, it's mixed with enough other ingredients so that 1 pound will easily feed six people. In the summer at Philadelphia's 100-year-old culinary treasure, the Reading Terminal Market, you can buy little bags of freshly shelled baby limas from Amish farmers. What a treat! I love anything made with crab, corn, Jersey tomatoes, and field-grown basil, and this dish has it all. For a vegetarian version, simply omit the crabmeat. In that case, you will have about 4 cups of the gratin mixture, so place it in a smaller dish to bake.

—————————— *Serves 6 (Makes one 6-cup gratin)* ——————————

1 pound shelled fresh baby lima beans

1 bunch scallions, white and green parts, sliced into 1-inch lengths

4 tablespoons (½ stick) unsalted butter, melted

1 pound jumbo lump crabmeat, carefully picked over

4 cups sweet white corn kernels (about 8 ears)

4 large, ripe beefsteak tomatoes, seeded and diced

1 cup shredded basil leaves (about 1 bunch)

½ cup heavy cream

Salt and freshly ground black pepper

1 cup fresh white bread crumbs

1. Place the lima beans in a medium saucepan with enough cold water to cover. Bring to a boil. Reduce the heat and simmer for about 10 minutes, or until bright green and almost tender. Drain and reserve.

2. Preheat the oven to 400°F. In a small skillet, cook the scallions in 2 tablespoons of the melted butter, just until bright green. Remove from the heat and combine in a large bowl with the limas, crabmeat, corn, tomatoes, basil, and cream. Season to taste with salt and pepper. Spoon the mixture into an ungreased 6-cup, shallow gratin dish.

3. Combine the bread crumbs and the remaining 2 tablespoons butter in a small bowl. Sprinkle evenly over the top of the gratin. Bake for 20 to 30 minutes, or until bubbling and browned on top.

Pasta Primavera with Sugar Snaps

(VEGETARIAN)

When Sirio Maccioni of the world-class New York restaurant Le Cirque first introduced pasta primavera to American diners back in the seventies, he had an extraordinarily long-lasting and widespread effect. For a time it seemed like every self-respecting chef in America made a version of this dish. Each ingredient here plays a role in providing color, texture, and juiciness. Don't leave anything out and you'll understand why it was such an instant hit.

Serves 4

1 pound linguine
1 tablespoon chopped garlic
½ head broccoli, cut into small florets
2 tablespoons olive oil
1 pint ripe red cherry tomatoes, halved
½ pound fresh sugar snap peas, trimmed
1 bunch scallions, cut into 1-inch lengths
½ cup heavy cream
1 bunch fresh basil, leaves washed and
    roughly torn (about 1 cup leaves)
½ cup grated Parmigiano-Reggiano
    cheese
Salt and freshly ground black pepper
¼ cup toasted pine nuts

1. Bring a large pot of salted water to a boil. Add the linguine and cook until firm but tender, about 7 minutes. Drain and reserve in the pot to keep warm.

2. While the pasta is cooking, sauté the garlic and broccoli in the olive oil in a large skillet for 2 to 3 minutes, or until crisp-tender. Add the cherry tomatoes and cook for 2 minutes. Stir in the sugar snaps, scallions, and cream. Bring the mixture to a boil; then turn off the heat. Add the basil and cheese. Add most of the vegetable mixture to the pot of pasta. Toss to coat evenly. Season to taste with salt and pepper, sprinkle with the reserved vegetable mixture and pine nuts, and serve immediately.

CHAPTER EIGHT

Main Dishes

Red Bean and White Hominy Chili

(VEGETARIAN)

This vegetarian chili, which I developed for the takeout department of a specialty foods store, makes a knockout presentation when served in steamed acorn squash halves. The chili is even better when you reheat it a day or two later. Giant white hominy is known as mote pelado *in the Andean countries of Peru and Bolivia. Hominy,* mote, *and* posole *are all the same food—corn that has had the outer hull removed by a special process using wood ash, crushed seashells, or other materials containing lime, then air-dried, so that it has a chewy texture when cooked. It dates back to the time of the Incan empire, which before the Spanish conquest included the coastal and mountain regions of Ecuador, Peru, Bolivia, and northern Chile and Argentina. You can find giant white hominy at South American groceries and at some Web sites (see Sources, page 341).*

—————— *Advance preparation required. Serves 8 to 10* ——————

1 pound hominy (dried giant white corn)
8 cups (2 quarts) cold water
4 bay leaves
½ cup olive oil
1 pound onions, chopped
1 pound carrots, diced
¼ cup chopped garlic
2 (28-ounce) cans chopped Italian plum tomatoes
1 celery root, diced
1 rutabaga, diced
1 small butternut squash, peeled, seeded, and cubed
Salt and freshly ground black pepper
¼ cup chopped chipotle chile in adobo sauce (including sauce)
2 teaspoons ground allspice
2 tablespoons dried oregano
2 tablespoons ground toasted cumin seeds (see Toasting Seeds, page 225)
4 cups cooked black beans or 1½ cups dried black turtle beans, cooked and drained (see Basic Cooking Chart, page 58)
4 cups cooked kidney beans or 1½ cups dried red kidney beans, cooked and drained (see Basic Cooking Chart, page 58)
1 cup cilantro sprigs (about 1 bunch), for garnish

1. In a large bowl, soak the hominy in enough cold water to cover for 12 hours.

2. Drain the hominy, rinse, and place in a large pot. Cover with the cold water and add the bay leaves. Bring to a boil, cover, and reduce the heat to a bare simmer. Cook for 2 hours, or until firm but cooked through. Drain, discarding the bay leaves, and reserve.

3. Heat the olive oil in a large Dutch oven. Add the onions and carrots and cook over medium heat for 3 to 5 minutes, until tender but still crisp. Add the garlic and cook 3 minutes longer. Add the chopped tomatoes, celery root, and rutabaga and bring to a boil. Reduce the heat, cover, and simmer for 15 minutes; then stir in the squash and bring back to a boil. Cover and simmer 15 minutes, stirring occasionally. Season to taste with salt and pepper.

4. Add the chipotle chile, allspice, oregano, and cumin and stir to mix well. Add the black beans, red beans, and cooked hominy. Bring to a boil. Reduce the heat and cook for 20 minutes, stirring often, until the chili has thickened. Taste for seasoning, adding more salt if necessary. Serve garnished with chopped cilantro.

COOK'S NOTE

This makes a large batch of chili, but it freezes so beautifully, it doesn't make sense to prepare less. After cooling the chili, divide it into quart-size plastic freezer bags, label, and freeze.

Seared Salmon with Sugar Snaps
and Rhubarb Sauce

Here are three springtime treats in one dish—salmon, sugar snap peas, and rhubarb. Because the salmon is slightly oily, the crunchy, fresh sugar snaps and the tart rhubarb with its hint of sweetness both serve to cut the richness of the fish and make this a perfectly balanced dish. It's an easy, quickly cooked, and eye-catching entrée for a dinner party. You can prepare the rhubarb sauce up to 2 days ahead of time, reheating gently just before serving. Note that field-grown rhubarb will be brighter in color than the hot-house type, which is the first kind that comes into season.

Serves 4 (Makes 1½ cups sauce)

Rhubarb Sauce

1 bunch rhubarb (about 1 pound), trimmed and stems cut into 1-inch lengths, or 1 (12-ounce) package frozen rhubarb

2 bay leaves

¼ cup honey

6 star anise pods

½ cup heavy cream

Salt and freshly ground black pepper

Salmon and Sugar Snaps

1 tablespoon olive oil

2 pounds salmon fillet, pin bones removed, cut into 4 portions

Salt and freshly ground pepper

1 cup trimmed sugar snap peas

1. Prepare the Rhubarb Sauce: Combine the rhubarb, bay leaves, honey, and two of the star anise pods in a medium pot. Simmer over medium heat until the rhubarb is soft, about 5 minutes. Add the cream, increase the heat, and bring to a boil. Remove from the heat. Season to taste with salt and pepper. Remove and discard bay leaves and star anise.

2. Prepare the Salmon and Sugar Snaps: Lightly oil the salmon fillets and season with salt and pepper. Preheat a large nonstick pan over medium-high heat. Arrange the salmon fillets in the pan, skin sides down, and cook until the skins are well browned and crisp, about 3 minutes. Turn and cook on the other side until the salmon is medium to medium-rare. Remove from the pan and drain on paper towels.

3. In a small saucepan, bring 2 cups of water to a boil. Add the sugar snap peas and cook until bright green, about 2 minutes. Remove from the water, drain, and reserve. Ladle the rhubarb sauce onto 4 large, heated dinner plates. Place one portion of salmon, skin side up, on each plate. Surround the salmon with the reserved sugar snaps and garnish with the remaining four star anise.

COOK'S NOTE

Rhubarb leaves are toxic because they contain so much oxalic acid. Normally they are removed before being sold. If you grow your own, be sure to remove the leaves.

Adriatic Grilled Shrimp
with Cranberry Beans, Broccoli Rabe, and Sweet Red Pepper Sauce

In Italy, at seafront restaurants along the Adriatic near Rimini, locally caught shrimp and other crustaceans are tossed with a mixture of olive oil, chopped garlic, and a little fresh bread crumbs, and then grilled. Here, I've taken that basic idea and added lemon zest, chopped thyme, and saffron. I've been making shrimp this way for more than 20 years and people just keep loving them. I like to serve the shrimp with a ragout of cranberry beans and sharp, biting broccoli rabe—a vegetable you either love or hate—on a bed of sweet red pepper sauce, as bright as a sunset. The whole dish makes an outstanding presentation and the tastes are surprising to the palate. Make this when you want to "wow" your guests.

——————————————— *Serves 6* ———————————————

Marinated Shrimp and Broccoli Rabe

½ teaspoon crumbled saffron

Juice and grated zest of 2 lemons

¼ cup bread crumbs, preferably Japanese *panko* (see Sources, page 341)

2 tablespoons extra-virgin olive oil

1 tablespoon chopped garlic

2 teaspoons chopped fresh thyme

½ teaspoon crushed hot red pepper flakes

1 teaspoon kosher salt

½ teaspoon finely ground black pepper

¼ cup chopped parsley

2 pounds large (16–20 count) shrimp, peeled and deveined, tail shells left on

½ bunch broccoli rabe, trimmed and cut into 1-inch lengths

1. Make the Marinated Shrimp: Crumble the saffron threads and soak briefly in the lemon juice. Place the bread crumbs, olive oil, lemon zest, garlic, thyme, red pepper flakes, salt, and pepper into the bowl of a food processor. Process to a fine paste. Transfer to a nonreactive glass or stainless-steel bowl and stir in the lemon juice–saffron mixture and chopped parsley. Add the shrimp and toss to combine. Cover and refrigerate for at least 2 hours and up to 24 hours.

2. Bring a medium pot of salted water to a boil. Add the broccoli rabe and cook for 1 to 2 minutes, or until bright green. Drain, run under cold water, and reserve.

3. Make the Red Pepper Sauce: In a large skillet, sauté the red peppers and shallots in the olive oil until soft. Add the basil, white wine, Vegetable Stock, and *pimentón*, and simmer together until the liquid has thickened and the vegetables are soft, about 15 minutes. Remove from the heat and discard the basil. Purée in a blender until the sauce is very smooth, and if desired, strained it through a sieve for an even smoother texture. Season to taste with salt and pepper and keep warm.

4. When ready to serve, preheat a charcoal or gas grill, or a broiler. Remove the shrimp from the marinade and grill, turning once, until just cooked through.

Sweet Red Pepper Sauce

2 red bell peppers, seeded and coarsely
    chopped
2 shallots, peeled and sliced
2 tablespoons extra-virgin olive oil
3 sprigs fresh basil, wrapped in string
½ cup dry white wine
½ cup **Vegetable Stock** (see page 323)
    or water
2 teaspoons *pimentón* (smoked Spanish
    paprika; see Sources, page 341)
Kosher salt and black pepper to taste
2 tablespoons extra-virgin olive oil
2 teaspoons chopped garlic
2 cups Cooked Fresh Cranberry Beans
    (see page 294), or 2 cups cooked
    dried white beans, *emergo* beans,
    or *borlotti* beans (see Basic Cooking
    Chart, page 58)

5. To assemble the dish, heat the 2 tablespoons olive oil in a large skillet over medium heat. Add the garlic and cook until sizzling. Add the reserved broccoli rabe and Cooked Fresh Cranberry Beans. Cook together until thoroughly heated. Place amound of the broccoli-bean mixture in the center of each plate. Surround with the Red Pepper Sauce. Arrange the grilled shrimp over the sauce, surrounding the bean mixture. Serve immediately.

Black Sea Bass with French Green Lentils
and Tarragon

This recipe was given to me by the renowned Lyonnais chef Pierre Orsi, who makes it with gilt-head bream (dorade). Because dorade, a royal member of the porgy family prized by the French, is almost unattainable in the United States (unless you are a restaurant chef with access to the finest imported fish), you'll probably need to substitute black sea bass, striped bass, grouper, tilefish, or even Chilean sea bass. It's a relatively easy dish to make and is sure to garner rave reviews, as it has when I've prepared it for my cooking classes.

Serves 4

½ pound (1 cup) dried French green
   lentils
½ medium onion
½ carrot
1 sprig fresh thyme
Fine sea salt and freshly ground black
   pepper
6 tablespoons olive oil
1 shallot, peeled and sliced
¼ cup red wine vinegar
¼ cup heavy cream
4 black sea bass fillets, about 10 ounces
   each
1 tomato, peeled, seeded, and diced
1 sprig fresh tarragon, chopped
2 tablespoons snipped fresh chives
   (about ½ bunch)

1. Place the lentils in a large pot and add the onion, carrot, thyme, and enough water to cover by about 1 inch. Bring to a boil; then reduce the heat and simmer for about 30 minutes, or until cooked through but still firm. Drain and discard the onion, carrot, and thyme, then season to taste with salt and pepper.

2. Heat 4 tablespoons of the olive oil in a medium pot over medium heat. Add the shallot and cook until softened but not colored. Add the lentils and the red wine vinegar. Bring to a boil, reduce the heat, and simmer for about 10 minutes to evaporate the excess liquid. Add the cream and return to a boil. Season to taste with salt and pepper. Reserve in a warm place.

3. If the fish fillets are thicker than ½ inch, cut 2- to 3½-inch-deep slashes in them using kitchen scissors so they will cook faster. Grouper and Chilean sea bass are firmer and could benefit by this treatment; black sea bass, however, is a delicate-fleshed fish that won't need slashing.

4. Heat the remaining 2 tablespoons olive oil in a large nonstick skillet over high heat. Place the fish fillets, skin sides down, in the skillet and cook for 3 minutes on each side, or until flaky but still moist. Season to taste with salt and pepper.

5. When ready to serve, add the tomato, tarragon, and chives to the reserved lentils and mix well. Place the fish fillets, skin sides down, onto 4 large, heated dinner plates. Surround the fish with the lentils and their sauce. Serve immediately.

Salmon Scaloppine
with Chinese Black Bean Sauce

Here is a crowd-pleasing, quick-cooking dish of salmon scallops in an orange-scented fermented black bean sauce. Inspired by a dish served at Susanna Foo, a nationally celebrated restaurant on Philadelphia's prestigious Restaurant Row, it is a perfect mélange of the Chinese ingredients and French techniques that Chef Foo has made her trademark. By cutting the salmon fillet on the bias into thin slices that resemble veal scallops, 1 pound of salmon will easily feed four people. Serve with Sesame Sugar Snaps (see page 269), if desired.

——————————— *Serves 4* ———————————

¼ cup chopped shallots

2 tablespoons chopped garlic

¼ cup chopped fresh ginger

2 tablespoons peanut oil

2 cups dry white vermouth

½ cup frozen orange juice concentrate, thawed

2 tablespoons molasses

2 teaspoons coriander seeds, crushed

1 cup fermented black beans (available in Asian markets)

2 tablespoons grated orange zest

½ pound (2 sticks) unsalted butter, softened

1 pound salmon fillet

¼ cup thinly sliced fresh chives or Chinese chives (about 1 bunch)

1. Combine the shallots, garlic, ginger, and peanut oil in a medium stainless steel or enameled saucepan and cook over medium heat until the shallots are transparent. Add the vermouth, juice concentrate, molasses, and coriander seeds and bring to a boil. Reduce the heat and simmer until the liquid has reduced by half. Transfer to a food processor or blender and purée until smooth. Strain through a food mill or sieve.

2. When ready to serve, bring the sauce to a boil, cooking until thick bubbles appear all over the surface. Stir in the black beans and orange zest; then beat in the butter a little at a time. Reserve the sauce in a warm place.

3. Slice the salmon on the diagonal into 8 (2-ounce) scallops. Heat a large nonstick skillet over medium-high heat until hot. Working in batches, arrange the salmon slices in the hot pan in a single layer, without crowding, and cook until browned, about 2 minutes. Turn each scallop and cook until browned but still juicy and not quite cooked through in the center, 2 to 3 minutes. Using a flat spatula, remove the salmon from the pan and drain briefly on paper towels.

4. Arrange 2 salmon scallops on each plate and ladle about ¼ cup of the sauce on top. Sprinkle with the chives and serve immediately.

COOK'S NOTE

To make the sauce ahead, prepare up to Step 2, but don't add the butter. Allow the sauce to cool, and refrigerate it for up to 4 days. Reheat over low heat until bubbling; then stir in the butter. Continue as directed.

Grilled Cured Tuna on a Bed of Beluga Lentils

To enhance the flavor of the tuna, I cure it for a day in a mixture of spices. If you prefer, serve the lentils topped with simply grilled tuna and sprinkled with fresh herbs. The beluga lentils called for here are, naturally, tiny, black, caviar-shaped lentils that make a beautiful bed for the tuna. Beluga lentils absorb flavors very easily. If you can't find them, the best substitute is the French green or Spanish pardina lentils. Fresh tuna tastes best when cooked to no more than medium-rare in temperature; cook it longer and it's apt to be dry.

Advance preparation required. Serves 6 to 8

Tuna

¼ cup kosher salt (not table salt)

¼ cup packed dark brown sugar

½ cup chopped mixed fresh herbs, such as dill, thyme, marjoram, tarragon, and/or chervil

3 shallots, chopped

2 teaspoons crushed black peppercorns

2 teaspoons crushed coriander seeds

1 tablespoon crushed fennel seeds

¼ cup brandy

1 (2- to 3-pound) piece center-cut fresh tuna loin, blood line and dark flesh removed and discarded

Olive oil, for brushing

1 bunch scallions, white and green parts, sliced on the bias

2 tablespoons (¼ stick) butter

3 cups Basic Cooked French Green Lentils, made using beluga lentils (see page 298)

1 cup diced yellow and red tomatoes

2 tablespoons chopped mixed tender herbs, such as thyme, basil, tarragon, chervil, and/or Italian parsley

Kosher salt and black pepper

¼ cup extra-virgin olive oil

2 tablespoon lemon juice (about 1 lemon)

1. Prepare the Tuna: In a small bowl, combine the kosher salt, brown sugar, herbs, shallots, crushed black pepper, coriander, fennel, and brandy to form a thick paste. Spread the paste all over the tuna. Place on a wire rack (such as a cooling rack) over a pan to catch the drippings. Cover with plastic wrap, place another pan on top, and add several cans to the top pan to weight down the fish. Refrigerate for 24 hours to cure. When ready to proceed, remove the tuna from the pan, draining off and discarding any excess liquid that has accumulated.

2. Thoroughly heat a grill. Quickly rinse the tuna and pat dry, wiping off most of the spices on the surface with paper towels. Cut into 6 to 8 portions, keeping in mind that the thicker the fillet, the easier it will be to char it on the outside while keeping it rare to medium-rare inside.

3. Lightly brush both sides of the tuna with olive oil; then lay them on the grill at an angle on the racks. Grill for 5 to 6 minutes, or until the tuna releases easily from the grill when prodded with a spatula. Rotate to produce crosswise grill marks and cook for 2 to 3 minutes longer. Turn over and grill until cooked to your taste (medium-rare is pink in the middle; medium-well flakes apart).

4. Meanwhile, in a medium saucepan, sauté the scallions briefly in butter. Add the Basic Cooked French Green Lentils and diced tomatoes and cook for several minutes, or until hot and slightly thickened. Keep warm.

5. Just before serving, stir the chopped herbs into the lentils and season with salt and pepper to taste. Place a mound of lentils on each of 4 dinner plates. Lightly whisk together the olive oil and lemon juice. To serve, spoon a mound of beluga lentils onto each plate, cover with a portion of tuna, and drizzle with the olive oil–lemon mixture.

Thai Shrimp and Green Beans
in Orange–Red Curry Sauce

This impressive, quickly prepared meal blends crunchy bright green beans with succulent shrimp in a sweet-spicy curry sauce. The intense flavor of the red curry paste is tempered with orange juice and butter to produce a rosy pink sauce that's spicy but not too fiery. Haricots verts, sugar snap peas, or edamame make great substitutes for the green beans. The galangal (or galanga or galingale) called for here is a first cousin to ginger and an important seasoning in Southeast Asian cooking, used to flavor curries, soups, and stews. It is hotter than ginger, with a sharper bite and a tangy flavor reminiscent of hot mustard. Fresh galangal is occasionally found in natural foods and Asian markets, and may also be called laos *(its Indonesian name). Substitute fresh ginger root if galangal is not available.*

Serves 6

Orange–Red Curry Sauce
2 shallots, chopped

1 (2-inch) length fresh ginger, chopped

1 (1-inch) length fresh galangal, peeled and chopped, or 1 (1-inch length) fresh ginger, peeled and chopped

2 tablespoons curry powder

2 tablespoons (¼ stick) unsalted butter

2 tablespoons Thai red curry paste

½ (6-ounce) can frozen orange juice concentrate, thawed

Grated zest of 1 orange

¾ cup heavy cream

1 tablespoon salt

Shrimp and Green Beans
1½ pounds fresh green beans, trimmed

1 tablespoon vegetable oil

1½ pounds large shrimp, peeled and deveined, with tails intact

2 tablespoons chopped fresh cilantro leaves

2 tablespoons shredded fresh basil, preferably Thai purple basil

3 cups cooked rice, for serving (optional)

1. Make the Orange-Red Curry Sauce: In a large pan or wok over low heat, cook the shallots, ginger, galangal, and curry powder in the butter for 10 minutes, or until softened. Whisk in the curry paste and cook for 3 minutes longer. Add the orange juice concentrate and zest. Bring to a boil, reduce the heat, and simmer until the liquid is slightly reduced and thickened. Stir in the cream and salt.

2. Make the Shrimp and Green Beans: Bring a large pot of water to a boil. Add the beans and cook for 2 minutes, or until they turn bright green. Rinse under cold water and reserve.

3. Heat the oil in a wok or large skillet over high heat until it shimmers. Add the shrimp and reserved green beans, and stir-fry until the shrimp are opaque, about 4 minutes. Add the curry sauce and bring to a boil. Stir in the cilantro and basil, and serve immediately over cooked rice, if desired.

COOK'S NOTE
I prefer the flavor of shrimp mixed with other ingredients rather than by itself. Also, in a quantity like the one called for in this recipe, you can afford to buy better shrimp, such as South American pinks, rather than the less expensive warm-water tiger shrimp from Asia. The pinks have a more intense flavor and a firmer texture.

Seven-Vegetable and Chicken Couscous

(VEGETARIAN OPTION)

Couscous is actually small balls of semolina flour rolled around a core of coarse semolina, although sometimes it is made from whole wheat flour or toasted barley grits. All types of couscous—from vegetarian to lamb, poultry, seafood, and even sweet versions—are popular in the cuisines of Tunisia, Morocco, and Algeria. Here seven vegetables (including the chickpeas) are used—the same lucky number used in Tex-Mex Seven Layer Salad.

As the former chef of a Mediterranean bistro owned by two Tunisian-born brothers, I learned how to prepare couscous, harissa sauce, chakchouka (a dish of roasted vegetables mixed with egg), brik, and preserved lemons. It's only in the past few years that I've started seeing these dishes and ingredients served commonly. For a vegetarian version, omit Step 2—roasting the chicken—and use Vegetable Stock (see page 323) instead of the chicken stock. Serve the vegetable mixture over the couscous, topped with the cooking juices.

--- *Serves 6 to 8* ---

3 pounds chicken thighs
Salt and freshly ground black pepper
5 cups Rich Chicken Stock (see page 322)
2 cups couscous
6 tablespoons extra-virgin olive oil
Salt
1 small onion, diced
1 large butternut squash, peeled, seeded, and cut into 1-inch dice
1 rutabaga or white turnip, peeled and cut into 1-inch dice
1 (12-ounce) package frozen artichoke hearts, thawed and drained
1 (12-ounce) package frozen baby limas, thawed and drained
3 cups Basic Cooked Chickpeas (see page 299)
1 small head savoy cabbage, shredded
½ cup chopped fresh cilantro (about ½ bunch), for garnish
½ cup Tunisian Harissa Sauce (see page 316)

1. Preheat the oven to 350°F. Arrange the chicken thighs on a baking sheet and sprinkle with salt and pepper. Roast for 45 minutes, or until thoroughly cooked and tender. The juices should run clear when the thighs are pierced in their thickest parts. Reserve in a warm oven.

2. While the chicken is roasting, pour 3 cups of the Rich Chicken Stock into a medium pot. Arrange a sieve or colander over the pot. Pour the couscous into the sieve. Cover tightly with a lid or a double layer of heavy-duty aluminum foil, so the steam doesn't escape. Bring to a boil, reduce the heat, and steam for about 20 minutes, or until small white dots appear on the couscous. Transfer the steamed couscous to a large bowl. Add 2 tablespoons of the oil and season to taste with salt. Using your clean hands, work the oil and salt into the couscous until all the lumps disappear and the grain is fluffy. Return the fluffed couscous to the sieve set over simmering stock. Cover and steam for 20 minutes longer.

3. Meanwhile, in a large pan, heat the remaining 4 tablespoons olive oil. Add the onion, squash, rutabaga, artichokes, and limas, and cook until tender but still crisp, about 10 minutes. Add the remaining 2 cups Rich Chicken Stock, the Basic Cooked Chickpeas, and the cabbage. Bring to a boil and cook for 5 to 10 minutes at high heat to reduce the liquid.

4. To serve, place a pyramid-shaped mound of the couscous in the center of each plate. Place one roasted chicken thigh on each plate and cover with some of the vegetable mixture and a generous ladleful of cooking juices. Sprinkle with the chopped cilantro and serve accompanied by a bowl of Tunisian Harissa Sauce.

COOK'S NOTE

If you're short on time, you can prepare the couscous without steaming it, although it won't be quite as fluffy. Simply heat the Rich Chicken Stock with the olive oil and about 2 teaspoons salt to boiling. Stir in 2 cups of couscous, stir gently to combine, and remove from the heat. Cover and set aside for a few minutes to allow the grain to absorb the liquid. Stir to fluff up the couscous and serve.

COOKING WITH A COUSCOUSIER

A couscousier is an ancient, two-part steaming pot of Berber origin used to make the many versions of couscous, the national dish of north Africa. The grain is steamed in the upper section of the pot over a flavorful broth or stew in the bottom section. The couscousier I use is made of hammered copper with a tinned interior and brass fittings, and comes from Tunisia. It is not necessary to use an authentic couscousier to make good couscous. However, it does make it easier, and the eye appeal is wonderful. (See Sources, page 341.)

Roasted Pigeons with Baby Fava Beans
(*Pigeonneau Rôti aux Fèvettes*)

I had the great pleasure of spending several days in the kitchen of Chef Pierre Orsi's charming eponymous restaurant in Lyons. Chef Orsi was a generous and hospitable host, and he patiently answered my many questions about his kitchen and cuisine. He shared two of his recipes with me, which I've adapted for those of us who don't have professional kitchens (and their staffs) at our disposal. The French love pigeon (pigeonneau means "young pigeon") though Americans generally steer away from it. Try this elegant dish and you'll find out just how wonderful this dark, richly flavored bird—also known as squab when it is young—can be. You can buy game birds like pigeon from D'Artagnan (see Sources, page 341). I have also found frozen fava beans, though not as small as I'd prefer, in the frozen food section at my local Asian market.

Serves 4

4 whole young pigeons, about 3 pounds total
Salt and freshly ground black pepper
10 tablespoons (1¼ sticks) unsalted butter
½ cup vegetable oil
¼ cup dry white wine
½ cup Light Chicken Stock (see page 320)
2 tablespoons Cognac
4 slices country-style white bread, crusts trimmed and cut into neat oval shapes
½ cup wild rice, cooked according to package directions (1½ cups cooked)
½ cup blanched and skinned fresh young fava beans (see About Young Fava Beans, opposite)
2 tablespoons fresh basil leaves, snipped into fine shreds

1. Preheat the oven to 400°F. Rinse and dry the pigeons. Remove the giblets, reserving the livers. Sprinkle the birds inside and out with salt and pepper; then tie each with butcher's string into a neat compact shape.

2. In a large Dutch oven, heat about 6 tablespoons of the butter with the oil until foamy. Add the pigeons and brown on all sides. Place the pigeons, still in the pan, into the oven and roast for 10 minutes, basting several times.

3. Remove the pan from the oven and transfer the pigeons to a cutting board, draining and reserving any juices. Reduce the oven temperature to 300°F. Using a heavy knife or kitchen shears, cut down along both sides of each pigeon's backbone. Remove and reserve the bone. Turn the pigeon halves over and use your fingers to pull out the rib cage and reserve. Reserve the semi-boned pigeon halves on ovenproof platter and cover with foil.

4. Pour most of the fat from the Dutch oven into a small sauté pan and reserve. Add the wine to the Dutch oven, place over medium heat, and bring to a boil, scraping up any browned bits with a wooden spoon. Add the Light Chicken Stock and the reserved pigeon bones and juices and bring to a boil. Reduce the heat and simmer for 30 minutes; then strain the liquid, discarding the bones. Pour the liquid into a small pan and boil until reduced by about half. The liquid should be slightly syrupy. Season to taste with salt and pepper.

5. Heat the sauté pan of reserved roasting fat. Add the pigeon livers and cook over high heat until well browned. Season with salt and pepper. Remove the livers to a small bowl with a slotted spoon. Add 2 tablespoons of the butter and mash. Add the Cognac and mash again until fairly smooth. Stir this mixture into the reduced pigeon liquid to make the sauce.

6. In a small pan over low heat, heat the remaining 2 tablespoons butter until foamy. Add the bread ovals and lightly brown on both sides. Remove the bread ovals from the pan and reserve.

7. Reheat the wild rice, if necessary (you can do this in the microwave oven). When ready to serve, have ready 4 large, heated dinner plates. Place the platter with the pigeon halves into the 300°F oven to reheat for about 10 minutes. At the last minute, bring the pigeon sauce to a boil, add half the fava beans, and simmer for 2 minutes.

8. Place one bread oval in the center of each dinner plate. Place two pigeon halves onto the bread and baste with some of the pigeon sauce. Surround the pigeon with a ring of wild rice and sprinkle with some of the remaining fava beans, the basil shreds, and the remainder of the pigeon sauce. Serve immediately.

ABOUT *FÈVETTES* (YOUNG FAVA BEANS)

Tender young fava beans are a springtime legume. Before you cook them, it is necessary to blanch them in salted water and refresh them in ice water in order to remove the outer skin, which is not edible. Then, separate each bean into two halves.

Skillet-Roasted Chicken
with Black-Eyed Peas, Country Ham, and Savory

If you think supermarket chicken is boring, try a grain-fed or organic bird to remind yourself of just how special chicken can be. A strong, cured country ham, like a Smithfield ham, is perfect here. I love the little black-eyed peas and ham with the chicken. Try to find fresh savory for this dish—it's a wonderful herb with poultry and especially well suited to beans. For this recipe, you'll need two cast-iron skillets to weight down the chicken so it browns thoroughly. Or use a foil-wrapped brick as a weight, as is done in Italy, especially Tuscany, where a similar dish is called pollo al mattone.

Serves 4 to 6

2 chickens, preferably grain-fed or
    organic (4 to 5 pounds total), halved
    and flattened, backbones removed
Salt and freshly ground black pepper
Olive oil, for coating the skillet
2 tablespoons vegetable oil
¼ pound country ham, cut into small dice
½ pound fresh or frozen black-eyed peas
1 bunch scallions, white and green parts,
    cut diagonally into 1-inch lengths
1 cup Light Chicken Stock (see page 320)
½ cup dry white vermouth
1 tablespoon chopped fresh savory
    leaves, or 1 teaspoon dried
2 tablespoons unsalted butter

1. Assemble two well-seasoned cast-iron skillets, each about 10 inches in diameter. Cut two or three slashes in each chicken thigh. Season the chicken halves with salt and pepper.

2. Preheat one skillet and coat the inside with a little olive oil. Cooking in two batches, place the chicken halves, skin side down, in the skillet and cover with the second skillet to weight down. Cook over medium heat for about 10 minutes; until well-browned on one side, then turn and cook for about 10 minutes longer, until well-browned on the other side. When chicken halves are cooked through, remove them from the skillet and keep warm in a 200°F oven. Pour off and discard any excess fat from the skillet.

3. In a small skillet, heat the vegetable oil over high heat, add the diced ham, and quickly cook until crispy. Add the black-eyed peas and scallions and cook for a few minutes. Remove the ham-pea mixture from the pan and scatter over the chicken.

4. In the same skillet, combine the Light Chicken Stock and vermouth and bring to a boil. Cook until reduced to a syrupy consistency. Stir in the savory and the butter. Ladle the sauce over the chicken and serve immediately.

Indonesian Lamb Saté
with Spicy Peanut Dipping Sauce

This classic saté of lamb might be sold by an Indonesian street vendor with a small charcoal brazier. Try serving this quick, easy make-ahead dish at your next cookout. If you use natural hardwood charcoal for grilling, the flavor will be even better. Here, strips of lean lamb are marinated in tamarind (a tart tropical fruit), ginger, and soy sauce and then threaded on bamboo skewers. The lamb is grilled and accompanied by a spicy peanut sauce. This is an inexpensive and tasty dish that your guests will snap up and you won't even need any silverware. For a variation, you can make this with beef strips.

Serves 8

2 tablespoons tamarind pulp
2 pounds boneless leg or shoulder of
   lamb
1 small onion, coarsely chopped
2 cloves garlic, chopped
2 tablespoons mushroom soy sauce
¼ teaspoon cayenne
1½ teaspoons ground coriander
1 (2-inch) length fresh ginger, peeled
   and chopped
2 tablespoons peanut oil
1 cup Spicy Peanut Dipping Sauce
   (see page 317)

1. Prepare the tamarind pulp according to the directions on page 10.

2. Place the lamb in the freezer for about 30 minutes to chill and firm. Remove and trim off any surface fat. Cut the meat into thin strips, 2 to 3 inches long, and reserve. In a shallow glass dish, combine the meat, onion, garlic, soy sauce, cayenne, coriander, ginger, tamarind pulp, and oil. Cover and marinate in the refrigerator for 24 hours.

3. Drain and discard the marinade. Thread the meat strips accordion-style on bamboo skewers. Cover and refrigerate the skewered meat until ready to cook no more than 8 hours.

4. When ready to serve, heat a grill, preferably with hardwood charcoal, until white hot. Grill the skewers until browned and crusty, about 5 minutes on each side. Serve the skewers with the Spicy Peanut Sauce.

Ragout of Flageolets, Chicken-Basil Sausage, and Spinach

Chef Alfonso Contrisciani, captain of the 2000 U.S. Culinary Olympic Team, is one of only fifty-three Certified Master Chefs in the United States, a title earned in a grueling 10-day examination. He is also a skilled charcutier and believes in making everything in his kitchen from scratch, including his own chicken-basil sausage. This ragout—which is just a fancy French name for stew—features delicate flageolet beans in a rich broth topped with grilled portobello mushrooms and homemade chicken-basil sausage. Feel free to substitute any of the imaginative chicken sausages sold in markets ranging from Costco to Whole Foods. Like many a chef's creation, this one depends on advance preparation of all ingredients. Once you've assembled all the components, it's relatively easy to complete the dish.

Serves 6

1 tablespoon olive oil

1 teaspoon chopped garlic

1 tablespoon chopped shallot

¼ cup diced onion

1 cup quartered white mushrooms

1 cup sliced shiitake mushroom caps

1 teaspoon chopped fresh thyme leaves

1 tablespoon chopped fresh basil leaves, plus ¼ cup shredded basil leaves, for garnish

¼ teaspoon hot red pepper flakes

½ teaspoon dried oregano

2 tablespoons brandy

3 cups Basic Cooked Flageolets (see page 302)

1 cup Rich Chicken Stock (see page 322)

¼ cup dry white wine

3 tablespoons olive oil

2 tablespoons balsamic vinegar

6 large portobello mushroom caps

1½ pounds chicken-basil sausage or other chicken sausage (see Sources, page 341)

1 (12-ounce) bag fresh spinach leaves, stems removed

4 tablespoons unsalted butter

1 cup sliced bottled, imported roasted red peppers, for garnish

6 Crostini (see page 65), for serving

1. In a medium saucepan, heat 1 tablespoon olive oil over medium-high heat. Add the garlic and shallot. Stir-fry until the garlic turns golden; then add the onion and the white and shiitake mushrooms, stirring to combine. Add the thyme, 1 tablespoon basil, red pepper flakes, and oregano. Continue to stir-fry until the onion is translucent, 3 to 4 minutes.

2. Add the brandy and, keeping your face away from the flame, carefully light the mixture with a match to flambé. When the flames die down, add the Basic Cooked Flageolets, the Rich Chicken Stock, and the white wine. Simmer over high heat to reduce and thicken the liquid slightly, about 5 to 10 minutes. Reserve the sauce until ready to finish the dish. (It can be made up to 1 day ahead of time, covered, and refrigerated.)

3. To cook the portobello mushrooms and sausage, prepare a grill to high heat. If using natural hardwood charcoal, wait until the flames die down.

4. In a small bowl, whisk together 2 tablespoons of the olive oil and the balsamic vinegar. Brush the portobello mushroom caps with the mixture and grill, starting with the top sides down, for about 5 minutes on each side, or until grill marks are visible. Remove the mushrooms from the grill, reserving on a plate to collect the juices. Grill the sausage until cooked through, about 10 minutes. Cool slightly, and cut into ¼-inch diagonal slices.

5. In a medium pan, heat the remaining 1 tablespoon olive oil over medium heat. Add the spinach and cook just until wilted but still intensely green. Drain and reserve.

6. To finish the ragout, reheat the reserved sauce and gradually stir in the ¼ cup basil and the butter. Divide the ragout among 6 large, shallow soup plates, heated if possible. Place one grilled portobello mushroom cap on each, drizzling with any accumulated juices. Top with the sausage slices, roasted pepper strips, and wilted spinach. Serve immediately with one Crostino on the side of each plate.

COOK'S NOTE

For the home cook, I recommend purchasing one of the fine commercially made chicken sausages available in specialty meat departments (see Sources, page 341). If you can't find basil-flavored chicken sausage, substitute plain chicken sausage, or one flavored with sun-dried tomatoes.

Spiced Duck in Port Wine Sauce with Green Lentils
and Savoy Cabbage

This lovely, fancy dish would be an excellent choice for a special wintertime dinner. It encompasses everything that I adore about French cuisine: the contradictory combination of earthy cabbage and lentils with the elegant, medium-rare duck breast in its deep ruby-colored sauce. I fell in love with the cabbage confit after tasting Chef Georges Perrier's version. The large moulard-type duck breasts are available at specialty meat markets or from the D'Artagnan company (see Sources, page 341). The sauce, cabbage, and green lentils can all be made up to 2 days ahead of time. On the day of your dinner, the only thing you'll need to do is reheat them, and sear and carve the duck.

——————————— *Advance preparation required. Serves 6* ———————————

Spiced Duck

1 tablespoon ground cinnamon
1 tablespoon ground coriander
1 tablespoon ground anise seeds
1 tablespoon kosher salt
2 teaspoons freshly ground black pepper
6 large boneless moulard duck breast
    halves, fat pricked all over (without
    piercing the flesh)

Savoy Cabbage Confit

1 head savoy cabbage
¼ cup duck fat (see Sources, page 341),
    bacon fat, or butter
1 teaspoon kosher salt
¼ teaspoon freshly ground black pepper

Port Wine Sauce

½ cup chopped shallots
2 tablespoons (¼ stick) unsalted butter
¼ cup sugar
¼ cup cider vinegar
2 cups port wine
1 quart Rich Chicken Stock (see page
    322), or duck stock
2 tablespoons chopped fresh thyme
    leaves (about ¼ bunch)
Salt and freshly ground black pepper
3 cups Basic Cooked French Green
    Lentils (see page 298), warmed

1. Prepare the Spiced Duck: Combine the cinnamon, coriander, anise, salt, and black pepper. Rub lightly into both sides of the duck breasts. Cover and refrigerate for 8 hours.

2. Prepare the Savoy Cabbage Confit: Bring a large pot of salted water to a boil. Cut the cabbage into quarters. Trim off and discard a triangle-shaped piece of the core and the larger ribs from each quarter. Add the cabbage leaves to the boiling water and blanch for 5 minutes; then drain in a colander. Combine the duck fat, cabbage, salt, and pepper in a medium pot over low heat and cook for 20 minutes. Strain the cabbage in a colander or sieve to drain off the fat. Pat dry on paper towels and reserve.

3. Prepare the Port Wine Sauce: In a small pan over medium heat, sauté the shallots in 1 tablespoon of the butter until browned. Stir in the sugar and cook until the sugar melts and caramelizes (it will turn brown and smell like caramel). Add the vinegar and cook for 2 minutes. Add the port wine, Rich Chicken Stock, and thyme. Bring to a boil and cook until the liquid is reduced to 1½ cups. Whisk in the remaining 1 tablespoon butter and season with salt and pepper to taste. Strain through a fine sieve and reserve in a warm place.

4. Place the spiced duck breasts in a cast-iron skillet, skin sides down, and sear on low heat to render the excess fat. Drain the fat once or twice, reserving it for another use. When the skin is evenly and lightly browned, remove the duck breasts from the skillet and cover with foil. Allow them to rest for 5 to 10 minutes, so the juices settle back into the meat.

5. Have ready 6 large, heated dinner plates. Place a mound of Basic Cooked French Green Lentils in the center of each plate. Surround with the cabbage. Carve the duck into thin slices, using an electric knife if available. Arrange the duck slices over the lentils and ladle over about ½ cup of Port Wine Sauce for each portion.

COOK'S NOTE

The Moulard duck is a crossbreed between a Muscovy male and a Pekin
female, and is raised especially for its enlarged liver, or foie gras. The large
breasts of these ducks are suitable for cooking rare and serving thinly sliced,
like a steak.

Maccheroni Rustica

(VEGETARIAN OPTION)

This satisfying, boldly flavored dish was quite popular, especially with the men, at the trattoria Stella Notte, in Philadelphia's Chestnut Hill section, where I served as executive chef. It's a low-cost, highly flavored dish with lots of chunky textural appeal. Serve it at an informal gathering of friends, perhaps a Super Bowl buffet or Father's Day supper, and you'll find that it's a winner. The browned sausage, Caramelized Garlic, Oven-Roasted Plum Tomatoes, and Oven-Cooked Italian-Style Beans can (and should) all be made as much as 3 days ahead of time. Assembly is then quick and easy. For a vegetarian version, omit the sausages and use Oven-Cooked Vegetarian Beans.

Serves 4

½ pound Italian sweet sausage

½ pound Italian hot sausage

2 tablespoons olive oil

½ cup Caramelized Garlic (recipe follows)

8 Oven-Roasted Plum Tomatoes, cut in half lengthwise and then lengthwise into strips (see page 309)

2 cups Oven-Cooked Italian-Style Beans (see page 294), made with cranberry beans

1 pound maccheroni pasta (preferably Martelli; see Sources, page 341), or ziti or rigatoni

¼ cup chopped Italian parsley

Salt and freshly ground pepper

½ pound fresh mozzarella, cut into small dice

½ pound smoked mozzarella, cut into small dice

1. Preheat the oven to 350°F. Arrange the sausages on a baking sheet. Bake for 20 minutes, or until browned on the outside and cooked through. Chill and then slice into rounds.

2. In a large skillet, brown the sausage slices in the olive oil. Add the Caramelized Garlic, Oven-Roasted Plum Tomato Strips, and Oven-Cooked Vegetarian Beans to the pan and heat.

3. Meanwhile, heat a large pot of salted boiling water. Add the pasta and cook until al dente. Drain, reserving about 1 cup of the cooking water. Toss the pasta with the sausage and bean sauce and the parsley. Season to taste, thinning the sauce as desired with the reserved pasta cooking water. Serve in a large preheated pasta bowl topped with both kinds of mozzarella.

CARAMELIZED GARLIC

1 cup peeled garlic cloves
1½ cups olive oil

Combine the garlic and oil in a small heavy-bottomed pot just large enough to hold them. Heat until the oil bubbles vigorously. Reduce the heat and cook for about 10 minutes longer, with the oil still slightly bubbling, until the garlic cloves begin to brown on the outside. Turn off the heat and allow garlic to cool in the oil. Drain, saving both the oil (excellent for roasting vegetables) and the garlic separately. Both the garlic and the oil will keep for about 2 weeks in the refrigerator.

CHOOSING GARLIC

I'm a garlic lover, so I'm particular about the garlic I buy. I really despise the bitter taste of commercial chopped garlic in oil. On the other hand, even I don't always have the patience to peel my own, though if I come across heads of hard-necked, pink-skinned fresh garlic full of juicy cloves, I don't pass up the opportunity to enjoy garlic at its best. Chefs have been able to buy high-quality peeled garlic cloves for a long time, but it's only recently that I've seen whole peeled garlic cloves in the produce section of my market. If you spot creamy-looking, smooth, pearly cloves, buy them for this hearty, soul-satisfying dish.

Toto's Pasta "Fazool" *(Pasta e Fagioli)*

Toto Schiavone, owner of the stylish Center City Philadelphia restaurant Toto, has had a major influence on my life. As direttore *(managing director) of the original Ristorante DiLullo where I served as chef for six years, Toto was the king of maître d's. A born restaurateur, his generous and outgoing nature endeared him to customers, who continued coming back for both the food and his legendary hospitality. As a boy growing up in Taranto, the instep of the Italian boot, Toto ate the traditional rustic foods of the region, including calamari and mussels, and this rib-sticking cold-weather pasta with beans (prepared in so many different ways throughout Italy). I always loved it when he cooked this dish for me, and so I asked him to share his mother's recipe. He makes it using pork broth, but I've substituted chicken broth.*

—————————— *Serves 6* ——————————

¼ cup plus 2 tablespoons extra-virgin olive oil

6 individually cut pork ribs

½ red onion, chopped (about ¼ cup)

½ fennel bulb, finely chopped

1 cup crushed fresh tomatoes

3 cups Oven-Cooked Italian-Style Beans (see page 294) prepared with *borlotti* or pinto beans

3 cups Light Chicken Stock (see page 320)

½ cup finely diced carrots

1 pound Durum Pasta Dough (see page 325), cut into maltagliati shapes, or 1 (1-pound) package small dried pasta shells

½ cup finely shredded arugula leaves (about 1 bunch), washed thoroughly

2 teaspoons salt

¼ teaspoon freshly ground black pepper

½ cup grated Parmigiano-Reggiano cheese

1. Heat ¼ cup of the olive oil in a large, heavy-bottomed pan. Add the pork ribs and cook over medium heat until brown. Remove from the pan. Add the onion and fennel. Cook until the vegetables are soft. Add the tomatoes and simmer for 7 to 10 minutes.

2. Add the Oven-Cooked Italian-Style Beans, mix well, and stir in the Light Chicken Stock. Bring to a boil, reduce the heat, and simmer for 30 minutes, adding the carrots during the last 5 minutes. Remove the pork ribs from the pot. Cool; then remove the meat from the bones. Remove about 1 cup of the bean mixture to a bowl and mash with a fork. Return the pork meat and the mashed beans to the pot.

3. Bring a large pot of salted water to a boil. Add the pasta and cook until firm to the bite (2 to 3 minutes for fresh pasta; 8 minutes for dried). Drain, reserving ½ cup of the pasta cooking water.

4. Add the reserved pasta water to the bean mixture along with the arugula, salt, pepper, and grated cheese. Let the mixture rest for 5 minutes and then serve, dividing the meat among the plates. As Toto says, "Drizzle each plate with a hair [remaining 2 tablespoons] of oil."

About "Fazool"

I always wondered about the Southern Italian dialect word *fazool*, used instead of the classic Italian word *fagioli*. Where did this word come from? It was not until I traveled to Greece several years ago and learned that their word for beans is *fasoulia*. Because southern Italy was once part of the Greek Empire—when it was known as Magna Grecia—the Greek name *fasoulia* was adopted and transformed to the word *fazool* that is used today in this part of Italy. *Fasoulia* is also the Arabic word for "beans."

Country-Style Ziti (*Ziti alla Contadina*)

(VEGETARIAN)

About 10 years ago, I was asked by Gabriel Marabella to develop a new fast Italian food concept with him. Gabe's parents had started the Philadelphia area's famous Marabella's restaurants many years before, and later the three brothers ran the rapidly expanding business with the help of their mother. After most of the original restaurants were sold, Gabe decided it was time to venture out on his own. His concept was Parma, where he served "Old World food" prepared from scratch quickly and at moderate prices. I developed this dish for the original Parma as a hearty, satisfying vegetarian pasta. Though not a vegetarian myself, I adore all kinds of vegetables, including the delicious bitter-edged broccoli rabe called for here.

Serves 6

4 cups Oven-Cooked Vegetarian Beans (see page 296), or Oven-Cooked Italian-Style Beans (see page 294), prepared with cannellini beans

1 pound ziti, preferably ridged (rigati)

1 bunch broccoli rabe, bottom 2 inches of stem discarded

¼ cup extra-virgin olive oil

1 tablespoon chopped fresh garlic

½ teaspoon hot red pepper flakes

12 to 16 Oven-Roasted Plum Tomatoes, cut into strips (see page 309)

½ cup grated aged Pecorino Romano cheese

1. In a blender or food processor purée half of the Oven-Cooked Vegetarian Beans, leaving the remaining beans whole.

2. Bring a large pot of salted water to a boil. Cut the broccoli rabe into ½-inch pieces. Add to the pot and cook for 1 minute, or until bright green. Using a skimmer or slotted spoon, scoop out the broccoli rabe, drain, and reserve. Bring the water back to a boil. Add the pasta and cook for about 9 minutes, or until al dente. Drain and reserve.

3. In a large, heavy-bottomed pan, heat the olive oil over medium heat. Add the garlic and red pepper flakes. Cook until the garlic sizzles and gives off its aroma. Stir in the broccoli rabe and cook 5 minutes more. Add the puréed and whole cooked beans and the Oven-Roasted Plum Tomato strips. Bring the sauce to a boil. Add the pasta, toss to combine, and sprinkle with the cheese. Serve immediately.

Kofte (Grilled Lamb Patties)
with Turkish White Bean Salad and Marinated Carrots

In the early seventies, I visited Istanbul and stayed in the old section of the city, near the souk and across from the famous Blue Mosque. Every night we played shesh-besh *(backgammon) in the hotel's courtyard. In spite of my limited funds, I ate extremely well, enjoying Istanbul's varied offerings, a mélange of Turkish, Eastern Mediterranean and North African dishes. Most days I would go to the same restaurant to enjoy this dish, their working man's lunch special. Accompany with warmed pita bread and, as they did in Istanbul, bottles of ice-cold spring water.*

———————————— *Serves 4* ————————————

Marinated Carrots

1 pound carrots, peeled and shredded
½ cup fresh lemon juice (about 4 lemons)
½ cup extra-virgin olive oil
1 sweet onion (such as Vidalia or Texas 100) or white onion, thinly sliced
Salt and freshly ground black pepper
2 teaspoons sumac (optional; see Chef's Note)

Lamb Patties

1 pound ground lamb
1 egg
1 teaspoon finely chopped garlic
1 small onion, grated
2 teaspoons chopped fresh mint leaves, or ½ teaspoon dried
¼ teaspoon hot red pepper flakes
¼ teaspoon ground cinnamon
¼ teaspoon ground allspice
2 teaspoons salt
¼ teaspoons freshly ground black pepper
Olive oil, for brushing
Kosher salt, for grilling
2 cups Turkish White Bean Salad (see page 86)

1. Prepare the Marinated Carrots: In a bowl, combine the carrots, lemon juice, olive oil, onion, and salt and pepper to taste, mixing well. Refrigerate until needed, up to 3 or 4 days. Just before serving, toss the carrots again to distribute the dressing, and sprinkle with the sumac.

2. Prepare the Lamb Patties: In a large bowl, combine the lamb, egg, garlic, onion, mint, red pepper flakes, cinnamon, allspice, salt, and black pepper. Knead together by hand until well combined. Form into 8 oblong patties. Cover and refrigerate for 30 minutes or up to 1 day.

3. When ready to cook, preheat a grill. Lightly brush the lamb patties with olive oil and sprinkle with kosher salt to help keep them from sticking. Place the patties on an angle on the grill and cook 5 to 7 minutes, or until they release freely from the grill when you try to turn them. Rotate the patties a half-turn and continue to grill for 5 minutes; then turn them over and repeat, cooking for 5 to 7 minutes longer. The patties should be medium to medium-rare when cooked.

4. To serve, place a mound of the Turkish White Bean Salad on each plate. Top with two grilled lamb patties and surround with 3 to 4 small mounds of the marinated carrots.

CHEF'S NOTE

Sumac, which is sold ground, is a tart, fruity spice that is brick red to deep purplish red in color. The berries of a bush that grows wild in the Middle East and elsewhere, sumac is commonly used in Middle Eastern cooking as a colorful astringent accent. It can be found in Middle Eastern markets or at Penzeys (see Sources, page 341) and other spice purveyors.

Mustard-Crusted Rack of Lamb
with Spinach and Cranberry Bean Ragout

When you really want to celebrate, serve this rack of lamb with its crunchy coarse-grain mustard crust. If you can find fresh cranberry beans, in season sporadically from the early spring through the fall, use them here for their firm yet smooth and creamy texture. Marinate the lamb, and cook the cranberry beans up to 2 days ahead of time. For best results, allow the lamb to come to room temperature before roasting, and make sure your oven is good and hot so you'll get a well browned crust on the outside, with a juicy red to pink interior, depending on how you like your lamb cooked. Shelled fresh cranberry beans freeze perfectly, so anytime you spot them, buy a few pounds, shell them, and freeze in a double zipper-lock freezer bag until ready to use.

--- *Serves 4* ---

Lamb

½ cup chopped garlic
½ cup vegetable oil
¾ cup coarse-grain mustard
¾ cup Dijon mustard
1 bunch fresh oregano, leaves chopped
2 tablespoons kosher salt
2 teaspoons ground black pepper
2 racks of lamb, trimmed of all outside fat and silverskin cut away

Ragout

½ cup veal demi-glace, purchased (see Sources, page 341) or homemade
1 cup dry red wine
2 cups Cooked Fresh Cranberry Beans (see page 294), or 2 cups cooked dried white beans, emergo beans, or borlotti beans (see Basic Cooking Chart, page 58)
½ cup Caramelized Garlic (see page 207)
½ cup Oven-Roasted Plum Tomato halves, cut lengthwise into strips (see page 309)
1 (10-ounce) bag cleaned spinach

1. Prepare the Lamb: In a food processor, combine the garlic, oil, mustards, oregano, salt, and black pepper. Blend until well combined. Spread about ½ cup of the mustard mixture over each rack of lamb, including the rib portion.

2. Preheat the oven to 425°F. Place the racks of lamb, flesh side up, in a baking pan. Roast about 20 minutes, or until rare to medium rare inside. (An instant-read meat thermometer inserted into the thickest part of the meat should read 125°F for rare and 145°F for medium-rare.) Remove the lamb from the oven and allow to rest in a warm place, covered with foil, about 10 minutes before cutting into individual chops.

3. Prepare the Ragout: Meanwhile, in a small saucepan, simmer the demi-glace with the red wine until syrupy. Turn off the heat and transfer the sauce to a larger skillet. Add the Cooked Fresh Cranberry Beans, Caramelized Garlic, and Oven-Roasted Plum Tomato strips and bring to a boil. Just before serving, stir in the spinach and remove the pan from the heat. The spinach will wilt in the residual heat.

4. Transfer the ragout to individual large, shallow serving bowls or plates. Arrange 4 lamb chops for each person, half from the smaller end of the rack and half from the larger end with the bone end forming a pyramid shape over the ragout. Serve immediately.

Roasted Gigot of Lamb
with Flageolet Gratin

Flageolets and lamb are a classic combination in France, where the gigot, or leg of lamb, is much appreciated for its robust flavor. We Americans eat relatively little lamb, but are starting to get to know it better as a result of the huge wave of new Mediterranean restaurants. Assertively flavored lamb rubbed with resinous herbs, like rosemary, thyme, and oregano, marries very well with creamy textured legumes. Start this dish the day before you plan to serve it so the meat has a chance to absorb the flavors of the rub. The flageolets can be prepared up to the point of baking them as much as 3 days ahead. While flageolets are traditional in this dish, navy beans may be substituted.

——————— *Advance preparation recommended. Serves 8* ———————

Lamb

¼ cup chopped fresh rosemary leaves
　(about ¼ bunch)
¼ cup chopped fresh thyme leaves
　(about ½ bunch)
2 tablespoons chopped garlic
Grated zest of 2 lemons
1 tablespoon kosher salt
1 teaspoon freshly ground black pepper
¼ cup olive oil
1 (8- to 10-pound) leg of lamb, trimmed
　of exterior fat (see Cook's Note)

Flageolet Gratin

1 (12-ounce) package imported flageolets
1 peeled medium onion, stuck with
　4 whole cloves
1 (3- to 4-inch) strip lemon zest
2 bay leaves
6 cups water
½ cup extra-virgin olive oil
½ cup sliced shallots
2 tablespoons chopped garlic
2 tablespoons chopped fresh thyme
　leaves (about ¼ bunch)
3 cups Light Chicken Stock (see page 320)
1½ cups fresh bread crumbs, prepared
　from country-style white bread
1 cup dry white vermouth
1 cup water

1. Prepare the Lamb: Combine the rosemary, thyme, garlic, lemon zest, salt, and pepper in a small bowl. Stir in the oil and rub the seasoning paste all over the surface of the lamb. Place the lamb in a roasting pan just large enough to hold it, cover lightly, and refrigerate for at least 4 hours or overnight. (You could use a disposable foil roasting pan for this.) About 3 hours before you plan to serve the lamb, start the flageolets.

2. Prepare the Flageolet Gratin: Place the flageolets, clove-studded onion, lemon zest, and bay leaves in a medium, heavy-bottomed pot. Add the 6 cups water to cover and bring to a boil. Skim off and discard the white foam impurities that rise to the surface. Reduce the heat to a bare simmer and cook slowly for about 1 hour, or until the beans are almost tender. Remove from the heat and pour off and reserve the liquid. Discard the onion, lemon zest, and bay leaves. Reserve the beans and their cooking liquid.

3. Heat ¼ cup of the olive oil in a sauté pan. Add the shallots, garlic, and thyme and cook for 2 to 3 minutes, stirring constantly. Add the Light Chicken Stock and bring the mixture to a boil. Add the reserved flageolets along with their cooking liquid, and remove from the heat.

4. Lightly rub the inside of a 2-quart, shallow, oval gratin dish or large, shallow baking dish with a little oil. In a separate bowl, combine the remaining ¼ cup oil with the bread crumbs. Fill the gratin dish with the bean mixture, spreading it evenly with a spoon. Sprinkle generously with the bread crumbs. (If desired, cover and refrigerate for up to 3 days at this point.)

5. About 2 hours before serving, preheat the oven to 375°F. Place the marinated lamb on the bottom shelf of the oven and roast for about 1 hour, or until it reaches 100° to 110°F on a meat thermometer. Place the gratin on the top shelf of the oven and cook with the lamb for about 1 hour longer, or until the top of the gratin is browned and bubbly and the lamb reaches 135°F on a meat thermometer inserted into its thickest part (for medium-rare).

6. Remove the lamb from the oven, place on a cutting board, drape with foil, and allow it to rest for about 15 minutes before carving it into thin slices. Arrange the slices on a platter. Pour off and discard the excess fat from the roasting pan. If the pan is metal, place it directly over a burner. (If not, add the vermouth and place the pan back in the oven to soften the browned bits.) Add the vermouth and water. Bring to a boil, scraping up the browned bits with a wooden spoon. Strain through a sieve into a small saucepan. Cook for 5 to 10 minutes to reduce the liquid by one-fourth. Transfer it to a gravy boat.

7. To serve, place a scoop of the gratin, including some crust, on each plate and top with several slices of lamb. Pour the juices over the top.

COOK'S NOTE

Ask your butcher to completely trim the fat from the leg of lamb, and to remove the aitch bone (the partial hip bone at the large end of the leg) to make it easier to carve. If you have the butcher remove the shank meat, the leg will have a smaller yield, but the meat will be more tender. You should see little or no outer connective tissue, with the muscle meat exposed. Lamb fat has a strong flavor, and the herb rub won't penetrate if you skip this step.

Brazilian Feijõada Completa

Feijõada, *from the Portuguese word* feijõas, *meaning "beans," is the national dish of Brazil, known as "The land of beans.". It is based on a dish of black beans surrounded by a large variety of smoked and cured meats, traditionally including pigs' ears and tails. I once held a tasting party for a take-out food project I was working on. Seventy-five or so guests came, tasted a menu of about twenty items, and then had to fill out a survey. This dish was the all-around favorite.*

If you have access to a home smoker and you want to include the amazing Spiced and Smoked Short Ribs and the Home-Smoked Chorizo, you'll need to start this dish three days ahead of time. Otherwise, simply substitute corned beef or smoked pork butt and smoked kielbasa. Here, I serve the black beans surrounded with the spiced ribs, smoked chorizo, Brazilian rice, and braised greens, and accompanied by the spicy Lemon-Pepper Mojo, a type of Brazilian salsa.

———————— *Advance preparation required. Serves 12 to 16* ————————

Meat

3½ pounds Spiced and Smoked Short Ribs (recipe follows), or 3 pounds cooked corned beef or smoked pork butt (see Cook's Note)

2½ pounds Home-Smoked Chorizo (recipe follows), or 3 pounds smoked kielbasa, cut into ¾-inch diagonal slices (see Cook's Note)

Black Beans

6 cups Basic Black Turtle Beans (see page 297)

2 large white onions, diced

2 tablespoons chopped garlic

1 tablespoon ground toasted cumin seeds (see Toasting Seeds, page 225)

¼ cup bacon fat or olive oil

1 (28-ounce) can plum tomatoes, seeded and diced, juice strained and reserved

½ cup malt vinegar, or cider or sherry vinegar

1 tablespoon Mexican oregano

2 tablespoons hot pepper sauce

2 tablespoons salt

1. Prepare the Meat: Make the Spiced and Smoked Short Ribs and the Home-Smoked Chorizo.

2. Prepare the Black Beans: Preheat the oven to 300°F. In a large, heavy Dutch oven with a lid, cook the onions, garlic, and cumin in the bacon fat until softened but not browned. Stir in the tomatoes, vinegar, oregano, hot sauce, and salt, and bring to a boil. Stir in the cooked beans, cover, and transfer to the oven. Bake for 2 hours, or until the beans are soft and plump.

3. Prepare the Brazilian Rice: Bring the Light Chicken Stock, saffron, water, salt, and pepper to a boil in a medium pan. Remove from the heat and cover. In a large, heavy Dutch oven, cook the onion in the olive oil until softened but not browned. Add the rice and sauté until transparent but not browned. Add the hot stock mixture and tomatoes to the rice and bring to a boil. Reduce the heat and simmer, covered, for 15 to 20 minutes, or until all the liquid has been absorbed.

4. To serve, arrange the beans in the center of a large platter. Place the reserved short ribs on one side of the beans and the chorizo on the other. Garnish the platter with the orange and grapefruit slices. On a second large platter, arrange the rice on one side and the Mixed Greens with Garlic and Olive Oil on the other. Place the Lemon-Pepper Mojo in a bowl alongside.

Brazilian Rice

2 cups Light Chicken Stock (see page 320)

½ teaspoon saffron threads

2 cups water

Salt and freshly ground black pepper

1 medium onion, peeled and thinly sliced

2 tablespoons olive oil

2 cups long-grain rice

1 (28-ounce) can chopped plum tomatoes

Orange slices and ruby red grapefruit slices, for garnish

6 cups Mixed Greens with Garlic and Olive Oil (see page 318)

1½ cups Lemon-Pepper Mojo (see page 304)

COOK'S NOTE

If using corned beef instead of beef ribs, purchase a 5- to 6- pound corned beef brisket. Remove it from the package, drain well, and place in a large soup or braising pot. Cover with chicken, beef, or vegetable stock, or water, and bring the liquid to a boil. Reduce the heat and simmer very gently for 3 hours, or until the meat is tender when pierced with a fork. Cool in its cooking liquid for juiciest results and reserve the liquid. To serve, slice thinly across the grain of the meat and reheat in the reserved cooking liquid. Cover and reserve in a 200°F oven.

If using smoked pork instead of beef ribs, purchase a 4-pound boneless smoked pork loin. To cook, preheat the oven to 325°F. Place the meat in a roasting pan with about 3 cups of liquid (white wine, beef or chicken stock, or water). Cover with foil and bake for 1 hour, or until steaming hot. Remove from the oven and cool for about 10 minutes before slicing. Cover and reserve in a 200°F oven.

If using kielbasa instead of chorizo, brown the slices in a skillet over medium heat. Drain and reserve in a 200°F oven.

SPICED AND SMOKED SHORT RIBS

— Makes 3½ pounds smoked ribs —

2 tablespoons kosher salt

2 tablespoons molasses

2 tablespoons sugar

2 tablespoons grated fresh ginger

1 tablespoon cracked black peppercorns

½ cup chopped garlic

2 tablespoons cracked coriander seeds

2 tablespoons ground fennel seeds

5 pounds cross-cut short ribs of beef

Combine the salt, molasses, sugar, ginger, peppercorns, garlic, coriander, and fennel in a blender or food processor and process to a paste. Rub all over the surface of the short ribs. Cover and refrigerate for 3 days to cure the meat. When ready to cook, wipe off the excess paste and hot-smoke according to your smoker manufacturer's directions for 4 hours, or until tender and well browned. Cover and reserve in a 200°F oven.

HOME-SMOKED CHORIZO

— Makes 2½ pounds smoked chorizo —

3 pounds raw chorizo links

Hot-smoke the chorizo according to your smoker manufacturer's directions for 1 hour, or until it bubbles inside when pricked with a fork and is evenly browned. Cover and reserve in a 200°F oven.

Beef Stir-Fry
with Snow Peas and Bean Sprouts

This quick stir-fry is a popular choice for lunch at a longtime favorite Philadelphia restaurant called Friday Saturday Sunday. (Originally it was open only those days. More than 20 years later, it's now open 7 days.) Crunchy bean sprouts and sweet snow peas represent the legume family here. The large, white, mild daikon radish called for is sold in many supermarkets. It's a versatile vegetable, delicious shredded raw in salads or cooked in stir-fries. Substitute white turnip if daikon isn't available.

Serves 4 to 6

1 tablespoon roasted Japanese
   sesame oil
¼ cup soy sauce
¼ cup molasses
½ teaspoon hot red pepper flakes,
   preferably Korean red pepper flakes
   (see Korean Red Pepper Flakes,
   page 61)
2 tablespoons cornstarch
2 tablespoons peanut or soybean oil
1 pound beef London broil, cut into thin,
   2- to 3-inch strips
2 tablespoons chopped fresh ginger
2 tablespoons chopped garlic
1 large white onion, cut into strips
1 red bell pepper, cut into ½-inch-wide
   strips
½ pound daikon radish, peeled and cut
   into half-moon slices
¼ pound snow peas, trimmed
1 pint fresh bean sprouts, trimmed
3 cups steamed rice, for serving
   (optional)

1. In a small bowl, whisk together the sesame oil, soy sauce, molasses, red pepper flakes, and cornstarch.

2. Heat the peanut oil in a wok or a large skillet until it just begins to smoke. Add the beef and stir-fry for about 5 minutes, or until browned. Remove from the pan and reserve in a warm place.

3. In the same pan, cook the ginger and garlic for 1 minute. Add the onion, bell pepper, and daikon. Stir-fry for 2 minutes; then add the reserved beef, snow peas, cornstarch mixture, and bean sprouts. Cook until the sauce thickens and the snow peas turn bright green. Serve with steamed rice, if desired.

A WORD ABOUT SNOW PEAS

The French term *mangetout* (literally "eat-it-all") usually refers to young beans that are eaten pods and all and that are known in this country as snow peas. In England, the same term is applied to the relative newcomers known as sugar snap peas. Snow peas, which have been cultivated for at least 300 years, have pods with no hard inner skin. They are picked before the peas inside grow large enough to be visible from the outside. The pea pods used to be called "pea cods," as in codpiece.

Israeli Couscous
with Eggplant Rolls and Chickpeas
(VEGETARIAN OPTION)

In the early sixties, much of Morocco's large Jewish population left the country and settled in Paris, bringing along their highly developed cuisine. On a trip to Paris in 1964, I tasted my first couscous in a kosher restaurant in the Moroccan Jewish quarter and loved the way the fluffy bits soaked up the subtly spiced cooking juices. Later, my mother's Moroccan Jewish friend in Washington, D.C., taught her how to make her version of couscous, which I've adapted here, using the large-grain couscous popular in Israel and Lebanon. For a vegetarian version, make the eggplant rolls without their beef filling, and substitute Vegetable Stock (see page 323) for the chicken stock.

―――――――――― *Serves 8* ――――――――――

Eggplant Rolls

1 large eggplant, sliced into 16 (⅜-inch) rounds

1 pound ground beef

1 teaspoon salt

¼ teaspoon black pepper

2 eggs, lightly beaten

1 cup unbleached, all-purpose flour, seasoned with salt and freshly ground black pepper

Olive oil, for frying

2 cloves garlic, crushed

2 pounds beefsteak tomatoes, seeded and diced, juices reserved

3 cups cooked and drained chickpeas, (see Basic Cooking Chart, page 58)

2 cups Light Chicken Stock (see page 320)

Israeli Couscous

2 tablespoons olive oil

2 cups Israeli large-grained couscous

4 cups Light Chicken Stock (see page 320), simmering

2 teaspoons salt

1. Prepare the Eggplant Rolls: Lay the eggplant slices on a clean flat surface and salt lightly. After 30 minutes, pat the eggplant slices dry. In a large bowl, combine the ground beef with the salt and pepper and form into 16 walnut-sized oblong meatballs. Place a meatball in the center of each eggplant slice. Roll the eggplant around the meat to form a tube, securing with a toothpick or skewer. When all the eggplant slices have been stuffed, dip them first in the egg and then roll them in the seasoned flour, shaking off the excess. Reserve on a platter.

2. Heat a ½-inch depth of olive oil in a large skillet over medium heat. Add the eggplant rolls and brown on both sides; then remove from the pan and reserve. Pour off and discard almost all the oil.

3. Reduce the heat and add the garlic to the pan, stirring to cook evenly. Add the tomatoes and juice, cooked chickpeas, and Light Chicken Stock. Increase the heat and bring to a boil. Place the eggplant rolls in the stock mixture, reduce the heat, and simmer for 30 minutes, or until tender.

4. Prepare the Israeli Couscous: Heat the olive oil over medium heat in a medium saucepan. Add the couscous and cook, stirring constantly, until lightly browned. Add the simmering Light Chicken Stock and salt. Bring to a boil and cover. Reduce the heat and cook for about 15 minutes, or until the stock has been absorbed.

5. To serve, mound the couscous in the center of a large platter, preferably heated. Surround it with the eggplant rolls. Serve topped with the remaining sauce from the pan.

Classic Chili con Carne

Chili con carne seems to have originated in the early 1800s in towns near the Mexican border, like San Antonio, Texas. By the turn of the century, a German immigrant from New Braunfels, Texas, had invented chile powder, which is a blend of ground red chiles, seasoned with oregano, cumin, allspice, and garlic. Each manufacturer has its own secret blend, so taste and compare to find one you like, and check the ingredient labels to be sure there are no additives. After the invention of chile powder, chili con carne started to become popular throughout the rest of the country, leading to innumerable chili cook-off contests. The classic version of this dish, according to many chili authorities, is made with meat only, with the beans served on the side. The beef should be coarsely ground to provide good texture. This is best done by your butcher.

Serves 8

¼ cup vegetable oil

2 pounds coarsely ground beef chuck

3 cups thinly sliced onions

1 tablespoon chopped garlic

3 cups tomato sauce (purchased or homemade)

2 tablespoons yellow cornmeal

2 teaspoons dried oregano

¼ cup prepared chile powder (hot or mild)

2 teaspoons salt

½ teaspoon freshly ground black pepper

Steamed white rice, for serving (optional)

3 cups (½ recipe) Earthenware-Cooked Beans (see page 300), made with pinto beans

Chopped white onion, shredded Cheddar cheese, and diced tomato, for garnish (optional)

1. In a large Dutch oven, heat the oil. Add the beef in small batches and cook over high heat until browned; then reserve. Pour off most of the fat from the pan and add the sliced onions. Cook until the onions are brown, stirring often. Add the garlic and cook for 2 minutes longer.

2. Stir in the tomato sauce, cornmeal, oregano, chile powder, and beef. Bring to a boil. Reduce the heat, cover, and simmer for 1½ hours, stirring occasionally, or until the fat rises to the top. Remove from the heat. Stir in the salt and black pepper. Serve with the steamed white rice, Earthenware-Cooked Beans, and small bowls of the optional garnishes.

Five-Way Cincinnati-Style Chili

Fantastically funny food maven Calvin Trillin writes about Cincinnati chili in his book American Fried. *According to Trillin, a Greek immigrant named Kiradjieff introduced Cincinnati-style chili in his Empress Diner in 1922. The Skyline Diner was also famous for its version of this unique chili. I believe that the unusual seasoning derives from the Greek practice of seasoning meats, especially lamb, with cinnamon. In Cincinnati, the cinnamon and allspice–accented chili is served three-way (chili and cheese over spaghetti), four-way (chili and cheese over spaghetti topped with chopped onions), or five-way, which includes all of the above, plus beans. If you use the dark red kidney beans known as* badi rajma *in Indian markets, the color will be more striking.*

Serves 6 to 8

5 medium onions, chopped

2 tablespoons vegetable oil

1 clove garlic, minced

2 pounds ground beef

Spice sachet (4 whole dried chiles, 36 whole allspice berries, and 5 bay leaves tied in a cheesecloth bag with kitchen string)

1 quart water

2 tablespoons white vinegar

1 (12-ounce) can tomato paste

2 tablespoons mild chile powder

1 tablespoon ground cinnamon

1 teaspoon Tabasco sauce

2 dashes Worcestershire sauce

Salt and freshly ground black pepper

1 pound spaghetti

2 cups cooked kidney beans, rinsed and drained (¾ cup dried red kidney beans; see Basic Cooking Chart, page 58)

½ pound sharp Cheddar cheese, shredded, for serving

1. In a large, heavy-bottomed pot or Dutch oven, cook 4 of the onions in the oil over medium heat until lightly browned. Stir in the garlic and cook for 1 minute. Add the beef and cook until the meat is browned. Add the spice sachet, water, vinegar, tomato paste, chile powder, cinnamon, Tabasco, and Worcestershire sauce; season to taste with salt and pepper, and bring to a boil. Reduce the heat and simmer for 1 hour, stirring occasionally. Taste for seasoning and keep hot. Remove and discard the spice sachet.

2. Bring a large pot of salted water to a boil. Add the spaghetti and cook for 7 minutes, or until firm but cooked through. Drain and place on the bottom of a large serving bowl. Spoon the reserved beans on top and then ladle the chili over the spaghetti. Cover with the cheese and remaining chopped onion, and serve immediately.

Miso-Marinated Glazed Halibut

This delicately flavored glazed fish was popularized by Japanese chef Nobu Matsuhisa at his restaurants Matsuhisa in Los Angeles and Nobu in New York. Originally made with Pacific black cod (also known as Alaska cod, black sablefish, and butterfish), it is also good with firm white halibut or the richer but still white-fleshed Chilean sea bass. Miso is a Japanese fermented soybean paste that comes in many varieties, each with its own characteristic color and flavor. The shiro miso used here is light yellow and mild-tasting. Mirin is a sweet, syrupy Japanese cooking wine available in Asian markets. Because the fish must marinate for 2 days to absorb the flavors and produce the golden brown, caramelized glaze, this is an excellent dish to make when you buy fresh fish but don't want to eat it the same day.

—————————— *Advance preparation required. Serves 4* ——————————

½ cup shiro (white) miso
¼ cup sugar
¼ cup saké
¼ cup mirin
1½ pounds halibut or cod fillet, cut into
    4 pieces

1. Thoroughly combine the miso, sugar, saké, and mirin in a small, heatproof mixing bowl with a wooden spoon until smooth. Place over a saucepan of simmering water and simmer for about 30 minutes, until hot and fragrant. Remove from the heat and cool to room temperature. Pour half the marinade into a shallow glass or ceramic dish. Arrange the halibut over the marinade in the dish; then cover with the remaining marinade. Cover and refrigerate for 2 days.

2. When ready to serve, preheat the broiler. Remove the fish from the marinade, allowing the excess to drip off. Arrange the fish pieces, skin sides up, on a broiler or shallow baking pan and place under the broiler, 6 to 8 inches from the heat source. Broil for 10 minutes; then turn and broil about 3 minutes longer, or until the fish flakes easily.

CHAPTER NINE

One-Pot Meals

Venetian Rice and Peas *(Risi e Bisi)*

(VEGETARIAN OPTION)

If you prepare this on April 25, you will be carrying on an ancient tradition that dates from the days of the Republic of Venice. This springtime dish of creamy rice and peas was, and still is, made in Venice and its surroundings area to celebrate the feast day of its patron, Saint Mark. Almost the consistency of a soup, risi e bisi *should be served as a course of its own. In days past,* risi e bisi *was presented on Saint Mark's Day with much ceremony to the doge, the leader of Venice. You can streamline this dish by using frozen small peas. To get the delicate flavor of the pea pod–scented stock, substitute about ¼ pound fresh sugar snap peas for the pea pods. For a vegetarian version, substitute Vegetable Stock (see page 323) for the chicken stock and omit the prosciutto.*

Serves 6

---

2 quarts Light Chicken Stock (see page 320)

2 pounds fresh, young English green peas, shelled, pods reserved

½ pound imported prosciutto including the fat, cut into small dice

1 large yellow onion, finely diced

6 tablespoons (¾ stick) unsalted butter

2 cups arborio or other short-grain Italian rice, such as carnaroli

½ cup dry white vermouth

1 tablespoon salt

½ teaspoon freshly ground black pepper

¼ pound Parmigiano-Reggiano cheese, grated (about 1 cup)

2 tablespoons chopped Italian parsley

1. In a 3-quart pot with a lid, combine the Light Chicken Stock and pea pods. Bring to a boil, reduce the heat, and simmer, partially covered, for 30 minutes to flavor the broth with the pea pods. Strain and reserve the broth, discarding the pods.

2. In a large, heavy-bottomed saucepan over medium heat, cook the prosciutto and onion in 4 tablespoons of the butter, stirring constantly, until the onion is translucent, about 5 minutes. Add the rice and stir to coat with the butter. Add the vermouth and about 2 cups of the reserved broth. Bring to a boil; then reduce the heat and simmer until the liquid is absorbed, stirring occasionally. Continue to add the broth in 2-cup increments, stirring occasionally and waiting until the previous addition is absorbed before adding more.

3. When about half the broth (4 cups) has been added, stir in the peas, salt, and pepper. Continue to cook until all the liquid has been added and the dish is creamy and almost soupy. Remove from the heat, and stir in the cheese, parsley, and remaining 2 tablespoons butter. Serve immediately.

Baked Anasazi Beans with Ancho Chile

(VEGETARIAN OPTION)

The Anasazi beans called for here are medium-sized and oblong, with vivid streaks of deep red over cream. The beans were given their romantic name after the lost tribe of Anasazi Indians, who lived in cliff dwellings in Arizona. (Read more about the Anasazi people in Tony Hillerman's mysteries that take place in this region.) In natural food stores, I've bought the trademarked organic Anasazi beans packed by Colorado's Adobe Milling Company (www.anazazi.com). You can certainly substitute pinto, cranberry, or pink beans because this delicious dish—fragrant with orange zest, ancho chile, and roasted cumin and mellowed with molasses—is a real winner. Because the sweet tomatoes and oranges juice toughen the skins of the beans and prevent them from absorbing water and softening, the beans must be precooked. For a vegetarian version, substitute ½ cup olive oil for the bacon when sautéing the vegetables in Step 2.

Serves 6

1 pound (2 cups) dried Anasazi, pinto, pink, or cranberry beans, soaked (see Soaking Chart, page 57)

½ pound bacon, diced

1 large onion, diced

3 carrots, diced

2 tablespoons chopped garlic

2 tablespoons ground ancho chile or 1 whole ancho chile, seeded, soaked in cold water until soft (about 30 minutes), and minced

2 tablespoons ground toasted cumin seeds (see Toasting Seeds, page 225)

½ cup molasses

Grated zest of 1 orange

Juice of 1 orange

1 (28-ounce) can plum tomatoes, chopped

1½ teaspoons freshly ground black pepper

1 tablespoon salt

1. Drain the beans. In a large pot, cover the beans with cold water and bring to a boil. Cook for 5 minutes; then drain, discarding the water. Cover the beans with cold water and bring to a boil again. Simmer for 1 hour, or until half cooked (a bean cut in half will still have a hard center). Drain the beans, discarding any liquid.

2. Cook the bacon in a saucepan over low heat until crispy. Transfer the bacon to paper towels and reserve. In the same pan, cook the onion, carrots, and garlic in the bacon fat until softened. Add the chile, cumin, molasses, orange zest, and juice. Cook for 3 minutes.

3. Preheat the oven to 300°F. Add the reserved beans, tomatoes, and bacon to a large Dutch oven with a lid. Bring to a boil on top of the stove. Cover and bake in the oven for 2 hours, or until the beans are almost soft. Season the beans to taste with the pepper and salt. Stir well, cover, and return to the oven. Bake for 30 minutes longer, or until the beans are soft and the liquid has been absorbed. If the water has been absorbed before the beans are done, add 1 to 2 cups water to the beans while baking.

ABOUT *PIMENTÓN*

If you can find it, vary the basic recipe by substituting 1 tablespoon *pimentón* (oak-smoked paprika grown exclusively in Spain's Extremadura region) for 1 tablespoon of the chile ancho powder. Lately, I've been able to find this extraordinary wood-smoked paprika—in mild, medium, and hot versions—in specialty food shops and on the Internet (see Sources, page 341).

Chickpea and Eggplant Moussaka
with Goat Cheese Topping
(VEGETARIAN)

Years ago, I worked as the chef at the well-known White Dog Cafe, an eatery and gathering place near the University of Pennsylvania. For our many vegetarian customers, I developed this hearty casserole based on three of my favorite foods—eggplant, chickpeas, and goat cheese. It is my version of the popular meatless Arabic musakka'a *(better known by its Greek name, moussaka), to which I added the tangy goat cheese topping. Many people are afraid of cooking eggplant because it's so oil-hungry. I've found this method of hot-roasting eggplant cubes prevents oil absorption—and it's easy and tasty, too.*

———————————— *Serves 6* ————————————

1 large onion, diced

1 tablespoon chopped garlic

½ cup extra-virgin olive oil

1 (28-ounce) can plum tomatoes, chopped

½ cup dry white vermouth

1 tablespoon ground toasted cumin seeds (see Toasting Seeds, opposite)

1 tablespoon ground toasted coriander seeds (see Toasting Seeds, opposite)

3 bay leaves

Salt and freshly ground black pepper

1 (1-pound) firm, shiny eggplant, cut into 1-inch cubes

¼ cup extra-virgin olive oil

2 tablespoons chopped fresh marjoram leaves, or 1 tablespoon dried oregano

1 tablespoon chopped garlic

2 teaspoons kosher salt and ½ freshly ground black pepper

1 teaspoon hot red pepper flakes or Korean red pepper flakes

2 cups cooked chickpeas, rinsed and drained (¾ cup dried chickpeas; (see Basic Cooking Chart, page 58)

¼ pound mild goat cheese, crumbled

1. Preheat the oven to 400°F. In a medium saucepan, cook the onion and garlic in the olive oil over medium heat, until softened but not browned. Add the tomatoes, vermouth, cumin, coriander, and bay leaves. Bring to a boil. Reduce the heat and simmer until thickened, stirring occasionally, about 20 minutes. Discard the bay leaves and season to taste with salt and pepper.

2. Toss the eggplant cubes with the olive oil, marjoram, garlic, salt and black pepper, and red pepper flakes in a large bowl. Spread out in a single layer on a large, shallow baking pan. Roast for 20 minutes; then shake the pan to release the eggplant and turn the pieces over so they cook evenly. Return to the oven and bake for 20 minutes longer, or until the eggplant is brown and crusty on the outside and creamy on the inside. Spread on the bottom of either a 2-quart, shallow baking dish or 6 individual ovenproof casserole dishes.

3. Stir the chickpeas into the onion mixture and cook about 10 minutes, or until somewhat thickened. Spread the chickpea mixture over the eggplant, and then top with the crumbled goat cheese. (The dish may be prepared to this point up to 2 days before finishing. Cover and refrigerate.)

4. When ready to serve, preheat the oven to 400°F. Bake for 30 minutes, or until the mixture is bubbling and the cheese is browned. Allow the dish to cool for 5 to 10 minutes before serving.

TOASTING SEEDS

I toast whole seed spices such as cumin, coriander, allspice, fennel, anise, and nigella to intensify their flavors. To toast, heat a small, dry skillet (preferably uncoated, such as steel or cast iron) until quite hot. Add about ¼ cup of the whole seeds and toast, shaking occasionally, just until the seeds are lightly browned and fragrant, about 4 minutes. Watch the spices carefully at this point; you don't want blackened seeds, which will be bitter. Remove from the heat and cool to room temperature. Grind in a small coffee grinder, preferably one reserved for spices. Alternatively, crush the seeds using a mortar and pestle. Using a funnel, pour into a small glass jar, such as an empty spice, mustard, or jelly jar, and cover tightly. The toasted spices will keep quite well for 2 to 3 months.

Bean-Pebbled Paella

(VEGETARIAN OPTION)

Although we usually think of paella as saffron rice with seafood, sausage, and chicken, in the style of Valencia, Spain, the dish is actually made in many versions. This colorful paella has a striking pebbled appearance because of the yellow, red, and black beans. For extra color, look for dark red kidney beans rather than the more common pale kidney beans. You'll need a 15-inch steel paella pan that serves six to eight people (see Sources, page 341). The Web sites Tienda.com and The Spanish Table, which sell the pans, also carry the special callasparra and bomba varieties of short-grain rice particularly suited to paella. You could substitute Italian arborio rice, but be sure to use short-grain pearly rice, not American long-grain rice. My thanks to Penelope Casas, author of many wonderful books about Spanish cuisine, including Paella!, *from which this recipe is adapted. For a vegetarian version, substitute Vegetable Stock (see page 323) for the chicken stock, eliminate the ham, increase the beans to ¾ cup of each kind, and increase the* pimentón *to 1 tablespoon and the cumin to 1½ teaspoons.*

─────────────── *Serves 6* ───────────────

½ cup cooked chickpeas, plus cooking liquid (see Basic Cooking Chart, page 58)

½ cup cooked dark red kidney beans, plus cooking liquid (see Basic Cooking Chart, page 58)

½ cup cooked black beans, drained and rinsed, liquid discarded (see Basic Cooking Chart, page 58)

About 2½ cups Light Chicken Stock (see page 320)

¼ teaspoon crumbled saffron threads

¼ cup olive oil

1 bunch scallions, white and green parts, trimmed and thinly sliced

2 tablespoons chopped garlic

1 cup diced piquillo peppers (see Sources, page 341), or 1 large red bell pepper, diced

½ pound boneless ham, diced

3 cups rinsed and thinly sliced Swiss chard leaves and stalks (about ½ bunch)

1 ripe tomato, diced

¼ cup chopped Italian parsley

2 teaspoons *pimentón* or paprika

1. Preheat a gas oven to 425°F or an electric oven to 450°F.

2. Drain the chickpeas and kidney beans, reserving their liquid. Rinse the chickpeas and kidney beans and mix with the drained black beans. Combine the reserved bean liquids in a medium pot with enough Light Chicken Stock to make 4 cups. Bring the liquid to the boil, turn off the heat, add the saffron, and reserve.

3. Heat the oil in the paella pan over medium heat. Add the scallions, garlic, piquillo peppers, and ham, and sauté until the chiles are slightly softened. Add the Swiss chard, tomato, and parsley, and cook 1 to 2 minutes longer; then stir in the *pimentón* and cumin.

4. Stir in the rice and coat well with the pan mixture. Pour in the reserved hot chicken stock mixture and bring to a boil. Add the beans and the salt and black pepper to taste. Continue to boil, stirring and rotating the pan occasionally, until the rice is no longer soupy, about 5 minutes.

5. Transfer the paella pan to the oven and cook, uncovered, for 12 to 15 minutes in a gas oven or 15 to 20 minutes in an electric oven, until the rice is almost al dente and the liquid has been absorbed. Remove to a warm spot, cover with foil, and let rest for 5 to 10 minutes, until the rice finishes cooking and is tender but still firm.

1 teaspoon ground cumin

2 cups short-grain rice, such as arborio, callasparra, or bomba

Salt and black pepper to taste

ABOUT PAELLA PANS

Inexpensive slope-sided paella pans of carbon steel have been used for centuries in Spain. These dimpled, flat-bottomed pans conduct heat evenly and quickly to create perfectly cooked paella, with firm, fluffy, moist rice. After using, wash the paella pan by hand, wipe dry, and coat lightly with oil to prevent rusting. The pan will darken and absorb flavor as it is used and will develop a coating that makes it less susceptible to rust. It can be used over direct heat (including a charcoal or gas grill) or in the oven. Use the paella pan to make outstanding Black Bean Nachos (see page 67), or to roast vegetables, potatoes, or even cut-up chicken.

Spanish One-Pot Soup (Cocido)

There are numerous versions of this dish in Spain, all invariably containing chickpeas. This meal simmered in a big pot is closely related to French pot-au-feu, *Italian* bollito misto, *and even New England boiled dinner, all of which contain a variety of meats and hearty root vegetables simmered in a rich broth. Traditionally, this soup is served in three separate courses: first the broth alone in a soup tureen accompanied with fresh crusty bread for dunking, then the vegetables and chickpeas, and finally, the assorted meats. Cooked fine noodles, called* cabello de angel, *or "angel's hair," are often added to the broth. See Sources (page 341) for information on La Tienda and The Spanish Table, both of which sell special varieties of garbanzos (the Spanish name for chickpeas) that will cook up plump and tender yet firm for* cocido. *This dish, though less well known in the United States, rivals the popularity of paella and gazpacho in Spain and may be made with a variety of meats, but must always include chickpeas.*

Serves 8 to 10

1 pound (2 cups) dried chickpeas, soaked
   (see Soaking Chart, page 57)
4 pounds chicken legs with thighs
2 smoked ham hocks
2 pounds sliced veal shank, cut into 1- to
   2-inch rounds
2 quarts Light Chicken Stock (see page
   320)
2 cups dry white wine
1 quart cold water
2 pounds smoked chorizo
1 large onion, chopped
1 tablespoon chopped garlic
½ pound yellow potatoes, peeled, diced,
   and placed in a bowl of cold water
½ pound parsnips, peeled, diced, and
   placed in a bowl of cold water
½ pound carrots, peeled and diced
2 bay leaves
2 tablespoons hot paprika or *pimentón*
   (Spanish smoked paprika)
Salt and freshly ground black pepper

1. Drain and rinse the chickpeas. Place in a large soup pot. Add the chicken, ham hocks, veal shank, Light Chicken Stock, white wine, and water. Bring to a boil, skim off the white foam impurities that rise to the surface, and reduce the heat. Simmer for 2 hours. Add the chorizo, onion, garlic, potatoes, parsnips, carrots, bay leaves, and paprika. Return to a boil, reduce the heat, cover, and simmer for 1 hour longer.

2. Remove the ham hocks and veal shanks from the soup. Remove and discard the bay leaves. When cool enough to handle, remove the meat from the bones. Add the meat back to the pot and season to taste with salt and pepper. Serve immediately, making sure that each guest gets one piece each of the chorizo and chicken.

Smoked Turkey Chili with Black-Eyed Peas

This chili is tasty, relatively low in fat, and great to feed a hungry crowd. It's also inexpensive. I like to play around with my outdoor smoker, so I brine and then smoke inexpensive turkey thighs on the bone. Check out the recipe below, which I make using the outdoor smoker I bought for about $50 from Home Depot. I then pull the meat from the bone and use the bones to make a fabulous soup stock for black bean or split pea soup. You can also use purchased smoked turkey, preferably thigh meat, which will be the juiciest.

—————————————— *Serves 8* ——————————————

¼ cup olive oil

1 large Spanish onion, diced

2 large carrots, diced

4 bell peppers (preferably a mix of red, yellow, and orange), seeded and diced

2 pounds poblano chiles, seeded and diced

1 tablespoon chopped garlic

1 teaspoon ground allspice

1 tablespoon ground cinnamon

1 tablespoon dried oregano

2 tablespoons ancho chile powder

2 tablespoons salt

1 teaspoon freshly ground black pepper

2 tablespoons all-purpose unbleached flour

1 cup Light Chicken Stock (see page 320)

4 pounds smoked turkey parts on the bone, or 2 pounds boneless smoked turkey, preferably thighs

2 (12-ounce) packages frozen black-eyed peas or 3 cups cooked black-eyed peas (see Basic Cooking Chart on page 58)

3 cups tomato sauce, purchased or homemade

½ bunch fresh cilantro sprigs, for serving

1 cup sour cream, for serving

¼ pound sharp Cheddar or pepper Jack cheese, shredded, for serving

1 red onion, thinly sliced, for serving

1. In a large Dutch oven, heat the olive oil over medium heat. Add the onion, carrots, bell peppers, poblano chiles, and garlic, and cook until softened but not browned, about 7 minutes. Stir in the allspice, cinnamon, oregano, chile powder, salt, and black pepper. Cook for about 5 minutes, or until the aromas are released, stirring to combine.

2. Stir in the flour and cook for 2 to 3 minutes, stirring until well mixed. Add the Light Chicken Stock and bring to a boil, stirring occasionally, to make a smooth, thick sauce. Stir in the smoked turkey, black-eyed peas, and tomato sauce. Reduce the heat and simmer for 30 minutes, or until the turkey is tender and the chili has thickened.

3. When the chili is done, serve it immediately, garnishing each portion with cilantro, sour cream, cheese, and red onion. (If you want to serve the chili within the next few days, chill it in an ice water bath, especially if you make this recipe during hot, humid weather when beans tend to ferment easily. Cover and refrigerate until ready to use.)

HOMEMADE SMOKED TURKEY THIGHS

For 10 pounds of turkey thighs on the bone, combine 2 cups molasses, 6 tablespoons kosher salt, and 2 tablespoons each ground coriander, ground juniper berry, ground fennel seed, and ground allspice in a large bowl. Combine with 3 quarts water, add the turkey, and refrigerate the turkey in the brine mixture for 8 hours or up to 2 days. Drain and smoke the turkey thighs according to your smoker manufacturer's directions using fruitwood chips, such as cherry or apple, for 5 hours, or until the thighs are tender.

Boston Baked Beans
with Steamed Boston Brown Bread

What could be more frugal than a pot of baked beans and steamed brown bread? Thrifty colonial New England cooks knew how to make the most out of the few ingredients in their pantries. Yankee traders in the West Indies brought home barrels of inexpensive molasses left over from the sugar refining process, and New Englanders developed an enduring taste for its mellow, dark sweetness. What's surprising is how good the combination of baked beans and brown bread is: simple but satisfying. Interestingly, the Puritans were very strict about not working on their Sabbath, which was Sunday. As the Jews did with their Sabbath casserole, cholent, *the Puritans sent the family's bean pot to the baker's oven, usually in the cellar of a nearby tavern. The baker returned the baked beans complete with a bit of brown bread on Sunday morning. Note that the bread tastes best when made with whole-grain flours. You will need an empty 1-pound coffee can to bake the bread in its traditional cylindrical shape.*

———————————— *Serves 8 (Makes 1 loaf of bread)* ————————————

Boston Baked Beans

1 pound (2 cups) dried Great Northern
　　beans
5½ quarts cold water
1 large onion stuck with 5 whole cloves
1 cup molasses
1½ cups packed dark brown sugar
1 tablespoon dry mustard
1 tablespoon ground ginger
1 teaspoon salt
1½ teaspoons freshly ground black
　　pepper
½-pound piece salt pork, scored in
　　diamond shapes

Steamed Boston Brown Bread

1 cup rye flour
1 cup cornmeal
1 cup oat flour
2 teaspoons baking soda
1 teaspoon salt
2 cups buttermilk
¾ cup molasses

1. Prepare the Boston Baked Beans: Place the beans in a large pot and add 8 cups of the cold water. Bring to a boil and cook for 5 minutes. Remove from the heat and allow the beans to soak for 1 hour. Drain the beans; cover with another 8 cups of the cold water. Bring to a boil, reduce the heat, and simmer for about 1 hour, until partially cooked (a bean cut in half will still have a hard center). Drain the beans, discarding any liquid.

2. Preheat the oven to 275°F. Place the onion in the bottom of a large bean pot or Dutch oven and cover with the partially cooked beans. In a large bowl, combine the molasses, 1 cup of the brown sugar, the mustard, ginger, salt, pepper, and the remaining 6 cups of cold water. Whisk together to combine; then pour this mixture over the beans. Add the salt pork, skin side up, pushing it slightly beneath the surface. Cover tightly and bake in the center of the oven for 4 hours.

3. Prepare the Steamed Boston Brown Bread: Butter a clean, empty 1-pound coffee can and two 24 x 12-inch pieces of heavy-duty foil, doubled over. Whisk together the rye flour, cornmeal, oat flour, baking soda, and salt in a large bowl. In another medium bowl, combine the buttermilk and molasses. Stir into the dry ingredients until the mixture is well combined and resembles a thick pancake batter. Scrape the batter into the buttered can. It should fill the can by two-thirds. Cover tightly with the buttered doubled foil and, without puncturing the foil, secure the foil to the can by tying with a string.

4. Place a round wire rack, trivet, or two empty tuna cans with both ends removed in the bottom of a tall pot with a lid. (This is to keep the bread mold off the bottom of the pot.) Place the mold upright on the rack in the bottom of the pot. Add enough hot water to reach halfway up the side of the can. Cover the pot, bring the water to a boil, and reduce the heat to a simmer. Steam for 2½ to 3 hours, or until a skewer inserted into the center of the bread comes out clean. Check the water level occasionally, since it may need to be replenished. When done, remove the foil cover, and allow the steam to escape. Carefully remove the can from the pot. Allow the bread to cool for 10 minutes in the can; then turn upside down. The bread should slide right out. Cool to room temperature on a rack.

5. When the beans have cooked for 4 hours, remove the cover and sprinkle with the remaining ½ cup brown sugar. Bake for another 30 minutes and serve directly from the Dutch oven. Using a serrated knife, cut the cooled brown bread into thin slices. Serve with butter and the baked beans.

ABOUT BEAN POTS AND BREAD MOLDS

Boston is known as "Beantown" in honor of the significance of beans in the Bostonian diet. I adapted the Boston baked bean and brown bread recipes from the 1923 edition of Fanny Farmer's *The Boston Cooking-School Cook Book*. According to Farmer, "The fine reputation which Boston Baked Beans have gained has been attributed to the earthen bean-pot with small top and bulging sides in which they are supposed to be cooked." If you don't have one of these half-glazed brown bean pots, it's a good item to look for at flea markets. Farmer adds, "Equally good beans have often been eaten where a five-pound lard pail was substituted for the broken bean pot." These beans will taste great no matter what pot you use. If you have a traditional steamed pudding mold with a cover, use it to make the brown bread in an appealing shape.

Italian New Year's Eve Cotechino with Lentils

Like the dish called Hoppin' John (rice studded with black-eyed peas; see page 238), served in the American South on New Year's Day, cotechino (or zampone) with lentils is served at midnight on New Year's Eve in Italy to ensure good fortune for the coming year. Cotechino is a thick pork sausage with a rich, somewhat gelatinous filling. Zampone, a stuffed pig's trotter with the same filling, is prepared for the winter holidays. Both cotechino and zampone can be found partially cooked in Italian delicatessens close to the New Year. The lentils and sausage are just as good and just as traditional served the next day at lunch. Lentils represent money (coins) and the zampone, the container that will hold the wealth. Zampone and cotechino, both made from pig, are eaten for the new year because it is said that animals like the pig that move forward while eating bring good luck.

Serves 6 to 8

1 *cotechino* or *zampone* sausage, about 2 pounds

1 pound Italian Castelluccio lentils or French green lentils

2 ribs celery, diced

1 whole onion, one half left whole, one half diced

3 to 4 slices pancetta, frozen until firm and cut into small pieces, or prosciutto fat or bacon

Salt and pepper to taste

Extra-virgin olive oil, for serving

1. If you buy precooked *cotechino* or *zampone*, you'll need to simmer either for about 30 minutes, or until tender and thoroughly heated. If you buy uncooked *cotechino*, prick it all over and simmer it for 3 hours in enough water to cover. For the uncooked *zampone*, prick it all over and wrap tightly in a double thickness of cheesecloth, tied with kitchen twine. Place the *zampone* on its side in a large pot and cover with 4 inches of cold water. Bring the water slowly to a boil, and then reduce the heat and simmer for 2 to 4 hours, depending on the size of the *zampone*; allow about 1 hour per pound. Add boiling water as needed to keep the *zampone* covered. To keep the *zampone* warm, remove the cloth, wrap it in foil, and place it in a 250°F oven. Reserve some of the cooking liquid from either the *cotechino* or the *zampone*.

2. Meanwhile, add the lentils, celery, and the onion half to a large pot and cover with 2 quarts salted water. Bring to a boil; then reduce the heat and simmer for 30 to 45 minutes. Combine the diced onion with the pancetta in a large pan and sweat until the onion is tender. Drain the lentils, add to the pan with 2 cups of reserved sausage cooking liquid, and season with salt and pepper. Simmer until the lentils are tender and most of the liquid has been absorbed, about 20 minutes longer.

3. Drain any excess liquid from the lentils and transfer them to a large, shallow, heated bowl. Drain the *cotechino* or *zampone* and cut into thick slices. Arrange the sausage slices on top of the lentils. Serve piping hot with a carafe of extra-virgin olive oil to drizzle over the lentils.

CASTELLUCCIO LENTILS

Tiny and delicate, the best lentils in Italy come from Castelluccio, in central Italy's Umbria region, south of Tuscany. The town is one of the highest in the region, with an elevation of 4,800 feet, and it overlooks two broad plains where these special lentils are grown. Much of the harvesting is done by hand because the plants are too delicate to withstand trampling by animals or machines. These lentils, favored since the Etruscan era, are best cooked simply and served with a drizzle of fine extra-virgin olive oil. Through century-old methods of crop rotation, their cultivation has always been organic: lentils are cultivated one year, wheat the next, and the land is kept as pasture during the third. Then the process starts all over again. Since 1998, Castelluccio lentils have been awarded the I.G.T. (Protected Geographical Indication) by the Italian government.

Diner-Style Baked Beans
with Bacon

What good is a diner without baked beans? I developed this simple but delicious recipe while consulting for the Country Club Diner in Philadelphia. The second-largest diner ever built, this well-established eatery has been a local institution for 40 years for everyone from families with young children to older customers who've been loyal from the beginning. The dish reheats and freezes perfectly.

Serves 12

2 pounds (4 cups) dried Great Northern
    beans
1 pound bacon, sliced into thin strips
3 medium onions, cut into small dice
1 cup dark corn syrup
1 cup prepared German-style mustard,
    such as Gulden's
1 cup Worcestershire sauce, preferably
    Lea & Perrins
1 cup ketchup
1 cup tomato purée
1 tablespoon salt
½ teaspoon freshly ground black pepper

1. Place the beans in a large pot and add enough cold water to cover. Bring to a boil and cook for 5 minutes, skimming off and discarding any white foam. Drain the beans, and then cover with cold water. Bring to a boil again, reduce the heat, and simmer for about 1 hour, until half done (a bean cut in half will still have a hard center). Drain the beans, discarding any liquid.

2. Cook the bacon in a large pan over medium heat until crisp, stirring to prevent burning. Transfer the bacon to paper towels to drain, reserving the fat. In the same pan, cook the onions in the bacon fat until transparent.

3. In a large bowl, whisk together the corn syrup, mustard, Worcestershire sauce, ketchup, tomato purée, bacon, and onions. Add to the reserved beans.

4. Preheat the oven to 325°F. Place the bean mixture in a large Dutch oven, cover and bake for 2 hours. then season the beans with salt and pepper. Do not season before 2 hours, or the beans won't cook properly. Cover and bake for 2 hours longer, or until the beans are tender and have absorbed the liquid.

HEINZ BAKED BEANS

An older version of baked beans, introduced by the H.J. Heinz Company of Pittsburgh, Pennsylvania, became one of the first popular brand-name canned foods. While other brands of pork and beans had appeared in tins as far back as 1880, they really started to take off under the Heinz name. The company tried to introduce these profitable beans into England in 1905, without much success. In the 1920s, the head of the British branch of Heinz is said to have vowed, "I'm going to manufacture baked beans in England, and they're going to like it!" Well, they did. In fact, one of the most common dishes at British cafes is the ubiquitous beans-on-toast, made using a can of "Heinz 57."

"Liz Taylor" Beef and Black Bean Chili
Topped with Corn Bread

When I first moved to Philadelphia from Washington, D.C., in the late sixties, good restaurants were few and far between. It was quite a change from the full array of ethnic eateries that Washington had to offer. Then came the Philadelphia "restaurant renaissance," when brave entrepreneurs opened storefront restaurants. The recipe for this dish was passed around the restaurant community at that time with many claimants to the title of original. It is based on the chili recipe at the late, great Chasen's restaurant in Los Angeles, which sent this chili to the set of Cleopatra *when Liz Taylor was filming and had a craving for it. I'm not sure where the corn bread topping came from; maybe it was a local addition.*

Serves 8

¼ pound dried New Mexico chiles, or 2 whole ancho chiles, or ¼ cup ancho chile powder

1 cup vegetable oil

2 pounds boneless stewing beef (chuck or top rib), cut into ½-inch cubes

2 medium onions, cut into ¼-inch dice

2 tablespoons chopped garlic

2 jalapeño peppers, seeded and chopped

2 tablespoons ground toasted cumin seeds (see Toasting Seeds, page 225)

2 tablespoons dried oregano

1 tablespoon ground toasted allspice seeds (see Toasting Seeds, page 225)

1 (15-ounce) can plum tomatoes, seeded, drained, and chopped

1½ tablespoons salt

3 cups Basic Black Turtle Beans (see page 297)

4 cups (½ recipe) Buttermilk Corn Bread batter (see page 328)

1. Soak the chiles in warm water to soften.

2. In a large Dutch oven over medium-high heat, heat ¼ cup of the oil, add the beef, and brown it in small batches, adding more oil as needed. Transfer to a plate and reserve. Drain the excess fat from the pan. In the same pan, using the remaining ¼ cup of peanut oil, brown the onions, garlic, and jalapeños. Stir in the cumin, oregano, and allspice, and cook for 3 minutes. Remove from the heat and reserve.

3. Preheat the oven to 325°F. Drain the soaked chiles, reserving the water. Seed and discard the stems. In a blender, purée the chiles with the reserved soaking liquid. Transfer the chile purée to the pan with the onion mixture. Add the tomatoes and bring to a boil. Add the reserved browned meat and salt, bring back to a boil, and transfer to the oven. Cover and bake the chili for 2 hours, or until the meat is quite tender. Check several times and add more water if the chili begins to stick to the bottom of the pan. (The chili can be prepared to this point and reserved for later. Cool the pot of chili quickly in an ice bath and refrigerate, tightly covered. It will keep up to 5 days.)

4. When ready to serve, preheat the oven to 375°F. Spread a layer of the Basic Black Turtle Beans on the bottom of a shallow 8-quart glass or ceramic baking dish, or in 8 individual deep casseroles. Top with the chili, leaving 1 inch of space at the top. Pour the Buttermilk Corn Bread batter over the chili. Place the dish on a baking sheet and bake for 30 to 40 minutes, or until the corn bread is golden brown and the chili is bubbling hot.

Because gold prospectors' diets consisted mainly of beans, they gave the beans wishful names, such as "Alaska strawberries."

Cassoulet with Duck Confit, Lamb,
and Haricots Lingots

Cassoulet is an ancient dish, a rich baked stew of white haricot beans and meats that originated in southwestern France. The French word cassoulet *shares its origin with a word that has become as American as apple pie,* casserole. *It's probably the original potluck casserole. Three towns in the Languedoc area claim to produce the most authentic version of this endlessly varied dish. In Toulouse, cassoulet features breast of mutton and the famous local sausage. In Carcassonne, they add pork chops, along with partridge during hunting season. In Castelnaudary, whose cassoulet is deemed classic by the* Larousse Gastronomique, *preserved duck or goose is included, and perhaps garlic sausage. In another town, Corbières, it would be sacrilege to make cassoulet without lightly salted pig's tail and ear. These days, the regional differences have been blurred. I make my cassoulet with what I think are the tastiest in this panoply of meats: duck confit, lamb, bacon, and smoked pork sausage. Be aware that if you plan to make the Confit of Duck Legs, you will need to prepare them 1 week in advance.*

——————————— *Advance preparation required. Serves 12* ———————————

Beans

2 pounds (4 cups) dried *haricots lingots* or cannellini beans, soaked (see Soaking Chart, page 57)

2 quarts Light Chicken Stock (see page 320)

2 quarts cold water

4 pounds smoked ham hocks

3 large yellow onions, peeled

1 bunch fresh thyme, tied with kitchen string

6 bay leaves

1 head garlic, ½ inch sliced off the top to expose the cloves

½ pound pork rind, bacon rind, or prosciutto skin (optional)

Meats

½ pound thick-cut smoked bacon, cut into ½-inch strips

1 pound boneless lamb shoulder, cut into 2-inch chunks

1 pound garlic pork sausages (kielbasa, *cotechino*, or *saucisson*), sliced ½ inch thick

12 Confit of Duck Legs (see page 329), or purchased (see Sources, page 341)

1 pound yellow onions, diced

1. Prepare the Beans: Place the beans in a large stockpot and add enough cold water to cover them. Bring to a boil, and cook for 2 minutes. Drain and discard the liquid.

2. In the same stockpot, combine the Light Chicken Stock, water, ham hocks, onions, thyme, bay leaves, garlic, and pork rind; bring to a boil. Reduce the heat and simmer for 2 hours. Strain through a sieve, reserving the liquid and the ham hocks and discarding the other solids. Cool the ham hocks; then remove the meat from the bones. Save the meat and discard the bones. Clean out the pot.

3. Combine the strained stock, reserved beans, and ham hock meat in the cleaned pot. Bring to a boil, reduce the heat to a simmer, and cook until the beans are tender but still firm, about 2 hours. They should have a hard center kernel when cut in half, but otherwise they should be soft.

4. Prepare the Meats: In a large pan, render the fat from the bacon over medium heat, reserving both the fat and the crisp bacon bits. In the same pan with the fat, brown the lamb on all sides. Remove and reserve. Brown the sausages, pricking in several places. Remove and reserve. Brown the duck confit legs. Remove and reserve.

5. In the same pan, brown the onions over medium heat in the remaining fat. Add the garlic and thyme, and cook for 2 to 3 minutes. Add the tomatoes and vermouth, and season to taste with salt and pepper. Bring the liquid to a boil and cook for 10 minutes, or until slightly thickened.

1 tablespoon chopped garlic

¼ cup chopped fresh thyme leaves
(about ½ bunch)

1 (28-ounce) can plum tomatoes, seeded
and diced, liquid strained and
reserved

2 cups dry white vermouth

Kosher salt and freshly ground black
pepper

2 cups fresh bread crumbs
(country-style bread)

⅛ cup melted duck fat, bacon fat, or lard

½ cup chopped Italian parsley leaves
(about ½ bunch)

6. Preheat the oven to 300°F. In a small bowl, combine the bread crumbs, duck fat, and parsley.

7. In a large Dutch oven, arrange a layer of half the meats, followed by half the beans. Repeat the layers. Pour the tomato-vermouth sauce on top. There should be enough liquid to just cover the beans. If not, add a little water. Cover and bake for 1 hour.

8. Sprinkle the top of the cassoulet with the reserved bread crumb mixture. Bake, uncovered, for 2 hours longer, or until the crust is crunchy and most of the liquid has been absorbed. Remove from the oven and cool slightly before serving directly from the Dutch oven.

THE HOLY WAR OF CASSOULET

According to French food historian Maguelonne Toussaint-Samat, in her magnum opus *The History of Food*, "Ever since the persecution of Protestants and the Albigensian Crusade in Languedoc, a holy war has been waged in that part of France, and it is nowhere near dying out. The various ways of making cassoulet are the issue at stake. For there is not just one cassoulet. The dish exists in several versions, each of which has its fanatical supporters, vehemently defending their faith. Each little district proclaims that it alone practices the true rite—for rites rather recipes are involved in the perfect preparation of this baked beans dish." However, they are in agreement about these points: The dish's name comes from *cassole*, the name of a special earthenware pot that is made in a town near Castlenaudary. Before the discovery of New World *haricot* beans, cassoulet was made with fava beans, known as *favolles*. Now the preferred *haricot* bean to use is the monk-bean or *mounjete*, a plump bean supposedly resembling a plump Capuchin friar. Toussaint-Samat tells us, "The beans must be cooked in two lots of water, the dish itself must finished off in the oven and its crust of breadcrumbs should be broken six times. The seventh crust (seven is a magical number) is the sign of the apotheosis of the dish."

Hoppin' John

This Southern dish of rice with black-eyed peas, pigeon peas, or cowpeas, all legumes of African origin, is traditionally served on New Year's Day—and must be eaten before noon—to ensure good luck for the year. Hoppin' John became a staple of African slaves who populated Southern plantations where rice was the most important crop, especially those of the Gullah country of South Carolina. Earlier versions were made with pigeon peas, which, although prolific in the West Indies, did not flourish in the United States, so the sweet and delicate black-eyed pea came to be used instead.

Serves 8
---

1 pound (2 cups) dried black-eyed peas,
    soaked (see Soaking Chart, page 57)
½ pound salt pork or thick-cut bacon,
    cut into small dice
1 medium onion, chopped
1 clove garlic, chopped
1 sprig fresh thyme
2 quarts water
Salt and freshly ground black pepper
1½ cups long-grain rice

1. Drain the soaked black-eyed peas. Reserve.

2. In a large, heavy-bottomed pot, cook the salt pork, onion, garlic, and thyme over medium-high heat until the vegetables are soft. Add the soaked peas and water, and bring to a boil. Cover, reduce the heat, and simmer for 1 hour. Season generously with salt and pepper.

3. Stir in the rice. Continue to cook for 30 minutes, or until the beans and rice are cooked through and the liquid has been absorbed. Add more water if the liquid is absorbed before the beans and rice are completely cooked.

HOPPIN' JOHN

The origin of the name "Hoppin' John" is obscure, and some theories about its meaning seem more reliable than others. According to the detailed research of John Thorne, author of *Simple Cooking*, the name most likely came from a corruption of *pois à pigeon* (meaning "pigeon peas"), a French-Caribbean term for a similar dish. According to Thorne, "Certainly, there was movement of slaves from the rice plantations in the West Indies to those in South Carolina, the area traditionally associated with the dish, especially Gullah country in back of Charleston. Historically, the famous Southern rice and bean dishes are most closely associated with the rice-growing areas of the Carolinas and Louisiana. Today, however, Hoppin' John is common across the whole South, and there are as many versions as there are cooks."

Tunisian Fava Bean Stew
with Merguez Lamb Sausage *(Bisara)*

Tunisia is a land with an ancient history. It has been influenced at one time or another by just about every civilization surrounding the Mediterranean, including the indigenous Berber peoples, the Phoenicians—founders of the city of Carthage—and the Romans during the height of their empire. Later came the Arabic tribes, Ottoman Turks, the French, and Italians, all of whom contributed to the cuisine. Tunisian food is based on sun-ripened products of the earth, including highly fragrant olive oil. Tunisians also favor spicy merguez lamb sausage. Two sizes of fava beans are called for here; the smaller will dissolve into the sauce and the large ones will remain whole.

Serves 6

1 pound (2 cups) dried split fava beans, preferably half small and half large, soaked (see Soaking Chart, page 57)
¼ cup extra-virgin olive oil
2 tablespoons tomato paste
4 or 5 ripe plum tomatoes, diced
3 cloves garlic, finely chopped
3 cups water
1 pound merguez sausage (see Sources, page 341)
2 teaspoons ground coriander seeds
1 teaspoon ground caraway seeds
2 teaspoons salt
1 teaspoon cayenne (optional)

1. Drain and rinse the soaked favas.

2. In a Dutch oven, heat the olive oil over medium heat. Add the tomato paste and cook for 5 minutes, stirring to combine. Stir in the tomatoes and garlic, and cook for 5 minutes longer. Add the water and bring to a boil. Add the reserved favas and cook for 25 minutes. Add the sausage, coriander, caraway, salt, and cayenne. Continue cooking for 15 minutes, stirring occasionally, or until the favas are tender and the sausage is thoroughly cooked.

COOK'S NOTE

If only whole caraway is available, grind it in a clean coffee grinder or use a mortar and pestle to crush it finely.

Jewish Sabbath *Cholent*
(Sabbath Beef, Bean, and Barley Casserole)

Observant Jews don't light a fire on the Sabbath, relying instead on an oven or burner left on low heat from sundown Friday until 1 hour after sundown on Saturday, when the Sabbath is over. In times past, when gas and electric stoves didn't exist and fires had to be kept stoked, Jewish cooks turned to their neighborhood bakers. After the bread baking was finished for the day, the baker would allow people to bring their dishes (usually hermetically sealed with a flour-and-water paste) and place them in the still-hot hearth oven. The dishes would cook slowly overnight in the retained heat of the baker's oven. It's easy to see how the cholent, *though made with beef and perhaps goose, could have evolved into the southwest French masterpiece cassoulet. Just like the word "chowder," even the name* cholent *is probably derived from* chaud *in French, meaning "hot," and* lent, *meaning "slow."*

Although not traditional, to make the cholent *more easily digestible, soak the baby limas and kidney beans separately in cold water to cover overnight; then rinse. Place the limas and kidney beans in separate saucepans. Cover with cold water, bring to a boil, and cook for 5 minutes. Rinse and drain before proceeding with the recipe.*

--------------------------- *Serves 8* ---------------------------

1½ pounds beef chuck, trimmed of
  excess fat and cut into 2-inch cubes
3 tablespoons paprika, preferably
  Hungarian
2 teaspoons ground ginger
2 tablespoons kosher salt
1½ teaspoons freshly ground black
  pepper
4 large carrots, sliced
2 large onions, diced
2 tablespoons chopped garlic
3 ribs celery, sliced
1 cup dried baby limas
1 cup dried red kidney beans
1 cup medium pearl barley
2 pounds all-purpose potatoes, peeled
  and cut into 1-inch half-moons

1. Preheat the oven to 250°F. In a large bowl, toss the beef with 1 tablespoon of the paprika, 1 teaspoon ground ginger, 1 tablespoon of salt, and 1 teaspoon of pepper.

2. In a large Dutch oven, arrange the following ingredients in four layers, sprinkling each layer with some of the remaining 2 tablespoons paprika, 1 teaspoon ground ginger, 1 tablespoon salt, and ½ teaspoon pepper: layer 1 is the carrots, onions, celery, and garlic; layer 2 is the beef; layer 3 is the limas, kidney beans, and barley; layer 4 is the potatoes.

3. Add enough cold water to cover the potatoes by about 2 inches. Cover and bring to a boil on top of the stove; then bake for at least 8 hours and no longer than 10 hours. Check the water level once or twice, adding more if all of the liquid has been absorbed. When the dish is done, the water should be almost completely absorbed and the potatoes should be browned and soft. Serve piping hot.

> During World War II, a person who waited on tables was known as a "bean jockey," no doubt a reference to this common staple in a soldier's diet.

A 1918 Recipe for Cholent

This recipe for *schalet* or *tscholnt* appeared in the highly influential 1918 edition *International Jewish Cookbook* by Florence Greenbaum: "Wash one pint of white haricot beans and one pint of coarse barley and put them into a covered pot or pan with some pieces of fat meat and some pieces of marrow bone, or the back of two fat geese, which have been skinned and well spiced with ginger and garlic. Season with pepper and salt and add sufficient water to cover. Cover the pot up tightly. If one has a coal range it can be placed in the oven on Friday afternoon and let remain there until Saturday noon. The heat of the oven will be sufficient to make the schalet if there was a nice clear fire when the porridge was put in the oven. If this dish cannot be baked at home it may be sent to a neighboring baker to be placed in the oven there to remain until Saturday noon when it is called for. This takes the place of soup for the Sabbath dinner."

Individual Chicken Potpies
with Assorted Legumes

It seems that in every restaurant I've cooked or consulted for, I've developed a signature potpie recipe. I admit that this dish is a bit time-consuming to make because of the preparation of the chicken, vegetables, sauce, and pastry. However, potpies are always received with pleasure by grown-ups and children alike, and can be varied endlessly to suit your taste and the vegetables you have on hand. This is a potpie for legume lovers because it calls for green beans, black-eyed peas, and sugar snap peas. Prepare the chicken through Step 3 and the pastry a day or two ahead of time.

Makes 8 to 12 individual pies

1 quart Rich Chicken Stock (see page 322)

3 pounds boneless, skinless chicken thighs

8 tablespoons (1 stick) unsalted butter

½ cup unbleached all-purpose flour

½ cup dry white vermouth

Salt, freshly ground black pepper, and cayenne

½ cup diced onion

½ cup diced carrot

½ cup diced celery or celery root

1 cup diced peeled sweet or yellow potato

1 cup fresh green beans, cut into 1-inch lengths

1 (12-ounce) package frozen black-eyed peas, rinsed and drained

1 cup trimmed sugar snap peas

¼ cup chopped fresh tarragon leaves (about ¼ bunch)

½ cup chopped fresh dill (about ½ bunch)

1 pound Buttermilk Pastry Dough (see page 324), or 1 (17-ounce) package puff pastry sheets (preferably all-butter), defrosted in the refrigerator

2 egg yolks

¼ cup heavy cream

1. Heat the Rich Chicken Stock in a large pot. Add the chicken thighs and bring to a boil. Skim off and discard the white foam impurities that rise to the surface. Reduce the heat to a simmer and cook for 20 minutes, or until tender. Remove the chicken from the stock and cover with damp paper towels. Strain the stock through a sieve or cheesecloth and then wipe out the pot. Return the stock to the pot.

2. In a small pan, make a roux by melting 4 tablespoons of the butter over low heat, then stirring in ¼ cup of the flour and cooking for 5 to 10 minutes, stirring occasionally. Whisk the roux into the strained chicken stock. Bring to a boil, stirring occasionally, and boil until the stock thickens. Add the vermouth and continue to cook until thick enough to coat a spoon. Season the sauce generously with salt, black pepper, and cayenne.

3. Shred the cooked chicken meat into large pieces, removing and discarding any gristle, fat, or bone. Add to the sauce and proceed with the recipe. (Otherwise, if making this dish ahead, place the large pot in an ice bath to cool it quickly; then cover and refrigerate until ready to use.)

4. In a large skillet, melt the remaining 4 tablespoons butter and add the onion, carrot, celery, potato, and green beans; sauté until tender but still crisp. Remove from the heat and stir in the black-eyed peas and snap peas. Cool the vegetables to room temperature and then stir into the chicken mixture with the tarragon and dill. (Or, if making ahead, cool and reserve, covered, in the refrigerator up to 1 day.)

5. On a lightly floured surface, roll out the Buttermilk Dough to a ⅛-inch thickness. Wrap in plastic wrap and refrigerate for at least 30 minutes. Assemble 8 to 12 large ovenproof bowls or individual casserole dishes. Cut the chilled dough into shapes to match the dishes, making them 1 inch larger all around than the dishes. Chill the pastry cutouts if they become too soft to handle.

6. In a small bowl, lightly beat together the egg yolks and heavy cream to make an egg wash. Spoon the chicken filling into the ungreased individual serving dishes. Brush the outside edges of the dishes with the egg wash. Carefully lay a pastry cutout over each bowl or casserole. Press down on the outside of the dish to seal. Brush the tops of the pastry with the remaining egg wash to make a glaze. Using a sharp knife, cut a 2-inch cross into the pastry top of each potpie. (If desired, cut out leaves or other decorative shapes from any dough scraps, place on top, and brush with the egg wash.)

7. When ready to bake, preheat the oven to 350°F. Place the potpies on a baking sheet and bake for 30 minutes, or until the tops are brown and the filling is bubbling. Remove from the oven and cool for 5 to 10 minutes before serving.

Cook's Note

To make the potpies ahead of time, make the Rich Chicken Stock and the Buttermilk Dough in advance and refrigerate or freeze until ready to proceed. You can also make the filling up to the point of adding the chicken (but without the vegetables) and refrigerate or freeze it. Add the vegetables fresh, finish with the pastry, and you'll have a perfectly tasty dish. Before stirring in the vegetables, be sure to defrost the filling if it has been frozen.

Rice Stick Noodles with Shrimp, Bean Sprouts, and Peanuts (*Pad Thai*)

(VEGETARIAN OPTION)

Pad thai *is made in many versions, but this classic recipe given to me by the owners of one of Philadelphia's finest Thai restaurants, Thai Garden, is outstanding. Thai cooks and prep people formed the backbone of Philadelphia's first restaurant renaissance, which flourished in the early seventies. Many of the early restaurants couldn't have operated without their large contingent of Thai staff, a number of whom went on to open their own establishments. For a vegetarian version, omit the shrimp, substituting firm tofu if desired.*

—————————— *Serves 2 (or 4 as an appetizer)* ——————————

½ pound dried rice stick noodles

2 tablespoons *nam pla* (Thai fish sauce)

1 teaspoon Thai *sriracha* sauce, or 1 tablespoon chili sauce

4 teaspoons sugar

4 tablespoons soybean oil

2 tablespoons coarsely chopped garlic

¾ pound large shrimp, peeled and deveined, tail shell left on

2 eggs, lightly beaten

¼ cup coarsely chopped roasted peanuts

2 cups fresh bean sprouts

1 bunch scallions, white and green parts, diagonally sliced into 1-inch lengths

2 limes, quartered

2 tablespoons shredded Thai purple basil, or 1 tablespoon shredded sweet basil plus 1 tablespoon shredded mint

1. Soak the noodles in warm water to cover for 15 minutes, or until soft and limp. Drain well.

2. Combine the *nam pla, sriracha sauce*, and sugar in a small bowl, stirring until the sugar is dissolved.

3. Heat a wok or large skillet, such as a cast-iron skillet, over medium-high heat. Add 2 tablespoons of the soybean oil and heat until very hot. Add the garlic and stir-fry until golden, about 30 seconds. Add the shrimp and stir-fry until pink and opaque, about 1 minute. Remove from the wok and reserve.

4. Add the beaten eggs to the wok and spread out into a thin sheet. As soon as the eggs set, stir to break them up into small chunks. Remove from the pan and set aside with the shrimp.

5. Wipe out the pan with paper towels. Add the remaining 2 tablespoons oil to the wok and heat until very hot. Add the softened noodles. Using a spatula, spread the noodles in a thin layer. Allow them to cook for 1 minute; then scrape up the noodles and spread them out again into a thin layer. Cook for 1 minute. Repeat once again, and then add the reserved *nam pla* mixture and most of the peanuts. Toss together until the noodles are evenly coated.

6. Reserving a few for garnish, add the bean sprouts, scallions, and shrimp and eggs to the noodle mixture. Cook for 1 minute, turning often. Transfer the noodles to the serving platter and squeeze the juice of half the limes on top. Garnish with the remaining bean sprouts, 1 tablespoon peanuts, lime wedges, and basil. Serve at once.

PAD THAI VARIATIONS

Basic *pad thai* consists of rice stick noodles sautéed with bean sprouts, garlic, peanuts, and shrimp. It's made in many versions and can include more exotic ingredients like dried shrimp, salted radish, tamarind, and brown bean sauce. In Thailand, *pad thai* is served with small bowls of chopped peanuts, ground dried chiles, sugar, lime wedges, and fresh Chinese chives.

CHAPTER TEN

Side Dishes and Relishes

Fagioli all'Ucceletto (Bird-Style Beans)

(VEGETARIAN OPTION)

The people of Tuscany are known as mangiafagioli, *or "bean-eaters." This is a poor man's version of a dish featuring the olive oil, whole sage leaves, and garlic cloves traditionally used in cooking the wild game birds once so plentiful in the Tuscan hills. Cranberry or pink beans are closest to the Tuscan favorite,* borlotti. *For a real treat, prepare this dish in October and November, when fresh cranberry beans in their pink and white pods are in season. After shelling the fresh beans, cover them with Light Chicken Stock only, no water, and cook for 15 minutes. Proceed with the recipe as directed. For a vegetarian version of this dish, substitute Vegetable Stock (see page 323) for the chicken stock.*

Serves 6

1 pound (2 cups) dried borlotti, cranberry, or pink beans, soaked (see Soaking Chart, page 57)

3 cups Light Chicken Stock (see page 320)

3 cups water

½ cup olive oil

8 cloves garlic, peeled

¼ cup whole fresh sage leaves (about ¼ bunch)

1 pound ripe plum tomatoes, peeled, seeded, and diced, or 1 (15-ounce) can chopped plum tomatoes

2 teaspoons salt

Freshly ground black pepper

1. In a large pot, combine the dried beans, Light Chicken Stock, and water. Bring to a boil and skim off any white foam impurities that rise to the surface. Reduce the heat and simmer until the beans are half-cooked, about 30 minutes. Remove from heat.

2. Preheat the oven to 325°F. Place the olive oil, garlic, and sage in the bottom of a heavy Dutch oven. Cook over low heat for about 5 minutes, or until the garlic becomes golden. Add the beans with their liquid, the tomatoes, and salt. Bring to a boil. Cover and transfer to the oven. Bake for about 30 minutes; then stir gently. Cover and bake for 30 minutes longer, or until the beans are quite soft, but still juicy. Remove from the oven and season to taste with more salt and pepper. Serve piping hot as an accompaniment to grilled meats or poultry.

Pennsylvania Dutch Chow-Chow

(VEGETARIAN)

The name of this brightly colored, prominently spiced version of the traditional sweet-and-sour bean relish is thought to derive from the Cantonese word tsap, *meaning "food mixture." Shipments of spices and mixed pickles from China became known as "chow-chow," which today may be either a ginger-spiced fruit preserve or a mustard-flavored mixed vegetable and pickle relish. Chow-chow is served as one of the huge array of "seven sweets and seven sours" on the Pennsylvania Dutch table. It became a fixed tradition of Dutch hospitality for the woman of the family to put precisely seven sweet relishes and seven sour relishes on the table, especially for "company."*

Serves 32 (Makes 1 gallon)

Vegetables

1 pound green beans, cut into 1-inch lengths

1 head cauliflower, cut into small florets

4 cups fresh yellow, white, or bi-colored corn kernels (about 8 ears), or 3 (10-ounce) packages frozen corn kernels

1 (10-ounce) package frozen baby lima beans

2 cups cooked dark red kidney beans, rinsed and drained (¾ cup dried dark red kidney beans, cooked and drained; see Basic Cooking Chart, page 58)

2 cups cooked black turtle beans, rinsed and drained (¾ cup dried black turtle beans, cooked and drained; see Basic Cooking Chart, page 58)

½ rib celery, cut into ½-inch lengths

2 red bell peppers, seeded and cut into 1-inch strips

2 yellow bell peppers, seeded and cut into 1-inch strips

Spiced Syrup

2 cups sugar

4 cups cider vinegar

2 cups water

¼ cup kosher salt

2 tablespoons turmeric

2 tablespoons black peppercorns

1 (2- to 3-inch) stick cinnamon

1 tablespoon allspice berries

6 whole bay leaves

2 red chiles

¼ cup yellow mustard seeds

1 tablespoon celery seeds

1. Prepare the Vegetables: Steam the green beans and then the cauliflower for 5 minutes each. If using fresh corn, steam for 3 minutes. Drain and rinse with cold water to stop the cooking. Place the limas and corn (if using frozen) in a colander and rinse under lukewarm water to separate the pieces. Rinse the kidney and black beans; then drain and combine with the green beans, cauliflower, limas, corn, celery, and bell peppers in a large bowl.

2. Prepare the Spiced Syrup: In a large saucepan, bring the sugar, cider vinegar, water, salt, turmeric, peppercorns, cinnamon, and allspice to a boil. Simmer 30 minutes. Strain out the spices and pour the syrup back into the saucepan. Add the bay leaves, chiles, mustard seeds, and celery seeds. Simmer for 10 minutes longer. Pour the syrup over the vegetables and mix well. Cool.

3. Spoon the chow-chow and syrup into clean glass jars and store in the refrigerator for 1 week before serving. (The chow-chow keeps at least 1 month in the refrigerator.) Remove the bay leaves before serving.

Tricolor Succotash

(VEGETARIAN)

Succotash is made in many versions with a long history. Originally, it was an Algonquin Indian dish consisting of butter beans (large limas) and corn kernels cooked together in bear fat. The Narragansett Indians called it misckquatash *and made it with kidney beans instead of limas. It may have been one of the first recipes taught to the settlers at Plymouth Rock. The recipe in my 1923 Boston Cooking-School Cook Book couldn't be simpler: "Cut hot boiled corn from cob, an equal quantity of hot boiled shelled beans; season with butter and salt; reheat before serving." As they do at Georgia Brown's Restaurant in Washington, D.C., serve this dish as a bed for Maryland-style crab cakes.*

Serves 8

¼ cup (½ stick) unsalted butter

2 cups cooked kidney beans, rinsed and drained, or ¾ cup dried dark red kidney beans, cooked and drained (see Basic Cooking Chart, page 58)

2 cups cooked shelled fresh lima beans (see Basic Cooking Chart, page 58), or 2 cups frozen baby limas, rinsed

4 cups fresh yellow, white, or bi-colored corn kernels (about 8 ears), or 3 (10-ounce) packages frozen yellow corn

Salt and freshly ground black pepper

Freshly grated nutmeg

1. In a large, heavy-bottomed pan, melt the butter. Add the cooked kidney beans, fresh or frozen limas, and fresh or frozen corn. Stir or toss to coat evenly with the butter and cook over medium heat for 5 to 10 minutes, until bubbling hot. Season to taste with salt, pepper, and nutmeg. Serve immediately.

Indian-Spiced Chickpeas

(VEGETARIAN)

The exotic flavors of Indian cooking are finally starting to gain the attention of American chefs and diners. I haven't been in England recently, but I can still taste the wonderfully complex dishes served in the fine Indian restaurants I visited. The fresh chutneys, raitas, *and breads were outstanding. Although I served Indian-inspired dishes as a chef all during my career, not enough customers understood or appreciated the food. Finally, it has become truly popular. It's about time! If desired, serve these spicy vegetarian chickpeas over rice sprinkled with black sesame seeds for a simple garnish. The* amchur *called for here is dried mango powder, used for its acidic qualities.*

Serves 8 (Makes 6 cups)

¼ cup vegetable oil

1 large onion, chopped

2 tablespoons chopped garlic

1 fresh green chile, such as jalapeño, chopped

1 tablespoon chopped fresh ginger

1 tablespoon ground coriander

1 tablespoon ground cumin

2 teaspoons turmeric

1 tablespoon sweet paprika

1 (15-ounce) can chopped plum tomatoes

4½ cups cooked chickpeas (1½ cups dried chickpeas, cooked and drained; see Basic Cooking Chart, page 58)

2 teaspoons homemade Garam Masala (see page 313), or purchased

1 tablespoon *amchur*, or juice of 2 limes

Salt

Black sesame seeds, for garnish

1. Heat the oil in a large pan with a lid. Add the onion, garlic, chile, and ginger. Cook gently until lightly browned. Add the coriander, cumin, turmeric, paprika, and tomatoes. Bring to a boil.

2. Add the drained chickpeas, Garam Masala, and amchur, and season to taste with salt. Reduce the heat and simmer for 5 to 10 minutes, or until the sauce has thickened. Sprinkle with black sesame seeds before serving.

Black Turtle Beans with Epazote and Cotija Cheese

(VEGETARIAN OPTION)

It's hard to believe now, but it wasn't that long ago when fresh herbs, other than curly parsley and maybe dill, were difficult to come by. We owe their current availability to folks like Paul Tsakos, an herb and exotic vegetable grower at Overbrook Herb Farm in Lansdale, Pennsylvania. Long ago, he came into a kitchen where I was chef with an assortment of fresh herbs to sell. I snapped them up and started buying from him every week. He's still the only grower I know in my area who sells fresh epazote, a strong-tasting resinous herb in the oregano family that's a natural partner to black beans in Mexican cookery. Epazote is commonly available fresh in supermarkets in Texas and other parts of the southwestern United States, but is more often found dried in Mexican markets and online. Cotija cheese is known as the "Parmesan of Mexico" because it is aged, strongly flavored, firm, and perfect for grating, especially over bean dishes like this. It is available from Mexican groceries and online (see Sources, page 341). For a vegetarian dish, substitute vegetable stock for the chicken stock and sauté the vegetables in step 2 in ¼ cup olive oil instead ot bacon fat. Eliminate the crumbled bacon.

Serves 6

1 pound (2 cups) dried black turtle beans, soaked (see Soaking Chart, page 57)

4 cups Light Chicken Stock (see page 320) or Vegetable Stock (see page 323)

2 large sprigs fresh epazote, or 2 tablespoons dried

4 cups cold water

½ pound thick-sliced bacon, diced

1 large onion, diced

2 carrots, diced

2 ribs celery, diced

4 cloves garlic, chopped

1 tablespoon pure red chile powder, such as from ancho chiles or New Mexican chiles

1 tablespoon ground toasted cumin seeds (see Toasting Seeds, page 225)

2 tablespoons salt

12 (6-inch) corn tortillas, for serving

¼ pound cotija cheese, French feta, or ricotta salata, crumbled for garnish

¼ cup chopped pickled jalapeño peppers, for garnish

½ pound bacon, cooked and crumbled, for garnish

1. Preheat the oven to 300°F. Drain and rinse the black beans. Place the beans, Light Chicken Stock, epazote, and cold water in a large Dutch oven. Bring to a boil on top of the stove; then transfer to the oven. Cover and bake for 2 hours.

2. Meanwhile, in a large skillet, cook the bacon over medium heat until it is crisp and the fat is rendered. Remove and reserve the bacon, leaving the fat in the pan. Add the onion, carrots, celery, and garlic. Cook over medium heat until the vegetables are softened but not browned.

3. Remove the pot of beans from the oven and uncover. Taking care not to touch the hot pot or lid, stir the cooked vegetable mixture into the beans with the chile powder, cumin, and salt. Cover and bake for 1 hour longer, or until the liquid has been absorbed and the beans are thoroughly cooked.

4. Preheat a grill pan over medium-high heat. Add the tortillas and grill on each side until lightly charred, about 3 minutes. Serve the beans accompanied by the grilled tortillas. Garnish each portion with the cheese, pickled jalapeños, and crumbled bacon.

ABOUT EPAZOTE

The strong, almost turpentine-like smell of epazote is off-putting at first, but I swear it grows on you. This annual herb with a pungent odor is also a natural carminative, meaning that it prevents gas, always a consideration when eating black beans. You can buy dried epazote from many herb companies.

Flageolets with Fennel, Tomato, and Green Olives

(VEGETARIAN)

A recipe for flageolets that once appeared in a Williams-Sonoma catalog immediately caught my eye. It was on the same page as a pressure cooker, and I'm a big fan of pressure-cooked beans. I adapted the original recipe to suit my taste for the Mediterranean flavors I crave, including the wonderful preserved lemons from North Africa. Substitute small navy beans if you must, but there is nothing like the elegant, pale green flageolets grown only in France. I've added tomatoes for color and to balance the saltiness of the lemons and olives. Because flageolets have such tender, thin skins, it is not necessary to soak them.

Serves 6
---

1 (12-ounce) package (1½ cups) flageolet beans

2 bay leaves

2 sprigs fresh thyme

1 head garlic, ½ inch sliced off the top to expose the cloves

4 cups Light Chicken Stock (see page 320)

1 large fennel bulb, trimmed

2 tablespoons fresh lemon juice (about 1 lemon)

¼ cup extra-virgin olive oil

½ cup dry white vermouth

1 cup chopped plum tomatoes, fresh or canned

2 tablespoons chopped fresh thyme leaves (about ½ bunch)

¼ cup diced preserved lemon rind (see Sources, page 341)

½ cup coarsely chopped, pitted green olives

2 tablespoons chopped Italian parsley leaves

Freshly ground black pepper

1. Drain and rinse the soaked flageolets. In a large pot, combine the flageolets, bay leaves, thyme, garlic, and Light Chicken Stock. Bring to a boil. Reduce the heat and simmer for 1 to 1½ hours, or until tender but still firm. Cool slightly; then discard the bay leaves, thyme, and garlic.

2. Meanwhile, cut the fennel bulb into small dice and toss with the lemon juice to prevent discoloration. In a large stainless-steel or enameled saucepan, heat the olive oil; then add the fennel and stir-fry for 3 to 4 minutes, or until lightly browned. Add the vermouth, tomatoes, chopped thyme, preserved lemon rind, and olives. Simmer for 5 minutes; then add the flageolets and any cooking liquid. Return to a boil, reduce the heat, and simmer for 10 minutes, or until the liquid has almost completely evaporated and the flageolets are firm yet tender.

3. Sprinkle with the parsley before serving, either hot or at room temperature. Season to taste with pepper. You might need salt, but taste first as both the olives and preserved lemon are salty.

Mexican Drunken Beans
(Frijoles Borrachos)

(VEGETARIAN OPTION)

There is a whole family of "drunken" dishes, called borracho *in Mexico or* ubriaco *in Italy, that are cooked in copious amounts of alcoholic beverages, usually beer or wine. Here, it refers to cowboy-style pinto beans cooked in dark beer with roasted poblanos and tomatoes. Serve them over rice or as an accompaniment to charcoal-grilled skirt steak or flank steak. For a vegetarian option, simply omit the chorizo.*

Serves 6 to 8

1 pound (2 cups) dried pinto beans,
    soaked (see Soaking Chart, page 57)
2 (12-ounce) bottles dark beer
4 cups cold water
1 large onion, quartered
2 poblano chiles
2 ripe beefsteak tomatoes
½ pound chorizo sausage, casing
    removed
Salt
½ cup chopped fresh cilantro leaves
    (about ½ bunch)

1. Drain and rinse the soaked pinto beans. Place in a large, heavy-bottomed pot with a lid. Add the beer and water and bring to a boil. Cover, reduce the heat, and simmer for about 1 hour, or until the beans are cooked through but still firm.

2. Over a gas flame or directly on an electric coil, char the onion, poblano, and tomatoes until the skins are blackened but the flesh is still firm. Place in a bowl to cool. When cool enough to handle, rub off and discard the blackened skins. Seed the peppers and tomatoes. Chop the vegetables and combine in the bowl.

3. Place the chorizo in a hot skillet and cook over medium heat until well browned, breaking up the meat as it cooks.

4. Add the charred vegetables and the browned chorizo, along with its fat, to the cooked beans. Season to taste with salt and cook, stirring occasionally, for 30 minutes, or until the sauce thickens and the beans are tender. Remove from the heat and taste for seasoning. Stir in the cilantro and serve.

The original term "beanfeast" came from the practice of 18th-century English employers giving their workers an annual blowout party in which beans with bacon were a major part of the menu. "Beanfeast" gradually came to be used for any celebration, especially a free party. In printers' jargon, the word was shortened to "beano" (which is now the commercial name of an effective anti-flatulence remedy).

Tuscan Beans Cooked in a Flask
(Fagioli al Fiasco Toscana)
(VEGETARIAN)

In Tuscany, it was an old custom to cook shelled fresh white beans in a heavy glass wine flask buried in the cinders of a hardwood fire. The beans would cook slowly, absorbing all the flavor inside the bottle because the steam would condense on the sides of the narrow neck and fall back into the beans. This dish is an example of Italian cooking at its best: the simplest of ingredients cooked slowly to make an exquisite dish. Tuscan bean lovers serve this dish instead of potatoes as an accompaniment to a rare grilled T-bone steak seasoned alla Fiorentina, *or rubbed with chopped fresh rosemary, garlic, sea salt, and black pepper. If you don't have a fireplace, cook the beans as slowly as possible using an earthenware bean pot or a cast-iron Dutch oven in a conventional oven. If you'd like to try cooking the beans authentically in a glass wine flask buried in fireplace embers, refer to the detailed instructions in William Rubel's wonderful book* The Magic of Fire.

—————————— *Serves 6* ——————————

4 cups shelled fresh white beans or fresh
    cranberry beans
½ cup extra-virgin olive oil, preferably
    Tuscan
1 bunch fresh sage
4 cloves plump, young garlic
3 cups cold water
Sea salt and freshly ground black pepper

1. Preheat the oven to 325°F. Combine the beans, oil, sage, garlic, and cold water in an earthenware bean pot or Dutch oven. Cover and place in oven. Reduce the heat to 275°F and cook for 3 hours, or until the beans are plump and tender.

2. Remove the beans from the oven, transfer them to a bowl, and season generously with salt and freshly ground black pepper. Serve piping hot or at room temperature.

Sardinian-Style Cranberry Beans
with Fennel and Savoy Cabbage
(VEGETARIAN OPTION)

This rustic, earthy dish comes from the Sardinia. Now home to ultra-exclusive resorts, in the past that island was extremely isolated, with little choice in foods. I've never been there, but I did spend several weeks on the neighboring island of Corsica, where the countryside is dramatic and the rocky landscape is thick with struggling herbs that develop extraordinary flavor. In Sardinia, this dish is prepared with dried beans, potent wild fennel, and the tender curly green verza, *or savoy cabbage. In California, wild fennel grows by the sides of many roads. If you can't find it, use domestic fennel spiked with ground fennel seeds. Note that fennel stalks provide much more of the heady licorice flavor than the bulbs, which are quite mild. For a vegetarian version, use olive oil in place of the pork fat.*

——————— *Serves 4* ———————

¾ pound (1½ cups) dried cranberry beans, soaked (see Soaking Chart, page 57)
2 wild fennel bulbs, or 2 small domestic fennel bulbs, including stalks
2 tablespoons ground fennel seeds
1 small head savoy cabbage, shredded
1 large onion, sliced
3 or 4 cloves garlic, peeled
¼ pound fresh pork fat, chilled to make it easier to chop, or olive oil
½ cup imported Italian tomato paste
Salt

1. Drain and rinse the soaked cranberry beans. Combine in a large pot with enough fresh cold water to cover by 2 to 3 inches. Bring to a boil. Reduce the heat and simmer until almost tender, about 1½ hours.

2. Trim and finely slice the fennel bulbs. Add to the bean pot along with the ground fennel seeds, cabbage, and onion. Simmer for 10 to 15 minutes, or until the vegetables are tender.

3. Chop the garlic and pork fat together (or mix the garlic with the olive oil) to form a paste. Stir into the beans and add the tomato paste. Season to taste with salt. Cook for 15 minutes longer, or until the beans and vegetables are tender and the flavors have blended.

Puerto Rican–Style Pink Beans
(Habichuelas Rojas)

This recipe was given to me by Guillermo Pernot, chef-owner of ¡Pasion!, the nationally acclaimed Nuevo Latino restaurant in Philadelphia. In his travels, Pernot—a native of Buenos Aires—learned to make this Puerto Rican dish using the firm orange calabaza squash common in Hispanic markets. You can easily substitute butternut squash. Pernot recommends serving this dish with a tangy green herb condiment called recaito criollo. *The Vitarroz brand is a good all-natural version available in Caribbean groceries.*

------------------------------- *Serves 6* -------------------------------

1 pound (2 cups) dried pink or kidney beans, soaked (see Soaking Chart, page 57)
2 tablespoons olive oil
¼ pound ham, diced
2 quarts cold water
3 medium onions, chopped
1 green bell pepper, seeded and chopped
½ pound calabaza or butternut squash, peeled and cut into ½-inch dice
½ pound all-purpose potatoes, peeled and cut into ½-inch dice
½ cup chopped Italian parsley leaves (about ½ large bunch)
1 chicken bouillon cube
2 tablespoons tomato paste
½ teaspoon ground cumin
½ teaspoon chopped Mexican oregano
1 teaspoon salt
Freshly ground black pepper
1 cup prepared *recaito criollo* (see Sources, page 341), for serving

1. Drain the soaked pink beans. In a large pot, heat the oil. Add the ham and cook for 5 minutes over medium heat. Add the pink beans and cold water. Bring to a boil. Reduce the heat, cover, and simmer for about 2 hours, or until the beans are tender.

2. Stir in the onions, green pepper, calabaza, potatoes, parsley, bouillon cube, tomato paste, cumin, and oregano. Simmer for about 10 minutes longer, or until the calabaza and potatoes are tender. Season to taste with salt and black pepper. Serve with the *recaito criollo*.

Spanish Names for Common Beans

Judía — Spain
Frijole — Mexico
Poroto — Chile, Argentina, Peru
Caraota — Venezuela
Habichuela — Puerto Rico

Trio of Savory Beans

(VEGETARIAN)

Savory, a member of the large mint family along with basil and sage, is the herb for beans. Use either the winter variety with fibrous leaves and a pungent flavor or the summer variety with tender leaves and a milder flavor. I've read that every little garden in Switzerland has a summer savory plant, called bohnenkraut, or "bean green," to be used for cooking beans. Both winter and summer savory seem to grow very easily in my front-yard herb garden with little or no attention. The blossoms of both are lovely and long lasting, though the lavender blossoms of winter savory are especially beautiful. If you happen to have them, sprinkle over this dish for garnish.

Serves 6

½ pound fresh green beans, cut diagonally into 1-inch pieces
½ pound shelled fresh fava beans or fresh baby lima beans
¼ cup extra-virgin olive oil
3 large shallots, chopped
1½ tablespoons chopped fresh savory leaves, or 1½ teaspoons dried
2 cups cooked cranberry beans, rinsed and drained (¾ cup dried cranberry beans, cooked and drained; see Basic Cooking Chart, page 58)
Salt and freshly ground black pepper
Fresh savory sprigs (with blossoms if available), for garnish

1. Bring a large pot of salted water to a boil. Add the green beans and cook for 2 minutes. Remove with a slotted spoon and rinse under cold water to set the color and stop the cooking. Return the water to a boil. Add the fava beans and cook for 2 minutes. Drain and rinse under cold water. Slip off each of the fava skins and discard, reserving the favas.

2. Heat the olive oil in a large pan over medium-low heat. Add the shallots and savory. Cook for 5 minutes, or until the shallots are softened and lightly browned. Add the cooked cranberry beans, green beans, and favas, and toss to coat evenly. Cook for 2 to 3 minutes, or until thoroughly heated; then season to taste with salt and pepper. Serve immediately, garnished with savory sprigs.

Chinese Yard-Long Beans
with Black Bean and Garlic Sauce
(VEGETARIAN)

Not for the faint of heart, these Asian long beans are stir-fried in a delightful, pungent fermented black bean sauce with plenty of garlic. Tangerine zest is sweeter and spicier than orange, and has a wonderful perfume. Yard-long beans are such an ancient vegetable that their place of origin is unknown, though it's probably Africa or Asia. They have been grown in China since prehistoric times, and remain an important crop there. Also eaten in Africa, the Mediterranean, and the Caribbean, they easily hold their own when combined with pungent flavorings, as in this dish.

— *Serves 6* —

¼ cup soy sauce

¼ cup rice wine, dry sherry, or Marsala

1 tablespoon sugar

2 teaspoons cornstarch

½ cup cold water

1 pound Chinese yard-long beans, washed, trimmed, and cut into 6-inch lengths

2 tablespoons vegetable oil

2 tablespoons coarsely chopped fermented black beans

Grated zest of 1 tangerine or ½ orange

1 (1-inch) length fresh ginger, grated

2 teaspoons chopped garlic

1 teaspoon hot chile paste or hot red pepper flakes

1. In a small bowl, combine the soy sauce, rice wine, sugar, cornstarch, and cold water.

2. Bring a pot of water to a boil. Add the long beans, return to a boil, and boil for 5 to 6 minutes, or until tender. Drain and rinse under cold water to set the color and stop the cooking. (The beans may be prepared to this point up to 1 day ahead.)

3. In a large skillet or a wok, heat the oil over medium-high heat until it just begins to smoke. Add the cooked, drained beans and stir-fry for 3 to 4 minutes, or until the color is intensified. Add the black beans, zest, ginger, garlic, and chile paste. Stir-fry for 2 minutes longer. Pour in the soy sauce mixture and stir to coat well. Bring to a boil, toss to combine well, and serve immediately.

COOK'S NOTE

Yard-long beans are pencil-thin, flexible pods that can grow as much as three feet long, though they are normally picked at half that length. They have a stronger bean flavor and a dense, solid texture that is chewy when cooked, rather than tender and herbal like green beans. Closely related to the black-eyed pea, they are best suited to stir-frying or braising. Choose thin, relatively smooth, blemish-free beans without noticeably developed seeds and with little to no shriveling at the ends. They are available year-round, primarily in Asian markets.

Lady Peas with Carolina Rice
and Green Tomato Relish

During a fabulous weekend of shopping, cooking, and eating with the Carolina Low Country culinary authority John Martin Taylor, or "Hoppin' John," I was introduced to this unpretentious dish. John decided to make it after passing a farmer's stand that sold the delicate lady peas it calls for. This smaller, more delicate version of black-eyed peas is found mostly at Southern farm markets and is not commercially grown. You can certainly substitute fresh or frozen black-eyed peas for dried ones. South Carolina's famous long-grain Carolina rice is now hardly grown there, though the rice plantations have a long and venerable history. After an absence of almost 100 years, commercial rice production has begun to start up again in South Carolina, although almost all Carolina rice is now grown in Texas, California, Louisiana, and Arkansas.

Serves 6

11 cups cold water
2 smoked ham hocks (about 1 pound)
4 cups fresh lady peas, or fresh or frozen
    black-eyed peas
1 teaspoon salt
1 tablespoon unsalted butter
1½ cups long-grain rice, preferably
    Carolina
Green tomato relish, *piccalilli* (see
    Sources, page 341), or Pennsylvania
    Dutch Chow-Chow (see page 247),
    for serving

1. Combine 8 cups of the cold water and the ham hocks in a large soup pot. Bring to a boil. Reduce the heat and simmer for 30 minutes, skimming off any white foam impurities that rise to the surface. Add the lady peas and return to a boil. Reduce the heat and simmer for 30 minutes, or until the peas are plump and tender. There should be several cups of liquid in the pot. Reserve, discarding the ham hock.

2. In a 2-quart, heavy-bottomed pot with a lid, bring the remaining 3 cups water, the salt, and the butter to a boil. Add the rice. Return to a boil, cover, and reduce the heat as low as possible. Cook for 15 minutes, or until the water is absorbed. Turn off the heat and allow the rice to steam for another 10 minutes. Uncover and fluff lightly with a fork or a rubber spatula.

3. Place a generous mound of steaming rice in the center of a salad-size plate. Make a well in the center, spreading the rice out into a ring. Ladle the peas and their cooking juices into the center. Serve with a bowl of green tomato relish.

Garden Peas à la Française

(VEGETARIAN)

This most delicate French springtime dish is worth making when you find sweet young garden peas in the pod. Tender Boston lettuce and scallions or spring onions both enhance the subtle, sweet taste of the peas. The lettuce shreds also form a sort of web that captures the flavors of mild scallions, sweet butter, and grated fresh nutmeg.

Serves 4 to 6

2 tablespoons (¼ stick) unsalted butter
2 pounds fresh garden peas, shelled
1 small head Boston lettuce, sliced into thin shreds
1 bunch scallions, white and green parts, sliced
Salt and freshly ground black pepper
Freshly grated nutmeg

1. In a medium saucepan pan over low heat, heat the butter until foaming. Add the peas, lettuce, and scallions. Cook until the peas turn bright green.

2. Season to taste with salt, pepper, and nutmeg, and serve immediately.

GARDEN PEAS

Choose garden peas with rounded, pearl-shaped peas that perfectly fill their pods but aren't bulging. Stay away from overgrown, starchy peas that are flattened against each other, resembling a set of teeth. Peas will maintain almost all of their sweetness for 3 to 4 days if they're placed in a closed plastic bag and refrigerated.

Georgian Green Beans in Walnut Sauce

(VEGETARIAN)

The Republic of Georgia reaches from the Black Sea to the Caspian Sea. It is a fabled land of bounty, with tucked-away mountain valleys and fertile lowlands. Often featured in ancient mythology, Georgia to this day maintains a strong national identity and a 2,500-year-old cuisine. The most famous of many sauces is this walnut sauce, satsivi. *It may be served with poultry, fish, or as in this recipe, with vegetables. According to Darra Goldstein, author of* The Georgian Feast, *the local sauces are so delicious that people say "with a Georgian sauce, you can swallow nails."*

--------- *Serves 6* ---------

2 pounds fresh green beans, cut into
    2-inch pieces
¼ pound light-skinned walnuts
2 cloves garlic
1 small onion, coarsely chopped
¼ cup fresh cilantro leaves, chopped
    (about ¼ bunch), reserving a few
    whole leaves for garnish
1 teaspoon ground coriander
2 tablespoons olive oil
2 tablespoons red wine vinegar
2 tablespoons fresh lemon juice (about
    1 lemon)
2 teaspoons sweet paprika, plus
    additional for serving
½ cup Light Chicken Stock (see page 320)
Salt

1. Bring a medium pot of lightly salted water to a boil. Add the green beans, return to a boil, and cook for 2 minutes. Drain and rinse under cold water to set the color and stop the cooking.

2. Combine the walnuts, garlic, onion, cilantro, coriander, olive oil, vinegar, lemon juice, and paprika in the bowl of a food processor. Process to a smooth paste, pouring in the chicken stock a little at a time so the mixture stays creamy. Season to taste with salt.

3. Arrange the green beans on a serving platter. Drizzle with the walnut sauce and sprinkle with the cilantro leaves and additional paprika.

Green Beans Amandine

(VEGETARIAN)

Is there anyone out there who doesn't love the tried-and-true combination of green beans with butter-toasted almonds? It may be simple but it certainly is delicious. If you happen across velvety, pencil-thin haricots verts in season, don't miss the opportunity to enjoy this classic. I prefer unblanched, sliced almonds, rather than the more common skinless, slivered nuts that taste and look bland. You can substitute pine nuts for a terrific variation. Mix wax beans with green beans for a more colorful dish.

Serves 6

1 pound young green beans, stem ends
    trimmed
¼ cup (½ stick) unsalted butter
½ cup unblanched sliced almonds
¼ cup chopped shallots
¼ cup water
1 wedge lemon
Salt and freshly ground black pepper

1. Steam the green beans until they turn bright green; then drain. (If you're preparing them ahead of time, run under cold water to set the color. If serving them immediately, this step is not necessary.)

2. In a medium skillet, melt the butter and cook until the solids are lightly caramelized and the butter starts to give off an aroma of hazelnuts. Add the sliced almonds and shallots. Sauté 1 to 2 minutes, or until the shallots are softened and the almonds lightly browned. Add the green beans and water, and cook over high heat until the beans are hot and coated with the sauce.

3. At the last minute, squeeze the lemon juice into the beans. Season to taste with salt and pepper, toss, and serve immediately.

Green Beans in Lemon-Marjoram Cream

(VEGETARIAN)

Except at roadside farmstands, old-fashioned hand-picked green beans are hard to come by. These days, unfortunately, most beans are machine picked—stem pieces still attached to the green beans are a sign of this. The combination of the lemon cream and the pungent marjoram makes this dish something special. Just be sure to combine the cream with the green beans and lemon right before serving to maintain their attractive bright color.

Serves 6

1 pound tender green beans or *haricots verts,* trimmed
¾ cup heavy cream
2 tablespoons chopped fresh marjoram leaves (about ¼ bunch)
Grated zest of 1 lemon
¼ cup fresh lemon juice (about 2 lemons)
Salt and freshly ground black pepper

1. Cook the green beans in a large pot in plenty of boiling salted water for 3 minutes, or until they turn bright green. Drain and immediately rinse under cold running water to stop the cooking and set the color.

2. In a small saucepan, heat the cream over medium heat, about 10 minutes, until it's thickened and bubbles appear over the entire surface. Transfer to a skillet and add the green beans, marjoram, lemon zest, and juice. Season to taste with salt and pepper. Quickly toss together and cook 1 to 2 minutes to reheat the beans. Don't cook any longer or the color of the green beans will fade.

Wax Beans with Dill

(VEGETARIAN)

Here's a simple, attractive way to prepare wax beans, the butter-colored variety of green beans. I like the contrast of the grassy green dill against the pale yellow wax beans. These beans can be on the tough side, so look for slender pods with small, unobtrusive seeds inside. They should be crisp enough to make a "snap" sound when broken in half. Wrap and refrigerate any remaining dill butter tightly in plastic wrap or place in a small freezer bag and freeze for another time. This butter is an excellent way to have fresh herb flavor on hand in a convenient form, as long as you don't stint on the dill.

—————————— *Serves 6* ——————————

¼ pound (1 stick) unsalted butter, softened

1 large bunch fresh dill, stems discarded, leaves washed and dried

2 shallots, peeled

2 teaspoons salt

½ teaspoon freshly ground black pepper

2 pounds fresh wax beans, stem ends trimmed

1. Combine the butter, dill, shallots, salt, and pepper in the bowl of a food processor. Process until well combined but not puréed. There should still be visible pieces of dill.

2. Bring a large pot of salted water to a boil. Add the beans and cook for about 5 minutes, or until bright yellow with no white spots. Drain and toss with about half the dill butter. Serve immediately. Refrigerate or freeze the remaining dill butter.

Green Soybeans with Cantonese Bacon

I first tasted this unexpected treat at Chef Philippe Chin's tiny original restaurant, Chanterelles, in Philadelphia. While I've never been much of a dried soybean fan, I've always loved fresh green favas, which these green soybeans resemble in texture, color, and flavor. The best part is, you can buy packages of inexpensive green soybeans, called Edamame or Vegetable Soy beans, in the frozen food section of many Asian and natural supermarkets, even if they're not in season. The Cantonese bacon is not smoked but it is cured—much like pancetta, which makes a good substitute. If you can find only smoked bacon, then par-cook it first in boiling water for 1 minute to reduce the smoked flavor, which would interfere with the oyster sauce in this recipe.

—————————————— *Serves 6* ——————————————

4 cups shelled fresh green soybeans
    (about 2 pounds whole beans), or
    frozen soybeans
½ medium onion, chopped
1 shallot, chopped
1 tablespoon unsalted butter
3 (¼-inch-thick) slices Cantonese or
    regular bacon, cut into small dice
1 teaspoon sugar
1 tablespoon balsamic vinegar
1 teaspoon soy sauce
2 tablespoons oyster sauce (see Cook's
    Note)
2 tablespoons chopped parsley leaves

1. Bring a large pot of salted water to a boil. Add the soybeans and cook for 2 minutes. Drain and rinse under cold water to set the color and stop the cooking. Drain and reserve. (The soybeans can be prepared to this point up to 1 day ahead.)

2. In a medium pan over medium heat, cook the onion and shallot in the butter for 5 minutes. Add the bacon and sugar, and cook until the mixture is golden brown.

3. Add the soybeans. Deglaze the pan with the vinegar and soy sauce, scraping up any brown bits with a spoon. Add the oyster sauce and parsley and serve immediately.

COOK'S NOTE

Oyster sauce is a thick, concentrated, dark brown liquid made from oysters, brine, and soy sauce. Used as both a stir-fry seasoning and a table condiment, it imparts a rich but not overpowering flavor. When choosing a brand, always look at the ingredients to make sure oyster is one of the first listed. It does not need to be refrigerated.

Provençal-Style Green Beans

(VEGETARIAN)

I happen to adore green beans prepared in almost any fashion, as long as the beans themselves are tender and brightly colored, with no developed seed straining against the pod. Here, young green beans are served in a lovely, light sauce made in the Provençal style with fresh tomatoes, garlic, and basil. Make this at the height of midsummer when greens beans and local vine-ripened tomatoes are at their best. In the colder months, it is best made with the aseptically packed chopped tomatoes under the Pomi name by Parmalat, sold in natural foods stores and specialty markets. These tomatoes that come in what looks like a cardboard box are less acidic and fresher tasting than the canned type.

Serves 6

1½ pounds green beans, stem ends trimmed
1 red onion, cut into slivers
2 tablespoons extra-virgin olive oil
3 or 4 large cloves garlic, thinly sliced
3 ripe beefsteak tomatoes (about 1 pound), cored, seeded, and diced
¼ cup shredded fresh basil leaves
Salt and freshly ground black pepper

1. Bring a large pot of salted water to a boil. Add the green beans and bring back to a boil, stirring so they cook evenly. As soon as the beans turn bright green but are still crisp, after about 3 minutes, drain and rinse under cold running water to set the color and stop the cooking.

2. In a medium pan, cook the red onion in the olive oil over medium heat until softened but not browned. Add the garlic and cook for 1 minute longer, or until the garlic releases its fragrance. Add the tomatoes and cook over high heat for about 5 minutes, or until they have softened but still hold their shape, shaking the pan occasionally to prevent sticking. (The dish can be prepared up to 1 day ahead at this point.)

3. Just before serving, reheat the tomato mixture if necessary and add the beans and basil. Toss to combine and cook for about 1 minute, or until the beans are thoroughly heated. Season with salt and pepper to taste, and serve immediately.

COOK'S NOTE

Because of the acid in the tomatoes, the beans will lose their bright green color quickly and turn a less attractive olive green color. That's why it's important not to combine them until ready to serve, although throughout the Mediterranean greens are stewed in tomato-based sauces until they turn dark olive green. Those dishes have their own honest appeal.

Minted Fresh Fava Beans

(VEGETARIAN)

As a driven young chef in my first major job, I did some crazy things in my search for authenticity, such as personally clean fifty-pound boxes of squid in order to obtain their tiny ink sacs to make my own black squid ink pasta. Perhaps my most notorious act was choosing to serve fresh green fava beans for the opening of the restaurant, an event to which several hundred guests had been invited. I joined the staff in cleaning about 6 bushels of favas, which involved opening the tough outer pods, removing the inner beans, blanching them, and then individually removing the skin from each bean. The task seemed endless, but the results were extraordinary because no one (for good reason) had ever been served fresh favas in a restaurant. Favas are best in season in early June. You could substitute edamame with good results here.

Serves 6

2 to 3 pounds fresh fava beans in their
  pods
¼ cup extra-virgin olive oil
¼ cup chopped fresh mint (about ½
  bunch)
¼ cup water
Salt and freshly ground black pepper

1. Remove the fava beans from their spongy outer pods and discard the pods.

2. Bring a large pot of salted water to a boil. Add the favas and cook for about 2 minutes, or long enough to loosen the outer skin. Drain and rinse under cold water. Slip the individual favas from their skins and reserve. If the favas are overly mature and have turned yellow rather than bright green, blanch them again in boiling water until tender.

3. In a medium pan, heat the olive oil and mint just until the mint gives off its aroma. Add the favas and water, and cook until the beans are tender and coated with mint oil. Season to taste with salt and pepper. Serve immediately.

Raw Baby Favas with Salt

(VEGETARIAN)

According to the renowned Provençal culinary authority Jean-Noël Escudier, it is an ancient custom in the region to enjoy the first, most tender green broad beans—called fèvettes—*right from their pods as an hors d'oeuvre, perhaps with a glass of the Riviera's beloved* pastis *(the aniseed-flavored liquor, similar to Pernod and Ricard). You will only be able to serve this delicacy if you grow your own favas or know a friendly farmer who does. Once the beans start to mature, they lose their fleeting sweetness and become too starchy. To serve eight as an hors d'oeuvre, you'll need about 1 pound of very young fava beans in their pods and a dish of French sea salt. Each person splits open the pods and slips the fava out of the inner skin, revealing the grass-green bean halves. Dip lightly into the salt and eat them as is.*

Piedmontese Red Beans in Red Wine

One of my first and still favorite Italian cookbooks written in English is Northern Italian Cooking *by Francesco Ghedini, an Italian nobleman who came to the United States as a journalist specializing in food. Published in 1973, this little book is a treasure of simple, authentic recipes. Unfortunately, Ghedini had only just completed this one book before his death. I adapted this recipe for red kidney beans cooked with red wine from my much-stained copy. I found a similar recipe in Escudier's Provençal cookbook. There must be an old connection between these two dishes dating from the days of the Kingdom of Savoy, which included Savoy, Piedmont, Monaco, and Nice.*

Serves 6 to 8

1 pound (2 cups) dried dark red kidney beans

4 cups cold water

2 cups dry red wine (preferably Piedmontese, such as Barbera, Barbaresco, or Gattinara)

½ pound prosciutto rind or salt pork, rinsed and drained

1 large onion, stuck with 2 whole cloves

2 bay leaves

1 tablespoon salt

½ pound pancetta or bacon, diced

2 tablespoons unbleached all-purpose flour

2 tablespoons (¼ stick) unsalted butter

Freshly ground black pepper

1. In a large pot, combine the kidney beans with enough cold water to cover. Bring to a boil, reduce the heat, and simmer for 5 minutes. Drain, discarding the water.

2. Combine the beans with the cold water, wine, prosciutto rind, onion, and bay leaves in the same pot. Bring to a boil, skim off any white foam impurities that rise to the surface, and reduce the heat. Simmer for 1 hour, covered. Add the salt, cover, and cook for about 30 minutes, or until the beans are soft but not mushy. Remove and discard the prosciutto rind, onion, and bay leaves.

3. In a small pan over medium heat, cook the pancetta to render the fat and brown the meat. Stir in the flour. Add this mixture to the cooked beans along with the butter, stirring to combine thoroughly. Season to taste with pepper. Bring back to a boil and serve.

Scarlet Runner Beans
in Brown Butter and Shallots

(VEGETARIAN)

My friends Mark and Judy Dornstreich have been growing extraordinary organic greens, herbs, edible flowers, and vegetables for more than 20 years at Branch Creek Farm in Bucks County, Pennsylvania. As their first restaurant customer, I take pride in having introduced other chefs to their produce. It's hard to describe the experience of handling, cooking, and eating what they grow. Their scarlet runner beans, for instance, are as decorative as they are delicious. Commonly planted as an ornamental (especially in England, where they thrive in the cool, damp climate) rather than an edible plant, scarlet runners have big, beautiful red blossoms. Lemon thyme has lovely variegated leaves of green and pale yellow, with a potent lemon aroma.

—————————————— *Serves 4 to 6* ——————————————

2 pounds fresh scarlet runner beans, shelled, or 2 cups (1 pound) fresh green lima beans
4 tablespoons (½ stick) unsalted butter
½ cup thinly sliced shallots
1 tablespoon chopped fresh lemon thyme, or 1 tablespoon regular fresh thyme plus 1 teaspoon grated lemon zest
Salt and freshly ground black pepper

1. Bring a large pot of salted water to a boil. Add the beans and return to a boil. Cook for 5 to 10 minutes, or until the beans are tender but not mealy. Drain and reserve.

2. Heat the butter in a medium pan and cook over medium heat until it begins to brown, shaking constantly. Add the shallots and sauté until caramelized on the edges. Stir in the beans and the thyme, and cook just until the beans are heated through. Season to taste with salt and pepper, and serve.

SCARLET RUNNER BEANS

This bean gets its name from the tendrils or runners it produces for support when climbing up the nearest convenient beanpole or lattice. It was first introduced into Britain in the 17th century as a decorative plant because of its attractive, bright red flowers. Around that time, it occurred to the British to eat the young pods, a habit that didn't catch on in other parts of the world where it was cultivated. At one time it was used as a mildly insulting slang name for an English soldier because of their red coats. It is also called "stick bean."

Sesame Sugar Snaps

(VEGETARIAN)

Sugar snap peas are versatile and make a good addition to any quickly cooked mixed-vegetable dish, such as a sauté or stir-fry. Here, served in a simple Asian-style sauce, they are flavored with sesame in two forms—the roasted oil and the seeds. Sugar snap peas wilt quickly, so plan on cooking them just before you're ready to serve them. Always cook sugar snaps briefly and at high heat for crispy texture and bright color.

Serves 4 to 6

1 pound fresh sugar snap peas
1 tablespoon sesame seeds
1 tablespoon roasted Japanese
    sesame oil
2 tablespoons unsalted butter
2 tablespoons soy sauce

1. Preheat the oven to 300°F. Trim the peas by removing the stem ends and side strings with your thumb and forefinger.

2. Lightly toast the sesame seeds in a small baking pan for 5 to 10 minutes, checking often.

3. In a wok or a large pan, heat the sesame oil and butter. Add the sugar snaps and toss, cooking for 1 to 2 minutes or until the peas turn bright green. Sprinkle in the soy sauce and toss. Serve immediately, topped with the toasted sesame seeds.

SUGAR SNAPS

Sugar snap peas have been around for about a hundred years, but didn't become famous until 1979, when Carl Lamborn of the Gallatin Valley Seed Company in Twin Falls, Idaho, crossed a thick-podded mutant green pea with a snow pea and made breeding history. The resulting offspring was a sugar snap pea that won the gold medal in the All-American selection. While these peas have been a favorite of home gardeners ever since, they are now commonly available in supermarkets. Look for crisp, unblemished beans with no visible peas bulging out. They should be brilliant green and smooth, with no cuts and with the same firm skin as snow peas.

Stir-Fried Snow Peas and Bok Choy with Ginger

(VEGETARIAN)

This simple, fresh-tasting stir-fry combines slightly chewy, sweet snow peas with juicy bok choy, a vegetable so mild it's hard to believe it's in the cabbage family. Make this dish when you can find fresh snow peas that have no round spots, which indicate spoilage. These can be hard to find because they're a relatively expensive specialty item, so supermarkets tend to move their inventories slowly. Even as little as a quarter pound of snow peas is noticeable in this dish, but a half pound is even better.

Serves 4

1 large head bok choy, or 1 pound baby
    bok choy
¼ cup rice wine
2 tablespoons soy sauce
2 teaspoons cornstarch
1 teaspoon Chinese five-spice powder,
    or a pinch each of ground cinnamon
    and ground cloves
2 tablespoons soybean oil
1 bunch scallions, white and green parts,
    sliced diagonally into 1-inch pieces
2 tablespoons finely chopped fresh ginger
½ pound snow peas, trimmed

1. Trim off and discard any wilted leaf ends of the bok choy. Cut crosswise into 1-inch-wide strips, discarding the white core near the bottom of the stalk. Wash in a large bowl of water; then scoop out and drain in a colander.

2. In a small bowl, stir together the rice wine, soy sauce, cornstarch, and five-spice powder.

3. In a wok or a large skillet, heat the oil over medium-high heat; then add the scallions and ginger. Stir-fry for 1 minute to release the flavors. Add the bok choy and snow peas and stir-fry for about 2 minutes, or until the bok choy begins to wilt and the snow peas are shiny green.

4. Stir the rice wine mixture and add to the pan. Bring to a boil, stirring to coat the vegetables. Serve immediately.

Haitian Red Beans and Rice

Growing up in Washington, D.C., I developed friendships with kids from around the world, including one close friend from Senegal and another from Haiti. The son of the military attaché to the Haitian Embassy, the second friend introduced me to Haitian-style music and the planter's punch that made it easy to dance to the music. I loved to eat dinner at his house, where their cook would make this dish. I don't know what there was about it, but I could never get my fill; the textural combination of nutty, almost dry red beans and creamy rice was delicious. From Caribbean friends like my neighbor from Belize, I picked up the habit of always serving a bottle of hot sauce to sprinkle on all rice and bean dishes. A related dish is a delicious and popular Louisiana dish traditionally served on Mondays, made with the ham bone left over from the previous day's ham dinner. Red kidney beans are most often used, but many purists feel their flavor is too strong and use the small red beans known as pequeños *in Spanish.*

Serves 6 to 8

1 pound (2 cups) dried small red beans
   (pequeños) or kidney beans
1 ham hock
2 bay leaves
2 quarts cold water
¼ pound sliced bacon, diced
1 large onion, diced
2 large shallots, chopped
1 green bell pepper, seeded and diced
1 hot green chile, such as jalapeño or
   serrano, seeded and minced
2 cups long-grain white rice
2 tablespoons salt
2 tablespoons (¼ stick) butter
Hot sauce, for serving (optional)

1. Combine the beans, ham hock, bay leaves, and water in a large, heavy-bottomed pot. Bring to a boil. Cover, reduce the heat, and simmer for 1½ to 2 hours, or until the beans are tender. Cool slightly; then drain the beans, reserving both the cooking liquid and the beans. Measure out 4 cups of the bean liquid, discarding any extra, and reserve. Discard the ham hock and bay leaves.

2. Preheat the oven to 300°F. In a large Dutch oven, cook the bacon over medium heat until most of the fat has been rendered. Add the onion, shallots, bell pepper, and green chile, and cook for 5 minutes, or until softened but not browned. Stir in the rice and cook for 2 minutes, or until translucent but not browned. Add the reserved beans, cooking liquid, and salt. Bring to a boil; then reduce the heat, cover, and place in the oven.

3. Bake for 20 minutes, or until the liquid has evaporated. Cool for about 10 minutes; then fluff lightly and stir in the butter. Serve with the hot sauce.

> The great Louis Armstrong, native of New Orleans, loved the Creole favorite red beans and rice so much, he signed his letters "Red Beans and Ricely Yours."

According to the 1901 edition of the classic *Picayune Creole Cookbook,* "In all the ancient homes of New Orleans, and in the colleges and convents, where large numbers of children are sent to be reared to be strong and useful men and women, several times a week there appear on the table either the nicely cooked dish of Red Beans, which are eaten with rice . . . The Creoles hold that the boys and girls who are raised on beans and rice and beef will be among the strongest and sturdiest of people."

Moros e Christianos
(Cuban Black Turtle Beans and Rice)

This popular dish is whimsically referred to as "Moors and Christians" owing to the black and white colors of the beans and rice. The culantro *called for here is a typical Cuban herb, widely used throughout the Caribbean, Latin America, and the Far East, though relatively unknown in this country. Sometimes called spiny or serrated coriander, it is often mistaken for its relative cilantro, or coriander, which can be substituted for a less pungent flavor, though the two don't resemble each other much, as* culantro *has long, flat serrated leaves. To make this into a Cuban one-dish meal, top each portion with a fried egg and garnish with pan-fried sweet plantain slices cut on the diagonal.*

Serves 6

½ cup olive oil

1 medium onion, chopped

1 green bell pepper, diced

½ cup diced roasted red bell peppers (see page 332), or purchased

1 bunch scallions, white and green parts, thinly sliced

2 tablespoons chopped garlic

4 cups Light Chicken Stock (see page 320)

2 teaspoons dried oregano

2 teaspoons ground cumin

Salt and freshly ground black pepper

2 cups long-grain rice

1 cup dried black turtle beans, cooked and drained (see Basic Cooking Chart, page 58)

¼ cup chopped fresh *culantro* or cilantro leaves (about ¼ bunch)

1. Preheat the oven to 300°F. Heat the olive oil in a large Dutch oven with a lid. Stir the onion, green pepper, roasted red peppers, scallions, and garlic. Cook for about 5 minutes, or until softened but not brown. Add the Light Chicken Stock, oregano, and cumin, and season with salt and black pepper. Bring to a boil. Stir in the rice and cooked beans, cover, and place in the oven.

2. Bake for about 25 minutes, or until the liquid has been absorbed. Remove from the oven and let stand for 5 to 10 minutes with the lid on to steam; then fluff with a fork, stir in the *culantro*, and season to taste with salt and black pepper.

Chickpea Spaetzle

(VEGETARIAN)

Spaetzle are known throughout the former Austro-Hungarian Empire. These tiny, free-form dumplings, made from a batter that is halfway between a pancake batter and a pasta dough, can be flavored with everything from chestnuts and chestnut flour to spinach, pumpkin, and chickpea flour. Spaetzle are an especially good side dish to serve at a party because they can be made ahead and then fried in butter until toasty brown. I first tasted these chickpea spaetzle at the Indian-inspired restaurant Tabla in Manhattan. I thought it was such a good idea that I had to try making them myself. Look for chickpea flour at Indian and Middle Eastern groceries and natural foods stores. Store it in the freezer.

Serves 6

---

2 cups unbleached all-purpose flour

2 cups chickpea flour

2 teaspoons salt

1 teaspoon freshly grated nutmeg

4 eggs

4 cups whole milk

4 tablespoons (½ stick) unsalted butter

1 cup soft bread crumbs

½ cup chopped Italian parsley leaves (about ½ bunch)

1. Combine the flour, chickpea flour, salt, and nutmeg in a large mixing bowl. Whisk together the eggs and milk in a large bowl. Beat the egg mixture slowly into the flour mixture until the dough is smooth and the consistency between a pancake batter and a dough.

2. Bring a large pot of water to a boil. Working in batches, press the batter through the holes of a colander or a spaetzle maker directly into the boiling water. Stir gently to prevent sticking. The spaetzle are ready when they float to the surface, after about 5 minutes. Remove with a slotted spoon and reserve.

3. Melt the butter in a saucepan over medium heat. Add the bread crumbs and cook until evenly toasted, stirring frequently. Toss the spaetzle with the toasted crumbs and parsley. Serve as a side dish with braised meats.

White Bean Purée

(VEGETARIAN OPTION)

Purées are a classic side dish in the elegant cuisines of France. Serve this smooth, flavorful purée as a hot side dish with roast chicken or roast beef. The exquisite creamy texture comes from combining the beans with potato and heavy cream. For a vegetarian version, substitute Vegetable Stock (see page 323) for the chicken stock.

Serves 6

1 pound (2 cups) dried white emergo beans, *haricots lingots, haricots soisson,* or other large creamy white beans, soaked and drained (see Basic Soaking Chart, page 58)

½ bunch fresh savory or thyme, tied with kitchen string

4 cups Light Chicken Stock (see page 320)

4 tablespoons (½ stick) unsalted butter

1 large onion, diced

2 tablespoons chopped garlic

1 teaspoon ground allspice

Grated zest of 1 lemon

2 russet potatoes, peeled and diced

1 cup heavy cream

Salt and freshly ground black pepper

1. Combine the beans with the savory and Light Chicken Stock in a large pot. Cover and bring to a boil. Reduce the heat and simmer for 1½ hours.

2. In a small pan, melt the butter. Add the onion, garlic, allspice, and lemon zest, and cook over medium heat until the onion is transparent. Add the beans and potatoes. Cook for 30 minutes longer, or until the beans are very soft. Remove from heat and discard the savory. (Some of the leaves will remain in the pot.) Drain and reserve any excess liquid.

3. Purée the bean mixture in a food processor. Pour in the cream and process again. If the mixture is still stiff, pour in up to ½ cup of the reserved cooking liquid to create a smooth, soft consistency. Season to taste with salt and pepper.

CHAPTER ELEVEN

Desserts and Sweet Treats

Japanese Red Adzuki Bean Ice Cream

(VEGETARIAN)

Ice cream and frozen fruit sherbets have a long history. Alexander the Great is said to have enjoyed snow flavored with honey, King Solomon was apparently fond of iced drinks during harvest season, and the Roman emperor Nero Claudius Caesar sent runners into the mountains for snow to be flavored with fruits and juices. A thousand years later, Marco Polo is believed to have returned from his travels in the Far East with a recipe that closely resembled that of sherbet. Somewhere around the 16th century, cream- and custard-based ice creams began to appear in Italy and France.

Modern Asian flavored ice creams made with ingredients like adzuki bean, ginger, and green tea were first offered to please American customers dining in Chinese and Japanese restaurants, who wanted to end their meal with a sweet dessert. When these flavors first began to show up in the ice cream shops of Asia, they were considered "exotic," although they have since become quite the rage.

Serves 8 to 12

3 cups whole milk
1 cup heavy cream
½ cup sugar
4 egg yolks
2 cups Red Bean Paste (see page 282)
Chopped crystallized ginger, for garnish
Chopped toasted peanuts, for garnish

1. Combine the milk and cream in a medium saucepan and bring to a simmer. In a mixing bowl, combine the sugar and egg yolks, and beat until the yolks turn thick and pale. Temper the yolk mixture by gradually pouring in the hot cream mixture while continuously stirring. Return the mixture to the saucepan and stir constantly over moderate heat until the custard thickens enough to coat the back of a wooden spoon, or until it reaches a temperature of 165°F on a candy thermometer.

2. Remove the custard from the heat, whisk in the Red Bean Paste, and then (optionally, for extra smooth texture) strain through a fine-mesh sieve into a clean container, preferably stainless steel or glass. Cover with plastic wrap, pressing down against the surface to prevent a skin from forming. Quickly chill the custard in a metal bowl set over a larger bowl filled with ice and water, or cool and then refrigerate overnight until cold to the touch. Freeze in ice cream maker according to manufacturer's directions. Transfer to an airtight container and freeze until ready to serve.

3. To serve, spoon the ice cream into bowls and garnish with chopped peanuts and crystallized ginger. Serve immediately.

COOK'S NOTE

Especially popular in Japan and Korea, adzuki beans are the second most important dry bean in Japan after soybeans. There, the color red is associated with happiness and luck, and adzuki beans, a deep burgundy that turns to dusky rose upon cooking, are often served at festivals. In fact, the majority of Japanese sweets contain adzuki beans.

Idaho Pinto Bean Pie

(VEGETARIAN)

Idaho is a major grower of beans in this country, so Idahoans have developed this pie with the flavor and creamy texture of pumpkin pie to use their abundant produce. Once you try it, you'll be very surprised at how delicious a bean pie can be. A similar pie, named after the Shabazz tribe that some say are ancestors of African Americans, was baked and sold to raise funds for Malcolm X's Nation of Islam and now appears on the menu in many soul-food restaurants. Serve this pie with unsweetened whipped cream because it's on the sweet side.

— *Serves 6 to 8* —

½ cup granulated sugar
1 cup dark brown sugar
2 eggs, beaten
¼ pound (1 stick) unsalted butter, softened
1 heaping cup cool, mashed pinto beans
    (strain to remove the skins if a
    smoother texture is desired)
¾ teaspoon ground cinnamon
½ teaspoon ground ginger
½ teaspoon grated nutmeg
½ teaspoon ground cloves
½ teaspoon salt
1 teaspoon vanilla extract
1 (9-inch) unbaked Shortcrust Pastry
    Shell (recipe follows), or purchased
Sweetened whipped cream, for serving

1. Preheat the oven to 375°F. In the bowl of an electric mixer, cream both sugars, eggs, and butter. Add the pinto beans, spices, salt, and vanilla, and beat again until well blended.

2. Pour the mixture into the pastry shell. Bake at 375°F for 20 minutes; then decrease the temperature to 350°F for an additional 25 minutes, or until a knife inserted in the center comes out clean.

SHORTCRUST PASTRY SHELL

— *Makes ³/₄ pound (Enough for 1 pie shell)* —

12 tablespoons cold unsalted butter
    (1½ sticks), cut into pieces
2 cups pastry flour (or all-purpose flour,
    preferably unbleached)
½ teaspoon salt
3 to 4 tablespoons ice water
1½ teaspoons cider vinegar

1. Place the butter, flour, and salt in a bowl and place in the freezer for 30 minutes. Using the flat beater attachment of an electric mixer, or by hand, cut the butter into the flour until the pieces are the size of peas.

2. Combine the ice water and vinegar. Sprinkle most of the liquid over the flour mixture while tossing with your hands to distribute it evenly. Pat the mixture together to form a ball. If necessary, add a few more teaspoons of liquid, but just enough to consolidate any dry ingredients remaining in the bowl.

3. Form the dough into a flattened round and wrap in plastic. Refrigerate for 1 hour. Flour the board and roll the dough into a circle about 12 inches in diameter. Pat into a pie plate, forming an attractive border and trimming off any excess dough. Chill while preparing the filling.

Creamy White Bean Ice Cream
with Molasses Caramel Sauce
(VEGETARIAN)

"Whoever heard of bean ice cream?" That's what my 17-year-old son said to me when I asked him to try my new concoction. Well, he was brave enough to try it, and he liked it! I got the idea for this super-creamy yet light ice cream from two very different sources. One was a recipe on the Web site maintained by the Northwest Bean Growers, which includes many creative bean recipes from chefs around the country (although, like many chef recipes, this one makes enough to serve a small army). Another version of this ice cream is included in a wonderful book I discovered on my last trip to Italy, called I Legumi, *a compilation of Italian chefs' recipes, historical recipes, and cooking instruction accompanied by mouth-watering photos. (See the Selected Bibliography, page 345, for more information.) Top this ice cream with warm molasses caramel sauce to make an indulgent delight suitable for the most decadent occasion.*

Serves 8 to 10

White Bean Ice Cream

1½ cups cooked white beans, drained and rinsed (a 15-ounce can, or ½ cup dried beans, soaked and cooked; see Basic Cooking Chart, page 58)

3 cups milk

1½ cups sugar

1 vanilla bean, split lengthwise, or 1 tablespoon vanilla extract

½ teaspoon ground cinnamon

¼ teaspoon ground allspice

1 cup heavy cream

6 egg yolks

Molasses Caramel Sauce

Makes about 1½ cups sauce

½ cup sugar

¼ cup water

6 tablespoons molasses

2 tablespoons honey

½ cup heavy cream

4 tablespoons (½ stick) unsalted butter

2 teaspoons vanilla extract

1. Prepare the White Bean Ice Cream: Combine the beans, 2 cups milk, ¾ cup sugar, vanilla bean (add the vanilla extract later, if using), cinnamon, and allspice in a medium enamel or stainless-steel saucepan. Bring to a boil; then reduce the heat and simmer uncovered for 10 minutes, stirring frequently to prevent sticking. Remove from the heat, stir in the vanilla extract, if using, and let stand, partially covered, for 1 hour. Remove and discard the vanilla bean; purée the bean mixture in a blender or food processor until smooth, and then strain through a sieve, discarding the solids.

2. Combine the remaining 1 cup milk with the cream and heat to scalding. (You can easily do this by placing it in a glass measuring cup and heating in the microwave.) Beat the remaining ¾ cup sugar and the egg yolks in a bowl until the yolks turn thick and pale. Temper the yolk mixture by gradually pouring in the hot cream mixture while continuously stirring. Return the mixture to an enamel or stainless-steel saucepan and stir constantly over medium heat until the custard thickens enough to coat the back of a wooden spoon, or reaches 165°F on a candy thermometer. Quickly chill the custard in a metal bowl set over a larger bowl filled with ice and water, or cool and then refrigerate overnight until cold to the touch. Freeze in an ice cream maker according to the manufacturer's directions.

3. Prepare the Molasses Caramel Sauce: Combine the sugar and water in a small, heavy-bottomed saucepan. Cook over medium heat until the sugar dissolves, shaking the pan occasionally. Do not stir, as that encourages the formation of crystals. Continue to boil gently until the sugar turns golden brown, while shaking the pan so it melts evenly. Do this carefully, as caramelized sugar is close to 400°F! When the sugar has evenly browned to a rich color and is just beginning to turn red, carefully pour in the molasses and honey; the mixture will bubble up. Swirl to combine and add the cream and butter. Stir over moderate heat until the mixture is smooth. Remove from the heat and stir in the vanilla. Serve warm over ice cream.

COOK'S NOTE

The Molasses Caramel Sauce can be kept cold and reheated in the microwave as needed, though it may need to be recombined by beating with a whisk until smooth and creamy again.

Molasses Caramel Corn with Peanuts

(VEGETARIAN)

In 1871, German immigrant F. W. Rueckheim brought the recipe for the delight that became known as Cracker Jack to Chicago. With his entire fortune of $200, Rueckheim started a small shop selling his specialty. The treat's popularity increased enormously in 1893, after it was introduced at the first World's Fair, held in the same city, and it's still being made today. Essential to this recipe are the small, round, red-skinned Spanish peanuts.

―――――――――――――――― *Makes about 16 cups (4 quarts)* ――――――――――――――――

8 tablespoons (1 stick) unsalted butter

1 tablespoon peanut oil

1 cup raw popcorn kernels

1 cup sugar

½ cup light corn syrup

¼ cup molasses

1 tablespoon vanilla extract

2 cups red-skinned Spanish peanuts, roasted and salted

1. Preheat the oven to 275°F. Rub a large roasting pan with 1 tablespoon of the butter. In a large (2-gallon), heavy-bottomed pot with a lid, heat the oil with 3 popcorn kernels, covered, over medium heat. When the kernels pop, add the remaining popcorn. Cover, shaking the pot occasionally, until the popping slows to several seconds between each pop. Remove from the heat, uncover, and cool to room temperature. Transfer to a large heatproof bowl.

2. In a medium, heavy-bottomed saucepan over medium heat, combine the sugar, remaining 7 tablespoons butter, corn syrup, and molasses, and bring to a boil. Cook over medium heat until the mixture reaches the soft-crack stage (275°F on a candy thermometer). If not using a thermometer, the syrup should form hard but pliable threads when dropped into a bowl of cold water. Remove from the heat and slowly stir in the vanilla, taking care as the syrup will bubble up.

3. Working quickly, add the peanuts to the hot syrup and stir to coat. Immediately pour the peanuts and syrup over the reserved popcorn and stir to combine, using a wooden spoon or a high-heat silicon spatula.

4. Spread the mixture out in the prepared roasting pan. Bake for 30 minutes, stirring every 10 minutes. The mixture should be the color of dark caramel. Remove from the oven, cool completely, and break into chunks. Store in an airtight cookie tin.

Caramel Apples
with Salted Peanut Crunch Coating
(VEGETARIAN)

This is a great snack for kids, either on the stick or cut into wedges with the seeds removed. If you serve it on a stick, you will need 8 short wooden dowels, available in most cookware stores or where candy-making supplies are sold. (You can substitute inexpensive wooden chopsticks cut into halves.) When choosing apples, look for the smaller ones that come packed in a 2- to 3- pound plastic bag. They're less expensive than the larger ones and will have a good apple-to-coating ratio. Make the caramel yourself, as in the recipe, or use 1 pound good-quality soft, chewy caramel candies, unwrapped and melted.

—————————————— *Makes 16 to 20 apples* ——————————————

1 (½-pound) can roasted salted peanuts
  (not dry-roasted)

Caramel
2 cups granulated sugar
1 cup brown sugar
⅔ cup white corn syrup
12 tablespoons (1½ sticks) butter
1 cup heavy cream
1 tablespoon vanilla extract
½ teaspoon salt
16 to 40 tart apples, such as Winesap,
  Jonathan, or McIntosh

1. Have ready a baking sheet covered with waxed or parchment paper. Twist the stems off the apples and insert a dowel or skewer 2 to 3 inches into the bottom end of each apple.

2. Coarsely chop the peanuts; then shake them through a wire sieve set over a bowl to remove any dusty bits. You should have only chunky nuts left in the sieve. Transfer the chopped peanuts in a bowl and reserve.

3. Prepare the Caramel: Combine the sugars, corn syrup, butter, cream, vanilla, and salt in a large (at least 4-quart), heavy pan over low heat, stirring frequently until the butter is melted and the ingredients are combined. Cook, stirring occasionally, until mixture reaches 240°F on a candy thermometer; this is the soft-ball stage, when a small amount of sugar syrup dropped into very cold water forms a ball that yields when pressed. (If using caramel candies, combine them with the vanilla in a deep microwaveable bowl. Microwave on medium power [50 percent] for 2 to 3 minutes; then stir. Microwave again for 2 minutes, or until almost liquid. Alternatively, place the caramels in a heatproof bowl and set over a pot of simmering water. Stir until melted and smooth. The mixture should be hot to the touch but not burning.)

4. Holding an apple by its wooden dowel, dip into the melted caramel, tilting the bowl and twirling the apple to coat completely. Allow any excess caramel to drip off; then dip the top of the apple into the bowl of reserved chopped peanuts. Place on the prepared baking sheet. Repeat with the remaining apples.

5. Chill in the refrigerator for 30 minutes, or until the caramel is set. Serve the apples as is or cut each into six wedges and remove the core, seeds, and dowels.

Fried Dessert Won Tons
with Red Bean Paste Filling
(VEGETARIAN)

In China, small red adzuki beans are reserved for sweet rather than savory dishes. The color red is said to bring good luck, which explains why dishes made with these beans are associated with festivals. Here, in a somewhat Westernized variation, the tiny, mild red adzuki beans are combined with chopped dates, vanilla, and brandy and cooked until they form a thick paste reminiscent of chocolate. Rather than using it to fill the more traditional Chinese steamed buns, I use the red bean filling to stuff won ton skins, and then deep-fry them. To make the stuffed won tons ahead, spread them out in a single layer on a baking sheet lined with waxed paper or parchment; then freeze until firm. Transfer to a zipper-lock freezer bag, pressing out the excess air before sealing. Freeze until ready to cook. Do not defrost before frying.

Serves 8 (Makes 48 won tons)

Red Bean Paste

1 pound (2 cups dried) red adzuki beans, soaked (see Soaking Chart, page 57)
6 cups cold water
½ pound pitted dates
1 cup boiling water
¼ pound (1 stick) unsalted butter
1 cup granulated sugar
1 teaspoon salt
2 tablespoons vanilla extract
¼ cup brandy

Won Tons

1 (4-ounce) package won ton skins, thawed if frozen
4 cups canola, peanut, or soybean oil, for frying
Confectioners' sugar, for serving

1. Drain the soaked adzuki beans. Place in a large pot and cover with the cold water. Bring to a boil; then reduce the heat and simmer for 1½ to 2 hours, or until the beans are soft but not mushy. The water should have evaporated by the time the beans are cooked. Drain and discard any remaining water.

2. Soak the dates for 15 minutes in the boiling water to soften.

3. Purée the cooked beans in a food processor to form a smooth paste, scraping down the side of the bowl several times. If desired, strain the puréed beans through a sieve or food mill to remove the skin pieces for a more refined texture. Transfer the beans to a bowl. Without washing the processor bowl, purée the dates and their soaking liquid until smooth.

4. In a large, heavy-bottomed saucepan, combine the butter and sugar over low heat, stirring until melted. Add the salt, reserved red bean purée, and date purée. Stir to combine, and cook, stirring frequently, to form a thick paste similar in texture to refried beans. Remove from the heat and immediately stir in the vanilla and the brandy. Cool, covered, and then refrigerate until chilled, about 1 hour. (The paste can be made 3 to 4 days ahead.)

5. To prepare the won tons, place 1½ teaspoons of the bean paste just below the diagonal center of each won ton skin. Do not get any filling on the edges. Using a finger dipped into a bowl of water, moisten the edges of the wrapper. Bring the wrapper up over the filling, forming a triangle, and press the edges to seal. Take the two points of the triangle along the bottom folded edge and bring them together, pinching tightly to form a stuffed ring shape with a pointy cap, like tortellini. As the won tons are finished, arrange them, not touching, on a baking sheet lined with waxed paper or parchment. Chill until ready to serve.

6. Heat the oil in a deep pan or wok until a light haze forms above it, about 365°F on a deep-frying thermometer. Carefully place 6 to 8 won tons, one at a time, into the oil. Fry for 2 to 3 minutes, turning them to cook evenly, until golden brown. Remove with a slotted spoon and drain on paper towels. Sprinkle generously while still warm with confectioners' sugar, and serve immediately.

ADZUKI BEANS

Known simply as red beans in China and adzuki or azuki beans in Japan, these small red mung beans are associated with sweets. They are prepared in a sweet bean paste filling for steamed buns or are cooked and sugar-coated as a confection. When these same beans, related to black-eyed peas, cow peas, and pigeon peas, are skinned and split, they become the Indian staple porridge bean, *dal*.

Peanut Butter and Jelly Sandwich Cookies

(V E G E T A R I A N)

I first made these cookies for a television presentation and I've been thinking about them ever since. The funny thing is, I always hated PB and J sandwiches. Somehow, in cookie form I find it an irresistible combination. To shape the cookie dough, you will need a fairly large (4-inch) round cutter, fluted if possible, and a small (1-inch) round cutter or the bottom of a metal pastry tip.

Makes 2 dozen sandwich cookies

5 cups (1¼ pounds) unbleached
   all-purpose flour
1 tablespoon baking powder
1 teaspoon baking soda
1 teaspoon salt
1 teaspoon ground allspice
2 cups chunky peanut butter
¾ pound (3 sticks) unsalted butter
2 cups confectioners' sugar
1 pound dark or light brown sugar
3 eggs
2 tablespoons vanilla extract
1 (15-ounce) jar good-quality raspberry
   or strawberry jam

1. In a large bowl, combine the flour, baking powder, baking soda, salt, and allspice.

2. In the bowl of an electric mixer, beat together the peanut butter, butter, confectioners' sugar, and brown sugar until light and fluffy. Beat in the eggs, one at a time. Add the vanilla. Stir in the dry ingredients. Wrap the dough tightly in plastic wrap and refrigerate for about 1 hour or until firm.

3. Preheat the oven to 325°F. On a floured board, roll out the dough, one portion at a time, ¼ inch thick. Using a 4-inch round cutter, cut out circles and place 2 inches apart on baking sheets lined with parchment. Refrigerate the cookie rounds for 30 minutes; or until firm enough to cut. You should have about 48 cookie rounds. Cut out the centers of half the chilled dough rounds with a 1-inch round cutter. (Reroll these small dough rounds or bake as is, for mini cookies, if you like.)

4. Bake the cookies for 15 minutes, or until lightly browned on the edges, turning the baking sheets after about 7 minutes for even browning. Remove from the oven and cool the cookies to room temperature on a rack.

5. Warm the jam for 2 minutes in the microwave oven on low (20 percent) power, or over low heat in a small saucepan for 2 minutes, until runny but not hot to the touch. To form each sandwich cookie, spoon 1 tablespoon of the warm jam into the center of each baked solid cookie round. Cool slightly to set, then lay a cutout top over the jam and press to adhere. Chill to set the filling. Bring to room temperature before serving.

GOOBERS

Peanuts are a member of the legume family and have many aliases. They have been called "goobers," a word of African origin from the Congo that has been used since the nineteenth century; groundnuts, a name used by botanists because the seed case of the plant burrows down into the earth to ripen; monkey nuts, because they were commonly fed to monkeys at zoos; earthnuts; and ground peas.

Chinese Firecracker-Jacks

(VEGETARIAN)

As a food consultant, I am sometimes hired to develop recipes for specialty foods companies. This generally means that I'm immersed in a particular food for a time while I try and retry recipes. Once it was lobster bisque and Guinness Irish stew; another time it was endless batches of bolognese sauce. For a time I worked on popcorn recipes for my friend Ronna Schultz, who owns the Society Hill Nut Company, which makes praline-coated nuts in giant old copper kettles. Ronna had the idea that flavored and coated popcorn was a natural extension of her existing line. This recipe is one of my favorites from that time, when I seemed to be always popping corn and making caramel.

———————————— *Makes 8 cups* ————————————

1 tablespoon peanut oil

1 cup raw popcorn kernels

2 cups salted, roasted peanuts, preferably with skins on

2 tablespoons sesame seeds

2 tablespoons grated fresh ginger

1 tablespoon dry mustard

Grated zest of 1 orange

2 tablespoons soy sauce

2 tablespoons roasted Japanese sesame oil

½ cup sugar

¼ cup orange marmalade

¼ cup light corn syrup

1½ tablespoons Korean red pepper flakes or hot red pepper flakes

1. In a large, heavy-bottomed pot with a lid, heat the oil and 3 popcorn kernels, covered, over medium heat. When the kernels pop, add the remaining popcorn. Cover, shaking the pot occasionally, until the popping slows to several seconds between each pop. Remove from the heat, uncover, and cool to room temperature. Combine the cooled popcorn and peanuts in a large, heatproof bowl.

2. Preheat the oven to 300°F. In an ovenproof pan, lightly toast the sesame seeds for about 10 minutes.

3. In a bowl, whisk together the ginger, dry mustard, orange zest, soy sauce, and sesame oil.

4. In a small, heavy-bottomed pot, combine the sugar, marmalade, and corn syrup and bring to a boil. Cook over medium heat until the mixture reaches 275°F on a candy thermometer. Slowly stir the spice mixture into the hot syrup, being careful not to get burned, as the mixture may bubble up.

5. Pour the hot syrup over the cooled popcorn and peanuts, and toss to mix. Sprinkle with the red pepper flakes and toasted sesame seeds, and toss again. Cool; then store in an airtight cookie tin.

Peanut Cream–Filled Chocolate Cups

(VEGETARIAN)

I don't know anyone who doesn't love chocolate peanut butter cups, and while the store-bought ones are good, this homemade version using high-quality dark chocolate is much better. You will need 2 dozen paper-lined foil cups or 1-inch muffin papers, also known as petit four cups, available at kitchenware and candy making supply stores or online (see Sources, page 341). Follow the directions for melting the chocolate carefully, to prevent temperamental chocolate from burning, separating, or turning dull.

——————— *Makes about 2 dozen miniature chocolate cups* ———————

Chocolate Shells

8 ounces high-quality semisweet couverture chocolate (see Cook's Note on page 289), broken into small chunks
1 tablespoon vegetable oil

Creamy Peanut Filling

1 cup creamy (or chunky) peanut butter
4 tablespoons (½ stick) unsalted butter
½ cup confectioners' sugar
2 teaspoons vanilla extract

1. Prepare the Chocolate Shells: Arrange 24 paper-lined petit four foils on a baking sheet. Combine 6 ounces of the chocolate and the oil in a microwaveable bowl or measuring cup. Heat on low power (20 percent) for 1 minute. Stir and microwave at 1-minute intervals until the chocolate has melted completely and is just barely warm to the touch, stirring between each interval. Remove from the microwave and stir in the remaining 2 ounces of chocolate. Continue stirring until the chocolate is completely smooth. Alternatively, combine the chocolate and oil in a heatproof bowl over a pot of simmering water and stir occasionally until melted; then remove from the heat.

2. Pour about 1 tablespoon of the melted chocolate into each paper-lined foil cup. Using a spoon, spread some of the chocolate up the side of each paper. Place the sheet of chocolate-lined cups in the refrigerator for 10 minutes, or until the chocolate has set. Keep the remaining chocolate warm.

3. Prepare the Creamy Peanut Filling: Combine the peanut butter, butter, confectioners' sugar, and vanilla in a food processor and process until smooth. Transfer the filling to a pastry bag fitted with a round piping tip or a heavy-duty plastic freezer bag with one corner snipped off. Pipe the filling into the prepared chocolate shells, snipping off ⅛ to ¼ inch more of the bag if necessary to make it easier to pipe.

4. Reheat the remaining chocolate in the microwave or over a pot of boiling water just until warm enough to pour. Transfer the melted chocolate to a separate pastry bag fitted with a small round piping tip or to a clean heavy-duty plastic freezer bag with a very small corner snipped off (just large enough for the chocolate to drizzle out using slight pressure). Drizzle the chocolate to cover the tops of the filled cups and refrigerate again until set. Store in the refrigerator until ready to serve.

As American as Peanut Butter

Because of their close association with slaves, peanuts were long considered lowly cousins of tree nuts and were often shunned by white consumers. About 100 years ago, the Kellogg brothers (of cornflake fame) began turning peanuts into paste. Peanut butter soon became a staple in the American pantry. More than half of our annual crop of peanuts gets turned into peanut butter. In fact, Americans consume about 700 million pounds of peanut butter a year.

All-American Peanutty Devil's Food Cake

(V E G E T A R I A N)

I've combined several American favorites here: deep, dark devil's food cake flavored with strong coffee, a peanut cream filling, and the the simplest chocolate icing of cream melted with the best high-quality couverture chocolate you can find. It's rich, delicious, and relatively easy to make. Why not make two cakes while you're at it? The devil's food layers freeze beautifully and just need to be defrosted overnight in the refrigerator before filling and icing. This cake is best served at room temperature, so that the chocolate icing melts in your mouth and the peanut filling tastes rich and creamy. Add the optional coffee granules if you like a pronounced coffee flavor. Make this cake one day ahead if possible. It will be easier to cut in neat wedges without crumbs.

——————————— *Serves 12 (Makes one 9-inch layer cake)* ———————————

Cake

½ cup Dutch-processed cocoa
1 cup hot, freshly brewed strong coffee
2 tablespoons instant coffee granules (optional)
1½ cups unbleached all-purpose flour
1 teaspoon baking soda
1 teaspoon salt
½ teaspoon baking powder
¼ pound (1 stick) unsalted butter, softened
1 cup dark brown sugar
½ cup granulated sugar
1 teaspoon vanilla extract
2 eggs

Chunky Peanut Filling

1½ cups chunky peanut butter
8 ounces cream cheese, softened
1 cup confectioners' sugar
2 teaspoons vanilla extract

Creamy Chocolate Icing

1½ cups heavy cream
12 ounces semisweet couverture chocolate, coarsely chopped (see Cook's Note)
1 cup coarsely chopped roasted, salted peanuts, for garnish

1. Prepare the Cake: Preheat the oven to 350°F. Spray a 9-inch cake pan generously with nonstick vegetable spray. In a small bowl, whisk together the cocoa, coffee, and coffee granules (if using) and set the mixture aside to cool to room temperature.

2. In a separate bowl, combine the flour, baking soda, salt, and baking powder.

3. In the bowl of an electric mixer, cream together the butter, brown sugar, granulated sugar, and vanilla until creamy and light. Beat in the eggs, one at a time. Alternately add the dry ingredients and the coffee mixture, beginning and ending with the dry ingredients and beating well after each addition.

4. Pour the batter into the prepared pan. Bake for 40 minutes, or until the cake comes away from the side of the pan and forms a slightly rounded top, and a toothpick inserted into the center comes out clean. Cool in the pan on a wire rack for 10 minutes. Remove the cake pan and refrigerate the cake until chilled before filling.

5. Prepare the Chunky Peanut Filling: In the bowl of an electric mixer, beat the peanut butter, cream cheese, and confectioners' sugar until light and creamy, scraping the sides of the bowl halfway through to prevent lumps. Add the vanilla and beat until well mixed.

6. Prepare the Creamy Chocolate Icing: Place the cream in a glass measuring cup (or other microwaveable container) and heat 1 to 2 minutes on high power. Add the chopped chocolate and allow it to melt in the heat of the cream. Stir until completely melted. (If not completely melted, microwave for 30 seconds longer and then stir again until melted.) Cool and then refrigerate, stirring occasionally, until the icing reaches a spreadable consistency, about 30 minutes.

7. Using a long, serrated knife, cut the cake horizontally into two layers. Spread the peanut filling on one layer. Top with the second layer, cut side down. Smooth the sides and chill the cake for 20 minutes in the freezer. Remove from the freezer and spread the top and sides with the icing. Sprinkle the top with the chopped peanuts and refrigerate again until ready to serve. Cut the cake using a sharp knife dipped in hot water and wiped dry before each cut, and wipe the blade clean after cutting each piece.

COOK'S NOTE: COUVERTURE CHOCOLATE

Couverture, which means "covering" in French, is the type of chocolate used to coat candies and make shiny rich glazes for cakes, as in this recipe. It has a higher percentage of expensive cocoa butter than ordinary chocolate, which makes for glossier coatings and a richer flavor. Less expensive chocolate may have other vegetable fats added for enrichment that lack the crucial property of cocoa butter: it melts at lower than body temperature, giving couverture chocolate its extraordinary mouthfeel. Any high-quality semisweet chocolate bar can be used here.

MEET MR. PEANUT

Amedeo Obici, an Italian immigrant, founded the Planters Peanut Company. In 1918, he turned a sketch by a Virginia schoolboy into Mr. Peanut, the monocled, top-hatted mascot of his company, who became famous around the world.

Tunisian Chickpea Cookies *(Ghraiba)*

(VEGETARIAN)

These unusual cookies are made from toasted chickpea flour and rolled in white sesame seeds. Chickpeas are particularly high in soluble fiber and are quite high in protein. So, not only do these cookies taste good, they're also very healthful and nourishing. In Tunisia, they are typically served with a glass of hot, sweet mint tea. The name ghraiba *means "foreign," indicating that the original recipe was brought to Tunisia from somewhere else, perhaps the Middle East. Toasted chickpea flour is inexpensive, and is available at Middle Eastern and Indian groceries and natural food markets (see Sources, page 341). Untoasted chickpea flour will not produce the same results.*

—————————— *Makes 2 dozen cookies* ——————————

1½ cups toasted chickpea flour
½ cup unbleached all-purpose flour
¼ teaspoon baking powder
½ cup sugar
¼ cup olive oil
6 tablespoons (¾ stick) unsalted butter, melted
1 to 2 tablespoons water
½ cup hulled white sesame seeds

1. Preheat the oven to 325°F. In a blender or food processor, combine the toasted chickpea flour, all-purpose flour, baking powder, and sugar. Add the olive oil and butter and process to combine. Gradually add the water, using only enough to moisten the dough. As soon as the dough comes together into a ball, it is ready.

2. Remove the dough from the blender and knead briefly on a lightly floured surface until smooth. Divide the dough into six equal portions. Roll each portion into a log about ¾ inch in diameter. Spread the sesame seeds out evenly on a baking sheet.

3. Lightly roll the dough logs in the sesame seeds until coated. Cut the rolls diagonally into 2-inch-thick slices. Arrange on a separate baking sheet lined with parchment paper. Bake for 15 minutes, or until lightly browned. The cookies should be crunchy on the outsides and soft on the insides. Transfer the cookies to a cooling rack and let cool. To store, place in a cookie tin. (Cookies keep up to 4 days.)

> "Dog's body," a most unsavory-sounding dish, was nineteenth-century British naval slang for pease pudding boiled in a cloth.

Viennese White Bean and Hazelnut Torte

(VEGETARIAN)

This unusual Viennese-style torte uses not only the usual ground nuts to replace the flour, but also contains white bean purée, which makes it moist. It's easy to make and not too sweet because it is filled with apricot jam rather than covered with an icing. I recommend using a high-quality imported jam, such as Hero brand from Switzerland, for the most intense fruit flavor. To prevent nuts from becoming oily when ground, freeze them first. As long as the nuts are cold, the oil can't escape. For the neatest results when cutting the layers, bake the cake a day ahead of time so it has time to become firm.

—————————— *Serves 10 (Makes one 10-inch round cake)* ——————————

2 cups cooked navy beans, rinsed and drained (⅔ cup dried navy or Great Northern beans, cooked and drained; see Basic Cooking Chart, page 57)

4 eggs, separated

1 cup sugar

1 tablespoon vanilla extract

3 tablespoons dark rum, or brandy, whiskey, or bourbon

1½ cups finely ground toasted, skinless hazelnuts or almonds

½ cup apricot jam

⅓ cup confectioners' sugar

1. Pass the cooled beans through a food mill to make a smooth, thick purée.

2. Preheat the oven to 350°F. Coat the inside of a 10-inch springform pan with nonstick vegetable spray.

3. In a large bowl, beat the egg yolks with ½ cup sugar, vanilla, and rum until light and fluffy. Fold in the bean purée and ground hazelnuts.

4. In a medium bowl, beat the egg whites until soft peaks form. Gradually add the remaining ½ cup sugar, beating between each addition, until the whites are firm and glossy and the meringue sticks to the side of the bowl.

5. Fold one-third of the egg white mixture into the yolk mixture to lighten; then fold in the remaining egg whites in two parts. Pour the batter into the prepared pan. Bake for about 1 hour, or until the torte is set and has begun to shrink away from the side of the pan. Cool thoroughly in the pan at room temperature, preferably for at least 8 hours.

6. To finish the torte, cut it horizontally into two even layers using a large serrated knife. Melt the apricot jam in a small saucepan over low heat until warm and runny, but not hot. Spread the jam over the cut side of the bottom layer. Cover with the top layer, cut side down. Dust generously with the confectioners' sugar and cut the cake into 10 pieces with a serrated knife.

Roasted Peanut–Macadamia Brittle with Bourbon

(VEGETARIAN)

The last time I made this homemade brittle, I had to give away the second half of the batch because I couldn't stop eating it. Although I've outgrown the demanding sweet tooth I had as a child, there are still a few candies that tempt me. This brittle is one of them. The combination of the bourbon with the indulgently rich macadamia nuts is perfectly balanced by the salted, toasted peanuts.

Makes 3 pounds

1 (1-pound) can roasted and salted peanuts (not dry-roasted)

4 cups sugar

½ cup light corn syrup

¼ pound (1 stick) unsalted butter

1 teaspoon baking soda

2 teaspoons vanilla extract

¼ cup bourbon

¼ pound salted, roasted macadamia nuts, halved

1. Preheat the oven to 200°F. Shake the excess salt off the peanuts and spread the peanuts on a baking pan. Warm the nuts in the oven while making the brittle.

2. Generously coat two 15 x 10-inch jelly roll pans with nonstick vegetable spray. In a medium, heavy (not nonstick) saucepan with a lid, combine the sugar and the corn syrup. Cover and cook over medium heat, stirring occasionally with a wooden spoon. Heat until the sugar has melted and is no longer grainy. Increase the heat to medium-high and cook, without stirring, to the hard-crack stage (300°F on a candy thermometer; see note below), about 10 minutes.

3. Stir in the butter, which will reduce the temperature. Cook until the mixture returns to the soft-crack stage (275°F on a candy thermometer) and then remove from the heat.

4. In a small bowl, combine the baking soda, vanilla, and bourbon. Stir the soda mixture into the candy pot, continuing to stir as the mixture foams. Remove the peanuts from the oven and quickly stir in the warm peanuts and macadamias, using a wooden spoon. Carefully pour the mixture onto the two prepared jelly-roll pans. Use spring tongs to spread out the brittle to fill each pan; then flip the brittle over. Allow the brittle to cool enough to handle (gingerly) and stretch it thinner, like taffy. Allow the brittle to cool completely; then break into large shards. Store in an airtight cookie tin.

TESTING CANDY AT THE HARD-CRACK STAGE

To test without using a candy thermometer, have ready a small bowl filled with cold water. Drop a small spoonful of hot sugar syrup into the bowl. Remove and squeeze the ball. The syrup should form a rigid ball when pressed between your fingers.

CHAPTER TWELVE

Basic Bean Cookery

Cooked Fresh Cranberry Beans

(VEGETARIAN)

Fresh cranberry beans can be found sporadically throughout the year at well-stocked supermarkets, farmers' markets, and Asian markets. The striking red and white streaked pods are filled with colorful beans. Buy cranberry beans when you see them, then shell and freeze in double zipper-lock bags until needed. They will cook up plump and firm, with no soaking necesary.

Serves 6 to 8 (Makes 6 cups)

3 pounds fresh cranberry beans, shelled
    (3 to 4 cups shelled beans)
1 quart cold water
1 small onion, peeled
1 head garlic, outer skin removed and
    1 inch cut from the top end
2 bay leaves
4 sprigs fresh thyme
½ teaspoon ground allspice

1. Combine the cranberry beans with the cold water, onion, garlic, bay leaves, and thyme in a medium pot. Bring to a boil, reduce the heat, and simmer very slowly for about 30 minutes, or until the beans are tender.

2. Cool and drain the beans. Once cooled, they may be frozen for up to 3 months.

Oven-Cooked Italian-Style Beans

If you live near an Italian neighborhood, you can probably find prosciutto bones, trimmings, and tail ends for a low price. Prosciutto is a valuable ingredient in cooking beans because it provides not only a good deep flavor but also a smooth, unctuous texture. If you buy a prosciutto bone, make sure it is whole and not cut; the fat inside is likely to be rancid from the aging process. The rind of the prosciutto (called la cotenna *in Italian) is also wonderful for the velvety, creamy quality it imparts to slow-cooked beans.*

Serves 6 to 8 (Makes 6 cups)

1 pound (2 cups) dried red kidney beans
    or cannellini beans, soaked (see
    Soaking Chart, page 57)
½ pound prosciutto trimmings and uncut
    bones (or *cotenna*)
1 small onion, peeled
1 head garlic, ½ inch sliced off the top to
    expose the cloves
1 bunch fresh marjoram, tied with
    kitchen string
2 quarts cold water

1. Preheat the oven to 300°F. Drain and rinse the beans. In a large pot, cover the kidney beans with cold water and bring to a boil. Cook for 5 minutes; then drain, discarding the water.

2. Combine the beans, prosciutto trimmings, onion, garlic, and marjoram in a Dutch oven with a tight-fitting lid and add the water. Bring to a boil over medium heat. Cover and bake for 2 to 2½ hours, or until the beans are tender when pierced with a fork.

3. Remove beans from the oven, cool slightly, and then drain any remaining cooking liquid (or save for soup stock) and remove the prosciutto trimmings, onion, garlic, and marjoram. Once cooled, the beans may be frozen for up to 3 months. Simply rinse and use as needed in recipes calling for cooked beans.

Oven-Cooked Country-Style Beans

Ham hocks are just about the least expensive way of flavoring and enriching beans. You can buy them in most grocery stores and ethnic markets. They freeze quite well, so it makes sense to buy 5 pounds and keep the extra frozen. Aside from the smokiness, the hocks add a velvety, creamy quality to slow-cooked beans. Because this is a basic recipe to be used in many dishes, you may want to double it and cook 2 pounds of beans at a time, freezing the extra in double zipper-lock freezer bags. Just be sure to label and date the bags and use the frozen beans within 3 months. A smoked turkey leg can be substituted for the ham hock.

—————————— *Serves 6 to 8 (Makes 6 cups)* ——————————

1 pound (2 cups) dried cannellini, borlotti, cranberry, or pinto beans, or black-eyed peas, soaked (see Soaking Chart, page 57)

1 ham hock

1 small onion, peeled

1 head garlic, ½ inch sliced off the top to expose the cloves

1 bunch fresh thyme, tied with kitchen string

2 quarts cold water

Salt and freshly ground black pepper

1. Preheat the oven to 300°F. Drain and rinse the beans. In a large pot, cover the beans with cold water and bring to a boil. Cook for 5 minutes; then drain, discarding the water.

2. Combine the beans, ham hock, onion, garlic, and thyme in a Dutch oven with a tight-fitting lid and add the cold water. Bring to a boil over medium heat. Cover and place in the oven. Bake for 1½ hours. Season to taste with salt and pepper. Continue baking for about 1 hour, or until the beans are tender when pierced with a fork.

3. Remove from the oven, cool briefly, and then drain the cooking liquid. Remove the onion, garlic, and thyme. If you wish, pull the gelatin-rich meat from the ham hocks, discarding any connective tissue and bone, and add to the beans.

Oven-Cooked Vegetarian Beans

(V E G E T A R I A N)

Here is a full-flavored, meatless method of cooking larger dried legumes, such as red kidney beans or cannellini beans. If you can buy natural wood-smoked Spanish paprika (pimentón, see page 339), you'll find it adds a natural smoky flavor to the beans without meat. Or if you like spicy food, add a chipotle chile (smoke-dried ripe jalapeño). Serve these beans hot or at room temperature—but not cold, which dulls their flavor—as a side dish, or dress them while still warm with Cumin-Lime Citronette Dressing (see page 315), Roasted Red Bell Pepper Vinaigrette (see page 306), Lemon-Garlic Vinaigrette (see page 307), or French Tarragon–Shallot Vinaigrette (see page 308).

Serves 6 to 8 (Makes 6 cups)

1 pound (2 cups) dried dark red kidney beans, or cannellini beans, soaked (see Soaking Chart, page 57)

1½ quarts cold water

¼ cup extra-virgin olive oil

1 peeled onion, stuck with 4 whole cloves

1 head garlic, ½ inch sliced off the top to expose the cloves

3 bay leaves

½ bunch fresh thyme, tied with kitchen string

1 (3- to 4-inch) strip lemon zest

1 whole dried red chile, or 1 tablespoon *pimentón* (Spanish smoked paprika)

1 teaspoon ground allspice

Salt and freshly ground black pepper

1. Preheat the oven to 300°F. Drain and rinse the soaked kidney beans. In a large pot, cover the beans with cold water and bring to a boil. Cook for 5 minutes; then drain, discarding the water.

2. In a large Dutch oven with a lid, combine the beans, cold water, olive oil, onion, garlic, bay leaves, thyme, lemon zest, chile, allspice, and salt and pepper to taste. Bring to a boil on top of the stove. Cover and bake for 3 hours for large beans or about 2 hours for smaller beans. Remove from the oven, uncover, and cool briefly.

3. Discard the onion, garlic, bay leaves, thyme, lemon zest, and chile. Cool without stirring, to avoid breaking up the beans. Once cooled, they may be frozen for up to 3 months.

Basic Black Turtle Beans *(Frijoles Negros)*

Most American-grown dried beans don't need much sorting. However, some imported beans are not cleaned very well and should be picked over carefully. For some reason, dried black turtle beans are especially likely to have foreign matter mixed in, perhaps because the dirt clumps or little stones are easily missed during packaging. Before proceeding with the recipes, pick over the beans carefully. Mexican cooks always add the highly resinous herb epazote to their pot of black beans to make them more digestible. Be sure not to add the salt until the beans are at least half-cooked because salt toughens their skins and keeps them from softening.

Serves 8 (Makes 6 cups)

1 pound (2 cups) black turtle beans, soaked (see Soaking Chart, page 57)

1 ham hock, or 1 teaspoon Liquid Smoke

1 peeled onion, stuck with 6 whole cloves

2 bay leaves

2 to 3 sprigs fresh epazote, tied with kitchen string, or 2 to 3 sprigs fresh oregano, or 2 teaspoons dried oregano

1½ cups water

2 teaspoons salt

1. Rinse the soaked black beans under cold water. Place in a large pot and cover generously with cold water. Bring to a boil; then drain, discarding the water.

2. Add the ham hock, onion, bay leaves, and epazote sprigs. Cover with the 1½ quarts water and bring to a boil again. Reduce the heat and simmer for about 2 hours, and then stir in the salt. Cook for 1 hour longer, or until tender to the bite.

3. Remove from the heat and allow the beans to cool. Remove the ham hock, pick the meat from the bone, and add it to the beans. Discard the ham hock, onion, bay leaves, and epazote. Once cooled, the beans may be frozen for up to 3 months.

Basic Cooked French Green Lentils or Beluga Lentils

(VEGETARIAN)

The special French green lentils, called lentilles du Puy, *are raised in the Puy, a region of southwest France. They are small, speckled deep green, and firm when cooked—and they cook quickly. Because of their attractive appearance and ease of cooking, they are the darlings of French and American chefs. Use these basic cooked lentils in French Green Lentil Salad with Bacon and Tomato (see page 94), French Green Lentils with Black Truffles and Caramelized Shallots (see page 170), and Spiced Duck in Port Wine Sauce with Green Lentils and Savoy Cabbage (see page 204). This same recipe may be used to cook the even smaller beans called beluga lentils.*

—————————— *Serves 6 (Makes 3 cups)* ——————————

1 (12-ounce) package (1½ cups) imported *lentilles du Puy* (French green lentils) or beluga lentils

3 bay leaves

½ bunch fresh thyme, tied with kitchen string

½ peeled onion, stuck with 4 whole cloves

1 head garlic, top ½ inch cut off and discarded

2 teaspoons salt

1 quart cold water

1. Combine the lentils, bay leaves, thyme, onion, garlic, and salt in a medium pot. Add the cold water and bring to a boil. Skim off any white foam and discard. Cover, reduce the heat, and simmer for 45 minutes to 1 hour, or until the lentils are soft but still whole and not mushy.

2. Remove from the heat and discard the bay leaves, thyme, onion, and garlic. Cool slightly; then drain off and discard any excess liquid. Once cooled, the beans may be frozen for up to 3 months.

Basic Cooked Chickpeas

(VEGETARIAN)

Dried chickpeas are the most challenging of legumes to cook. Shriveled, dried-out chickpeas will never get soft, no matter how long you cook them. Check that your chickpeas come from a source that sells its stock quickly. I buy mine from Hispanic, Indian, or Middle Eastern groceries because those cuisines have many dishes made from chickpeas. More than any other type of legume, chickpeas need to cook in softened water, without a lot of minerals. Most tap water is too hard—acidic and mineral laden—to cook them properly. To ensure that your water is soft enough to cook chickpeas, add a pinch of baking soda. If the beans are still hard after cooking 2 hours, add more. Too much baking soda, though, makes the beans mushy and their skins will slip off. You can buy excellent plump chickpeas by mail order or online (see Sources, page 341). All chickpeas produce a great deal of white foam impurities when cooked. To ensure that this foam doesn't end up in your final product, cook them briefly before the final cooking step.

Serves 8 (Makes 6 cups)

1 pound (2 cups) dried chickpeas, soaked
   (see Soaking Chart, page 57)
2 quarts cold water
1 tablespoon salt
¼ to ½ teaspoon baking soda, depending
   on hardness of water
2 bay leaves
1 whole red chile

1. Drain and rinse the soaked chickpeas. Cover with cold water and bring to a boil. Boil for 3 to 5 minutes, skimming off and discarding the foam that rises to the top; then drain.

2. In a large pot, cover the par-cooked chickpeas with the cold water. Bring to a boil, along with the salt, smaller quantity of baking soda, bay leaves, and chile. Skim off and discard the white foam that rises to the top. Cover, reduce the heat, and simmer for 2 to 3 hours, or until the chickpeas are tender to the core but not mushy.

3. Cool and drain the chickpeas. Remove and discard the bay leaves and chile. Once cooled, the beans may be frozen for up to 3 months.

COOK'S NOTE

Because they give off so much foam, it's not a great idea to cook chickpeas in a pressure cooker. It's possible, though unlikely, that the valve could get clogged. If you're short on time and wish to use your pressure cooker, make sure that you don't fill it more than half full, to give the beans plenty of room to expand, and press down on the valve occasionally to unclog it. Add 1 tablespoon of oil to reduce foaming.

YOU SAY GARBANZO

The word *garbanzo*, which supposedly derives from Greek and prehistoric German, is the Spanish name for the chickpea. In seventeenth-century England, the word evolved into *calavance*, a term first used for chickpeas and eventually for all types of legumes. The old English word for chickpeas was *chichis*, similar to the Latin and Italian word *ceci*.

Earthenware-Cooked Beans
(Frijoles de Olla)

These soupy cooked beans are served at Mexican meals after the main course or alongside it in a small separate bowl. Diners soak up the yummy liquid by mopping it with a fresh corn tortilla. These beans taste even better reheated the next day, after the flavors have had a chance to mellow. In the old style, these beans were cooked in an earthenware pot, or olla, *nestled in the coals of a live fire. According to Rick Bayless, author of* Authentic Mexican, *"Those who've tasted the beans that come from it know that the olla and its contents share an earthy exchange of flavors."*

Serves 8 (Makes 6 cups)

1 pound (2 cups) pinto, dark red kidney, or black turtle beans

1½ quarts cold water

¼ pound bacon, finely chopped

1 medium onion, chopped fine

1 tablespoon seeded and chopped red chile

1 tablespoon chopped garlic

1 tablespoon salt

1. Rinse and drain the beans if they appear at all sandy. In a large pot, cover the beans with cold water and bring to a boil. Cook for 5 minutes; then drain, discarding the water.

2. Return the beans to the pot. Add the 1½ quarts cold water, bacon, onion, chile, garlic, and cold water. Bring to a boil. Reduce the heat, partially cover, and simmer, stirring occasionally, for 2 hours.

3. Stir in the salt and simmer for about 1 hour longer, or until the beans are very tender and the cooking liquid has thickened. Taste for seasoning and serve as is, or cool to use for refried beans. Once cooled, the beans may be frozen for up to 3 months.

PAINTED BEANS

The pinto bean is a variety of kidney bean speckled with brownish red blotches. Its name means "painted" in Spanish. Another colloquial name is crabeye beans, because they supposedly resemble the beady, bean-shaped eye of a crab.

Refried Beans
(Frijoles Refritos)

These mashed and fried beans are called refritos *because they are "recooked" by frying after the first preliminary cooking stage. Although the lard called for here has suffered a bad reputation healthwise, new research indicates that it is not the villain it was once thought to be. Though it's completely nontraditional, I've also used duck fat with excellent results. I always make a large batch of refried beans because they freeze so well. Use them in Chile Ancho Empanadas with Frijoles Filling and Huevos Rancheros (see page 175).*

Serves 8

¼ cup lard, or melted duck fat (see About
    Duck Fat, page 329), or olive oil
1 cup finely chopped onion
6 cups Earthenware-Cooked Beans
    (see page 300)

1. Heat the lard in a large cast-iron or nonstick skillet over medium heat. Add the onion and cook for 2 to 3 minutes, or until transparent but not browned.

2. Stir in one-fourth of the beans. As the beans begin to bubble, crush them with a potato masher. Cook the beans until thickened, stirring often with a wooden spoon and mashing. Add another one-fourth of the beans and repeat, cooking until thickened. Add the remaining beans in the same fashion. Cook the beans until they resemble mashed potatoes. (These beans reheat quite well in the microwave and freeze perfectly for up to 3 months.)

Basic Cooked Flageolets

(VEGETARIAN)

A dish of these simple lemon- and thyme-flavored flageolets makes an elegant side dish for roasted chicken or meat. Because they have such thin and delicate skins, it's important to cook the flageolets gently at low heat and not to overcook them, or the skins will float off and the beans will lose their svelte shape. It's best to add salt from the beginning of cooking so the flageolets don't become mushy.

Serves 6 (Makes 4 cups)

1 (12-ounce) package (1½ cups) dried
    flageolets
1 peeled onion, stuck with 4 whole cloves
1 (3- to 4-inch) strip lemon zest
2 bay leaves
½ bunch fresh thyme, tied with kitchen
    string
2 teaspoons salt
1½ quarts cold water

1.Combine the flageolets, onion, lemon zest, bay leaves, thyme, and salt in a medium, heavy-bottomed pot. Cover with the cold water and bring to a boil. Skim off and discard the white foam impurities that rise to the top. Reduce the heat to a bare simmer and cook slowly for about 1 hour or until the beans are almost tender.

2. Remove the pot from the heat, drain off any remaining liquid, and discard the onion, lemon zest, bay leaves, and thyme. Once cooled, the beans may be frozen for up to 3 months.

CHAPTER THIRTEEN

Pantry Recipes:
Dressings, Sauces, Stocks, and More

Adobo Colorado Marinade

(VEGETARIAN)

A versatile and delicious marinade from the Yucatán, adobo colorado *("red mixture") not only imparts a great flavor and beautiful red-gold color to grilled foods like chicken and tuna also tenderizes dark meat chicken, making it as moist and succulent as can be. Serve adobo-marinated chicken or tuna as an accompaniment to Black Turtle Beans with Epazote and Cotija Cheese (see page 250) or make it a full meal with a side of Refried Beans (see page 301) and a basket of warm, fresh tortillas. You can order inexpensive* achiote condimentato *through the Internet (see Sources, page 341).*

─── *Makes about 1 cup* ───

½ cup *achiote* paste (available at most
    supermarkets)
¼ cup vegetable oil
½ cup cider vinegar
1 tablespoon ground toasted cumin
2 tablespoons finely chopped garlic
1 tablespoon dried oregano
1 teaspoon ground allspice
2 teaspoons salt

In a bowl, blend together the *achiote*, oil, vinegar, cumin, garlic, oregano, allspice, and salt; reserve. (Freeze any extra *achiote* and use to marinate boneless, skinless chicken thighs, chicken breasts on the bone or off, or firm fish such as tuna, swordfish, and mahi mahi.) Use to marinate chicken for 6 to 48 hours, and fish for 2 to 6 hours, before grilling.

Lemon-Pepper Mojo

(VEGETARIAN)

Mojo *or* môlho *is a Brazilian term for a fresh salsa. Serve this* mojo *with Black Turtle Beans with Epazote and Cojita Cheese (see page 250), Chile Ancho Empanadas with Frijoles Filling (see page 68), or with lime- and chile-marinated grilled fish or shrimp. This* mojo *is the traditional accompaniment to Bahian Acarajé Fritters (black-eyed pea fritters; see page 164).*

─── *Makes 1½ cups* ───

¼ cup drained and chopped pickled
    jalapeño peppers
½ cup finely diced white onion
1 teaspoon chopped garlic
¼ cup fresh lemon juice (about 2 lemons)
½ cup diced, drained imported roasted
    red bell peppers
¼ cup diced green bell pepper
¼ cup chopped fresh cilantro leaves

In a small bowl, combine the jalapeños, onion, garlic, lemon juice, roasted red peppers, and green pepper. Cover and refrigerate until chilled. Stir in the cilantro just before serving so it keeps its color. The mojo will keep for 4 to 5 days in the refrigerator.

Barley Malt Vinaigrette

(VEGETARIAN)

This is kind of a "macho" dressing, strong and bold in flavor and not meant for the fainthearted. It is especially suited to bean salads because the flavor of milder dressings tends to get lost when absorbed into the starchy beans. Substitute cider vinegar if malt vinegar is not available.

Makes about 2 cups

½ cup malt vinegar
1 tablespoon Dijon mustard
1 tablespoon Pickapeppa sauce
2 tablespoons barley malt syrup or honey
1 teaspoon hot pepper sauce
2 large shallots, coarsely sliced
1 teaspoon salt
½ teaspoon freshly ground black pepper
¼ cup chopped marjoram
1½ cups peanut oil or sunflower oil

Combine the vinegar, mustard, Pickapeppa sauce, malt syrup, hot sauce, shallots, salt, black pepper, and marjoram in a mixing bowl. Whisk until creamy. Slowly pour in the oil, whisking constantly, until well combined. This keeps in the refrigerator for up to 2 weeks.

Pepita-Tomatillo Sauce

(VEGETARIAN OPTION)

This is a rich, creamy, light green sauce made with ground pumpkin seeds (pepitas) and the Mexican green-husked tomatoes called tomatillos. The lemony tasting, crisp-tender tomatillos are counterbalanced by the rich creaminess of the pumpkin seeds. The method of using ground nuts to thicken sauces can be traced back to the Spanish colonists who brought the technique from the Mediterranean, where they were more likely to use almonds or pine nuts. The green pumpkin seeds are a New World food that became adapted to Old World methods. Look for them in Mexican groceries and natural food stores. For a vegetarian version, substitute Vegetable Stock (see page 323) for the chicken stock.

Makes 4 cups

½ cup diced onion
2 teaspoons chopped garlic
½ pound tomatillos, cored and husked
2 tablespoons olive oil
1 cup shelled green pumpkin seeds
   (pepitas), lightly toasted
2 sprigs epazote (optional)
½ cup fresh cilantro leaves
1 jalapeño pepper, chopped
2 cups Light Chicken Stock (see page 320)

In a medium saucepan, heat the onion and garlic in the olive oil until transparent. In a blender, purée the tomatillo, pumpkin seeds, epazote, cilantro, jalapeño, and Light Chicken Stock. Combine with the onion mixture. This sauce can be refrigerated for up to 3 weeks.

Roasted Red Bell Pepper Vinaigrette

(VEGETARIAN)

For this dressing I use roasted red bell peppers, either fresh or from a jar. I prefer the bottled bell peppers that are imported from Europe. Greece, Spain, and Italy all produce firm, slightly smoky, bottled roasted peppers. The peppers have a couple of functions: they impart a beautiful orangy red color and sweet pepper taste, and they also thicken the dressing, thereby keeping the other ingredients from separating. Drizzle this dressing over a plateful of Oven-Cooked Italian-Style Beans (see page 294), Oven-Cooked Vegetarian Beans (see page 296), or steamed green or wax beans.

Makes about 2 cups

1 teaspoon chopped garlic

¼ cup grated Pecorino Romano cheese

1 cup roasted red bell peppers (see page 332), or 1 (15-ounce) jar roasted red peppers, well drained

1 tablespoon chopped fresh marjoram leaves

1 teaspoon salt

½ teaspoon freshly ground black pepper

½ cup balsamic vinegar

1½ cups extra-virgin olive oil

1. In a small bowl with a hand-held blender, or in a standard blender, combine the garlic, cheese, roasted peppers, marjoram, salt, pepper, and vinegar. Then, with the blender running, slowly drizzle in the oil until it is completely absorbed and the dressing is creamy.

2. Pour into a glass jar with a lid and refrigerate until needed. The dressing will keep well for up to 2 weeks if tightly covered and refrigerated.

Lemon-Garlic Vinaigrette

(VEGETARIAN)

This dressing includes grated lemon zest. The oil contained in the tiny pockets of a lemon's skin provides a marvelous sunny aroma. Sometimes I make the dressing in a slightly Eastern Mediterranean style with garlic and lemon juice but no shallots and sherry vinegar, which give more of a Western European cast. If you use straight lemon juice, increase the quantity to 1 cup. Be sure the garlic is plump, juicy, and white without any bitter-tasting green sprout in the center. Don't use bottled lemon juice, which has a metallic aftertaste that is especially noticeable in a dressing like this. Enjoy this versatile dressing on Niçoise Pasta Shell Salad with Green Beans, Chickpeas, and Tuna (see page 95) and in Provençal Chickpea Salad with Tuna Caviar (see page 90).

──────────────── *Makes 2 cups* ────────────────

2 cloves garlic
1 large shallot, coarsely chopped
½ teaspoon freshly ground black pepper
1 teaspoon salt
¼ cup sherry vinegar
Grated zest of 1 lemon
¼ cup fresh lemon juice (about 2 lemons)
1 cup olive oil

1. In a medium bowl with a hand-held blender, or in a standard blender, combine the garlic, shallot, pepper, salt, vinegar, and lemon zest and juice. With the blender running, slowly drizzle in the olive oil until it is completely absorbed and the dressing is creamy.

2. Pour into a glass jar with a lid and refrigerate until needed. The dressing will keep well for up to 2 weeks if tightly covered and refrigerated.

Chinese Shanxi Vinegar Dressing

(VEGETARIAN)

Here's an easy dressing to make with a well-balanced mix of pungent Chinese flavors. The mild Shanxi vinegar is fermented from barley, sorghum, and peas with a mellow, sweet taste reminiscent of balsamic vinegar, which makes the best substitute. Mushroom soy sauce has an extra depth of flavor from the dried mushrooms used to flavor it, although plain soy sauce could easily be substituted. I've found, though, that I use mushroom soy sauce more and more, especially for cold dishes where flavors tend to fade.

──────────────── *Makes 2 cups* ────────────────

2 shallots, chopped
1 (2-inch) piece fresh ginger, chopped
½ cup peanut oil
2 tablespoons roasted Japanese sesame oil
½ cup Shanxi vinegar, or Chinese black
　　vinegar, or balsamic vinegar
¼ cup mushroom soy sauce or soy sauce
Grated zest of 1 tangerine or orange

1. In a medium bowl with a hand-held blender, or in a standard blender, purée the shallots, ginger, oils, vinegar, soy sauce, and tangerine zest until smooth and creamy.

2. Pour into a glass jar with a lid and refrigerate until needed. The dressing will keep well for up to 2 weeks if tightly covered and refrigerated.

French Tarragon–Shallot Vinaigrette

(VEGETARIAN)

This is a classic French vinaigrette dressing flavored with the characteristic trio of culinary musketeers: shallots, tarragon, and Dijon mustard. Use it when making the French Navy Bean and Shrimp Salad (see page 93) and the French Green Lentil Salad with Bacon and Tomato (see page 94). This dressing is also wonderful as a light coating on strong-flavored salad greens, such as Belgian endive, arugula, frisée, and spinach.

Makes 3 cups

¼ pound shallots, coarsely chopped
½ cup tarragon vinegar
¼ cup Dijon mustard
1 cup extra-virgin olive oil
1 cup chopped Italian parsley leaves
    (about 1 bunch)
¼ cup chopped fresh tarragon leaves
    (about ½ bunch)
Salt and freshly ground black pepper

1. In a blender or food processor, purée the shallots, vinegar, mustard, and olive oil. Add the parsley and tarragon. Blend again until the herb leaves are in small pieces but not puréed. Season to taste with salt and pepper.

2. Pour into a glass jar with a lid and refrigerate until needed. The dressing will keep well for up to 2 weeks if tightly covered and refrigerated.

Cucumber-Yogurt Raita

(VEGETARIAN)

A raita is a refreshing salad based on yogurt that is a standard condiment at the table in India. Because yogurt is high in protein, it is especially important in vegetarian meals. Indian yogurt is thick, creamy, and a bit sweet. Traditionally, it is made from buffalo milk, which has a high fat content, and is drained through a cloth before using to thicken it. This raita is particularly cool and delightful because it is made from firm seedless cucumbers and refreshing mint.

Makes 3 cups

2 cups plain whole-milk yogurt
1 large seedless English cucumber,
    peeled
1 fresh green chile (such as jalapeño or
    pasilla), seeded and minced
1 teaspoon toasted ground cumin seeds
    (see Toasting Seeds, page 225)
2 tablespoons chopped fresh mint leaves
1 teaspoon salt

1. Place a sieve lined with a cheese cone (yogurt cheese funnel), or clean dampened cotton, linen, cheesecloth, or a muslin napkin, over a large bowl. Place the yogurt in the lined sieve and allow it to drain for about 1 hour. (This step is optional, but it makes for a thicker *raita* with more body.)

2. Grate the cucumber into a medium bowl, and add the chile, drained yogurt, cumin, mint, and salt. Cover and refrigerate for at least 30 minutes before serving. The sauce will keep refrigerated for only 2 days; after that the cucumbers will become soggy.

Oven-Roasted Plum Tomatoes

(VEGETARIAN)

Make these wonderful tomatoes when large, ripe plum tomatoes are plentiful. It's really not worth making in quantities of less than 5 pounds of tomatoes because they shrink so much when baked. When the tomatoes are all used, strain the olive oil and reserve in the refrigerator. The oil is fabulous in pasta sauces, but must be kept refrigerated or it will spoil.

Makes about 6 cups

5 pounds ripe plum tomatoes, tops sliced off, halved lengthwise

3 tablespoons kosher salt

¾ cup olive oil

¼ cup chopped fresh oregano (about ½ bunch)

¼ cup chopped fresh rosemary (about ¼ bunch)

¼ cup chopped fresh thyme (about ½ bunch)

¼ cup chopped garlic

1. Preheat the oven to 225°F. In a large bowl, combine the tomato halves, cut side up, with the remaining ingredients. Arrange in a single layer on jelly-roll pans and slowly roast for 3 hours, or bake for 8 hours in an oven with the pilot light on. The tomatoes should be dried and wrinkly looking, but still plump.

2. Remove the tomatoes from the oven and cool to room temperature. Transfer to a covered container. The tomatoes will keep in the refrigerator for up to 1 week.

Date-Tamarind Chutney

(VEGETARIAN)

Unlike the well-known, commercially made mango chutney, which is chunky with pieces of chewy mango, this recipe from Bombay (now known as Mumbai) is a smooth, thick, dark condiment. This simple, fat-free chutney is made from a combination of dates and tamarind, two ingredients that have an ancient history in the East. Serve with Dosa (Yellow Split Pea and Rice Pancakes) (see page 72) or with Pappadums (Crispy Lentil Wafers) (see page 64). Tamarind is usually sold in small 12-ounce blocks. The fruit pulp and large seeds are dried and pressed into a block that will keep indefinitely. You must soak the block to soften it and then strain out the solids to obtain the usable fruit pulp.

Makes 1½ cups

1 cup pitted dates, soaked overnight in cold water
½ cup dried tamarind (see Preparing Tamarind, below), soaked for 8 hours in 1 cup cold water, seeds removed
1 teaspoon salt
1 teaspoon ground coriander seeds
1 teaspoon dark brown sugar

1. In a blender or food processor, purée the dates with the softened, seeded tamarind, including the soaking liquid. Strain through a sieve to remove any fibers. Stir in the salt, coriander, and brown sugar.

2. Pour into a glass jar with a lid and refrigerate until needed. The chutney will keep for up to 2 weeks if refrigerated.

PREPARING TAMARIND

To quick-soak the dried tamarind, place the entire block in hot water to cover for about 30 minutes, or until softened. While it is soaking, break the pulp up with your hands to speed the process. Rub the tamarind with the soaking liquid through a sieve or food mill, discarding the fibers and seeds. The strained tamarind liquid is ready to use and will keep for at least 1 month in the refrigerator. If you prefer, substitute ½ cup dried tamarind with 6 tablespoons soaked prunes puréed with 2 tablespoons lemon juice. Indian groceries also sell pre-made tamarind concentrate. If you use this, reduce the amount of salt in this recipe. If you can find fresh tamarind pods, available in spring at Asian markets, simply open the pods and remove the pulp and seeds to a sieve. Rub through to remove the seeds, and discard the pods.

Fresh Coconut–Cilantro Chutney

(VEGETARIAN)

This dip is great with Pappadums *(Crispy Lentil Wafers) (see page 64) or with Indian Spiced Chickpeas (see page 249). I was so happy when I discovered Goya's brand of frozen grated coconut in my local Latino market. I had been making this extraordinary fresh chutney with coconut meat that I removed from the shell, peeled, and then grated. While fresh coconut is a wonderful thing, miles from packaged, dried coconut, it is a lot of work to hammer open that coconut and pry out the meat. Now I've got the best of both worlds: fresh coconut taste and quick preparation.*

Makes 4 cups

2 tablespoons peanut oil
1 tablespoon black mustard seeds
1 bunch fresh cilantro, leaves and roots,
  if available
2 jalapeño peppers, seeded and sliced
1 (2-inch) piece fresh ginger, sliced
4 cloves garlic
2 cups frozen or fresh grated coconut
  meat
1 cup plain yogurt
2 teaspoons salt
2 tablespoons fresh lemon juice
  (about 1 lemon)

1. Heat the oil in a small pan and add the mustard seeds. Cover and cook until the seeds pop. Cool.

2. Process the cilantro, jalapeños, ginger, and garlic to a paste in a food processor. Stir in the coconut, yogurt, salt, lemon juice, and cooked mustard seeds with their oil. Cover and refrigerate until ready to serve. The chutney will keep well if refrigerated for 3 to 4 days.

Yemenite Fenugreek *(Hilbeh)* Sauce

(V E G E T A R I A N)

In the 1950s, almost all of the members of the ancient Jewish community of Yemen were airlifted to Israel, where they have since made their home. They brought with them special foods like this sauce, which have become a part of the multifaceted cooking of Israel. Hot and spicy foods are particularly loved by the Yemenites, who flavor their exotic dishes with fenugreek, cardamom, black cumin, caraway, turmeric, and even saffron. Serve this sauce with Falafel (see page 74) or with Bitar's Pan-Grilled Falafel with Salad in Garlic Dressing (see page 76). It's also good spread on fresh pita or other flatbreads.

Makes 1 cup

2 tablespoons whole fenugreek seeds, soaked in cold water overnight
4 cloves garlic
½ cup chopped fresh cilantro (about 1 bunch)
2 teaspoons salt
¼ cup fresh lemon juice (about 2 lemons)
1 small dried hot chile, seeded

Drain the fenugreek seeds, which should be softened after soaking and have a jellied coating. Process in a blender or food processor with the garlic, cilantro, salt, lemon juice, and chile until the mixture becomes a coarse purée. This may be stored in the refrigerator for up to 1 week.

ABOUT FENUGREEK

Fenugreek is a spice that is actually a member of the pea family. These small, aromatic yellow-brown seeds are most commonly used in Indian cookery, though they are also popular in North Africa and Yemen. The ancient Egyptians probably used fenugreek in their cooking, but the name is derived from another use, as animal fodder. The Romans called this plant *fenum graecum*, which means "Greek hay." The tiny, pebblelike seeds are roasted to enhance their pungent aroma. They have a unique bittersweet, somewhat acrid taste and are quite powerful, so use in moderation. Ground fenugreek seems to lose its fragrance rather quickly, so check the quality before you use it. Fenugreek seeds tend to have a hard shell, so crush them in a mortar and pestle or with a hammer.

Garam Masala

(V E G E T A R I A N)

This versatile mix of roasted spices is used in many Indian dishes. It is made in various styles in different regions of India. Many spice companies make an excellent prepared version of garam masala, convenient if you're planning to use only a little bit. However, it is easy and fun to make, and the warm, sweet fragrance will perfume your house better than any aromatherapy candle. Store in a tightly sealed glass jar out of the light for up to 4 months. After that it will start to lose the subtleties of its aroma. Among the many additions to the basic formula are mace, nutmeg, fennel seeds, mustard seeds, and ajwain (carom or lovage) seeds.

—————————————— *Makes 1½ cups* ——————————————

3 (2- to 3-inch) cinnamon sticks
½ cup white or green cardamom pods,
   or 2 tablespoons ground cardamom
4 bay leaves
¾ cup coriander seeds
½ cup cumin seeds
¼ cup black peppercorns
4 bay leaves
1 tablespoon whole cloves

1. Using a hammer, break up the cinnamon sticks into small shards. Break open the cardamom pods, remove the hard black seeds, and discard the pods. Crumble the bay leaves.

2. Heat a small, dry skillet, preferably uncoated (such as steel or cast iron), over high heat. Add the cinnamon, cardamom seeds, coriander, cumin, peppercorns, crumbled bay leaves, and cloves. Toast, shaking the pan occasionally, until the spices are lightly browned and fragrant. Watch the spices carefully at this point so they don't turn black and become bitter.

3. Remove from the heat and cool to room temperature. Grind to a powder in a small coffee grinder, preferably one reserved for spices. Alternatively, crush the seeds using a mortar and pestle. Using a funnel, pour into a clean, dry, small glass jar, such as an empty spice, mustard, or jelly jar, and cover tightly.

Spicy Guacamole

(VEGETARIAN)

Homemade guacamole with plenty of fresh-squeezed lime juice is a real weakness of mine, even though I know it's full of fat from the oil-rich avocados—the only fruit that I know of that contains oils. It's definitely a challenge to buy and ripen avocados just right. If you buy green avocados, preferably the Hass variety, ripen them at room temperature for 1 to 2 days. When ready, they should be firm, with a dull skin, and the tip of the stem end should be easy to pull off. Also, when cutting an avocado, if the skin peels back from the flesh without sticking, it's at its peak.

Serves 6 to 8 (Makes 1½ cups)

2 firm but ripe Hass avocados (see Cook's Note)

¼ cup fresh lime juice (2 to 3 limes)

1 teaspoon salt

½ cup finely diced white onion, or thinly sliced scallions, white and green part

1 jalapeño pepper, seeded and finely diced, or 1 tablespoon drained and chopped pickled jalapeño

½ cup seeded and diced ripe plum tomato

¼ cup chopped fresh cilantro leaves (about ½ bunch)

1. Peel, pit, and quarter the avocados. In a medium bowl, mash together the avocados, lime juice, and salt, using a heavy whisk or potato masher. The finished mixture should contain small lumps. Stir in the onion, jalapeño, tomato, and cilantro.

2. Cover tightly, pressing plastic wrap directly on the surface of the guacamole, and reserve in the refrigerator for up to 2 days. After a few hours, the guacamole may discolor on top, due to oxidation. Simply scrape away the darkened layer, which will have an off taste, and use the remainder.

COOK'S NOTE

Hass avocados—the pebbly, black-skinned type—tend to be more buttery tasting than other types. Eighty percent of the avocados sold in the U.S. are of the Hass variety. Fuerte or Pinkerton avocados make a good substitute.

Avocado Mousse

(VEGETARIAN)

Here, I combine avocados with other ingredients that help preserve their color. The cream cheese coats the avocado with fat, and the limes and pickled jalapeños are acidic, preventing oxidation. Lay the plastic wrap or waxed paper directly onto the surface of the mousse to maintain the green color. Serve the mousse with the Three-Bean Salad Ring on page 99, or spread on crackers.

Makes 2 cups
---

4 ounces cream cheese, softened

4 firm but ripe Hass avocados, peeled and pitted

1 bunch scallions, white and green parts, chopped

2 pickled jalapeño peppers, chopped

2 tablespoons fresh lime juice (about 1 lime)

¼ cup chopped fresh cilantro leaves (about ¼ bunch)

Salt

1. Process the cream cheese in a food processor until smooth. Add the avocados and process until chunky. Add the scallions, jalapeños, lime juice, and cilantro, and process briefly to maintain the chunky texture. Season to taste with salt.

2. Transfer to a bowl and place a piece of plastic wrap directly on the surface of the mousse. The mousse will keep for 1 week if tightly covered and refrigerated.

Cumin-Lime Citronette Dressing

(VEGETARIAN)

Here's a dressing that combines three of my favorite flavors: lime, toasted cumin, and cilantro. Fresh lime juice is less acidic than vinegar, so I've combined it with nutty-sweet but strong sherry vinegar for a deeper level of acidity. You could also make the same dressing with lime juice only, increasing the amount to 1 cup. When using lime zest, it's especially important not to include any of the bitter white pith that lies under the green skin. Look for firm, rough-skinned limes for easier grating. If your limes are too soft to grate, omit the zest.

Makes 2 cups
---

2 teaspoons toasted ground cumin seeds (see Toasting Seeds, page 225)

2 teaspoons hot pepper sauce

1 teaspoon salt

¼ cup chopped fresh cilantro leaves (about ¼ bunch)

½ teaspoon grated lime zest

1 teaspoon dried oregano

1 cup peanut oil

6 tablespoons fresh lime juice (about 2 limes)

¼ cup sherry vinegar

Blend together the cumin, hot sauce, salt, cilantro, lime zest, oregano, oil, lime juice, and vinegar using a hand-held blender or a standard blender. Pour into a covered jar. This may be refrigerated for up to 3 weeks.

Tunisian Harissa Sauce

(VEGETARIAN)

I first learned how to make this spicy red pepper paste from the two Tunisian Jewish brothers who owned a Mediterranean bistro in Philadelphia where I was the chef during the eighties. They showed me how to combine three different types of hot and sweet red peppers and how to oven-roast them to concentrate the flavors. I learned that caraway, rather than the cumin called for in many recipes, was the seasoning of choice for harissa. Later, I discovered this somewhat simpler way to make harissa from Taieb Dridi, the Tunisian owner of a bakery in Philadelphia that specializes in Mediterranean-style flatbreads.

--------- *Makes about 1½ cups* ---------

3 large (about ¾ pound) roasted red bell peppers (see page 332), or 2 cups imported roasted red peppers, drained

2 ounces (about 4) fresh hot red chiles (such as red jalapeños, red Korean chiles, red Holland hot chiles, or pasillas), trimmed and seeded

½ cup sweet Hungarian paprika

¼ cup extra-virgin olive oil

6 garlic cloves

1 tablespoon ground caraway seeds, or 3 tablespoons whole seeds, freshly ground

1. Purée the roasted red bell peppers, chiles, paprika, olive oil, garlic, and caraway in a food processor.

2. Pour into a glass jar with a lid and refrigerate until needed. The harissa will keep well for 2 months if tightly covered and refrigerated.

Spicy Peanut Dipping Sauce

Americans take quite easily to Asian-style peanut sauces, which can range in textures from smooth, like this one, to chunky, to a creamy Southeast-Asian style, which combines peanuts with rich coconut milk. The nam pla *called for here is a thin, liquid sauce made from salted, fermented fish that is vital to Thai and Vietnamese cooking. It provides the characteristic undertone of flavor. Fish sauce takes a little getting used to because of its strong smell, but here it helps emphasize the savory qualities of the sauce.*

Makes about 2 cups

1 cup smooth peanut butter

1 tablespoon coarsely chopped fresh ginger

2 teaspoons coarsely chopped garlic

2 shallots, coarsely chopped

¼ cup dry sherry

¼ cup soy sauce

¼ cup roasted Japanese sesame oil

¼ cup packed dark brown sugar

2 teaspoons *nam pla* (Thai fish sauce)

2 teaspoons hot chile oil or hot red pepper flakes

¼ cup cilantro leaves (about ¼ bunch)

½ cup thinly sliced scallions (about ½ bunch), white and green parts

1. Process the peanut butter, ginger, garlic, shallots, sherry, soy sauce, sesame oil, brown sugar, *nam pla,* and chile oil in a food processor to a smooth paste, scraping down the sides of the bowl once or twice. Add the cilantro and scallions.

2. Use immediately or transfer the mixture to a storage container. If the sauce seems too thick, thin by whisking in a little cold water before serving. This will keep covered and refrigerated for up to 2 weeks.

ABOUT PEANUTS

It is the salted, roasted variety of peanuts that has become such a universally popular snack, second only to potato chips. Peanut butter was first concocted in the early 1900s and quickly became an American staple. Other cultures, particularly Indonesian and Thai, have long used ground peanuts as a key ingredient to enrich and thicken their sauces.

Mixed Greens with Garlic and Olive Oil

(VEGETARIAN)

I like to combine greens for more interesting texture and a rounder flavor. The three I use here are all quite different: the broccoli rabe is slightly bitter; the chard echoes the sweetness of its close relative, the beet; and the kale has a mild, broccoli-like taste. Other good greens to substitute would be Chinese broccoli for the broccoli rabe, beet greens for the chard, and if you like strong tastes, sharp mustard greens or Tuscan (sometimes called "dinosaur" kale) for the milder kale. Unlike most vegetable dishes, these greens reheat quite well. I also enjoy them at room temperature or cold drizzled with a little Shanxi or balsamic vinegar. Serve these greens with Oven-Cooked Italian Style Beans (see recipe on page 294.)

Serves 6

---

1 pound fresh broccoli rabe, bottom 2 inches of stalks trimmed and discarded

1 pound fresh Swiss chard, ribs removed and saved for another use, leaves trimmed

1 pound fresh kale, bottom 2 inches of stalks trimmed and discarded

¼ cup olive oil

¼ cup chopped garlic (about 6 cloves)

½ teaspoon hot red pepper flakes

2 teaspoons salt

1. Cut the broccoli rabe crosswise into strips 1 inch wide. Wash well and drain. Cut the Swiss chard crosswise into strips 1 inch wide. Wash and drain. Remove and discard the center ribs of the kale and cut the leaves into strips 1 inch wide. Wash and drain the kale. Steam or boil all the greens together until bright green and fully wilted, about 5 minutes. Drain the greens, rinsing them under cold running water to set the color. (The greens can be cooked up to 2 days ahead and refrigerated.)

2. Heat the olive oil in a large pan over medium heat. Stir in the garlic, red pepper flakes, and salt. Cook for 3 minutes. Add the greens and heat until they are piping hot and the liquid has evaporated, about 8 minutes. Serve immediately.

Pico de Gallo Salsa

(VEGETARIAN)

This uncooked salsa's name translates to "rooster's beak," and is so called in the American Southwest and West because of its bright colors. In Mexico, it's known simply as "salsa Mexicana." Whatever the name, I could eat this salsa every day and not get tired of it, especially when local tomatoes are in season. If using larger beefsteak tomatoes, it's a good idea to sprinkle them with the salt and allow them to drain for 15 to 20 minutes to draw off the excess water. It's not necessary to do this step with meatier plum tomatoes.

— *Makes 2 cups* —

1 pound ripe plum or beefsteak tomatoes, seeded and cut into small dice
1 sweet white onion, cut into small dice
2 fresh or pickled jalapeño peppers, seeded and finely chopped
¼ cup fresh lime juice (about 2 limes)
1 tablespoon salt
½ cup chopped fresh cilantro leaves (about ½ bunch)

In a large bowl, combine the tomatoes, onion, jalapeños, lime juice, salt, and cilantro. Season to taste and then cover tightly, pressing plastic wrap directly on the surface of the salsa. Refrigerate until ready to serve. The salsa will keep for 2 to 3 days, but will become more watery each day as the liquid is released from the tomatoes and onions. If necessary, drain off this excess liquid before serving.

Light Chicken Stock

Do you really have to bother making your own stock? The answer is no, canned will do, and the brands sold in aseptic packaging (those rectangular containers) is even better. However, I get particular enjoyment out of making "stone soup," or something out of nothing. I save all the trimmings from onions (though not red onions because they give an off color to the stock), carrots, celery, tomatoes, and mushrooms as I prepare different dishes, along with stems of thyme, tarragon, and chives. I place the trimmings in a freezer bag and keep adding to my stash until I have enough to make a large pot of stock. I also save roasted chicken carcasses, chicken wing tips, backbones, and other trimmings and supplement as needed with inexpensive chicken legs, thigh, backs, and necks. After cooling the stock, I ladle it into 3 plastic 1-quart containers (or even freezer bags, sealed carefully) and freeze. The stock just needs a minute or two in the microwave to melt enough so that it slides right out of the bag and is ready.

--- *Makes 12 cups (3 quarts)* ---

5 pounds mixed chicken parts (necks, backs, wings, and legs), preferably from grain-fed chickens

4 quarts water

4 bay leaves

1 teaspoon coriander seeds

1 teaspoon fennel seeds

1 teaspoon black peppercorns

1 medium onion, peeled

2 carrots

2 ribs celery

A small handful of tender herb trimmings (parsley, chervil, tarragon)

1. In a large stockpot, combine the chicken parts, water, bay leaves, coriander, fennel, peppercorns, onion, carrots, celery, and herbs. Bring to a boil, skimming off and discarding the white foam impurities that rise to the surface. Reduce the heat to a bare simmer and cook, partially covered, for 8 hours, or until the chicken meat falls easily off the bones. Strain through a sieve into another pot, discarding the solids.

2. Place the pot of strained stock into a larger pot or deep pan containing ice water and allow the stock to cool for about 1 hour. Refrigerate overnight to solidify the fat. Remove and discard any fat from the surface. The stock will keep well in the refrigerator for 4 to 5 days. If desired, freeze the stock for up to 3 months. In that case, leave the layer of fat intact, for it helps keep the stock from spoiling. Scrape off the fat before reheating the stock.

Smoked Turkey Stock

I got the idea of making a smoked turkey stock because I learned that some people on a lighter or pork-free diet substitute smoked turkey legs for ham hocks. Flavorwise, it's not that different. You can find inexpensive smoked turkey legs, wings, and even necks in most supermarkets or ethnic markets. I buy extra and keep them in the freezer to use as needed. The turkey meat that's been cooked is delicious, but be careful when removing the bone-hard tendons.

Makes 12 cups (3 quarts)

5 pounds smoked turkey drumsticks, necks, and/or thighs

4 quarts water

4 bay leaves

1 teaspoon coriander seeds

1 teaspoon fennel seeds

1 teaspoon black peppercorns

1 medium onion, peeled

2 carrots

2 ribs celery

A small handful of tender herb trimmings (parsley, chervil, tarragon)

1. In a large stockpot, combine the turkey, water, bay leaves, coriander, fennel, peppercorns, onion, carrots, celery, and herbs. Bring to a boil, skimming off and discarding the white foam impurities that rise to the surface. Reduce the heat to a bare simmer and cook, partially covered, for 8 hours, or until the turkey meat falls easily off the bones. Strain through a sieve into another pot, discarding the solids.

2. Place the pot of strained stock into a larger pot or deep pan containing ice water. Allow the stock to cool for 1 hour. Refrigerate overnight to solidify the fat. Remove and discard any fat from the surface before using. If desired, freeze the stock at this point for up to 3 months.

Rich Chicken Stock

When you're looking for a more substantial foundation for a sauce or a soup, use this roasted chicken and vegetable stock. The caramelized roasted vegetables add a note of underlying sweetness. Use this stock for Hot and Sour Soup with Duck, Pea Shoots, and Fresh Tofu (see page 117), Moroccan Golden Split Pea and Pumpkin Soup (see page 126); and French Green Lentils with Black Truffles and Caramelized Shallots (see page 170).

——————————— *Makes about 12 cups (3 quarts)* ———————————

5 pounds mixed chicken parts (necks, backs, wings, and legs), preferably from grain-fed chickens

1 medium onion, unpeeled and coarsely chopped

2 carrots, cut up

2 ribs celery, cut up

16 cups (4 quarts) cold water

6 bay leaves

1 teaspoon coriander seeds

1 teaspoon fennel seeds

1 teaspoon black peppercorns

¼ bunch fresh thyme

¼ pound mushrooms or mushroom trimmings (optional)

A small handful of tender herb trimmings (parsley, chervil, tarragon)

1. Preheat the oven to 400°F. Arrange the chicken parts in a large roasting pan. Roast for 30 minutes, or until evenly browned. Add the onion, carrots, and celery, and roast for 30 minutes longer or until rich golden brown. Remove the pan from the oven and transfer the roasted chicken parts and vegetables to a large stockpot.

2. Place the roasting pan over a burner and add 4 cups of the water. Bring the liquid to a boil. Reduce the heat and simmer for 5 to 10 minutes, scraping up the browned bits with a wooden spoon. Pour the contents of the pan into the stockpot with the remaining 12 cups water. Bring to a boil, skimming off and discarding the white foam impurities that rise to the surface. Add the bay leaves, coriander, fennel, peppercorns, thyme, mushrooms, and herbs. Reduce the heat to a bare simmer and cook, partially covered, for 6 to 8 hours or until the chicken meat falls easily off the bones. Strain through a sieve into another pot, discarding the solids.

3. Place the pot of stock into another larger pot filled with ice water to cool for 1 hour. Refrigerate immediately. Remove and discard any fat that has solidified. If desired, freeze the stock at this point for up to 3 months, leaving the top layer of fat intact.

Vegetable Stock

(VEGETARIAN)

Here's a mild-flavored stock for vegetarians or others who enjoy the fresh flavor of vegetables. If you save the liquid from steamed vegetables, add it to this stock. Although it won't have the body that comes from gelatinous-rich meats, this stock will provide a flavorful foundation. Avoid adding strongly flavored members of the brassica family, such as broccoli, cauliflower, cabbage, and Brussels sprouts, though turnips add a pleasant, earthy sweet flavor. Do not use red onions (which tint the stock an unpleasant color). If you're adding herbs, rosemary and sage can be overpowering in this stock. If available, use bean cooking liquid, especially from chickpeas, for all or part of the liquid called for.

Makes 8 cups (2 quarts)

1 tablespoon black peppercorns
1 tablespoon coriander seeds
4 bay leaves
1 bunch fresh thyme, or 2 teaspoons dried
2 cups dry white vermouth or water
8 cups (2 quarts) water
2 cups chopped tomatoes, fresh or canned
2 cups coarsely chopped celery
4 cups coarsely chopped mushrooms, including the stems (shiitake, white, and/or cremini)
1 cup coarsely chopped yellow onion, including the skin
You might also include any or all of the following:
  Carrots
  White part of scallions
  Asparagus
  Celery root
  Green beans
  Pea pods
  Red pepper trimmings
  Fennel stalks
  Potatoes
  Turnips
  Tomatoes
  Squash
  Corn cobs
Herbs such as parsley, thyme, basil, marjoram, chives, lovage, or dill

1. In a large stockpot, combine the peppercorns, coriander, bay leaves, thyme, vermouth, water, tomatoes, celery, mushrooms, and onion, as well as any other vegetables listed. Bring to a boil, skimming off and discarding any white foam impurities that rise to the surface. Reduce the heat and simmer, partially covered, for 1 hour.

2. Strain through a sieve into another pot, pressing down well to extract the vegetable juices. Discard the solids. Cool and use as directed in soups or other dishes as a substitute for chicken stocks. This may be refrigerated for up to 4 days or frozen for up to 1 month.

Buttermilk Pastry Dough

(VEGETARIAN)

I've discovered that dry buttermilk powder, made by the Saco company and sold in many well-stocked supermarkets and specialty food stores, is a wonderful product to have on hand for baking. Not that different from the idea of powdered milk, this buttermilk powder makes a particularly flaky shortcrust dough. If you can't find the buttermilk powder, substitute ½ cup liquid buttermilk mixed with 1 egg for the ½ cup beaten eggs.

——— *Makes about 1 pound dough (enough for 16 potpies)* ———

3 cups (12 ounces) unbleached
   all-purpose flour
2 teaspoons salt
¼ cup dry buttermilk powder
¼ pound (1 stick) unsalted butter, cut
   into bits
½ cup eggs (about 3 large eggs), lightly
   beaten

1. In the bowl of an electric mixer, combine the flour, salt, and buttermilk powder and mix lightly. Top with the butter bits but don't mix in. Place the bowl in the freezer for 30 minutes, or chill for 1 hour if you're working on a really hot day.

2. Beat the chilled flour mixture until it resembles cold and crumbly oatmeal. Pour in the eggs and beat until the mixture just comes together in a ball. Place in a large, resealable plastic food storage bag and then flatten the dough to fill the bag. Chill for at least 30 minutes before rolling out. (The dough can be refrigerated for up to 2 days before using.)

3. Roll out the dough on a floured board to a thickness of from ⅛ to ¼ inch. Cut as needed. This dough freezes quite well if double-bagged in heavy zipper-lock freezer bags for up to 2 months. Defrost overnight in the refrigerator when ready to use.

Durum Pasta Dough

(V E G E T A R I A N)

Durum wheat flour, the golden yellow flour used to make Italian semolina bread, is the flour of choice for pasta. Its appealing color enhances the brightness of the egg yolks that enrich the pasta. Durum flour is sometimes sold as pasta flour. It is not the same thing as semolina, which is the hard germ of the same wheat kernel, and is mealy rather than fine, like durum flour. I especially like using durum flour because it produces a firm pasta with a bit of resistance to the bite, and the dough isn't sticky. Use this dough to make the Spring Greens Ravioli and Creamy White Bean Sauce (see page 178) or to make maltagliati for Toto's Pasta "Fazool" (see page 208).

Makes 1 pound

4 cups durum wheat flour
(about 1 pound)
5 large eggs, at room temperature

1. Place the flour in the bowl of a food processor. Add 4 eggs, one at a time, processing until the dough is crumbly. Add the fifth egg, processing just until the dough forms a ball. The dough will be quite stiff, so watch closely and stop processing immediately after it forms the ball.

2. Remove the dough to a floured board and knead by hand until smooth and elastic. Place the dough in a zipper-lock plastic bag, seal, and let rest at room temperature for at least 1 hour. You may refrigerate the dough at this point for up to 2 days, but be sure to allow it to come to room temperature before using.

3. Using a manual or electric pasta machine, roll about ½ cup of the dough at a time into thin (but not paper-thin) sheets. Feed the dough through the rollers, starting with a wide setting at number 1 and finishing with a narrow setting at number 6. Keep the sheets covered with plastic wrap until ready to use. Use this dough on the day you make it, or no longer than the day after, for best results.

SHAPING MALTAGLIATI

To make maltagliati, which means "badly cut" in Italian, lay a sheet of the pasta dough, rolled slightly thicker than for ravioli, onto a board. Cut parallel lines about 2 inches apart along the length of the dough. Cut crosswise strips on the diagonal to create rough diamond shapes from the dough, measuring about 1½ inches on a side. Spread out the cut pieces on a lightly floured surface to dry, making sure the pieces do not touch one another. When you're ready to cook the pasta, be sure to shake off the excess flour before adding the pasta to the cooking water.

Home-Grown Bean Sprouts

(VEGETARIAN)

Sprouts start to deteriorate as soon as they've been harvested, so freshly picked ones taste the best. If you don't have access to good-quality commercial bean sprouts, such as those sold fresh in Asian markets and natural food markets, sprouting your own is a good way to go. You can buy a commercial sprouter with separate racks that will allow you to sprout several different types of beans at once.

Bean sprouts are extremely nutritious and add a delightful crunchiness to stir-fries, salads, and sandwiches. They require anywhere from 3 to 5 days to grow, depending on the size of the bean and the room temperature. The sprouts are ready when they are about 1 inch long. The larger the bean, the smaller the sprout should be. If sprouts grow too large, they will lose their tenderness Stir delicate mung bean sprouts and stronger tasting soybean sprouts into clear soups several minutes before serving. Do NOT sprout lima beans or fava beans because they are toxic when raw.

Makes 3 quarts of sprouts

1 cup organically grown beans, peas, or lentils
4 cups tepid water

1. Have ready a large glass jar, some cheesecloth, and a rubber band. Pick through the legumes, discarding any damaged or moldy ones. Rinse the beans; then place them in a bowl covered by tepid water and allow them to soak overnight.

2. After soaking overnight, drain and rinse the beans. Place them in the glass jar. Cover the top of the jar with a piece of cheesecloth and secure it with a rubber band. Add water to the jar and rinse the beans again. Invert the jar to let them drain. Position the jar in a dark place, such as a closet, that is about 70°F. Store the jar on its side to spread the beans over a larger area. (Note that bright light or sunlight will make the seeds dry out, too high a temperature will promote mold, and too low of a temperature will prevent the seeds from sprouting.) The place you choose should be convenient because you will have to rinse the sprouts one to two times a day until the sprouts are fully developed, which will take from 4 to 7 days, depending on the type of bean. When the sprouts are ready to eat—about 1 inch long— rinse them in cold water to remove seed coats, roots and other residue. This rinsing is critical because it prevents fungus from growing on the sprouting seeds. *Never eat any sprouts that have even a trace of mold on them as they could be toxic.*

FDA Sprout Recommendations

According to the U.S. Food and Drug Administration (FDA), all raw sprouts, whether home or commercially grown, may pose a health risk, although alfalfa and clover sprouts tend to be the most problematic. Many illnesses have been attributed to contaminated seeds. If pathogenic bacteria are present in or on the seed, they can grow to high levels during sprouting even under clean conditions. To significantly reduce the risk of illness, the FDA recommends cooking sprouts first.

Cook's Note

• **Lentil sprouts** have a chewy texture and are small, only about ½ inch long.

• **Mung beans** and **soybeans** can take up to 1 week to sprout. Mung beans are especially easy to sprout and are delicious when added to almost any Asian-style stir-fry. These sprouts deteriorate quickly once they reach their full size of 1 to 2 inches long. For the best taste and texture, use mung bean sprouts within 1 day of picking, and cook them if they are more than 1 day old.

• **Soybean sprouts** can be purchased in Asian markets. These larger sprouts with a yellowish head and 2- to 3-inch-long stem are difficult to grow at home because they ferment so easily. If you do sprout soybeans, be sure to rinse them frequently and thoroughly.

• **Pea sprouts taste** like fresh peas and make a lovely garnish for salads and a tasty addition to sandwiches.

Larger sprouted beans need to be boiled for 30 minutes to 1 hour, or until they are tender enough to eat. Once they have been harvested, you should refrigerate sprouts in a loosely covered container to give air a chance to circulate, until ready to use, for up to 2 days.

Buttermilk Corn Bread

(VEGETARIAN)

Maybe I'm overly particular about ingredients, but if you make this corn bread with standard granulated cornmeal, you just won't get the same corn-rich taste and mouth-pleasing texture as with the whole-grain cornmeal. Whole-grain cornmeal is to granulated cornmeal as whole wheat flour is to white flour. It is particularly important to store whole-grain cornmeal in the freezer or refrigerator to keep bugs out of its rich nutrients. Rumford is the only brand of aluminum-free baking powder on the market these days. I prefer it because it doesn't leave that faintly metallic aftertaste that other baking powders can. Try to find whole-milk buttermilk for the richest flavor and texture.

Serves 12 (Makes one 13 x 9-inch pan)

3 cups sifted unbleached all-purpose flour
1½ cups whole-grain yellow cornmeal
1 tablespoon baking powder
1 teaspoon baking soda
¼ cup sugar
2 teaspoons salt
2 cups buttermilk
¼ pound (1 stick) unsalted butter, melted and cooked
6 extra-large eggs

1. Preheat the oven to 350°F. Spray a 13 x 9-inch baking pan with nonstick vegetable spray. Combine the flour, cornmeal, baking powder, baking soda, sugar, and salt in a large bowl and make a well in the center.

2. Lightly beat together the buttermilk, melted butter, and eggs. Pour the liquid mixture into the well in the center of the dry ingredients and whisk together until mostly combined. Using a rubber spatula, fold the batter together until no dry spots remain. Don't overbeat or you will toughen the cornbread.

3. Spread the batter in the prepared pan. Bake for 40 minutes, or until a toothpick inserted in the center comes out clean and the cornbread comes away from the sides of the pan. Cool slightly; then cut with a serrated knife and serve with butter.

Confit of Duck Leg

Confit is a wonderful method long used by frugal cooks in southwestern France to preserve duck parts like legs and even gizzards (delicious, believe it or not). These ducks have already have sacrificed their engorged livers for foie gras. Their breasts are pan-seared and served rare, carved like a steak. What's left is the plentiful duck fat and the leg-thigh portions, destined for confit. The duck is first cured by salting and spicing, then cooked ever so slowly in a large pot of duck fat. It is then aged in the same duck fat, which seals and helps to preserve it. After 2 weeks, the spices have mellowed and the duck is tender enough for the meat to fall off the bone when it is crisped in a pan. You can also purchase duck confit (see Sources, page 341).

Makes 4 pounds

¼ cup kosher salt
2 tablespoons ground coriander seeds
2 tablespoons ground ginger
2 tablespoons ground anise seeds
2 tablespoons ground allspice
2 tablespoons crushed bay leaves
2 tablespoons crushed black peppercorns
5 pounds duck leg-thigh pieces,
    preferably from large Moulard ducks
24 garlic cloves (about ½ pound),
    separated but not peeled
2 pounds duck fat, goose fat, or lard

1. Combine the salt, coriander, ginger, anise, allspice, bay leaves, and peppercorns in a small bowl. Rub generously onto each duck leg, coating completely. Arrange the duck legs on a wire rack set over a pan. Cure in the refrigerator for 48 hours, turning after 24 hours. Drain off and discard any excess liquid from the pan.

2. Preheat the oven to 300°F. Rinse the spice mixture off the legs, pat dry, and arrange in a large roasting pan. Add the garlic cloves and duck fat to the pan and cover with foil. Bake for 2 to 3 hours (or 1 to 2 hours if using the smaller Pekin duck legs), or until very tender. Test for tenderness by jiggling a thigh bone; it should move easily in the joint. Remove the pan from the oven, uncover, and let the duck legs cool.

3. Using a large fork or tongs, remove the duck legs from the pan and arrange in a heatproof container. Strain the fat and pan juices through a sieve into the container. You should have enough fat to cover the legs completely. Push the legs down to cover, if necessary, and rap the container to eliminate air pockets. Cover and refrigerate for at least 2 weeks to allow the flavors to mature and the duck to become even more tender. As needed, remove legs from container, wiping off excess fat. (Duck confit will keep refrigerated for at least 2 months, if fully covered in duck fat.)

ABOUT DUCK FAT

Duck fat is a delicious cooking fat suitable for many legume dishes. If you roast your own duck, save the drippings and pour into a small, narrow container. Chill overnight. The fat will have congealed to a hard white substance. Remove and reserve the layer of fat, discarding the jellied cooking juices. Simmer the reserved duck fat in a saucepan over very low heat, skimming often to remove any foam impurities, until the fat is clear. (Refrigerate for 3 months or freeze for up to 3 months.)

Mexican Tomato Sauce with Allspice

(VEGETARIAN OPTION)

This Mexican-style sauce is perfect for Huevos Rancheros (Ranch-Style Eggs with Refried Beans) (see page 175), or as an alternative sauce when making Black Bean Quesadillas with Pepita-Tomatillo Sauce (see page 75). Although the recipe calls for lard, which gives it an authentic flavor, you can use bacon fat or olive oil. If you have fresh, ripe plum tomatoes, use them for the sauce, but strain through a food mill or sieve after cooking to remove the rather tough skin pieces. For a vegetarian version, substitute olive oil for the lard or bacon fat.

Makes 6 cups

---

1 large onion, peeled and cut into quarters
4 cloves garlic, peeled
2 jalapeño peppers
2 (28-ounce) cans plum tomatoes
1 teaspoon ground allspice
½ teaspoon ground cinnamon
2 teaspoons salt
¼ teaspoon freshly ground black pepper
¼ cup lard, bacon fat, or olive oil

1. In a food processor or blender, process the onion, garlic, and jalapeños until chunky. Add the tomatoes with their liquid, allspice, cinnamon, salt, and black pepper, and process again quickly to maintain a chunky texture.

2. Melt the lard over medium-high heat in a skillet. Pour the tomato mixture into the lard, stirring carefully so it doesn't spatter. Cook for about 20 minutes, or until the oil rises to the top. To store, let cool and transfer to a glass container with a lid. This may be stored in the refrigerator for up to 1 week, or frozen for up to 3 months.

Notes on Ingredients

ROASTED RED BELL PEPPERS

There's nothing like a freshly roasted bell pepper. The object in roasting peppers is to char, or blacken, the skin while keeping the flesh firm and uncooked. Charring gives the peppers an extra dimension of smoky intensity. Beyond flavor, there are two reasons for removing the skin: ripened red bell pepper skin is especially thick, and it's indigestible. For best results, char red bell peppers over direct heat. Ideally, grill the peppers on an outdoor barbecue over hardwood charcoal burned down to coals. If you're lucky enough to own an indoor electric grill, this also works well. For those who struggle with an electric range, try placing the peppers directly on pre-heated electric coils. On a gas range, turn the flame up high. Alternately, roast the peppers under a preheated broiler, though this is not ideal. Since the peppers are not placed directly on the heat source, they tend to collapse from overcooking. If your heat source is less than intense, try rubbing the peppers lightly with oil. The oil helps the pepper skins char more easily.

Place the peppers side by side on a preheated grill. Char for about 5 minutes; the time depends on the quantity and initial heat. As the skins blacken, turn the peppers with a pair of tongs. If the peppers are thin-walled or overcooked, there won't be much flesh left after roasting. After evenly roasting the peppers on all sides, turn them so the stalk end chars a few minutes (trimming off the stem first, if necessary). Then turn upside down so the blossom end also chars.

Place the peppers in a large stainless-steel bowl and cover with plastic wrap. Or put them in a plastic bag and seal. The peppers will steam as they cool, making it easier to remove the skins. Working near a sink, rub off the charred skins. Rinse the blackened skin pieces from your hands under running water. Avoid rinsing the peppers themselves as water dilutes the flavor. Store covered in the refrigerator for up to 1 week.

SALT

I prefer to use kosher salt in the kitchen for a number of reasons: the large flakes make it easy to pick up in a pinch in my fingers and to distribute it evenly. Kosher salt is also relatively mild so you won't be likely to use too much. Because it's unmistakable as salt, you won't ever get it mixed up with the sugar, which happens more often than you might think in restaurant kitchens. Kosher salt is, however, only half as strong as the heavier, fine-crystal table salt. I've tested all these recipes using kosher salt or table salt, available in most supermarkets. If you prefer sea salt, go ahead and substitute it. Just remember that sea salt is the strongest and most concentrated of all the salts and you must use it judiciously.

HERBS

I'm kind of a fanatic about using fresh herbs, though these dishes will certainly taste good if you substitute half the amount of dried for the fresh. I can't cook happily without lots of fresh, chopped herbs and toasted home-ground spices. I wash herbs only if they feel sandy as many of them come from greenhouses these days. Local field-grown herbs, such as basil, dill, and cilantro, can be loaded with dirt, but their pungent aroma and strong healthy leaves make the washing worth the extra effort.

FLOUR

In recipes using flour, I prefer—and have tested these recipes using—a good unbleached, all-purpose flour, such as Ceresota, Hecker's, or King Arthur brands. For these recipes, sift before measuring.

CORNMEAL

I love the taste of natural cornmeal and recommend a ground whole-kernel corn variety from Arrowhead Mills in Texas. Compared to commercial cornmeal, it's like using whole wheat flour versus white.

BUTTER

I always specify unsalted butter because it must be fresher than salted butter (the salt in butter acts as a preservative). You can certainly substitute salted butter or margarine, but be sure to taste before adding any additional salt to the recipe. I recommend Land O' Lakes brand for its quality and availability.

OILS

I fry with a combination of oils depending on the flavor I'm trying to achieve. I prefer soybean oil for general frying because it's light and mild and has a relatively high smoking point. For vegetable tempura, I blend roasted Japanese sesame oil into the soybean oil for its nutty flavor and aroma. I like peanut oil for frying stronger flavored foods like fish and calamari. I use a strong extra-virgin olive oil that comes from North Africa for all of my Mediterranean-flavored dishes. I find most French and Ligurian olive oils too bland for my tastes. When I refer to Japanese sesame oil in these recipes, I mean roasted sesame oil used as a seasoning. Almost all of this roasted sesame oil is imported from Japan. I recommend Kadoya brand. Do not substitute the clear cold-pressed sesame oil sold in natural foods stores.

ONIONS

I call for three basic types of onions in this book: yellow-skinned or Spanish; white-skinned or sweet, like Vidalia or Texas 100s; and red-skinned or Bermuda onions. A standard medium onion will work for most recipes. I specify "sweet" onions when I want their special flavor and crisp texture. I use red onions in many salads for their color—and I like the rich flavor they add to Mediterranean dishes. You can substitute when necessary, as long as your onions are firm and without odor—an indication of spoilage.

Glossary

Achiote Paste

An orangy-red seasoning paste from the Yucatan, *achiote* is made from a combination of crushed red annatto seeds and an assortment of seasonings, such as oregano, garlic, black pepper, cumin, and cloves. I combine the prepared *achiote* paste with more fresh seasonings to make a marinade that I rub over chicken thighs, swordfish, and tuna before roasting or grilling. The *achiote* not only flavors the meats, it also makes them juicy and tender. *Achiote* paste is available from Mexican and Latino groceries. I use Del MayaB, available from www.DelMayaB.com.

Aleppo Pepper (Near East Pepper)

This mildly hot, very aromatic, deep red ground pepper comes from Aleppo in Syria. Its warm, rich flavor is highly sought after among Middle Eastern cooks. Because it contains only the dried pepper flesh and no seeds, Aleppo pepper has a more vegetal flavor. Its attractive color is another plus. Buy Aleppo pepper from Middle Eastern and Indian groceries. Keep refrigerated.

Amchur (or Amchoor)

Amchur is a dried and powdered form of unripe mango. This pale, beige-colored powder has a mangolike flavor and a tangy, sour taste. It is used much like lemon juice in Indian cookery, and because of India's hot climate and lack of refrigeration, it is preferred over fresh, perishable citrus juice.

Ancho Chile, Ancho Chile Powder

Ancho, also called mulato and, in California, pasilla (a misnomer), is the name for the red, ripe dried form of the dark green, fresh poblano peppers. A relatively mild, smoky, and sweet-tasting powder is made from the crushed peppers. Use along with toasted cumin, garlic, and oregano for a homemade chile powder. Seed and stem the dried form before soaking in hot water to soften or grinding to a powder.

Annatto Seeds

Very hard, deep red, triangular seeds commonly used in Caribbean cookery for color and a mild flavor. The Mexican name for them, *achiote*, is also the name for a seasoning paste made from crushed annatto seeds, garlic, oregano, and other spices. In Puerto Rico, the seeds are lightly cooked in oil and then strained out. This red oil is then used for cooking.

Asafetida

A super-powerful, even evil-smelling spice extracted from the sap of the asafoetida, a member of the parsley family. The spice is sold in lump and powdered form. It is used in minute quantities in Indian cookery as a flavor enhancer and as a substitute for onions. It is used especially in legume dishes because it is reputed to be an antiflatulent.

Asian Shrimp Wafers (Krupuk)

These Indonesian "crackers" are sold in thin, flat oblongs that resemble uncooked potato chips. They will keep a long time if uncooked and stored in a cool, dry spot. To prepare *krupuk*, heat about 2 inches of oil in a wok; then drop in the crackers one at a time. After about 15 seconds they will puff up to two or three times their original size. Remove from the oil and drain. Serve them as a snack chip or as a garnish for salads.

Bacala (Bacalao, Bacalhau)

The Italian, Spanish, and Portuguese terms for dried salt cod are very similar. *Bacala* was originally used by Portuguese and Scandinavian fisherman as a way of preserving cod during the long sea voyage home from the Grand Banks fishing grounds east of Canada. Because of its strong aroma and stringy consistency, *bacala* is somewhat of an acquired taste. *Bacala* must be soaked in cold water, changing the water several times if it is extremely salty. If you buy *bacala* fillet, you only need to soak the fish, not clean it.

Bean Thread (Cellophane Noodles)

These very fine, translucent threads are made from the starch of green mung beans. Sold dried in Asian markets, they must be soaked in water to soften before using. They generally don't need to be precooked.

Black Mustard Seeds

The two main types of mustard seeds are white and brown. Whole brown mustard seeds (commonly called black mustard seeds) are ubiquitous in Indian cookery. They are popped in oil before using, like popcorn, which transforms the seeds from hot to sweet and nutty.

Black Sesame Seeds

This variety of sesame seed is sold with black hulls intact. Black sesame seeds are popular in Japanese and Chinese cookery and have become more common here because many chefs like their dramatic look and mild flavor.

Bottarga

This preparation of strong-flavored, pressed and dried mullet or tuna roe is used in the south of France and along the Italian Mediterranean coast. It's also known as *poutarge*.

Caper Berries

Caper berries are the fruit of a caper bush and have a similar flavor to the tiny pickled flower buds from the same bush, called nonpareil capers. The berries have a large oval shape and are pickled complete with their stems.

Chickpea Flour

There are two kinds of chickpea flour, raw and toasted. The raw kind, called gram flour, is sold in Indian groceries. The toasted kind is tan, with a nutty aroma, and is sold in Middle Eastern groceries. Store this flour in the freezer.

Chile Paste (Sambal oelek)

Sambal oelek is a hot, vermilion red paste from Indonesia made from cooked red chile peppers and their seeds. The chiles are crushed to a chunky paste with salt and a little vinegar. There are also Chinese versions of chile paste, some flavored with garlic and other spices. Purchase chile paste in Asian groceries and specialty food markets. Once opened, keep the chili paste refrigerated. Use judiciously as this product can be extremely hot.

Chipotle Chiles, Chipotle Chile Powder

Chipotle peppers are smoke-dried jalapeño chiles. When purchased whole, they smell quite smoky, even through the package. Chipotles are light brown in color, brittle, and wrinkled, with the shape of a fresh jalapeño. Philly Chili Company produces an excellent chipotle. (See Sources, page 341.)

Chipotle Chiles in Adobo Sauce

These are dried, smoked, red jalapeño peppers that are rehydrated in a spicy tomato-based sauce and packed in small cans. Both the chipotles (with or without their seeds) and the packing liquid are used. Many specialty and Hispanic groceries carry this product. La Preferida, Embasa, and San Marcos are among the many good brands available.

Chorizo (Chouriço)

This highly seasoned, coarsely ground pork sausage is flavored with garlic and paprika. It is widely used in different versions in Mexico, Spain, and Portugal. Chorizo is available fresh, smoked, and dried.

Cotenna

The skin of a prosciutto or other cured pork product, *cotenna* is used for the large amounts of natural gelatin it contains. Cooking beans with *cotenna* gives them a rich, creamy, smooth texture. Pork or bacon rind imparts an equivalent texture, though not the same proscuitto flavor.

Culantro

This is a wide-leaved relative of the herb we call cilantro. It has an even more pronounced pungent flavor than cilantro and is sold fresh in Hispanic markets. Like cilantro, *culantro* must be used fresh because it doesn't dry or freeze well. Cilantro leaves may be substituted.

Demi-Glace

This rich classic French base for meat sauces, which means "half-glaze," is a concentration of veal stock and veal bones that requires two levels and many hours of slow roasting and cooking to achieve a rich, brown, thick, flavorful sauce. To obtain the desired richness in this sauce, 1 gallon of the veal stock must be reduced to 1 quart of demi-glace. Few home cooks make this sauce from scratch. There are a number of excellent commercial demi-glace sauces available (see Sources, page 341).

Epazote

A wild herb and common weed, epazote is also known as wormseed, goosefoot, and Jerusalem oak. It has spiky, 2- to 3-inch-long leaves with a strong, almost turpentine-like flavor that can get quite addictive. It is reputed to be an antiflatulent and is a requisite ingredient in Mexican bean cookery, especially with black turtle beans.

Fenugreek Seeds

A legume plant common in Indian cookery, fenugreek is used for both its greens and its seeds. You might recognize its aroma as being reminiscent of curry.

Fermented Black Beans

These salted black beans are a Chinese specialty, made of small black soybeans (not black turtle beans) that have been preserved in salt. They have a strong, pungent, salty flavor, and are available in most Asian markets.

Foie Gras

Literally translated, the word "foie gras" means "fat liver." It's a very delicate and unctuous tasting specialty of France, especially Alsace and the southwest region. Foie gras has been well-loved in France for centuries, where Alsatian farm women, many of them Jews, specialize in raising these geese. Even the Romans knew and prized foie gras. For a long time, the only form of foie gras available in this country was canned and sold as "pâté de foie gras." In the last 20 years, foie gras has been produced in the United States, originally only on one farm in New York started by Michael Ginor, author of a book called *Foie Gras.* Now it is also produced in California by Grimaud Farms, and much of what is consumed in France comes from Israel.

Genoa Salami

This is a type of uncooked, cured, and air-dried pork sausage originally from Genoa, Italy. Genoa-style salami is made with a mixture of beef and pork, boldly seasoned with garlic, and studded with white peppercorns.

Ghee

Ghee (or clarified butter) is the preferred cooking and seasoning fat in northern India, though these days vegetable shortenings are often substituted. To make ghee, butter is heated and skimmed of its white foam, then cooked very, very slowly until all the water evaporates and any remaining solids stick to the bottom of the pot. The clear cooked butterfat is then poured off and used for cooking. Ghee is especially important in India, where refrigeration is scarce to nonexistent, because once clarified, the butter will keep quite well even at room temperature.

Giant White Corn (White Hominy)

White hominy is made from dried white corn kernels from which the hull and the germ have been removed, making it easier to digest. In a process developed ages ago by Native Americans, the corn is soaked in some form of alkaline slaked lime such as fireplace ashes. At one time crushed oyster shells were used. The giant white corn hominy is a specialty of Peru and is sold by the Goya Company, Vitarroz, and Indian Harvest (see Sources, page 341).

Hazelnut Oil

This is a fragrant, sweet, and nutty oil pressed from hazelnuts and used mostly for salads. Most hazelnut oil comes from France and is rather expensive. Keep it in the refrigerator to prevent rancidity. You will still get the flavor of the oil if you blend it with bland oil such as soybean or canola.

Hoisin Sauce

A prepared sauce made from soybeans, spices, chile pepper, and garlic, hoisin is thick, reddish brown, and sweet. It is widely used in Chinese cooking. Once opened, it will keep indefinitely if tightly covered and refrigerated.

Jícama (Mexican Yam Bean)

The jícama is a turnip-shaped underground tuber of a plant in the legume family and can be eaten raw or cooked. Originally from Mexico, the plant was imported by the Spanish in Mexico to their colonies in the Philippines during the 17th century. From there it was quickly adapted by Chinese cooks. It has crunchy, juicy, ivory colored flesh with a texture very similar to that of fresh water chestnuts. Jícama must be peeled of its tough, beige outer skin before it is ready to eat. Look for jícama at the supermarket and in Asian groceries. It deteriorates quickly, so choose unblemished, plump jícama without any pockmarks or stickiness.

Kielbasa

This Polish smoked sausage is made from pork-flavored with garlic and sometimes with beef added. It is about 2 inches in diameter and is usually sold precooked.

French Green Lentils (Lentilles du Puy)

The tiny French *lentilles du Puy* are raised in a special region of France called Puy. They are small, dark green to brownish black in color, and firm when cooked. They take a short time to cook.

Maccheroni

These medium-large cut pasta tubes are often ridged and look similar to rigatoni. The artisanal Italian pasta manufacturer Martelli forms its pasta using brass rather than the more common Teflon-coated dies, and produces a firm, chewy, golden maccheroni (see Sources, page 341).

Merguez Sausage

This thin lamb sausage, popular in North Africa, is highly flavored with garlic and hot red pepper. It is available from specialty food stores (see Sources, page 341).

Mirin

Mirin is a very special Japanese rice wine used only in cooking. It adds a mild sweetness and glazes grilled foods when used in a basting sauce. Mirin has the consistency of a thin, golden syrup. Find it in Japanese and other Asian food stores. English labels read something like "sweet cooking rice wine." Only a few tablespoonfuls are needed to prepare most dishes, so it will last a long time. If you can't find mirin, says Shizuo Tsuji, author of *Japanese Cooking: A Simple Art,* try substituting 1 teaspoon of sugar for every tablespoon of mirin.

Molasses, unsulphured

A by-product of sugar refining, molasses is produced by squeezing the liquid from sugar cane or sugar beets and cooking it down to extract the sugar crystals. The remaining warm brown liquid is the molasses. Use light (from the first boiling) or dark (from the second boiling) for cooking. The type of molasses known as blackstrap is thick, very dark, and somewhat bitter. It's too strong for the recipes included here. I use Grandma's brand.

Mushroom Soy Sauce

Mushroom soy sauce is a seasoned black soy sauce flavored with dried Chinese black mushrooms. It has a rounded, almost meaty flavor.

Nam Pla (Asian Fish Sauce)

A thin, liquid sauce made from salted, fermented fish, *nam pla* is vital to Thai and Vietnamese cooking for its undertone of flavor. It has a strong aroma that dissipates after cooking. The closest comparison would be to anchovy paste. Squid Brand is easy to find and excellent quality.

Nigella Seeds

These angular black seeds called variously *negilla*, *kalonji*, and *charnushka* have a distinctive aroma and a mild flavor, acrid and nutty at the same time, that's a bit like a pungent poppy seed. Nigella is the seed of choice on Russian-style black bread and New York rye bread. The same seed is mixed with bread dough to make Indian nan bread and used to flavor lentil *pappadum* wafers. Purchase nigella seeds from Indian and Middle Eastern groceries like Kalustyan in New York and Bitar's in Philadelphia or from specialty spice companies like Penzeys (see Sources, page 341).

Oil-cured Black Olives (Sicilian-style)

These wrinkly looking, ripe black olives come from Sicily. They are cured first in salt and then in olive oil and resemble a dried raisin in consistency. Once the jar has been opened they can be refrigerated indefinitely. Press down with your thumb to flatten the olive and loosen the pit; then open into two halves to remove and discard the pit.

Oregano (Mexican and Greek)

Oregano is one of the few herbs that works as well when dried as when used fresh. Drying seems to concentrate its unmistakable aroma. Most commercial oregano is the Mediterranean type. If you can find Greek or Mediterranean oregano on the branch, it is wonderfully aromatic (see Sources, page 341). Mexican oregano is milder and more mintlike and is, in fact, a different variety than the European. In some Yucatan recipes it is toasted before using, which intensifies its flavor. Buy Mexican oregano from a Mexican grocer or from an herb and spice specialty company.

Pancetta

An Italian specialty product of pork belly, pancetta is the same cut as bacon, cured with salt and black pepper as for prosciutto, and then air-dried rather than smoked. Unlike bacon, pancetta is made without sugar.

Pickapeppa Sauce

This bottled savory sauce belongs to the family of British-inspired sauces like Worcestershire and A1 Steak Sauce. It comes from Shooters Hill in Jamaica and is used to add a sweetly pungent flavor that's jazzy but not hot to soups, meats, and seafood. Like Worcestershire and other bottled sauces, Pickapeppa sauce contains tamarind along with tomatoes, onions, raisins, vinegar, and other spices. Look for the bottle with the parrot on the label in the condiment aisle at the supermarket.

Pimentón (Spanish Paprika)

An extraordinary wood-smoked paprika produced from special peppers grown exclusively in Spain's Extremadura region, *pimentón* can be purchased from specialty food stores such as Caviar Assouline and The Spanish Table (see Sources, page 341). It comes in mild, medium, and hot versions and is available in beautifully decorated tins. Adding *pimentón* to vegetarian dishes is an excellent way to create natural smoked, meaty flavor without meat.

Popcorn Salt

This super-fine, almost powdery salt comes in a small container and is usually sold in the supermarket with the popcorn. It is ideal for salting any snack food because you can sprinkle on an even, fine coat without producing any overly salty spots. Substitute fine sea salt.

Preserved Lemon

A North African way of curing and preserving lemons is to soak them in a salt-water brine, or to salt and then layer them in olive oil to cure. Either way, the edible part is the yellow zest, not the lemon pulp, which is to be discarded. Available from specialty foods stores (see Sources, page 341).

Queso Añejo (Queso de Cotija)

A very dry, crumbly aged cheese that is a bit acidic and quite salty, *queso anejo* was originally made in the farming town of Cotija, Mexico. It is usually grated very finely and sprinkled on top of enchiladas and bean dishes.

Raw peanuts

You can buy creamy white, raw, shelled peanuts at most natural foods, many Asian markets, or specialty nut stores. Store raw peanuts in the freezer.

Recaito Criollo

This tangy green herb condiment of onion, green pepper, garlic, and cilantro is sold in Latino markets and used to enhance beans, soups, rice dishes, and stews.

Rice Stick Noodles (Pad Thai Noodles)

Rice noodles come in various shapes and widths. The flat, fettuccine-size noodles are sometimes labeled "chantaboon" and are perfect for *pad thai*.

Saké

This clear Japanese spirit made of fermented rice is sometimes referred to as rice wine or beer, though it has a character all its own.

Saucisson

This large French pork sausage is flavored with garlic and used in cassoulet or to wrap with brioche for an hors d'oeuvre. The closest easily available substitute is Polish kielbasa, though specialty sausage companies now produce French-style *saucisson* in many cities.

Sesame Seeds

These tiny, flat seeds are sold hulled (white) and unhulled (tan) in most grocery stores and Asian markets. Instead of toasting your own sesame seeds, you can buy unhulled, natural, light tan sesame seeds that have already been roasted in Asian grocery stores.

Shanxi Vinegar

This mild vinegar is fermented from barley, sorghum, and peas with a mellow, sweet taste reminiscent of balsamic vinegar. Made in a remote northern province of China, it has been brewed in the traditional way for thousands of years.

Sumac

These purplish red, ground dried berries of a special edible variety of sumac are used in Eastern Mediterranean cookery for their special acidity. Buy only from a Middle Eastern grocery or a spice company; do not attempt to pick your own wild sumac, as it can be poisonous.

Tamarind

Also known as an Indian date, tamarind is the large fruit pod of a tamarind tree. The sour, prune-flavored pulp surrounding the seeds is widely used as a flavoring in Middle Eastern, Indian, and Indonesian cuisines. Tamarind is available dried and in liquid form.

Tomatillos

Tomatillos resemble a green or acid tomato encased in a dry, parchmentlike, inedible husk. These Mexican "green tomatoes" aren't tomatoes at all but rather a variety of cape gooseberry or ground cherry, all in the *Physalis* family. Peel off and remove the husk, and lightly steam and purée or chop to make a salsa. Tomatillos keep for several weeks in the refrigerator, but they will eventually become sticky, indicating that they are beginning to break down.

Urud dal

These white, split gram beans look like tiny white seeds. They are closely related to green and red mung beans, and are used roasted as a spice in Indian cookery.

Za'atar

One of several varieties of thyme from Lebanon, *za'atar* has a longer, thinner leaf than traditional thyme and a fragrance somewhere between savory, oregano, and thyme. A blend of dried *za'atar* leaves, sumac, and sesame seeds, also called *za'atar*, is used to sprinkle on pita bread, salads, and kabobs.

Sources

Adobe Milling
P.O. Box 596, Dove Creek, CO 81324
Phone: 1-800-542-3623
www.anasazibeans.com
Anasazi beans, high-altitude-grown pinto beans, black beans, bean soup mixes

Aidell's Sausage Company
1625 Alvarado Street, San Leandro, CA 94577
Phone: 1-800-AIDELLS Fax: 510-614-2287
www.aidells.com
Large variety of fresh, all-natural sausages such as chicken and turkey sausage with sun-dried tomatoes and basil; available in two 3-pound packs of uncooked sausage, which freeze well if carefully wrapped

The Bean Bag
P.O. Box 567, Clarksburg, CA 95612
Phone: 1-800-845-BEAN (2326) Fax: 916-744-1870
www.beanbag.net
A family-owned business offering grower-direct beans; large selection of homegrown heirloom and exotic dry beans

Bitar's Specialty Food Store & Grill
947 Federal Street, Philadelphia, PA 19147
Phone: 215-755-1121 Fax: 215-755-8445
E-mail: pitahut@aol.com (Catalog available)
Source of Aleppo pepper, dried mint, dried yellow split favas, dried chickpeas, frozen green favas, nigella seeds sumac, tamarind, turnip pickle (torshi), za'atar leaves and mix, pita bread, za'atar pita, toasted chickpea flour

Caviar Assouline
505 Vine Street, Philadelphia, PA 19123
Phone: 1-800-521-4491 Fax: 215-627-3517
www.caviarassouline.com (Catalog available)
Chickpea flour, French white coco beans, French green lentils (lentilles de Puy), flageolets de Chevrier, haricots lingots, Shanxi vinegar, saffron (available by the ounce) hazelnut and walnut oils, pimentón (Spanish smoked paprika), preserved lemons, Martelli maccheroni pasta, merguez sausage

D'Artagnan
399-419 St. Paul Avenue, Jersey City, NJ 07306
Phone: 1-800-DARTAGNan Fax: 201-792-0588
www.dartagnan.com (Catalog available)
Duck fat, fresh foie gras, moulard duck breast and legs, game birds such as pigeon, chorizo sausage, merguez lamb sausage, duck confit

Dean & DeLuca
560 Broadway, New York, NY
Phone: 1-800-221-7714
www.dean-deluca.com
High-quality dried heirloom and specialty beans, spices, sun-dried tomatoes, olives, and many other gourmet items

Hoppin' John (The "King of Low Country Cooking")
Phone: 1-800-828-4412
www.hoppinjohns.com
Low Country foods, such as corn flour and green tomato relish to serve with lady peas and rice

Indian Foods Company
Phone: 952-593-3000
www.indianfoods.com
All kinds of Indian specialty legumes—gram, dal, and pappadums—plus spices like ajwain (carom or lovage seed), black cumin, and asafetida

Indian Harvest Specialtifoods, Inc.
P.O. Box 428, Bemidji, MN 56619-0428
Phone: 1-800-294-2433
www.indianharvest.com, (Catalog available)
Excellent variety of dried beans, peas, lentils, and chickpeas, including golden chickpeas; also heirloom and specialty beans, giant white corn (white hominy)

Kalustyan's
123 Lexington Avenue (between 28th and 29th Streets)
New York, NY 10016
Phone: 212-685-3451 Fax: 212-683-8458
www.kalustyans.com
Herbs, spices, and legumes—especially Indian and Middle Eastern items—such as nigella seeds, green chickpeas, black sesame seeds, yellow lentils, red lentils, tamarind, Aleppo pepper, amchur, white emergo beans, beluga lentils, and golden chickpeas, asafetida, and carom seeds

Landis Valley Museum—Heirloom Seed Project
2451 Kissel Hill Road, Lancaster, PA 17601
Phone: 717-569-0401
Catalog available of rare and endangered varieties of
historic plants, including many heirloom bean seeds

Melissa Guerra
5818 North Cage Rd., #28, Pharr, TX 78577
1-877-875-2665
fax: 1-956-380-3842
www.melissaguerra.com
High-quality Mexican, American, and European
kitchen equipment and authentic Mexican ingredients,
including chipotle chiles, chorizo, epazote, *frijoles
peruanos,* and tamarind pods.

Merieme Imports
c/o Farmer's Bakery, 4905 North 5th Street
Philadelphia, PA 19120
Phone: 215-329-2196 Fax: 215-329-9202
E-mail: farmersbakery@cs.com
Hand-hammered copper couscousiers, Tunisian products

More Than Gourmet
115 W. Bartges Street, Akron, OH 44311
Phone: 330-762-6652 Fax: 330-762-4832
www.morethangourmet.com
Excellent quality, all natural veal demi-glace, chicken
broth concentrate, beef broth concentrate, vegetarian
glace concentrate

Native Seeds/SEARCH
526 N. 4th Avenue, Tucson, AZ 85705
www.nativeseeds.com
A nonprofit organization dedicated to saving traditional crops—especially beans, squash, corn, and
melons—of the American Southwest and northern
Mexico. Annual membership $18, catalog available.

Penzeys Spices
19300 West Janacek Court
PO Box 924
Brookfield, WI 53008
Phone: 1-800-741-7787 Fax: 266-785-7678
www.penzeys.com (Catalog available)
Selection of exotic spices, including black cumin *(kala
jeera),* sumac, nigella, whole and ground chile ancho,
chipotle and ajwain seed

Republic of Beans
45 East 22nd Street, New York, NY 10010
Phone: 212-982-8274 Fax: 212-504-2775
www.republicofbeans.com
Selection of specialty heirloom Italian beans difficult or
impossible to find in the United States, now imported
by Cesare Casella, chef of Beppe Restaurant in New
York

Sadaf Middle Eastern Foods
Soofer Company, 2828 S. Alameda Street
Los Angeles, CA 90058
Phone: 1-800-852-4050 Fax: 323-234-2447
www.sadaf.com
Wide range of Middle Eastern and Persian products; all
types of dried favas, including large split yellow favas;
dark red kidney beans; yellow split peas

The Seed Savers Exchange (SSE)
3076 North Winn Road, Decorah, IA 52101
Phone: 319-382-5990
www.seedsavers.org
This is a network of mostly small-scale growers and
gardeners dedicated to preserving our heritage of open-
pollinated heirloom vegetables, fruits, and nuts. The
network's underlying purpose is to protect the genetic
diversity of our food crops. A large selection of unusual
heirloom bean seeds with photos is available on their
Web site. Write to receive a four-page color brochure
detailing SSE's projects and publications, enclosing $1
with your request.

The Spanish Table
1427 Western Avenue, Seattle, WA 98101
Phone: 206-682-2827 Fax: 206-682-2814
www.tablespan.com
Spanish products including dry and canned premium
beans and dry specialty varieties, wines, olives, piquillo
peppers, tuna packed in olive oil

La Tienda
3701 Rochambeau Road, Williamsburg, VA 23188
Phone: 757-566-9606 or 888-472-1022
Fax: 757-566-9603
www.tienda.com
Spanish food products, terra-cotta cazuelas, dried and
canned premium Spanish legumes, paella pans, *pimentón,* saffron, piquillo peppers, tuna packed in olive oil

Trader Joe's
www.traderjoes.com
Almost 200 stores across the U.S. carry all kinds of specialty foods at low prices, including excellent quality nuts, couverture chocolate from Belgium, truffle oil, frozen artichoke wedges, and pitted, oil-cured Moroccan olives.

Vann's Spices Ltd.
1238 E. Joppa Road, Baltimore, MD 21286
Phone: 800-583-1693 Fax: 800-583-1617
www.vannspices.com
Large variety of heirloom and specialty beans, grains, high-quality non-irradiated spices, and spice blends

Whole Foods Market
www.wholefoods.com
See web site for store locations
The world's largest natural and organic foods supermarket company has more than 150 stores, mostly in the U.S., but also in Canada and Great Britain. Good source for dried legumes, stone-ground cornmeal, molasses, and excellent quality cooked beans packed in glass jars and imported from Spain under the 365 Brand label.

Selected Bibliography

Algar, Ayla Esen. *Complete Book of Turkish Cookery.* London: Kegan Paul International, 1985.

Anderson, Jean. *The Foods of Portugal.* New York: William Morrow and Company, 1986.

Anthony, Dawn, Elaine, and Selwa. *The Lebanese Cookbook.* Sydney: Lansdowne Publishing Pty Ltd., 1978.

Ayto, John. *The Diner's Dictionary: Food and Drink from A to Z.* New York: Oxford University Press, 1993.

Berry, Elizabeth, and Florence Fabricant. *Elizabeth Berry's Great Bean Book.* Berkeley, Calif.: Ten Speed Press, 1999.

Boxer, Arabella, et al. *The Encyclopedia of Herbs, Spices and Flavorings.* London: Octopus Books Ltd., 1984.

David, Elizabeth. *A Book of Mediterranean Food.* London: John Lehman, 1950.

Davidson, Alan. *The Oxford Companion to Food.* Oxford: Oxford University Press, 1999.

der Haroutunian, Arto. *Middle Eastern Cookery.* London: Pan Books, 1984.

Escudier, Jean-Noël. *The Wonderful Food of Provence.* Translated by Peta J. Fuller. Boston: Houghton Mifflin Company, 1968.

Farmer, Fanny Merritt. *The Boston Cooking School Cookbook.* Boston: Little, Brown and Company, 1923.

Foo, Susanna. *Susanna Foo Chinese Cuisine.* Shelburne: Chapters Publishing Ltd., 1995.

Gavarini, Daniela. *I legume: Conoscerli, preparli, e cucinarli: Con le ricette dei grandi cuochi..* Lodi, Italy: Bibliotheca Culinaria SRL, 1999.

Ghedini, Francesco. *Northern Italian Food.* New York: Hawthorn Books Inc., 1973.

Gosetti della Salda, Anna. *Le Ricette Regionale Italiane.* Milan: Casa Editrice Solares, 1977.

Gray, Patience. *Honey from a Weed.* San Francisco: North Point Press, 1990.

GreenBaum, Florence Kreisler. *Jewish Cookbook.* New York: Bloch Publishing Co. Inc., 1933.

Grigson, Jane. *Jane Grigson's Vegetable Book.* Middlesex: Penguin Books Ltd., 1980.

Harris, Jessica B. *Tasting Brazil: Regional Recipes and Reminscences.* New York: Macmillan Publishing Company, 1992.

Hearn, Lafcadio. *La Cuisine Creole.* 1885. Reprint, New Orleans: Pelican Publishing House, 1967.

Herbst, Sharon Tyler. *Food Lover's Companion.* Hauppauge: Barron's Educational Series, Inc., 1990.

Idone, Christopher. *Brazil: A Cook's Tour.* New York: Clarkson Potter, 1995.

Johnson, Mireille. *The Cuisine of the Sun.* New York: Random House, 1976.

Kasper, Lynn Rossetto. *The Italian Country Table.* New York: Scribner, 1999.

Kennedy, Diana. *The Art of Mexican Cooking.* New York: Bantam Books, 1989.

Kouki, Mahomed. *Cuisine et Pâtisserie Tunisiennes.* Tunis: Le Patrimoine Tunisien, 1997.

LaFray, Joy. *Cuba Cocina.* New York: William Morrow and Company, 1994.

Lang, Jenifer. Harvey, ed. *Larousse Gastronomique.* New York: Crown Publishers Inc., 1988.

Mallos, Tess. *Complete Middle East Cookbook.* Willoughby: Weldon Publishing, 1979.

McGee, Harold. *On Food and Cooking: The Science and Lore of the Kitchen.* New York: Charles Scribner's Sons, 1984.

Miller, Ashley. *The Bean Harvest Cookbook.* Newtown: The Taunton Press, 1997.

Milorandovich, Milo. *The Art of Cooking with Herbs & Spices*. Garden City N.Y.: Doubleday & Company, 1954.

Ortiz, Elisabeth Lambert. *Complete Book of Caribbean Cooking*. New York: M. Evans and Company Inc., 1973.

Owen, Sri. *Indonesian Food and Cookery*. London: Prospect Books, 1986.

Perrier, Georges, with Aliza Green. *Georges Perrier: Le Bec-Fin Recipes*. Philadelphia: Running Press, 1997.

Raviv, Yael. *Falafel: A National Icon, from Gastronomica: The Journal of Food and Culture*. Berkeley: University of California Press, Summer 2003.

Roden, Claudia. *The Book of Jewish Food*. New York: Alfred A. Knopf Inc., 1996.

Rosengarten, David, with Joel Dean and Giorgio DeLuca. *The Dean & DeLuca Cookbook*. New York: Random House, 1996.

Rubel, William. *The Magic of Fire: Hearth Cooking: One Hundred Recipes for the Fireplace or Campfire*. Berkeley, Ten Speed Press, 2002.

Sahni, Julie. *Classic Indian Cooking*. New York: William Morrow and Company, 1980.

Senderens, Alain. *The Table Beckons: Thoughts and Recipes from the Kitchens of Alain Senderens*. Translated and adapted by Michael Krondl. New York: Farrar, Straus and Giroux, 1993.

Simon, André L. *Concise Encyclopedia of Gastronomy*. New York: Harcourt, Brace and Company, 1952.

Tsuji, Shizuo. *Japanese Cooking: A Simple Art*. Tokyo: Kodansha International, 1980.

Weaver, William Woys. *Heirloom Vegetable Gardening*. New York: Henry Holt and Company, 1997.

Withee, John E. *Growing and Cooking Beans*. Dublin: Yankee Inc., 1980.

Wolfert, Paula. *The Cooking of Eastern Mediterranean*. New York: HarperCollins Publishers, 1994.

For Our International Audience

Generic Formulas for Metric Conversion

Ounces to grams	multiply ounces by 28.35
Pounds to grams	multiply pounds by 453.5
Cups to liters	multiply cups by .24
Fahrenheit to Centigrade	subtract 32 from Fahrenheit, multiply by 5 and divide by 9

Metric Equivalents for Volume

U.S.	Imperial	Metric	
⅛ tsp.	—	.6 ml	
½ tsp.	—	2.5 ml	
¾ tsp.	—	4.0 ml	
1 tsp.	—	5.0 ml	
1½ tsp.	—	7.0 ml	
2 tsp.	—	10.0 ml	
3 tsp.	—	15.0 ml	
4 tsp.	—	20.0 ml	
1 Tbsp.	—	15.0 ml	
1½ Tbsp.	—	22.0 ml	
2 Tbsp. (⅛ cup)	1 fl. oz	30.0 ml	
2½ Tbsp.	—	37.0 ml	
3 Tbsp.	—	44.0 ml	
⅓ cup	—	57.0 ml	
4 Tbsp. (¼ cup)	2 fl. oz	59.0 ml	
5 Tbsp.	—	74.0 ml	
6 Tbsp.	—	89.0 ml	
8 Tbsp. (½ cup)	4 fl. oz	120.0 ml	
¾ cup	6 fl. oz	178.0 ml	
1 cup	8 fl. oz	237.0 ml	(.24 liter)
1½ cups	—	354.0 ml	
1¾ cups	—	414.0 ml	
2 cups (1 pint)	16 fl. oz	473.0 ml	
4 cups (1 quart)	32 fl. oz	—	(.95 liter)
5 cups	—	1185.0 ml	(1.183 liters)
16 cups (1 gallon)	128 fl. oz	—	(3.8 liters)

Oven Temperatures

Degrees Fahrenheit	Degrees Centigrade	British Gas Marks
200°	93.0°	—
250°	120.0°	—
275°	140.0°	1
300°	150.0°	2
325°	165.0°	3
350°	175.0°	4
375°	190.0°	5
400°	200.0°	6
450°	230.0°	8

Metric Equivalents for Weight

U.S.	Metric
1 oz	28 g
2 oz	58 g
3 oz	85 g
4 oz (¼ lb.)	113 g
5 oz	142 g
6 oz	170 g
7 oz	199 g
8 oz (½ lb.)	227 g
10 oz	284 g
12 oz (¾ lb.)	340 g
14 oz	397 g
16 oz (1 lb.)	454 g

Metric Equivalents for Butter

U.S.	Metric
2 tsp.	10.0 g
1 Tbsp.	15.0 g
1½ Tbsp.	22.5 g
2 Tbsp. (1 oz)	55.0 g
3 Tbsp.	70.0 g
¼ lb. (1 stick)	110.0 g
½ lb. (2 sticks)	220.0 g

Metric Equivalents for Length

(use also for pan sizes)

U.S.	Metric
¼ inch	65 cm
½ inch	1.25 cm
1 inch	2.50 cm
2 inches	5.00 cm
3 inches	6.00 cm
4 inches	8.00 cm
5 inches	11.00 cm
6 inches	15.00 cm
7 inches	18.00 cm
8 inches	20.00 cm
9 inches	23.00 cm
12 inches	30.50 cm
15 inches	38.00 cm

Index

A

B

E

F

M

S

Sabbath beef, bean, and barley casserole, 240

Salada de bacalhau e feijãos, 96

Salad dressings
  barley malt vinaigrette, 305
    for African black-eyed pea and okra salad with corn, 87
  black truffle vinaigrette, 174
  charmoula dressing, Moroccan, 102
  corn-saffron vinaigrette, 167
  cumin-lime citronette dressing, 315
    for Southwest black bean salad with baked spiced goat cheese, 98
    for Texas stuffed tomatoes with black-eyed pea salad, 100
  for curry noodle salad, 91
  for gado gado (Indonesian salad), 85
  garlic dressing and salad, 76
  herb mayonnaise, 90
  lemon-garlic vinaigrette, 307
    for Greek gigandas bean salad with grilled octopus, 84
    for Niçoise pasta shell salad with green beans, chickpeas, and tuna, 95
    for Provençal chickpea salad with tuna caviar, 90
  mustard vinaigrette, 101
  orange-honey dressing, 97
  preserved lemon aïoli, 104
  roasted garlic aïoli, 182
  roasted red bell pepper vinaigrette, 306
  Shanxi vinegar dressing, Chinese, 307
    Chinese noodle salad with snow peas, bean sprouts, and, 88
  sour cream dressing, 108
  for spinach and beef tip salad, 80
  tarragon–shallot vinaigrette, French, 308
    for French green lentil salad with bacon and tomato, 94
    for French navy bean and shrimp salad, 93
  white balsamic–truffle vinaigrette, 83
  for white bean salad contadina, 89

Salads
  black bean, with baked spiced goat cheese, Southwest, 98
  black-eyed pea, Texas stuffed tomatoes with, 100
  black-eyed pea and okra, with corn, African, 87
  borlotti bean and tuna, Florentine, 92
  chickpea, with tuna caviar, Provençal, 90
  emergo bean, with Moroccan charmoula dressing, 102
  French green lentil, with bacon and tomato, 94
  French navy bean and shrimp, 93
  gado gado (Indonesian salad), 85
  gigandas bean, with grilled octopus, Greek, 84
  haricots verts and beet, with balsamic–white truffle vinaigrette, goat cheese, and olivada crostini, 82–83
  kidney bean, in mustard vinaigrette, 101
  marinated bean sprouts and jícama, 81
  noodle, curry, with sugar snap peas and peanuts, 91
  noodle, with snow peas, bean sprouts, and Shanxi dressing, Chinese, 88
  pasta shell, with green beans, chickpeas, and tuna, Niçoise, 95
  pickled yellow wax beans in sour cream dressing, Tennessee, 108
  pinto bean, with smoked turkey sausage, 103
  raita, cucumber-yogurt, 308
  romano bean and navel orange, 97
  romano beans and sugar snaps, golden garlic aïoli with, 182–183
  salt cod and kidney bean, Portuguese, 96
  Spanish lentil, with salt cod fritters and preserved lemon aïoli, 104–105
  spinach and beef filet tip, with fermented black beans, 80
  sprouting bean, crunchy, 107
  tabbouli, with lentils, lemon, and mint, 106
  three-bean salad ring with avocado mousse, 99
  white bean, contadina, 89
  white bean, Turkish, 86

Salmon, seared, with sugar snaps and rhubarb sauce, 189

Salmon scaloppine with Chinese black bean sauce, 193

Salsa, pico de gallo, 319
  for black bean burgers on garlic toasted buns, 166

black bean nachos with guacamole and, 67

for Tex-Mex seven-layer salad with homemade tortilla chips, 73

Salt cod (bacala, bacalhau): about, 336

fritters and preserved lemon aïoli, Spanish lentil salad with, 104–105

and kidney bean salad, Portuguese, 96

Sandwich, Asian wrap, with shiitakes, bean sprouts, and hoisin sauce, 169

Sardinian-style cranberry beans with fennel and savoy cabbage, 254

Sauces and condiments

aïoli, preserved lemon, 104–105

aïoli, roasted garlic, 182

ajili mojili, 165

chutney, date-tamarind, 310

Bombay-style split chickpea cakes with, 176

chutney, fresh coconut–cilantro, 311

for pappadums (crispy lentil wafers), 64

fenugreek sauce, Yemenite, 312

falafel with, 74

harissa, Tunisian, 316

for seven-vegetable and chicken couscous, 196

hoisin, about, 338

mayonnaise, herb, 90

mojo, lemon-pepper, 304

for Brazilian feijõada completa, 214–215

molasses caramel sauce, 278

orange–red curry sauce, 195

peanut dipping sauce, spicy, 317

Indonesian lamb saté with, 201

spring rolls, shrimp and bean thread with, 184

pepita-tomatillo sauce, 305

for black bean quesadillas, 75

pesto

alla Genovese, 116

garlic-mint, 155

hazelnut sage, 120

Pickapeppa, about, 339

port wine sauce, 204

raita, cucumber-yogurt, 308

yellow split pea pancakes with, 72

rhubarb sauce, 189

salsa, pico de gallo, 319

for black bean burgers on garlic toasted buns, 166

black bean nachos with guacamole and, 67

for Tex-Mex seven-layer salad with homemade tortilla chips, 73

sweet red pepper sauce, 190–191

tadka, 112

tomato sauce with allspice, Mexican, 330

for ranch-style eggs with refried beans, 175

walnut sauce, 260

white bean and sage, creamy, 178

Sausage

cassoulet with duck confit, lamb, and haricots lingots, 236–237

chicken-basil sausage, flageolets, and spinach, ragout of, 202–203

chorizo (chouriço): about, 337

chile ancho empanadas with frijoles and, 68

and eggs, Portuguese green peas with, 168

home-smoked, 215

one-pot soup, Spanish, 228

cotechino with lentils, Italian New Year's Eve, 232

Italian, for *maccheroni rustica,* 206–207

kielbasa, about, 338

merguez: about, 338

lamb sausage, Tunisian fava bean stew with, 239

salami, Genoa, about, 338

saucisson, about, 340

Savory beans, trio of, 256

Savoy cabbage and fennel, Sardinian-style cranberry beans with, 254

Scallops, pan-seared, over autumn beluga lentil ragout with corn-saffron vinaigrette, 167

Scarlet runner beans: about, 39, 268

in brown butter and shallots, 268

Seafood. *See* Fish and seafood

Seeds, to toast, 225

Senate navy bean soup, 110

Seven-vegetable and chicken couscous, 196–197

Shanxi vinegar: about, 340

Shanxi vinegar dressing, Chinese, 307

Shellfish. *See* Fish and seafood

Y

Yam bean (jícama): about, 46, 338
    marinated bean sprouts and, 81
Yard-long beans: about, 44–45, 257
    with black bean and garlic sauce, Chinese, 257
    gado gado (Indonesian salad), 85
Yellow Indian woman beans, 34
Yellow split chickpeas. *See under* Chickpeas
Yellow wax beans. *See* Wax beans
Yemenite fenugreek sauce, 312
    falafel with, 74
Yin yang beans, 32

Z

Zebra beans, 34
Ziti alla contadina, 209
Zolfino pratomagno, 37